HOW TO BE A
SUCCESSFUL ECONOMIST

HOW TO BE A SUCCESSFUL ECONOMIST

VICKY PRYCE,
ANDY ROSS,
ALVIN BIRDI AND
IAN HARWOOD

Great Clarendon Street, Oxford, OX2 6DP,
United Kingdom

Oxford University Press is a department of the University of Oxford.
It furthers the University's objective of excellence in research, scholarship,
and education by publishing worldwide. Oxford is a registered trade mark of
Oxford University Press in the UK and in certain other countries

Published in the United States of America by Oxford University Press
198 Madison Avenue, New York, NY 10016, United States of America

British Library Cataloguing in Publication Data

Data available

Library of Congress Control Number: 2022943642

ISBN 978–0–19–886904–7

Printed in the UK by
Bell & Bain Ltd., Glasgow

Dedicated to Professor Peter Sinclair (1946–2020)

He was loved by the profession he loved

'I drifted into economics by accident but have never regretted it. If I had read this book, I would have chosen to be an economist. Unique in its insights into what life as an economist is like.'
Sir John Kay

Disclaimer

Apart from the authors, none of the individuals or organizations mentioned in or interviewed for this book are responsible for the information or views presented in it.

Preface

The authors believe in the power of economics to change the world for the better. To that end, we have spent our long careers promoting economics and championing good economists. We believe passionately that more economists would be a good thing, and so we hope that you too will become a professional economist. This book is a guide to help you:

- Decide to become an economist (Chapter 1)
- Choose your career choice as an economist (Chapter 2)
- Prepare for being an economist (Chapters 3 to 7)
- Get a job as an economist (see Chapter 9)
- Stay a successful economist (Chapter 10)

It is also a celebration, critique, and occasionally a chastisement of our profession. The bottom line is that a career as an economist is personally rewarding, both intrinsically and financially (Chapters 1 and 2) and can make the world a better place.

Overall, we praise the teaching of economics in the UK, but we also believe that there are often shortcomings, though there are also as often exemplars. There is no sharp dichotomy between academic and practitioner economists, but we do identify differences in approach (Chapter 3) and we advocate a more practitioner approach for first degrees. This would leave space for the broader skills required by economists in most of their career paths (Chapter 7) and for a more critical engagement with the subject (Chapter 8). We are certainly not advocating that economics degrees become more akin to the humanities, as the quantitative methods used by economists are a large part of the power of economics and these skills are highly prized by employers (Chapter 6). We do advocate, however, that more advanced techniques are deferred to higher degrees so that first degrees can concentrate on a deeper understanding of the fundamentals (Chapters 4 and 6) and a wider appreciation of the state of economics as a field of enquiry and where it is likely to be heading (Chapter 10). An undergraduate degree that skates over the limitations of economics or is designed only as a preparation for more technical higher degrees will sell most students short.

Our experiences are also that a critical and eclectic application (Chapter 8) of the basic insights of economics, and related disciplines, is the most reliable approach to policy. A weak grasp of sophisticated technique is the most unreliable approach (Chapter 6 and 10). Although we encourage universities to also employ practitioner economists experienced in working outside academia, if you do want to be a fully-fledged academic economist then you will need to immerse yourself in sophisticated techniques, usually through a Ph.D., and even as a practitioner economist you will still need to be aware of what these techniques do and what the current take-aways are from the body of academic research. That said, as we hope to demonstrate, there are many ways to serve as a good economist (Chapters 2, 3, 8, and 10).

All economists need to be acquainted with basic economic theory and data, and how data sets can be cracked open to, sometimes, reveal the economics therein. Theory without data is philosophy and data without theory is curatorship. Social Science brings theory and data together. All economists can also benefit from a knowledge of past events and policies, and increasingly an interdisciplinary awareness is fruitful (Chapter 8 and 10). We also look at the role of mathematics and formal models in economics (Chapter 6). We believe that 'low-brow' economics is best when it is well rooted in 'high-brow' economics. However, for many careers, economic journalism for example, a rounded grasp of the subject and its related subjects, and of course, compelling communication (Chapter 5), are more important than technical virtuosity. In academia (Chapter 3) and for some high finance careers (Chapter 2) you will usually need a lot of mathematics, and maths can be useful in public service too, but public policy is much more about 'dilemmas than lemmas'. If there were no opportunity costs, most economists would wish they knew more maths, but the amount of maths you will need will depend on what sort of economist you become (Chapter 2 and 6).

As with all the economists we interviewed for this book, your authors are pleased with the career choice we made to become economists. We want you, and many others besides, to become economists too. To that end, and for moral imperatives, democracy, and the better performance of economists, our chastisement of the profession is mostly reserved for its not being inclusive enough, both in thought and membership (Chapter 8). If more economists in the world would be a good thing then a larger and more diverse body of economists would be an even better thing. Whoever you are, we invite and welcome you to a career as an economist.

Vicky Pryce

The Authors

Professor Alvin Birdi is a leading authority on how and what economics is taught in UK universities.

He is a Professor of Economics Education in the School of Economics and Associate Pro-Vice Chancellor for Education Innovation and Enhancement at the University of Bristol. He is Director of the Economics Network, a national body that provides professional development for economics lecturers and promotes high quality and innovative teaching practice in the discipline within the higher education sector. Alvin was a member of the QAA subject benchmarks panel for economics and a lead panelist for economics in the Teaching Excellence Framework pilots. He has been a Director of the Bristol Institute for Learning and Teaching (BILT) and is a regular commentator and author on the teaching of economics.

Ian Harwood FAcSS has long been a leading economics practitioner in the City, focused upon global economic and financial developments.

Ian was enthused by Economics whilst at school before studying Economics at Bristol and Cambridge Universities. He became a macro-economist in the City of London in the late 1970s. Since then he has enjoyed a distinguished career, starting out as leading stockbroker Rowe & Pitman's first-ever economist and then becoming Chief Economist of SG Warburg (1986–94) and Dresdner Kleinwort (1994–2008). His work was highly valued by institutional investors world-wide. Indeed, prior to 'stepping-back' from full-time work in investment banking he was voted Number One in the Global Economics and European Economics categories of the annual Extel and Institutional Investor surveys respectively.

Ian has undertaken a wide range of economics-focussed, investment advisory and educational roles, and is currently Economics Adviser at Redburn, a stockbroking firm which focusses upon the provision of research advice to institutional investors; External Investment Adviser to insurer MS-Amlin, the BAE Systems Pension Fund, the Mineworkers' Pension Scheme and a Trustee Director of the UBS Pension Scheme. A Fellow of the Society of Professional Economists, he served on the Society's Council from 2008 to 2017, playing a leading role in pushing for substantive changes in the way Economics is taught in British universities. He served as an employer representative on the Quality Assurance Agency's Economics Degree Benchmarking Committee which reported in 2015. He also led the creation of the Society of Professional Economists' Continuing Professional Development programme and is currently the Society's Book Reviews Editor. He has been a member of the Royal Statistical Society's Statistics Users' Executive, a body responsible for liaising with the government's Chief Statistician about the quality of UK economic statistics, a Visiting Professor at Greenwich University and a member of the Management Board of the South-Western Universities' Doctoral Training Partnership since its inception in 2011.

(Visiting) Professor Vicky Pryce FAcSS is a famous economist whose career has been widely described in the media as 'stellar' and 'glittering'.

Chief Economic Adviser and Board member at the Centre for Economic and Business Research (CEBR) and a former Joint Head of the Government Economic Service, Vicky's other posts have included: Senior Managing Director at FTI Consulting, Director General for Economics at the Department for Business, Innovation and Skills. Before that, she was a partner at London Economics and Partner and Chief Economist at KPMG after holding senior economic positions in banking and the oil sector.

Vicky is primarily a practitioner but has also held a number of academic posts, including visiting professorships at Queen Mary, University of London, Imperial College Business School and Cass Business School. She has served on the Council of the Royal Economic Society, as a Visiting Fellow at Nuffield College, Oxford, member of the Council of the University of Kent and the Court of the London School of Economics, and was a trustee of the RSA. Currently, a Visiting Professor at Birmingham City University and Aston University, a Fellow of the Society of Professional Economists, a member of the Council of the Institute for Fiscal Studies. She is also a member of City AM's shadow monetary policy committee, on the Brexit Advisory Councils of techUK and CIPFA and on the Advisory Board of the central banking think-tank OMFIF. She also co-founded 'Good Corporation', set-up to promote corporate social responsibility and in 2010–11 became the first female Master for the Worshipful Company of Management Consultants in the City of London.

Her books include: *Women vs capitalism* (2019) *Greekonomics: The Euro crisis and Why Politicians Don't Get It* (2013) and *Prisonomics* (2013). Co-author of *Why Women Need Quotas* (2015). Joint author of *It's the Economy, Stupid—Economics for Voters*, with Ross and Urwin (2015); and *Redesigning Manufacturing Reimagining the Business of Making in the UK*, with Beverland, Nielsen and Hellmann. Vicky is a regular guest on radio and TV, giving commentary on economic matters including appearing on BBC Question Time and Today programmes.

(Visiting) Professor Andy Ross FAcSS is both an academic and practitioner economist a former Deputy Director in the Government Economic Service (GES) and Head of Professional Development for the GES and later for the Society of Professional Economists.

He is visiting professor at Birkbeck, University of London and recently Loughborough University, where he serves as a member of Loughborough's Business and Economics School Post-Graduate Programmes Advisory Board. Previously he was visiting professor at University of Reading, visiting research fellow at Leeds University, Recent Trustee and Director of the Academy of Social Sciences, where he still serves as Chair of the Practitioner Fellows Nominations Committee. Economist advisor to High Oak Enterprises. Patron of the Economics Network. Part-time lecturer at Birkbeck. Andy served for many years as the Chief Adviser for the Government Economic Service for their recruitment assessment centre. He has regularly trained the GES recruitment assessors for the GES in England, Scotland and Wales. He was an employer representative on the QAA subject benchmarks for economics and one of two employer representatives for the most recent Teaching Excellence Framework pilot for Social Science. Textbook joint author with the late John Beardshaw and author of many articles and several keynote speeches, particularly on practitioner economics. Andy was also joint author with Vicky Pryce and Peter Urwin of *It's the economy stupid* (2015) published by Biteback.

Acknowledgements

We are very grateful to all the economists who gave interviews for this book. They are listed on page xvi. Busy though they are, they gave their time and encouragement freely. They are of course not responsible for any shortcomings of this book.

The authors also particularly wish to thank Felicity Boughton of Oxford University Press. She did so much to improve the drafts by her diligent reshaping, insightful challenge and occasional scolding. Felicity really has a claim to be a fifth author, without any of the culpability.

We thank the economics students and faculty of Leeds University and Birkbeck, University of London, for supporting the vocational modules that gave rise to this book. Particular thanks go to Cathy Dolan, Giuseppe Fontana and David Spencer at Leeds University and Sandeep Kapur and Ron Smith at Birkbeck. Also, to Julia Bernhardt and Josephine Fox of Birkbeck who cheerfully lightened administration burdens with their helpful efficiency while this book was being written.

Thanks also to various members of the Government Economic Service and of the Government Economics and Social Research Team based at HM Treasury, for their checking of the details about the GES. Also, to Ashley Lait of the Economics Network for her reading of an early draft.

A thank you also to Catherine Connolly, previously at HM Treasury and now of the Society of Professional Economists and founder of *Economic Sense* https://www.economicsense.co.uk/, for her comments on the Cost Benefit Analysis material in Chapter 10.

Andy Ross wishes to express his special gratitude to Mr Rajaraman Durai, who is thankfully a successful oncologist surgeon.

And finally, our gratitude to James Sinclair for permission to dedicate this book to such a wonderful teacher of Economics, the late Peter Sinclair, who was tragically a victim of Covid-19.

Copyright Acknowledgements

The Times Higher Education for an extract from Reisz, Matthew, 2018. *Economists' communication problems extend to social media*, Times Higher Education (24th April). Available at: https://www.timeshighereducation.com/news/ economists-communication-problems-extend-social-media [last accessed 1 May 2021].

Interviewees

The authors are very grateful to all the economists who so generously gave of their time for the interviews for this book. Their experience and insights have been invaluable and they are drawn on throughout this book. Videos of their interviews are available for viewing at www.oup.com/he/pryce-ross1e.

Toju Anagboso is Global Head of Diversity, Equity & Inclusion at Harbour Energy. She has worked as an economist at the Office of National Statistics and had a twenty-year corporate career, spent working with senior executives across the UK government and private sector energy providers: Shell, the Oil and Gas Authority and an offshore helicopter operator (CHC). Founder of TOJU CONSULTING LTD, an Executive Coaching/Diversity Consultancy based in the Northeast of Scotland. Toju has an MSc in International Economics, Banking and Finance from Cardiff University, an MSc in Policy analysis and Evaluation from the University of London and a BSc in Economics and Statistics from the University of Benin.

Yasir Auckbur is a recent graduate in Economics from University of London who is now in his first job as a professional economist at the Office of National Statistics.

Dame Kate Barker is a business economist who was the Ford Motor Company's chief European economist and, subsequently, the CBI's chief economic adviser before becoming an External Member of the Bank of England's Monetary Policy Committee for three successive terms. During this period she led two major independent housing and planning policy reviews for the government. Since then, Dame Kate has pursued a plural career, including as a Non-Executive Director at Taylor Wimpey plc. She is currently chair of the British Coal Staff Superannuation and the Universities Superannuation Schemes.

Professor Alvin Birdi is co-author of this book. See 'The Authors'.

Sinéad Boultwood is an early career graduate. She entered Ofcom's graduate economist scheme and is currently the Economic Assistant to the Chief Economist. It is her first professional job as an economist after studying Economic and Social Policy at Birkbeck, University of London 2015–19.

Lizzy Burden is a reporter on the UK economy for Bloomberg. She also writes the weekly *Beyond Brexit* newsletter and contributes to Bloomberg TV, radio, podcasts and *Quicktake* social media channel. She was previously an economics reporter at *The Telegraph*, a graduate trainee at *The Times*, presented *CoronaNomics* TV and produced BBC Daily Politics. A regular guest on BBC, Sky News and Times Radio, she also hosts events, including for the Confederation of British Industry, the Institute for Fiscal Studies and British American Business. Before journalism, Lizzy was a fashion model for eight years. She graduated in History from the University of Cambridge.

Jonathan Coller and **Nathaniel Greenwold** are both in their early careers at Kraft Heinz and were involved in a 'Magic Breakfast' project for Pro Bono Economics (PBE). PBE is a charity providing free consultants in economics for charities and the third sector.

Catherine Connolly is the Founder of economicsense, a specialist economics training provider and consultancy, which also provides economics courses for the Society of Professional Economists (SPE). Catherine is also on the Council of the SPE. She teaches policy economics at Leeds University, and previously worked for HM Treasury.

Diane Coyle CBE has been Bennett Professor of Public Policy at the University of Cambridge since 2018. She was previously a Professor of Economics at the University of Manchester and has served on the BBC Trust, the Competition Commission, the Migration Advisory Committee and the Natural Capital Committee. She studied Economics at Brasenose College, Oxford and Harvard, and has been Economics Editor of the Independent newspaper, founded *The Enlightened Economist* consultancy and is the author of many well-received books on Economics. Her latest book is *Cogs and Monsters: What Economics is, and what it Should be* (2021) Princeton University Press.

Kevin Daly is co-head of CEEMEA Economics in Goldman Sachs. He was educated at the Universities of Cambridge, London and Dublin and joined Goldman Sachs in 2001. He is a member of the UK's Office for Budgetary Responsibility's advisory panel and of a steering group of independent experts advising the UK's Statistics Authority. He was also, until recently, Chairman of the Society of Professional Economists.

Gavyn Davies OBE is chairman of Fulcrum Asset Management and Co-Founder of Active Partners and Anthos Capital. He was Head of the Global Economics

Department at Goldman Sachs from 1987 to 2001 and Chairman of the BBC from 2001 to 2004. From 1979 to 2001, he was repeatedly ranked as the City's top UK, European or global economist in surveys of institutional investors. He has also served as an Economic Policy Adviser in Number 10 Downing Street, and an external adviser to the British Treasury. He is a Visiting Fellow at Balliol College, Oxford.

Melissa Davies has worked in the City as a macro-economist since leaving university in 2008. She was educated at Brasenose College, Oxford, where she read PPE, and followed this up with an MPhil in Economics. Melissa began her career as a practising economist at Lombard Research. Melissa subsequently moved to stockbroking research firm Redburn in 2013 where she is currently Chief Economist. She divides her time between her City role and looking after a young family.

Larry Elliott is a veteran commentator on economic and financial affairs and has been a journalist all his working life. After graduating from Cambridge with a history degree, he became a reporter with a local newspaper, moved to work for the Press Association for several years, and subsequently became Economics Editor of the *Guardian* in 1988—a position he has occupied ever since. Larry is also the author of seven economics-focused books.

Miatta Fahnbulleh is a Liberian-born British economist who is the Chief Executive at the New Economics Foundation (NEF). Before that, she was Director of Policy & Research at the Institute of Public Policy Research. Before this, she worked at senior levels for the Leader of the Opposition, the Cabinet Office, and the Prime Minister's Strategy Unit. Miatta has a Masters and PhD in economic development from the London School of Economics and a BA in PPE from Oxford.

Dame Rachel Griffiths As well as being a Research Director at the IFS, she was the Royal Economic Society's first female President in over 35 years and only the second woman to hold the post in its 129-year history. Professor of Economics at the University of Manchester, she is Fellow of the Econometric Society, the British Academy and the Academy of Social Sciences. Rachel won the Birgit Grodal award in 2014 and was awarded a CBE for services to economic policy. She has been Managing Editor of the *Economic Journal* and President of the European Economic Association.

Andy Haldane FAcSS FRS was Chief Economist at the Bank of England until mid-2021 and is now Chief Executive of the Royal Society of Arts. Having studied

Economics at the Universities of Sheffield and Warwick, he joined the Bank of England in 1989. He is a co-founder and trustee of Pro Bono Economics and Vice-Chair of the National Numeracy Charity. He has published extensively, having authored many articles and four books. Andy was recently appointed Head of the Government's 'Levelling-up' Taskforce.

Professor Sandeep Kapur is Head of Economics at Birkbeck, University of London. As the Director of the Department's Executive Training programme, he has designed and delivered training for many public and private sector organizations. Sandeep's current research interests span economic and financial regulation, and broad issues related to emerging economies. He has a PhD in economics from the University of Cambridge and has previously held teaching appointments at Cambridge and visiting appointments at Wharton (UPenn) and George Washington University.

Michael Littlechild studied European Studies at the University of Bradford University and then became a Research Fellow at the University of Strathclyde before finally deciding to study for his MSc in Economics at Birkbeck, University of London. He was a joint founder of *GoodCorporation* in 2000. GoodCorporation Ltd helps organizations to design, build, and embed ethics and compliance programmes and is regularly called upon to write and speak on business ethics and anti-corruption measures, drawing on his extensive experience and expertise across a wide range of sectors including mining, telecoms, defence, oil and gas, construction, and aviation. Formerly a partner at KPMG Consulting, he advised on strategy as well as policy formulation and implementation and led teams in Europe, the Middle East, Asia, Africa and the US. He has designed and evaluated many government programmes in developed and emerging economies. He is also a Trustee of Awards for Young Musicians.

Douglas McWilliams has focused his career upon making economics relevant to commerce and has specialized in economic forecasting and analysis. Douglas was Chief Economist for IBM UK, and then, the Confederation of British Industry's chief economic adviser. He subsequently set up the Centre for Economics and Business Research (CEBR) where he is now executive deputy chairman. He was also the Gresham Professor of Commerce from 2012 to 2014. He has published path-breaking books such as *The Flat White Economy: How the Digital Economy Is Transforming London and Other Cities of the Future* (2015) and an extraordinary combination of travel and economics exploration in *Driving the Silk Road: Halfway Across the World in a Bentley S1* (2019).

Lord Gus O'Donnell served as Cabinet Secretary from 2005 to 2011 and has since pursued a plural career including being Chairman of Frontier Economics, a trustee of The Economist Group, and a Visiting Professor at the London School of Economics and University College, London. Having studied Economics as Warwick University and Nuffield College, Oxford he taught the subject at Glasgow University for several years before joining the Treasury as an economist in 1979. He was appointed Head of the Government Economic Service in 1998 and became Permanent Secretary of the Treasury in 2002.

Mario Pisani is Deputy Director at HM Treasury. He has over fifteen years of experience working in economics, public policy, and financial management, and currently leads the Debt and Reserves Management team in the Fiscal Group at HM Treasury. He has also worked as an economics journalist for the *Financial Times* London. Mario has a BA in Economics with Econometrics from the University of Kent and an MPhil in Economics from the University of Oxford. He is also a professionally qualified accountant (ACMA/CGMA), and a Visiting Professor at King's College London. Mario also sits on the Council of the Society of Professional Economists.

(Visiting) Professor Vicky Pryce FAcSS is a co-author of this book—see above ('The Authors' page x).

Stephen Le Roux is Assistant Director in the Manufacturing Supply Chain Policy and International Policy Engagement in the Department for Business Energy and Industrial Strategy. He was a Fast Stream entrant to the Government Economic Service as an Economic Adviser to the Department of Work and Pensions' Health and Wellbeing Directorate. Stephen has a BA and an MA in Economics from the University of Exeter.

Andrew Smith is an independent consultant and commentator. Andrew is a former KPMG Chief Economist and before that Chief Economist and Investment Strategist at Credit Lyonnais Laing. He has served on the UK Government Secretary of State's Panel on the Economy and as a Board Member of the Centre for International Business and Management at the University of Bath. Andrew has an MA in Philosophy, Politics and Economics (PPE) and an M Phil in Economics from Oxford University.

Professor Lord Nicholas Stern is IG Patel Professor of Economics and Government and Chair of the Grantham Research Institute on Climate Change and the Environment at the London School of Economics (LSE). He initially pursued an academic career in Economics, becoming Professor of Economics at the

University of Warwick and, subsequently, the London School of Economics. He then became Chief Economist at the European Bank for Reconstruction and Development in 1994, Chief Economist of the World Bank in 2000 and in 2003 became head of the Government Economic Service and Second Permanent Secretary at HM Treasury, where he published his famous 'Stern Report' on the Economics of Climate Change in 2006. He is a former President of the British Academy and is currently co-chair of the Global Commission for the Economy and Climate.

Geoff Tily is a former Office of National Statistics and HM Treasury Economist, and is now a Senior Economist for the Trade Union Congress. He is an acknowledged expert in analysing UK economic trends and is the author of an influential book revisiting interpretations of J.M. Keynes: *Keynes Betrayed* (2007).

Kitty Ussher is the Chief Economist of Demos. She was MP for Burnley from 2005 until 2010, serving as Economic Secretary to the Treasury in the first phase of the global financial crisis, and prior to that as a Junior Minister in the Department of Work and Pensions. Since 2010 she has devised and delivered public policy thought leadership projects both as Managing Director of Tooley Street Research and through think-tanks, including being Director of Demos from 2010 to 2011. From July 2017 to August 2019 she took a two-year sabbatical to teach in inner-city schools. She studied Economics at Balliol College Oxford and Birkbeck College, London.

Romesh Vaitilingam is a writer and media consultant, Editor-in-Chief of the Economics Observatory and a member of the editorial board of VoxEU. He is the author of numerous articles and successful books in economics, finance, business and public policy, including *The Financial Times Guide to Using the Financial Pages* (FT-Prentice Hall). An expert in translating economic and financial concepts into everyday language, Romesh has advised a number of government agencies and international institutions, including the European Central Bank, the European Bank for Reconstruction and Development and the UK's Department for International Development.

Contents

PART ONE   Before you start

· · · ·●●●●●●· · · ·

CHAPTER 1   Why be an economist?   3

This chapter looks at the nature and importance of economics and why you too should become an economist, for the altruistic, intrinsic, and financial rewards of being an economist.

CHAPTER 2   Jobs you can do as an economist   25

An overview and description of a wide range of jobs open to economists in the private, public, and third sector. Also details on the sources for recruitment, with contacts and various employers' recruitment requirements.

CHAPTER 3   University and practitioner economics   67

This chapter looks at the similarities and differences between academic and practitioner economists, with insights on what it is like to work as a practitioner economist. It explores the difference in working to stakeholders in contrast with academic writing and research. Academics frequently end their journal articles with 'more research is required'. This is perfectly acceptable and often justified in academia, but in government, business and commerce, missing the deadline for a conclusion would more likely be deemed poor performance. Professional codes, such as for the civil service code, and ethics are also briefly explored.

CHAPTER 4   How useful are economics degrees?   87

This chapter explores the recent debates on whether academic economics is 'fit for purpose' and the skill gaps perceived in economics graduates as identified by employers. It will describe the generic skills that benefit all economics students and graduates, for example: good written and verbal communication skills; research skills; critical thinking skills; being an effective team player; self-motivation; self-awareness; and resilience—and those specialist skills that practitioners use most often in their professional work. These skill gaps are further explored in Part Two with exercises and additional sources.

PART TWO   Skills for success

· · · ●●●●●●● · · ·

CHAPTER 5   Communicating complexity simply   109

Good communication is vital for practitioner economists but is reported as a major skills gap among economics graduates by their employers. The advice on communication typically given at universities is excellent if one wishes to become an academic, but most students will not pursue that path. To be an effective professional practitioner economist one must practise communicating complexity simply, being concise, clear and convincing. It takes considerable practise to learn how to 'write-short'. This chapter outlines how academic writing differs from practitioner writing and provides tips on and examples of how to achieve the skills required.

CHAPTER 6   The importance of quantitative skills   153

As an economist, there is no escaping the need to interpret and present data effectively, but most practitioners, for example most of those working in the media, operational delivery, and policy, do not use nearly as much mathematics in their daily working lives as you will find in academic economic journals. This chapter puts this into perspective and outlines the quantitative and data skills most used by practitioners, including sections on presentation, common errors, and how to spot the statistical devices commonly used to mislead.

CHAPTER 7   The importance of broader and soft skills   182

This chapter emphasizes the importance of broader 'soft skills' required as complements to 'harder' quantitative skills and gives a brief overview of broader and soft skills, including how to 'manage upwards'.

CHAPTER 8   Towards a broader economics and a more diverse
body of economists   203

Eclecticism, interdisciplinarity, and historical perspectives are useful for pragmatic and successful policy formation. Practitioners must often be able to approach issues from various angles to be able to write from the perspective of their stakeholders and to defend their positions. This requires an eclectic approach to economics. This chapter looks at how different perspectives and world views can help inform policy formation. Learning about past economic policy is useful for understanding past policy mistakes and is a salutatory exercise for any practitioner of economics. The chapter looks at a recent debate between 'eclecticism v's pluralism' and student challenge to the curriculum. The chapter then looks at the need for greater diversity among economists themselves.

PART THREE   Planning for the future

· · · ●●●●●●● · · ·

CHAPTER 9   Applying for and passing interviews for economist posts   253

This chapter covers the process of applying for posts and how to approach interviews. It includes coverage of the most common errors when filling-in application pro-forma and gives suggestions for 'standing-out' from the crowd in a positive way. It gives advice on how to approach job interviews and provides guidance on 'What to do and what not to do' at interviews. It ends with reports from actual job interviews at a variety of organizations and interviews for economist jobs.

CHAPTER 10   How to stay a successful economist   281

Economics evolves and so there are constantly new challenges to rise to and opportunities for change. This chapter provides advice on how to keep abreast of new developments and up to date with data. There is an evaluation of the strengths and weaknesses of the main approaches used by economists and a brief overview of exciting new and revisited approaches to economics. Cost benefit analysis is given particular attention as it highlights many generic issues in microeconomics and as it is a ubiquitous tool in government and business, but one often overlooked at universities. The chapter ends with Andy Haldane, until recently Chief Economist at the Bank of England, explaining why it is a particularly good time to be an economist.

PART ONE

· · · · · · ● ● ● ● ● ● · · · ·

Before you start

CHAPTER 1

Why be an economist?

· · · ·●●●●●● · · ·

INTRODUCTION

This book will be useful to anyone considering studying economics or who just wants to know more about what economists do and how they do it, but it is particularly a guide for students of economics or recent graduates who are looking to work as a professional economist outside of academia, and most graduates do work outside universities.[1] It is best to start planning your career early on in your studies and this book has been written to help you decide to become an economist. It should also be invaluable for many academics who are interested in knowing more about working as an economist outside academia or who wish to help their students prepare for such 'practitioner' economist roles. Academic and practitioner economists are equipped with many of the same powerful tools, but they can be different trades in many ways, and so the skills required and the opportunities in these roles differ more than is often appreciated.

In this chapter we look at the nature and importance of economics and why you too should become an economist for the altruistic, intrinsic, and financial rewards. We start by exploring why you should study Economics in the first place. We ask what is the purpose of economics, what is its scope and impact? We then touch on why you should consider a career in economics before taking a deeper look at the career possibilities open to those with an Economics degree, in Chapter 2.

---

[1] If you do wish to become a successful academic economist you should read Weisbach, Michael S. (2021) The Economist's Craft (Skills for Scholars) Princeton University Press.

WHY STUDY ECONOMICS?

"Economics isn't just something you find in a textbook. It can be a potent tool to right past wrongs and improve people's lives."[2]

(Janet Yellen)

If you are already studying for an Economics degree—congratulations! You are most unlikely ever to regret your choice of degree subject. Eighty-five per cent of economics graduates said that, if they had their choice of degree again, they would still choose economics,[3] and all of the economists interviewed for this book said that they would still choose to be economists if they had their career choice again.[4]

If you are not yet studying Economics then read on a while, or visit http://whystudyeconomics.ac.uk, or https://www.discovereconomics.co.uk/, to see why you too should study for an Economics degree. If you have already completed a degree in another subject don't despair, not only do other subjects often complement economics but there are still routes available for you to become an economist, such as graduate diploma courses where you can in effect 'convert' your non-Economics degree to a recognized economics qualification in less time than it takes to do a first-degree. If you have yet to do a degree, then the Government Economic Service Apprenticeship Programme could actually pay you to work in government while studying for an Economics degree![5]

Economics is intellectually satisfying; vitally important; both topical and historical; extremely wide-ranging; interesting; and is likely to be more financially rewarding than degrees in almost all other subjects (see Chapter 2). Being an economist, like good food and music, should be a life-long pleasure. An Economics degree is an investment for life: you will draw on the knowledge and skills you gain if you become, as we urge, a professional economist, but also from the very wide range of roles and posts that graduate economists go on to occupy. For this book, we interviewed prominent economists, and some

---

[2] Janet Yellen was the first woman Chair of the US Federal Reserve and is now the first woman to head the US Treasury. The quote is from her Twitter account. https://twitter.com/SecYellen/status/1354147776880377862 (Accessed March 2021).

[3] In a survey of economics graduates by the Economics Network.

[4] With a few wistful asides about carpentry and being a marine biologist!

[5] The Government Economic Service Degree Apprenticeship Programme (GESDAP) https://www.gov.uk/government/publications/the-government-economic-service-degree-level-apprenticeship (Accessed March 2021).

recent graduates too.[6] As part of these, we asked our interviewees to reflect on their own careers and studies. We will quote from them throughout the chapters, and the full interviews are available to watch on the website that accompanies the book at www.oup.com/he/pryce-ross1e.

Lord Gus O'Donnell, an economist who went on to lead the UK civil service as Cabinet Secretary to three Prime Ministers, emphasized the lifelong return from an Economics degree:

"Throughout my career I've used economics and for me it's one of the great things about studying a subject in university that you can use for your life. I just worry about spending three years doing something and then never using it again. I mean, what a waste!"[7]

IS ECONOMICS A SCIENCE?

As this book has a particular focus on practitioner economics, we won't spend much time on such academic debates as to whether economics is a science or not.[8] However, given the often fierce debates on economics in the media, non-economists can be forgiven for thinking that the old joke about there being only two laws of economics rings true:

1st Law: For every economist there is an equal and opposite economist.
2nd Law: They are both wrong!

It is indeed true that much of economics is far from being settled science. Despite the still frequent anachronistic use of the term, there are no 'Laws of Economics'. In fact, there is hardly anything one can say in economics that is not conditional and/or heavily caveated. Instead of claiming universal laws 'It all depends on . . .' is a better maxim for economists. The work of economists ranges from technical research and application using the best data available, to more speculative exercises that are more akin to analysing international relations

---

[6] Yasir Auckbur, Sinéad Boultwood, Jonathan Coller, and Nathaniel Greenwold are all early career economists who spoke to us for the book. See Video 2: In conversation with Yasir Auckbur, Video 5: In conversation with Sinéad Boultwood, and Video 8: In conversation with Jonathan Coller and Nathaniel Greenwold available at www.oup.com/he/pryce-ross1e.

[7] Lord Gus O'Donnell in his interview for this book (see Video 19: In conversation with Lord Gus O'Donnell available at www.oup.com/he/pryce-ross1e).

[8] If you are looking for a book on epistemological metaphysics, this book is not it. But a good read is Alan Chalmers' *What is this thing called science?* 4th Edition (2013).

than science. That said, economists agree on far more than is appreciated by the general public. Indeed, economists often find that they are simultaneously being criticized for never agreeing with each other and for all being the same! The problems addressed by economists include the most important issues of our time. They can be complex and multi-dimensional, so the answers may not be easy and are unlikely to be certain, but to understand (Oh so many!) real-world issues we really do need economics.

Popular slogans used by some politicians such as, 'You can't borrow your way out of debt', or tabloid headlines such as 'Immigration leaves Brits unemployed' are far less 'obviously true' or 'just common sense' for real economists. So, despite all the uncertainties and lively debate that makes Economics such an exciting and dynamic subject, one thing all economists can do is spot a non-economist! Few, if any, economists believe that economics can match the scientific certainty of physics, but that is the nature of all social science, and there is no better alternative available. Of course, economics as a discipline can certainly be improved (see Chapter 4). Unfortunately, the world cannot stop and wait for a more definitive economics, and so, while some methodologists like to ponder such questions as 'Is Economics a Science?', this question is of no practical importance for practitioner economists. Practitioners are paid to get on with trying to find solutions to the pressing problems of the world, problems that do not wait for time nor tide or for better economic theory. In academia much time and effort are, rightly, devoted to advancing the great frontiers of knowledge that might one-day further advance the power and scope of economics. Practitioner economists must use the best of what we know so far, to decide what to do today for an uncertain tomorrow, using yesterday's limited information.

ECONOMICS IS RELEVANT FOR ISSUES PERSONAL TO GLOBAL

Almost all major events raise economic issues, as was so clear to all in the Covid 19 crisis, when economics and complementary behavioural sciences were as important for the best policy decisions as the medical sciences.[9] Economists have

---

[9] For example, see Lord Gus O'Donnell, *The Covid Tragedy: following the science or the sciences?* (2020) available at https://www.ifs.org.uk/uploads/IFS%20Annual%20Lecture%202020.pdf (Accessed March 2020).

the concepts and tools to make the most of every-day experience too. By shining a penetrating light into a huge range of phenomena and issues, economists often reveal things those non-economists struggle to see. Whereas a non-economist may complain that 'house prices are so high no-one can afford them', economists know the real questions are 'Who are the people buying the houses at these prices? Why are they doing it? and What impact does it have on others?'

The decisions economists make can impact everyday life for millions of people. In her interview for this book, Dame Kate Barker, a practical economist with a long and distinguished career, explains how she enjoyed being in jobs where she could see the effects of her decisions. Sometimes that could also be upsetting. She recalls a time, from when she was on the Monetary Policy Committee: 'We put interest rates up and I got home and my nanny was crying because she couldn't afford her mortgage anymore.'[10] Economists often have to consider the greater good over specific interests in this way. Economists have influence over the lives of others and usually, as with Dame Kate Barker, they take that responsibility very seriously indeed.[11]

Of course, there are no bigger world issues than poverty and climate change, together with the wider impacts of our lifestyles on the environment and biospheres that sustain us all. The implications for how we all live are profound and literally existential for very many millions of people, and for other species on our planet. This was known to science long before addressing climate change became part of the policy agenda, and as Vicky Pryce observes in her interview with Lord Nicholas Stern for this book, it was the economics of climate change in the 2006 'Stern Review'[12] that kicked climate change into mainstream politics. While academics were, rightly, still debating the technical elements[13] and the media were still presenting environmentalists as rather 'cranky', the Stern Review showed great leadership in combining economics and science to present the business case that drove home its central message about the urgency of addressing climate change. It used a business case format to engage with the language of those who had the power to act (see Chapter 5 on the importance of knowing your target audience). Lord Stern describes the

---

[10] Dame Kate Barker in her interview for this book (see Video 3: In conversation with Dame Kate Barker available at www.oup.com/he/pryce-ross1e).

[11] Even so, except for codes of conduct for members of the Royal Economic Society and the Government Economic Service, there is no binding ethnical code or exclusive professional body that prevents anyone from simply calling themselves an economist (see Chapter 3).

[12] N. Stern (2006), *The economics of climate change: The Stern Review*.

[13] Partly the 'correct' discount rate to use—see Chapter 10 of this book, page 313.

fascinating background to the Stern Review and how the emphasis has now shifted towards the possibilities for transformation towards sustainable production (see Chapter 10).

"The two subjects at the Gleneagles G7 summit in summer of 2005 were Africa and climate . . . most of the people there had thought quite a bit about Africa ahead of time and the challenges of growth, and the challenges of overcoming poverty across the board, but hardly anybody had thought about climate. They thought it was a marginal thing and they wondered why they were being asked to discuss it. It was a kind of cuddly environmental problem . . . on climate we got nowhere . . . And we concluded very quickly it's because the economics wasn't there.

People didn't see why it mattered so much, the lives and livelihoods, they didn't see what you could do about it, what it would cost to do something about it and were there other benefits to doing something about it, like reduced air pollution and better health? So, we decided very soon after the Gleneagles summit that this is what we needed to do . . . We put a very good team together of young people, mostly across government, but also one or two outsiders, and we tried to learn from the scientists. And we came up with two things which have absolutely lasted . . . which is that: the costs of inaction are far bigger than the costs of action, and this is a deep, deep market failure. Indeed, the biggest market failure the world has ever seen was the language we used.

Those two conclusions were absolutely central, but we've moved on a bit since then . . . we also see that changing the way we do things, to make things much more efficient, much cleaner will give us innovation, discovery, growth, and that it will give cities where we can move and breathe and be productive, ecosystems which are robust and fruitful. So, I think we actually see it in still more dynamic terms now that we have in our hands an alternative growth story. . . And in the last 15 years we've seen so much advance in what's possible now in terms of renewables"[14]

BUT DON'T ECONOMISTS THINK THAT ONLY GDP MATTERS?

Despite frequent accusations to the contrary, very few, if any, economists really believe that only GDP matters for human welfare. It's true that policy makers are often obsessed with GDP but there is nothing in economics that says

---

[14] Professor Lord Nicholas Stern in his interview for this book (see Video 24: In conversation with Professor Lord Nicholas Stern available at www.oup.com/he/pryce-ross1e).

we must prioritize GDP over everything else. In fact, economists understand what GDP does and does not measure much better than most people. Over 50 years ago, the economist Wilfred Beckerman wrote: 'Furthermore, for reasons which have been well known in the economic profession, GNP[15] is far from being a perfect measure of economic welfare'.[16] Indeed, you would be hard-pressed to find any introductory Economics tome that does not include a long list of why GDP is very inadequate as a measure of welfare. Today, it is still economists who write the most comprehensive and insightful critiques of what GDP is and what it is not, as in *GDP: A Brief but Affectionate History* by Diane Coyle.[17] (Diane Coyle is one of the leading economists interviewed for this book (see Video 9: In conversation with Diane Coyle CBE available at www.oup.com/he/pryce-ross1e). Economists at the UK's Office of National Statistics (ONS) are well-aware of what their GDP statistics do and do not measure and have been pioneers of working on developing better practical measures of economic welfare.[18] And in the same way that HM Treasury sponsored an eminent economist for the Stern Review and so pushed addressing climate change into mainstream policy, it is similarly to be hoped that their recent sponsorship of *The Economics of Biodiversity: The Dasgupta Review*, led by another eminent economist, Sir Partha Dasgupta, will do the same for the integration of the wider natural ecosystems and biospheres that all life and economic activity ultimately depend on.

Tellingly though, economists are also better informed than most about the consequences of neglecting GDP, such as on unemployment, poverty, the tax-base and the provision of public services. Even so, prominent economists have been leading advocates of wider metrics for capturing welfare and sustainability and for warning that an over emphasis on GDP can lead to ignoring things of greater importance (see Chapter 10): a warning often neglected by politicians who are eager for a 'hard statistic' to boast about in their electioneering. That said, for the poorer half of the world, it seems rather too easy for the well-off, living in rich countries, to be dismissive of economic growth. Billions of the world's people long for the sort of economic transformation described by

---

[15] We usually use GDP in place of GNP today.

[16] Wilfred Beckerman's *An Introduction to National Income Analysis* (1968, Weidenfeld and Nicolson).

[17] Diane Coyle's *GDP: A brief but affectionate history* (2014, Princeton University Press). Diane Coyle CBE FAcSS, Bennett Professor of Public Policy at the University of Cambridge.

[18] For example, see Richard Heys, *Building a bridge from GDP to Welfare: Next steps and first estimates* (July 2021), ONS https://www.escoe.ac.uk/building-a-bridge-from-gdp-to-welfare/ (Accessed July 2021).

economist Doug McWilliams where he explains how his upbringing in, what was then an impoverished Malaysia, led him to become an economist:

"People didn't have enough to eat. People died in their thirties and forties. Very few people lived on into their sixties unless they were fairly well off. And over just a short period of about 10 years this was transformed . . . So seeing what has created that change has been the thing that really excited me. Even as a little boy, I wanted to know why all this was happening. It seemed to be there was something almost magical in what was transforming the country and transforming people's lives for the better. And as far as I could see, it was economics . . . It seemed to me that economics was a sort of superpower and I wanted to have some of that superpower so that I could help improve other people's lives."[19]

Similarly, Liberian-born British economist Miatta Fahnbulleh, who is now the Chief Executive at the New Economics Foundation (NEF), describes how she was drawn to economics because she was interested in why some countries have developed and some countries haven't, what the past tells us about the present, and what potentially might give us insights into what you do in the future to try and make things better in those countries.[20] Sandeep Kapur, professor of economics at Birkbeck, London's evening university, describes how he grew up in India during times when there were huge variations in the economic policy regimes and there was a search for what would be the most appropriate policies for India.[21]

ECONOMICS IS UBIQUITOUS AND INTERDISCIPLINARY

We have noted that economics is relevant to issues from the personal to the global, and the practical bent of economics often leads to it being described as the 'science of choice'. It does provide very powerful decision-making tools. The most powerful of these is opportunity-cost, that constant reminder

[19] Doug McWilliams in his interview for this book (see Video 18: In conversation with Douglas McWilliams available at www.oup.com/he/pryce-ross1e).

[20] Miatta Fahnbulleh in her interview for this book (see Video 14: In conversation with Miatta Fahnbulleh available at www.oup.com/he/pryce-ross1e).

[21] Professor Sandeep Kapur in his interview for this book (see Video 17: In conversation with Professor Sandeep Kapur available at www.oup.com/he/pryce-ross1e).

to check if what you are doing or plan to do is the best that you can do with what you have available. Unfortunately for those economists who advise policy makers, the ubiquitous matter of opportunity cost must be frequently and repeatedly raised and asserted, and then reasserted, in order for good decision making to take place. This is in effect what an insistence on Cost Benefit Analysis does. Unfortunately, telling excited enthusiasts that there may a better use of resources than for their brainchild can feel like being a party-pooper: 'Yes, it is a good party, but is it the best party we could have?' is not always a welcome reality-check. Because of its ubiquity for practitioners and its sad neglect in universities, we look at Cost Benefit Analysis in Chapter 10.

Part of the attraction of economics is that it is so much more than even the vital job of making choices and problem solving. This is clear in the definition of Economics from a panel of economists for the UK Quality Assurance Agency for Higher Education (QAA) in its subject benchmarks for Economics:

> "Economics is the study of the factors that influence income, wealth and well-being. From this it seeks to inform the design and implementation of economic policy. Its aim is to analyse and understand the allocation, distribution and utilisation of resources and the consequences for economic and social well-being. Economics is concerned with such phenomena in the past and present and how they may evolve in the future."[22]

The scope of economics is huge.[23] Economics informs and interacts with business and politics, and with all the other social sciences, and is integral to our wider society both nationally and globally. As the QAA benchmarks add:

> "Economics is a major social science which draws on and influences other social sciences. It also links with other subject areas such as ethics, finance, geography, history, international relations, law, philosophy and psychology. It uses and interacts with mathematical and statistical methods and sciences such as environmental science, biology and medicine. As economics is integral to understanding business behaviour, strategy and corporate performance, it is also one of the core disciplines informing the study of business and management."[24]

---

[22] QAA, Subject Benchmark Statement Economics (2019). Available at https://www.qaa.ac.uk/docs/qaa/subject-benchmark-statements/subject-benchmark-statement-economics.pdf?sfvrsn=31e2cb81_5 (Accessed April 2021).

[23] Even though it is often confused with a narrower range of techniques and topics (see Chapters 4, 6, and 10).

[24] QAA, Subject Benchmark Statement Economics (2019), p.4.

Apart from the obviously economic things like economic performance, climate change, inequality and world poverty, economists have also helped shed light on many things non-economists might not consider as having much to do with economics at all. The range of topics studied by economists is astonishing, as Andy Ross once outlined in a speech to the delegates of the Economics Network's Developments in Economics Education Conference:

The topics economists study include:

- Auctions
- Sex and race discrimination
- Sport
- What you can and can't get on the NHS and why
- Competition and quality of education
- Value of time and life
- Happiness and well-being
- Inner-city dynamics
- Passenger safety
- Marriage and divorce—which partner gets the most in marriage?
- Crime and drugs
- Social exclusion
- Immigration
- Does performance-related pay make people work harder?
- Are we taxed too much?
- Is competition always good?
- Do people gamble rationally on the lottery and on quiz shows on television?
- What causes wars?
- Obesity
- How to match kidneys?
- Private returns to education (economists do particularly well!)
- Behavioural Economics
- Voting behaviour
- Social mobility
- Why are there so many junk media channels, all the same?

- Why aren't there petrol stations in the centre of cities?
- Are cities green?
- Why are cities so astonishingly productive? What are the agglomeration effects of human beings huddled together?
- Should we put folic acid in bread?
- Should nursery care be subsidized?
- Is Sure Start[25] off to an unsure start?
- Of course, there's the climate and the welfare of future generations and
- Yes, and all the stuff in 'Freakonomics' too.[26] Do teachers and Sumo wrestlers cheat? Did abortion reduce teenage crime?[27] Do doctors pump up their earnings by performing unnecessary operations?[28]

You will be able to greatly extend even this long list by looking at all the things that involve economics that are in the news today. Whether you take a business, political, social, philosophical, journalistic, statistical or mathematical approach, or combine all of these together as have some of the greatest economists, you will find economics a fascinating and fulfilling subject that allows enormous scope for personal and career development. Studying economics will need plenty of hard-work to master its concepts and techniques, but it is well-worth the effort as it rewards you with powerful insights into the world around you and opens a range of career opportunities unrivalled by most other degree subjects—it usually pays better too! This book has been written to help take you beyond university to get the best from your Economics degree.

WHY WORK AS AN ECONOMIST?

We have seen that the scope of economics is extremely broad. That is part of the reason why economics opens doors to such a wide variety of

---

[25] Sure Start is the name given to a UK initiative for early childcare.

[26] Steven D. Levitt and Stephen J. Dubner, *Freakonomics: A rogue economist explores the hidden side of everything* (2007).

[27] Probably not!

[28] Andy Ross (2007) *Economics in Action: What Economists Actually Do.* Keynote speech, Economics Network's Developments in Economics Education Conference, Cambridge. Available at http://whystudyeconomics.ac.uk/blog/2007/09/what-economists-actually-do/?shared=email&msg=fail (Accessed August 2021).

careers. The economists interviewed for this book often described how the power economics has for doing good is what attracted them to become economists, but the pros and perhaps cons of working as an economist will vary according to the particular job you choose. The easiest thing to quantify is earnings. Of course, this does not mean financial return is the most important thing that you should consider—as individuals we all have our own set of goals in life and success usually means much more than just money. That said, it is still nice to know that as an economist doing what you enjoy, you can still expect to earn, on average, more than most other graduates.

HOW MUCH WILL I EARN?

Despite much misperception and ill-informed criticism by non-economists, economists do know that there is much more to life than money alone. An all-too-common misperception among non-economists is that economists are a load of 'pale and stale males' talking only about money.[29] Depressingly, UCAS[30] still headlines its description of Economics degrees with 'Understanding the world's most powerful force: money'.[31] As a description of plutocracy this may have some merit, but it is a poor representation of economics.[32] Being an economist is also intrinsically satisfying and it can do a lot of good for others as well as for yourself. Yes, if you do want more money than you will ever need, at the possible sacrifice of work-life balance and family life, then an Economics degree can be a route to highly lucrative careers. But if you don't like what you would have to do, or put up with—or would miss the things you may have to neglect—to get loads of money, then fortunately a degree in economics opens the doors to very many other jobs too. This book also caters for, and particularly welcomes, those who are motivated by the good that economics can do for others while providing a satisfying and well-paid career for themselves.

---

[29] The Discover Economics initiative seeks to dispel this misperception and to increase the diversity of economics. See Chapter 8 and the Discover website at https://www.discovereconomics.co.uk/what-is-economics (Accessed March 2021).

[30] The UK's Universities and Colleges Admissions Service.

[31] UCAS Subject Guides/Economics. Available at https://www.ucas.com/explore/subjects/economics (Accessed September 2021).

[32] And as 'Discover Economics' found, is a far too common misperception about economics.

All that understood, surveys[33] do consistently confirm that the average financial return to an Economics degree compares very favourably indeed with that of other disciplines. In fact, the median starting salary for economics graduates is near the top of the official classification of degree subjects, and by five-years after graduation economics is in second place behind only medicine and dentistry[34] (see Table 1.1).

TABLE I.I   Median earnings of UK graduates 1 and 5 years after graduation

Tax year 17/18			
Degree subject	Median earnings £ pa 1 year after graduation	Degree Subject	Median earnings £ pa 5 years after graduation
Medicine and dentistry	36,500	Medicine and dentistry	49,300
Veterinary science	29,200	**Economics**	41,600
Engineering	26,600	Engineering	35,400
Economics	26,300	Mathematical sciences	34,300
Nursing and midwifery	25,900	Pharmacy, toxicology, and pharmacy	33,200
Physics and astronomy	24,800	Physics and astronomy	33,200
Architecture, building, and planning	24,800	Architecture, building and planning	33,200
Medical sciences	24,100	Veterinary science	32,800
Mathematical sciences	24,100	Medical sciences	31,000
Pharmacy, toxicology, and pharmacy	23,700	Computing	29,900
Computing	22,700	Chemistry	29,600
Chemistry	21,900	Politics	29,600
Allied health	21,200	Nursing and midwifery	28,500
Business and management	20,800	Languages and area studies	28,500

[33] See for example: The Sutton Trust *Earning by Degrees* (2014). Available at https://www.suttontrust.com/wp-content/uploads/2019/12/Earnings-by-Degrees-REPORT-1.pdf; 'How English domiciled graduate earnings vary with gender, institution attended, subject and socio-economic background' Institute of Fiscal Studies (2016); What Degree Will Get You Hired, Market Inspector (2018) https://www.market-inspector.co.uk/blog/2016/10/what-degree-will-get-you-hired and GOV.UK Graduate outcomes (LEO): outcomes in 2016 to 2017 https://www.gov.uk/government/statistics/graduate-outcomes-leo-outcomes-in-2016-to-2017). (All accessed March 2021).

[34] After ten years they are still in first and second place at £55 100 and £53 300 median earnings, respectively.

TABLE 1.1 (*Continued*)

Tax year 17/18

Degree subject	Median earnings £ pa 1 year after graduation	Degree Subject	Median earnings £ pa 5 years after graduation
Languages and area studies	20,800	Geography, earth and environmental studies	28,500
Politics	20,400	Business and management	27,700
Health and social care	20,400	Law	26,600
Combined and general studies	20,400	History and archaeology	26,600
Geography, earth and environmental studies	20,400	Philosophy and religious studies	26,600
Material and technology	19,000	Biosciences	26,300
Philosophy and religious studies	19,000	Allied health	25,600
Biosciences	18,600	Materials and technology	24,800
Law	18,600	English studies	24,800
History and archaeology	18,600	Sport and exercise sciences	24,500
Education and teaching	18,600	Health and social care	23,700
Agriculture, food and related studies	17,900	Education and teaching	23,700
General, applied and forensic sciences	17,900	Media, journalism and communications	23,700
Sociology, social policy, and anthropology	17,500	Psychology	23,400
Psychology	17,200	General, applied and forensic sciences	23,400
English studies	17,200	Sociology, social policy and anthropology	23,400
Media, journalism, and communications	16,800	Combined and general studies	23,400
Sport and exercise sciences	16,400	Agriculture, food and related studies	21,900
Creative arts and design	16,100	Creative arts and design	21,500
Performing arts	13,900	Performing arts	20,400

Source: Data from Official Statistics Graduate Outcomes (LEO): Tax Year 17/18 https://www.gov.uk/government/collections/statistics-higher-education-graduate-employment-and-earnings

FIGURE 1.1 Distribution of median earnings for each subject area five years after graduation

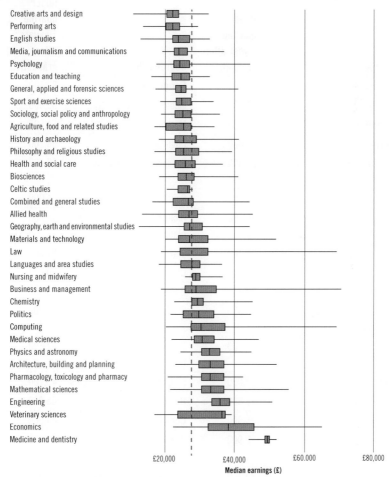

Source: Data from Official Statistics Graduate Outcomes (LEO): Tax Year 18/19

We can see the distribution of earnings for subjects in Figure 1.1 for earnings in Great Britain five years after graduation by subject, for the tax year 18/19, where we see the position of Economics is still second only to medicine and dentistry.

Of course, the median is merely the middle of the distribution, so highfliers may be more interested in the top of the distribution.[35] So, let's take a look at the upper quartile salary too, shown in Table 1.2.

---

[35] Of course, the range is not shown here and may be smaller for, say, medicine.

TABLE 1.2 Upper quartile earnings of UK graduates 1 and 10 years after graduation

Degree subject	Upper quartile 1 year after graduation	Degree Subject	Upper quartile 10 years after graduation
Medicine and dentistry	39,100	**Economics**	82,100
Veterinary science	32,500	Medicine and dentistry	69,000
Economics	32,100	Mathematical sciences	64,600
Engineering	31,800	Engineering	56,200
Architecture, building, and planning	30,300	Physics and astronomy	56,200
Nursing and midwifery	29,900	Politics	54,000
Mathematical sciences	29,600	Architecture, building, and planning	52,600
Physics and astronomy	29,200	Law	51,500
Combined and general studies	28,800	Computing	50,000
Computing	28,800	Business and management	50,000
Pharmacy, toxicology, and pharmacy	28,500	Medical sciences	47,800
Medical sciences	28,500	Pharmacy, toxicology, and pharmacy	47,100
Chemistry	27,000	Languages and area studies	46,700
Health and social care	26,600	History and archaeology	45,300
Politics	25,900	Chemistry	44,900
Business and management	25,900	Geography, earth and environmental studies	44,500
Languages and area studies	25,200	Philosophy and religious studies	43,800
Material and technology	24,800	Veterinary science	43,400
Geography, earth and environmental studies	24,800	Materials and technology	43,400
Allied health	24,100	Biosciences	43,400
Law	23,700	Sport and exercise sciences	39,400
Philosophy and religious studies	23,700	English studies	38,700
History and archaeology	23,400	Media, journalism, and communications	38,300

Degree subject	Upper quartile 1 year after graduation	Degree Subject	Upper quartile 10 years after graduation
Biosciences	23,000	Combined and general studies	38,000
Agriculture, food and related studies	22,300	Nursing and midwifery	37,600
General, applied and forensic sciences	21,900	Psychology	36,500
Sociology, social policy, and anthropology	21,900	General, applied and forensic sciences	36,100
Education and teaching	21,900	Sociology, social policy and anthropology	36,100
English studies	21,500	Health and social care	36,100
Psychology	21,200	Agriculture, food and related studies	35,800
Sport and exercise sciences	20,400	Allied health	35,400
Media, journalism, and communications	20,400	Education and teaching	34,700
Creative arts and design	20,100	Performing arts	34,300
Performing arts	18,200	Creative arts and design	33,900

Source: Data from Official Statistics Graduate Outcomes (LEO): Tax Year 2017/18 https://www.gov.uk/government/collections/statistics-higher-education-graduate-employment-and-earnings

Economics starts in third place close behind veterinary sciences. After 5 years it is in joint first place and economics then finishes after ten years in first place by quite some margin.[36]

'Glassdoor'[37] also collects small samples from subscribers and uses broad-terms that straddle both the private and public-sectors. For example, they report that for 2020 the post 'Chief Economist'[38] had an average base pay of £105,884.

[36] Where the available data ends.

[37] Glassdoor reviews employment opportunities and has a database of over 8 million company reviews, salary details, interview questions, and open job listings. It aims to help people make informed career decisions by increasing transparency about compensation and other previously 'taboo' information in the workplace.

[38] Glassdoor https://www.glassdoor.co.uk/Salaries/chief-economist-salary-SRCH_KO0,15.htm (Accessed March 2021).

TABLE 1.3 Society of Professional Economists: 2019 salary survey results

Total cash compensation (£k)	Percentage (%)
<=40	19
41–60	14
61–80	17
81–100	13
101–120	6
121–140	3
141–200	8
201–300	11
>300	8

Source: Society of Professional Economists—Salaries Report 2020
https://www.res.org.uk/resources-page/society-of-professional-economists-salaries-report-2020.html

The Society of Professional Economists (SPE)[39] annual salary survey gives an idea of the range of earnings of economists. The results from the 2019 survey are shown in Table 1.3.

Of course, age and length of career explain much of the range here. For example, the lower salaries will include early-career economists, and those earning below £40k includes young academic post-doctoral researchers wishing to build a research profile as preparation for an academic career. Such researchers may earn as little as £15k per annum but in effect are working through an apprenticeship. In the middle of the SPE range there will be academics and civil servants. At the top of the SPE scale there will be Chief Executive Officers (CEOs), and economists in finance and investment banking. We look at these jobs in Chapter 2, again noting that 'success' means different things for different people.

Most economists can expect their earnings to rise with years of experience, as Table 1.3 implies. *Salary Expert* reports that the average salary in the UK for an economist is close to £70k, although it does vary by region.[40] On the graduate

---

[39] The Society of Professional Economists (SPE) is the leading organization serving professional economists in the UK and Europe. See www.spe.org.uk.

[40] *Economist Salaries by City in United Kingdom*, Salary Expert https://www.salaryexpert.com/salary/browse/cities/job/all/economist/united-kingdom (Accessed March 2021).

development scheme at the Bank of England salaries start at around £30K[41] and, although senior officials at the Bank of England are more than just economists, it was reported in 2017 that almost one tenth of the staff at the Bank of England earned more than £100 000 before benefits and bonuses, according to the Bank's accounts.[42] Of course, many economists in the finance sector, much of it based in the City of London, earn considerably more than this. As an article from the *Independent* newspaper headlined 'City economists' salaries dwarf public servants' pay' pointed out,[43] the earnings of investment bankers can be double-figure multiples of even the most senior public appointments.

It is certainly the case that many economist civil servants work below the salaries they could earn elsewhere, mainly for reasons of job security, good pension, a civilized working environment and a commitment to public service.

Although we might personally like to believe it, the comparatively high earnings of economics cannot be wholly explained merely by claiming that economists are exceptionally bright:[44]

"When we account for different student intakes across subjects, only economics and medicine remain outliers with much higher earnings than one would expect given A-level performance as compared with their peers in other subjects (Institute of Fiscal Studies)."[45]

GENDER GAP IN ECONOMICS

While we are on the subject of earnings, we should acknowledge the gender pay gap. That is, that the median earnings of women across all jobs in an occupation are lower than for men, and this gap exists across all occupations.[46]

---

[41] See the Bank of England Careers website, available at https://www.bankofengland.co.uk/careers/early-careers/our-programmes (Accessed March 2021).

[42] Vivek Ahuja (2017), 'Six-figure earners on the rise at Bank of England', *FN Financial News*, 10th July. Available at https://www.fnlondon.com/articles/six-figure-earners-on-the-rise-at-bank-of-england-20170706 (Accessed March 2021).

[43] Sean O'Grady (2011), 'City economists' salaries dwarf public servants' pay', *The Independent*, 23 October. Available at https://www.independent.co.uk/news/business/news/city-economists-salaries-dwarf-public-servants-pay-2039041.html (Accessed March 2021).

[44] Though of course we are!

[45] Institute of Fiscal Studies *'How English domiciled graduate earnings vary with gender, institution attended, subject and socio-economic background'* (2016).

[46] The gender gap refers to the difference between average/median earnings of men and women across the jobs in an occupation. See for example: Vicky Pryce *Women vs Capitalism* (2019, C. Hurst & Co Ltd).

While there are many women economists in prominent positions, and women economists earn more than women in most other occupations, there is still a long way to go in terms of diversity and gender pay gap among economists:

> "It is also interesting to note that it is estimated that around 12 per cent of male economics graduates earned above £100,000 some ten years after graduation; by contrast, 6 per cent of those studying medicine or law earned more than £100,000. In terms of females, it is estimated that around 9% of economics graduates earned above £100,000 some ten years after graduation; by contrast, just 1 per cent of those studying medicine and 3 per cent of those studying law did so."[47]

We shall look at more aspects of diversity in economics in Chapter 8.

CONCLUSION: AM I GUARANTEED SUCCESS BY BEING AN ECONOMIST?

Of course not! Hard work, your personal attributes and behaviours, friends and networks, and even sheer luck can all play a part, as distinguished economist Dame Kate Barker modestly admits. Of course, she also adds 'You get a break because of those lucky things, but if you're no good in the position that luck runs out very, very quickly'.[48] Statistically, as Paul Johnson, former Deputy Director of the GES and Chief Microeconomist for HM Treasury and now Director of the Institute of Fiscal Studies, points out,[49] the average financial returns to degrees vary according to both what and where you study. As Chapter 7 explains, it takes more than an Economics degree, or even economics itself, to be a successful economist. Your renumeration will depend on more than just your degree, but as an economist you are at least more likely to do better in that respect than in other careers. More importantly, you will also enjoy the intrinsic satisfaction that comes with being an expert in a fascinating and useful discipline.

---

[47] Institute of Fiscal Studies cited *at Salaries for Economics Graduates* http://www.studyingeconomics.ac.uk/where-next/jobs-and-careers/money-you-could-earn/ (Accessed March 2021).

[48] Dame Kate Barker in her interview for this book (see Video 3: In conversation with Dame Kate Barker available at www.oup.com/he/pryce-ross1e).

[49] Paul Johnson, Graduate wage premium high but too variable? (2016). Available at https://www.ifs.org.uk/publications/8465 (Accessed March 2021).

SUMMARY

- Economics has a huge range and scope of enquiry and so should have something interesting for everyone.

- Personal decision making can be improved though economics and the most pressing problems of the world require an understanding of economics.

- The perception of non-economists as to what economics is, and what economists think and do, is often very wide of the mark.

- Economics interacts with a very wide range of other disciplines.

- Being an economist is both intrinsically and financially rewarding.

- There are a wide range of jobs open to economics graduates; each will have pros and cons according to your personal tastes and goals. (See the next chapter.)

- Women do comparatively well in economics compared to other subjects (but see Chapter 8).

QUESTIONS

1. What are the three most important aspects of a career that you aspire to and how well might a job as an economist match these aspirations?

2. Explain why economics is applicable to such a huge range of issues and problems and is central to government decision making.

3. Explain why economics and medical sciences were both vitally important for addressing the Covid-19 pandemic.

4. Why are economics and politics so often intertwined?

EXERCISES

1. Ask a few non-economist friends what they think economics is about. How well do their answers reflect what economics is actually about?

2. Borrow some introductory textbooks on economics, or simply look at those you may have already, do they emphasize the limitations of GDP?

3. Make a list of what you think are the three most important and pressing problems in the world. Now explain why economics is important to these problems.

4. Add at least three more topics that economists study to the list on page 12.

FIND OUT MORE

The Quality Assurance Agency for Higher Education (2019) *QAA Subject Benchmark Statement for Economics 2019*, available at: **https://www.qaa.ac.uk/docs/ qaa/subject-benchmark-statements/subject-benchmark-statement-economics.pdf** (accessed March 2021).

The 'Why Study Economics?' website: **https://whystudyeconomics.ac.uk/**.

CHAPTER 2

Jobs you can do as an economist

· · · · · ●●●●●● · · · ·

INTRODUCTION

The famous American economist and adviser to US Presidents, John Kenneth Galbraith, once joked, 'Economics is extremely useful as a form of employment for economists.'

In the previous chapter we saw economics is much more profound than JK Galbraith quipped, though in this chapter we will see that is indeed the gateway to a host of good jobs.

We might also joke that there are only two types of people in the world, economists and non-economists, but a constant frustration for economists is that almost everyone seems to think they are an economist! What seems so blindingly obvious to so many non-economists is often much more problematic and conditional to economists simply because they have a better understanding of what is involved. Fortunately, there are many ways to be a real economist, and an economics degree also boosts your general employability across a very wide range of industries and other occupations. It is pleasing that there is such a strong demand for economists. Although numerate graduates are generally prized by employers across the board, this is particularly so when combined with the transferable analytical and problem-solving skills of economists. If you can also learn how to communicate complexity simply and to work well with others, then even more opportunities are available. As Chapter 9 will explain, to succeed in getting a job in the career of your choice it is best to start thinking about your career choices early in your studies. This will inform your choice of option modules and bring focus to preparing the knowledge and skills that are most prized by your targeted careers, as well as rehearse for the recruitment regime you are likely to face.

An economics degree, combined with the skills we look at in Chapters 5 to 7, can open the door to and equip you for a host of great career opportunities. This chapter only looks at careers where you can expect to use and build on the economics you have learned from your degree—much as we wish you to become a professional economist, your career horizons as an economics graduate are not limited to economics. We explore economist roles in the private, public, and third sector by explaining what the jobs in different occupations might entail and by setting out the advantages and disadvantages to be considered. We also provide information on organizations and sectors that regularly seek to employ graduate economists. This should help you to decide on the careers that may interest you, and so also on where to focus your time and effort for further research into these careers. Such research is also invaluable to be successful at interview to get a job along your chosen career path (see Chapter 9). It is worth noting here, as does Dame Kate Barker in her interview for the book,[1] that even if you find out that you are not suited to your first few career paths you can still use them to learn things that turn out to be useful for your later chosen career, and still as an economist!

Additionally, we provide details on the sources for recruitment, with contacts and various employers' recruitment requirements. We finish the chapter by outlining some good websites for searching economist jobs and emphasize the use and importance of placements for helping you gain experience and get on to the career ladder.

The website Studying Economics www.studyingeconomics.ac.uk, also provides information on some job opportunities for economists.[2]

A WIDE RANGE OF CAREER OPPORTUNITIES ARE OPEN TO ECONOMICS GRADUATES

A good degree is a lifelong asset that can open many career doors. An excellent website for exploring this wider range of career opportunities is at www.prospect.ac.uk. The Prospect service is funded by the UK higher and further education and research funding bodies and their member institutions. As well

[1] See Video 3: In conversation with Dame Kate Barker available at www.oup.com/he/pryce-ross1e.

[2] Studying Economics http://www.studyingeconomics.ac.uk/where-next/jobs-and-careers/careers-in-the-private-sector/ (Accessed June 2021).

as supplying guidance and information on a wide range of jobs, Prospect provides a career planner, and you can register to receive updates by email. The Prospect website also includes lots of generic advice that will be useful for anyone seeking a graduate entry career. Again, as we are encouraging you to follow your degree in economics with a career as an economist, this book naturally focusses on economist jobs, but much of what we say, particularly in Chapters 5 to 9, will be valuable no matter what your career aspirations. It is also the case that many economist jobs also provide entry to other occupations that allow you to develop in other worthwhile ways. For example, as a manager, special adviser, or executive. Economists tend to do well in rising to senior positions wherever they go. For example, economists figure disproportionately across the top posts in the civil service. Although, as Chapter 7 explains, it typically takes a lot more than just economics for a successful career and to get to senior positions.

A broad picture of the careers economics graduates go into is provided by the Economic Network's alumni survey and their sister website 'Why Study Economics?' at www.whystudyeconomics.ac.uk. *Burning Glass Technologies* partnered with *Frontier Economics* to monitor, for *Discover Economics*,[3] 204,000 economics-specific or economics-related jobs advertised online in the UK in 2019.[4] This showed that nearly half of the jobs were located across the UK outside London and the South-East. They used a 'cloud' to represent the relative number of jobs adverts (shown in Figure 2.1).

Discover Economics (www.discovereconomics.ac.uk) is partnered with many of the major organizations in UK economics including the Royal Economic Society,[5] the Society of Professional Economists[6] and the Scottish Economic Society[7] and provides a chart (see Figure 2.2) illustrating the sort of jobs economics graduates go on to do.

---

[3] We look at the exciting and much needed 'Discover Economics' project in more depth in Chapter 8.

[4] Frontier Economics and Burning Glass Technologies (2020) *Career options for economics graduates Report for Discover Economics* https://www.frontier-economics.com/media/4351/career-options-for-economics-graduates.pdf (Accessed September 2021).

[5] The Royal Economic Society is one of the oldest and most prestigious economic associations in the world https://www.res.org.uk/ (Accessed March 2021).

[6] The Society of Professional Economists (SPE) is the leading organization serving professional economists in the UK and Europe https://spe.org.uk/ (Accessed March 2021).

[7] Successor from 1954 to the Scottish Society of Economists founded in 1897 http://www.scotecon.org/ (Accessed March 2021).

FIGURE 2.I   A cloud of the most advertised careers you can pursue with a degree in Economics

Source: Figure from page 8 of Frontier Economics and Burning Glass Technologies (2020) *Career options for economics graduates: Report for Discover Economics.* https://www.frontier-economics.com/media/4351/career-options-for-economics-graduates.pdf

FIGURE 2.2   What economists really do

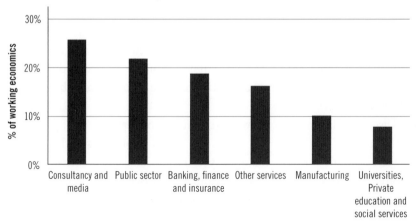

Source: Griffiths, R. (2019) *Communicating what economists really do* [PowerPoint presentation]. The Society of Professional Economists Annual Conference Report: The UK and Global Outlook—Weak Growth, Policy Changes, (14 October 2019). Available at: https://spe.org.uk/site/assets/files/7262/r_griffith_slides.pdf [Last accessed May 2022].

Having established the wide range of jobs that economist do, we will now look in more detail at specific occupations where graduates work as economists.

PRIVATE SECTOR CAREERS

CAREERS IN THE FINANCE SECTOR

Finance sector careers involve activities around very large sums of money. There are many roles that an economics graduate can go on to perform in the finance sector. Kevin Daly of Goldman Sachs gives this advice for anyone wishing to become a financial sector economist:

"Certainly, as a financial sector economist you need a broad range of different skills, you need to be academic, you need to be a good writer, you need to be a good presenter, you need forecasting skills . . . the two skills that I would highlight in particular . . . have been maths and writing."[8]

INVESTMENT BANKING

Investment banks are financial institutions that offer an extensive range of services such as advice on mergers and acquisitions, capital raising, economic forecasting and investment research, and trading financial instruments. Their typical clients will be large business corporations and 'buy-side' asset managers, who buy and sell large blocks of financial assets. Investment banks perform different functions from the traditional and commercial High Street banking that most of us use for our personal financial transactions and loans. Investment banks, by contrast, only deal with transactions where very large amounts of finance are involved.

There are a surprisingly large number of investment banks,[9] including the bigger better-known ones such as JPMorgan Chase, Goldman Sachs, Bank of America, Merrill Lynch, Morgan Stanley, Citigroup, Deutsche Bank and UBS. Also serving the same marketplace are a large selection of smaller companies which provide specialist advice in corporate finance, macroeconomics, and company research.

A career in investment banking is a popular aspiration for many students of economics. The comparatively high salaries and bonuses and intellectual challenge are an obvious attraction, but for many aspirants this should be

---

[8] In his interview for this book (see Video 10: In conversation with Kevin Daly available at www.oup.com/he/pryce-ross1e).

[9] A list of the largest ones can be found at www.relbanks.com/worlds-top-banks/top-investment-banks (Accessed March 2021).

balanced by also considering the long-hours, pressure, and a lack of security that may go with such jobs:

ADVANTAGES

- Can be a remarkably high starting salary compared to other economist job starting salaries
- A wide variety of work, albeit across finance
- The opportunity to work alongside and network with senior management
- A global outlook

DISADVANTAGES

- Highly competitive
- Employers may target certain universities, though this is less so than used to be the case
- You may need a postgraduate degree for entry as an economist to some investment banks
- Very long hours, weekend shifts often seen as obligatory
- Can be a high-stress environment
- Low job security

Every year investment banks draw a huge number of applications from economics students for their internship and graduate schemes. With starting salaries of £40,000+ and bonuses, it is easy to see why! Investment banks tend to recruit specialist economists, but many of the other positions offered by investment banks are well-suited to the wider skills of an economist. For example, a position on the trading floor may require graduates to analyse a particular firm or sector, to weigh up potential costs and benefits and understand risk. All these skills come naturally to students from an economics background. Furthermore, economics students are often much more aware of current issues surrounding the wider economy outside the banking sector than are non-economist bankers, and part of their job can be disseminating this knowledge around their organization and stakeholders. This might be why so many of the positions within this sector are filled by graduate economists.

However, as said, no undergraduate considering a career in investment banking should do so lightly. The financial sector makes money work as hard as possible and as it is a global activity there are financial markets open 24 hours a day, requiring constant monitoring and vigilance. Such jobs typically require an enormous amount of your time and effort. Roles in investment banking may also involve a large amount of international travel which can be punishingly exhausting. You may also be expected to study for the Chartered Financial Analyst's qualification, which constitutes a demanding challenge and is no pushover by any means. Consequently, if you do have your heart, or at least your bank balance, set on this career path then the earlier you begin planning and tailoring your CV the better (see Chapter 9). Securing a placement/internship, say in the summer of your second year of study, can be a great advantage for your preparation and networking.

Most graduates who gain a position at an investment bank do so through an internship (see page 62). These can be hard to obtain. To gain an internship your first-year academic results need to be outstanding. Investment banking has become determinedly meritocratic in its graduate recruitment practices compared with the days when entry was largely based on whom you knew and on having gone to the 'right' school and university. Don't be discouraged by these out-of-date attitudes from applying to this challenging, exciting, and highly rewarding industry. But be realistic: you are unlikely to find a position without at least a good 2:1 honours degree, and often outstanding A-levels or equivalent. And you should be aware of the sacrifices that may need to be made to be successful, which can be poor work-life balance, stress, a feeling of being on permanent probation, and the prospect of premature 'redundancy'. For others, the high-octane, high-reward environment suits them well.

For recruitment details view the individual websites of investment banking companies, such as Goldman Sachs (https://www.goldmansachs.com/careers/students/programs/index.html) or Morgan Stanley (https://www.morganstanley.com/people-opportunities/students-graduates), or use the job search engines listed at the end of this section.

ASSET MANAGEMENT

Asset managers invest money on behalf of a wide range of investors: pension funds; insurance companies; family offices; and retail investors (whether 'high net worth' individuals or for more modest Self-Invested Personal Pension (SIPP) and Individual Saving Account (ISA) investors[10]). The pressure to beat the competition is intense and unrelenting, though the risks to a healthy work/life balance are generally markedly less than in investment banks and associated 'sell-side' specialist service providers.

---

[10] SIPPs and ISAs provide advantages on moderate size investments, including tax-free returns and a breadth of portfolio options to invest in.

Many asset managers employ specialist economists. In addition, graduates with an economic background are especially suited to roles in asset allocation and FX/fixed income portfolio management. As with investment banks, economics graduates have the skills and knowledge which make them well-positioned for recruitment into other asset management roles.

Remuneration is generally lower than in investment banks, although the pay gap appears to have been narrowing in recent years.

ADVANTAGES

- Generally better work-life balance than investment banking
- Higher remuneration than most economist jobs

DISADVANTAGES

- Still a more high-pressure competitive job environment than for most other economist jobs
- Remuneration not as high as for investment banking

For asset management careers apply direct to the firms themselves, such as M&G (https://www.mandg.com/careers) and Baillie Gifford https://www.bailliegifford.com/en/uk/careers/current-opportunities/) or use the portals suggested below.

For more information on investment banking and asset management see:

Inside Careers : http://www.insidecareers.co.uk/professions/banking/

Target Jobs: https://targetjobs.co.uk/career-sectors/investment-banking-and-investment/advice/282489-how-to-get-a-banking-and-investment-graduate-job-the-basics

eFinancial Careers: www.eFinancialCareers.co.uk

CAREERS IN BUSINESS AND FINANCIAL CONSULTANCY

Economists are needed at the heart of the business world and in financial consulting. Their business roles vary widely, but economics graduates often find jobs in large and medium-sized business organisations providing relevant economic research, such as on specific market trends. Financial consultant economists fill similar roles, often working for multiple clients rather than just one organization. They will contribute to producing briefings and reports and advising on business strategy. Up-to-date specific industry knowledge and understanding of corporate finance are needed for these roles. For example, RSM is one of the world's largest networks of audit, tax, and consulting firms; its global network spans more than 120 countries. UK Capital Economics employs over 60 experienced economists and provides macroeconomic, financial market and sectoral analysis, forecasts and consultancy, from offices in London, New York, Toronto, and Singapore.

GENERAL ECONOMIC CONSULTANCY

If, later in your career, you achieve a successful track record as an economic adviser, you may set-up as an independent consultant. In his interview Doug McWilliams[11] explains how the consultancy he founded some thirty years ago, The Centre for Economic and Business Research (Cebr) has been called-in by a wide range of clients, not only commercial and those acting for government policy, such as in the Covid vaccine roll-out. He describes how there are more similarities than differences between being an economic adviser and an independent consultant, but that an economic adviser has to manage upwards (see Chapter 7) for a chance to make a difference whereas consultants tend to have the problem they are working on pre- specified.

CORPORATE AND RETAIL BANKING

These include familiar high street banks such as Barclays, NatWest, HSBC, RBS, and Lloyds. And they also have commercially orientated divisions for corporate customers. In fact, although corporate banking offers similar services to retail banks, the major distinction is the clientele and the amount of money and profit involved. Corporate banking services include corporate finance, credit management, asset management, cash management, and loan management.

There is generally lower remuneration than in investment banking but, typically, a better work-life balance.

PROFESSIONAL SERVICES

Professional services employ a range of expertise, including economists, to provide support to businesses and other organizations in the form of advice, analysis and tertiary roles. Their services include:

- Actuarial, for example, evaluating future financial risks.
- Audit, for example, checking and ensuring the validity and legality of financial records.

[11] In his interview for this book (see Video 18: In conversation with Douglas McWilliams available at www.oup.com/he/pryce-ross1e).

- Consulting, for example, advising on how to reduce costs or reorganize for better performance.
- Financial advice, for example, advising on investments and financial management.
- Project appraisal, advising on infrastructure investment, development, and sustainability.
- Tax, advising how to complete tax returns to reduce tax payments.

The 'Big Four' (PwC, Deloitte, KPMG and Ernst & Young) dominate the professional services sector, providing the full range of services listed above. Some others are also large globally as networks of independent accountants, auditors, tax advisers, and consulting firms and public sector entities. Grant Thornton and RSM are examples of this. Others are large but specialized, such as economic consultants on infrastructure investments employed by Arup (see below).

The 'Big Four' audit the vast majorities of companies in the FTSE 250 Index and help organizations with regular services and advice as well as change management, troubleshooting, and advice in times of rapid change, such as changes in an organization's economic circumstances or regulatory framework. As economists often have specialist knowledge it makes them especially attractive to professional services providers:

> "Our team of economic consultants work alongside a wide range of clients, using economic insights to inform strategic choices, guide the development of policy and assess the impact of major investments."[12]

As the economy impacts on almost all organizations, professional services often also employ macroeconomists to watch, evaluate, and forecast the course of the economy. For example:

> "The Chief Economist team at KPMG advises clients on the economic outlook and the implications for their business. Their analysis looks at the impact major changes, such as new technologies or shifts in preferences, could have on the economy as well as on individual businesses, and what policies could be used to support those negatively impacted. The team produces a range of reports

---

[12] PwC (2015) available at: https://www.pwc.co.uk/services/economics.html (Accessed March 2021).

on topical issues, as well as quarterly Economic outlook reports and weekly economic updates."[13]

ADVANTAGES

- High starting salary
- An emphasis on personal and professional development
- The opportunity to complete a professional qualification
- Good professional development opportunities

DISADVANTAGES

- Very competitive
- Many roles are exam orientated

The Professional Services industry recruits a large number of graduates from a wide range of degrees. The Big Four recruit on a rolling basis, so there are no strict deadlines, but once positions are filled recruitment can stop abruptly, so when there is an opening it is best to apply early.

One of the major benefits of this industry is that these firms take continuous professional development (CPD) very seriously (see Chapter 7 for the importance of CPD), and so make a large investment in knowledge and skills for all of their graduate recruits. Part of this investment is to put all their graduates through a professional qualification. These qualifications will usually be taken alongside your day-to-day responsibilities and can last from three years (ACA and CIMA[14]) to up to six (actuarial exams). Students studying Economics will often get exemptions from some of the exams in the first year of these qualifications. Economists will also find their degree very relevant to the modules they have to study in subsequent years for these qualifications and the projects their company will allocate to them.

Studying for a professional qualification may not be welcomed by some graduates who want to leave their exam-taking days behind them. Moreover, if you fail any of your exams twice, your contract with your employer may be terminated. This pressure can be very stressful, but, in addition to expanding

---

[13] Macroeconomic Strategy: Economic outlook and its impact on business strategy KPMG at https://home.kpmg/uk/en/home/services/advisory/strategy/macroeconomic-strategy.html (Accessed September 2021).

[14] ACA is the Association of Chartered Accountants and CIMA is the Chartered Institute of Management Accountants.

your skills repertoire, having one of these professional qualifications on your CV does look very impressive.

If you want to follow this career path then you need to spend a lot of time researching the particular service that you want to apply for and research each firm's core competencies. These factors are likely to be heavily emphasized in any interview you may get (see Chapter 9).

Watch Andrew Smith's (former Chief Economist at KPMG) interview for this book[15] where he talks about his experience working in the financial services and professional services sectors.

For more information on professional services and jobs see:

ARUP: https://www.arup.com/careers

Grant Thornton: https://www.grantthornton.co.uk/

KPMG Careers: https://www.kpmgcareers.co.uk/graduate

PWC: https://www.pwc.co.uk/careers.html

RSM: https://www.rsmuk.com/careers/students/choose-your-business-area/ consulting/economic-consulting

COMPETITION POLICY ECONOMIST AND REGULATORS

Competition policy draws on a rather specialized branch of economics, it can be lucrative but requires a very good knowledge of the relevant law and industrial organization, which is a field of economics dealing with the strategic behaviour of firms, regulatory policy, antitrust policy, and market competition. Competition policy is public policy aimed at ensuring that competition is not restricted or undermined in ways that are detrimental to the functioning of markets, and in particular to the consumer. It rests on the belief that competitive markets are central to consumer interests, investment, efficiency, innovation, and growth. The largest authority applying competition law in the UK is the Competition and Markets Authority (CMA),[16] which has staff in London, Edinburgh, Belfast and Cardiff. It expresses its purpose and activities succinctly as follows:

> "Competition is good for consumers and businesses. It means that people get better products at lower prices, and it helps ensure the most consumer-focused and innovative businesses are the ones that succeed."

[15] See Video 23: In conversation with Andrew Smith (available at www.oup.com/he/ pryce-ross1e).

[16] Competition and Markets Authority (CMA) https://www.gov.uk/government/organisations/competition-and-markets-authority/about (Accessed April 2021).

"We work to ensure that consumers get a good deal when buying goods and services, and businesses operate within the law.

We do this in a number of ways:

We investigate mergers between organisations, to make sure they don't reduce competition

We investigate entire markets if we think there are competition or consumer problems

We take action against businesses and individuals that take part in cartels or anti-competitive behaviour

We protect consumers from unfair trading practices

We encourage government and other regulators to use competition effectively on behalf of consumers."[17]

Economists work on competition policy both in the private and public sector: in the private sector, for companies and specialist consultancies which advise companies so that they do not infringe competition law—the fines for which can be very large indeed; in the public sector, for authorities such as the Competition and Markets Authority and the Financial Conduct Authority. Competition policy economists usually work side-by-side with specialist lawyers, which can be a challenge for both, as economists and lawyers tend to approach tasks with different perspectives and communication styles. For example, a competition economist once asked a competition lawyer 'What exactly are we attempting to maximise?' The reply was 'Maximisation doesn't come into it, we are simply here to apply the law'.

An attractive feature of competition policy is that practitioners quite often move in and out between the private and public sectors. 'Poachers turned gamekeepers' as they say! So long as all conflicts of interest are avoided, or at least declared and monitored, this can have advantages for all parties in that the perspectives and concerns of both regulators and business are better shared and so better understood and reconciled. The advantages and disadvantages of this work are very similar to those of the regulators.

THE REGULATORS

Closely related to competition policy is regulatory policy. For example, utilities companies are obliged to conform to legislation and guidance in their provision to customers. As this advert from Affinity Water shows:

[17] Ibid.

"When you join the Regulation & Strategy team at Affinity Water, you'll work as part of a small, expert team designed to analyse, understand and predict the business' regulatory performance. You'll assist the team's efforts to provide expert guidance to stakeholders when it comes to economic regulatory requirements, whilst supporting teams across the company on how to optimise performance against these compliance commitments."[18]

In addition to the well know regulators such as Ofcom, Ofgem, and Ofwat, there is a wide range of other regulators.[19]

Not surprisingly, as they tend to draw on the same pool of economists and graduates, the advantages and disadvantages for competition policy economists and regulators are similar:

ADVANTAGES

- Good starting salaries and career paths, the best may get poached by big firms for big money
- Good professional development opportunities
- Competition and regulation cases can be high profile in the financial media

DISADVANTAGES

- Rather a specialized field so fewer opportunities to develop as a rounded economist
- Lawyers often complain it's all economics and the economists complain it's all law!

For more information of competition and regulation policy jobs see

Financial Conduct Authority: https://www.fca.org.uk/about/promoting-competition

Frontier Economics: https://www.frontier-economics.com.au/disciplines/competition/

FTI Consulting: https://www.fticonsulting-emea.com/services/economic-and-financial-consulting/competition-policy

London Economics: https://londoneconomics.co.uk/

Morgan Hunt: https://www.morganhunt.com/job-search

---

[18] Affinity Water (2021) https://wearelanded.com/c/14748/68570 (Accessed March 2021).
[19] A comprehensive list of UK regulators can be found at https://en.wikipedia.org/wiki/List_of_regulators_in_the_United_Kingdom.

RBB Economics: https://www.rbbecon.com/

PCW: https://www.pwc.co.uk/services/economics/competition-economics.html

MULTINATIONAL COMPANIES

The types of organizations under this heading include many well-known giant companies, and although by definition they have branches in several, or many, countries, many are headquartered in the UK. Some are known mainly, or only, through their brands, which are household names. Large or giant multinationals headquartered in the UK include Associated British Foods (which owns brands such as Jordans cereals, Patak's curry pastes, Kingsmill bread, Ryvita crispbread, Silver Spoon sugar, Twinings tea, and many more); British Petroleum (BP), Pearson Education (Addison–Wesley, Peachpit, Prentice Hall, eCollege, Longman, Scott Foresman, and others); Vodaphone; AstraZeneca plc (a British Swedish multinational pharmaceutical and biopharmaceutical company). Other multinationals with their headquarters in other countries may still have a strong presence in the UK, such as Shell UK. More recently, giant multinationals actively looking to employ more economists include the 'Big Tech companies' like Amazon, FaceBook, Google and Microsoft. Economists are valued here for their skills in discerning market impacts and new trends and for working out the impacts of incentives.

The list of multinationals is long, and these firms have many roles which particularly suit economic students, such as for finance, strategy, and research. During a graduate placement, students will often get experience in more than one of these business areas. As well as the opportunity to experience different roles, by definition, multinationals offer posts overseas. As economics graduates tend to prioritize other job sectors, competition between economic students for placements in multinationals is relatively low, but there can still be fierce competition from students from other academic backgrounds. So, your analytical skills may be an important factor in gaining a post.

Like all jobs, there are also downsides, and in such large international organizations there can be layers of hierarchy, which means lots of bosses and perhaps less autonomy to be innovative. And, in common with many private sector concerns, the work you must do may seem far away from the organization's mission statement that might have attracted you in the first place. That said, economists can do well in such large companies, where the top salaries can be remarkably high by anyone's standards, and so perhaps multinationals do not get the consideration as a career that they deserve.

ADVANTAGES

- Good starting salary
- Comparatively high job security
- Under-applied to by economists
- Large number of roles
- International work opportunities

DISADVANTAGES

- Graduates may feel detached from senior management
- Work may not have much impact

For more information on multinational jobs see:

Amazon: https://www.amazon.jobs/en-gb/job_categories/economics

Unilever: https://careers.unilever.com/uk/en

Information from Studying Economics: http://www.studyingeconomics. ac.uk/where-next/jobs-and-careers/careers-in-the-private-sector/

OTHER CAREERS IN BUSINESS FINANCE AND COMMERCE

ACTUARIAL AND DATA ANALYSIS CAREERS

An actuary evaluates and advises on the impacts of financial risk and uncertainty. They provide reports and devise strategies on how to factor and reduce risks, and often have to look far into the future to offset any potential risks and trends. Most of the entry-level jobs are in pensions and insurance, but careers often later provide opportunities to move into banking, investment, and healthcare. Actuaries need to be good at mathematics, compiling statistics, and communicating complex data effectively to non-experts. You would also need the spreadsheet skills you have developed and to learn how to use specialist data analysis software. You should be able to join with just a good first degree, but there will be more exams to take to progress your career.

Hours are usually pretty regular, though you may need to work some weekends on more urgent projects. It can be lucrative: some experienced actuaries earn six-figure salaries, although www.prospects.ac.uk report that as a professional actuary you can expect to earn an average of £52,000 plus bonuses.

The 'big four' consultancies (PwC, EY, KPMG and Deloitte) sometimes offer actuarial internships. Smaller companies may not advertise, so it can be worthwhile simply to ask them directly about such opportunities. Actuarial Post Jobs (www.actuarialpostjobs.co.uk/) is a good source for job postings in this area.

ADVANTAGES

- Reasonable pay
- Regular hours
- Good development opportunities
- Important role
- Wide geographical choice

DISADVANTAGES

- More exams to pass
- Limited scope to develop as an economist

LARGE UK FIRMS

Many UK firms, for example well-known supermarket chains, offer management schemes that could be perfect for those economists who want to become future leaders. We can note that the legendary Cambridge macroeconomist Wynne Godley worked for the Metal Box Company in the 1950s, before becoming an influential critic of government economic policy contributing ideas that are still being developed today. Dame Kate Barker, earlier in her career, was Chief European economist at the Ford Motor Company in Brentwood (1985–94).

MARKET RESEARCH

This is another area of work where economists can put their econometric and statistical theory into practice. Marketing is described by the UK's Chartered Institute of Marketing as 'The management process responsible for identifying, anticipating and satisfying customer needs profitably'. But marketing techniques are also applicable to charities, not-for-profit organizations and public bodies, who will also wish to understand trends in their sectors and the motivations and needs of their stakeholders and clients. For more details see the information on jobs in marketing provided on the Prospects.ac.uk website at https://www.prospects.ac.uk/jobs-and-work-experience/job-sectors/ marketing-advertising-and-pr/jobs-in-marketing.

RATING AGENCIES

The rating agencies serve financial institutions by attaching their ratings of creditworthiness to sovereign nations, local and state governments, special purpose institutions, companies, and non-profit organizations. They use letter-based scores with plusses and minuses attached to indicate their assessment of whether there is a low or high default risk and the financial stability of its issuer. The level of the rating they decide to allocate to organizations and assets can affect even the ability, and the rate of interest, to issue further debt instruments, that is, IOUs.

It is fair to say that their reputations and influence were damaged somewhat by the financial crisis of 2007, when even assets given triple AAA ratings defaulted. Ratings agencies also report and provide commentary on things that do or might affect financial markets.

The credit rating industry is dominated by three big agencies, which control 95 per cent of the rating business. The top firms include Moody's Investor Services, Standard and Poor's (S&P), and Fitch Group. Fitch in particular has UK offices. A recent job advert from Fitch described the economist role as follows:[20]

> "Reporting to the Chief Economist, the successful candidate will play an active part in developing and communicating the team's forecast views and produce thought-provoking and insightful thematic global-macro research. The candidate will help support and develop the team's growing provision of analytical macroeconomic input and forecasts to the Sovereign and other credit rating teams in Fitch Ratings. Macroeconomic conditions are an important consideration in credit analysis. The candidate will also be expected to help represent the economics teams' views at conference presentations, panels and investor meetings and will likely work on a mix of both developed and emerging economies."

If you want to enter this sector straight from university, it's best to apply for a graduate traineeship, having ideally also done an internship at the same firm or at another financial institution.

---

[20] Fitch Group [2021] Career Opportunities: Director - Economics Team (28143). at:https://career5.successfactors.eu/career?career%5fns=job%5flisting&company=C0016306184P&navBarLevel=JOB%5fSEARCH&rcm%5fsite%5flocale=en%5fUS&career_job_req_id=28143&selected_lang=en_US&jobAlertController_jobAlertId=&jobAlertController_jobAlertName=&_s.crb=aqt12FbBfqeoPpTMUHx8KlxryEx6Pwa5i%2b5GrMcsaz8%3d (Accessed March 2021).

SPECIALIST CONSULTANTS

There are also large, multinational, specialist professional service companies that employ economists. These companies work in areas such as planning and development—such as Lichfield UK[21]—and services around the built environment. For example, Arup, a firm that provides engineering, architecture, design, planning, and project management services employs teams of economists. Founded by Sir Ove Arup in 1946, the firm is headquartered in London and has over 16,000 staff based in 96 offices across 35 countries around the world. Arup has advised on and designed some massive infrastructure projects.

In his interview for the book, Michael Littlewood[22] speaks about his different experiences of consultancy work. He started his consultancy career at KPMG before moving on to set up GoodCorporation Ltd,[23] a multinational organization which helps to design, build, and embed ethics and compliance programmes.

Frontier economics also employs a range of specialist economists across a variety of different areas, including behavioural economists.[24]

PUBLIC SECTOR CAREERS

The pay for comparable jobs, experience, qualifications, and responsibility in the private sector tends to be higher than in the public sector. However, the public sector can often offer a better work life balance, more intrinsically satisfying roles and responsibilities, often unrivalled pension schemes and generally better job security. In the private sector, the vagaries of markets can lead to many people losing their jobs, as Vicky Pryce relates was the experience of many of her former colleagues in an oil company:

"We were happily assuming a high oil price generally and making all our forecasts and investment decisions on that . . . and of course the price then collapsed . . . basically all production was stopped. And so Europe where I worked was closed, the offices in Stratton Street . . . so loads of people lost their jobs. That sort of thing

---

[21] Lichfield UK outline their company profile here: https://lichfields.uk/media/4983/lichfields_company-profile.pdf (Accessed September 2021).

[22] See Video 28: In conversation with Michael Littlechild available at www.oup.com/he/pryce-ross1e.

[23] See here for more information on GoodCorporation's services https://www.goodcorporation.com/ (Accessed May 2022).

[24] See here for more information on Frontier's services https://www.frontier-economics.com/uk/en/services/behavioural-economics/ (Accessed 2021).

doesn't happen in the public sector . . . you don't worry particularly about whether I'm going to lose my job tomorrow. There could be some reorganization, of course, but it's quite interesting because it changes the way in which you operate. And that is one of the main differences, I think when you come from the private sector where you're so aware of the, sort of, everyday movement in share prices and so on, to a public sector which has a completely different way of operating, and that is not to be underestimated.

. . . It isn't just that you weren't particularly worried about being . . . sacked the following day, but it is very much that you're the centre of . . . giving advice for things that really matter more widely."[25]

JOBS IN TEACHING AND ACADEMIA

A career in economics education can be very satisfying indeed. Early in his career, Andy Ross enjoyed five years teaching A-level economics in a further education college, having fun introducing people to the powerful insights of economics for the first time. However, some may find it a little tedious to teach the same syllabus each year. Later, after completing an MSc in Economics at Birkbeck, London University's evening university, Andy became a lecturer in higher education, which paid a higher salary, and he found more intellectually satisfying. Teaching at any level can sometimes be an exhausting vocation, especially at first when you need to prepare each new lecture and class session. And for most academics, the months outside term time are not nearly as leisurely as our press often portrays!

Although many professors earn quite a lot it can take years to reach that level, and only a minority of academics reach professorship. In fact, most lecturers earn surprisingly little considering that nowadays you mostly need a PhD to become a university lecturer. As with most economic data, it's worth drilling down to get a more detailed picture. For example, academic economists do not seem to do as well as other economists in terms of earnings, but this does not include the 'moonlighting' earnings of those academics who can earn lucrative consultancy and speaking fees. Some highly-regarded academics can command several thousand pounds per day, but it is fair to say that generally speaking academics are not 'in it for the money' and many professors

---

[25] In her interview for this book (see Video 21: In conversation with (Visiting) Professor Vicky Pryce FAcSS available at www.oup.com/he/pryce-ross1e).

must 'make-do' on their university pay of around 'only' £75 000, and, typically, they will have begun as low paid researchers and then spent years as lecturers earning much less than professors.

Overall, being an academic can be very fulfilling and with more autonomy than in most other economist jobs, and you will still earn a lot more than most people, albeit perhaps less than many other economists.

ADVANTAGES

- Relative autonomy
- Fulfilment from teaching
- Professional development opportunities
- Long periods with no teaching contact
- Jobs in most locations
- Relative job security once a permanent post has been secured
- A good pension (although not as certain as once was)

DISADVANTAGES

- Relatively low basic salary and comparatively slow career progression
- Increasingly more short-term jobs with inferior conditions, holding several part-time posts can be particularly onerous, and it can be difficult to secure tenure
- Often mischievously portrayed as leisurely when it is not—there are no core hours in teaching and nowadays there is the pressure of targets and inspections
- For teaching in state schools you will need to train for a teaching certificate and for universities you mostly need a PhD

For more information on teacher and lecturer jobs

Teaching jobs are often advertised on the general portals for economist jobs, listed at the end of this chapter.

For sites dedicated to jobs in education see *The Guardian* (https://jobs.theguard-ian.com/jobs/teacher/) jobs website and Tes (https://www.tes.com/jobs/).

For opportunities to train as a teacher while being paid see the *Teach First* website (https://www.teachfirst.org.uk/training-programme).

For a focus on jobs in higher education see *The Times Higher Education* website which has pages dedicated to university jobs (https://www.timeshigher-education.com/unijobs/).

JOBS IN THE GOVERNMENT ECONOMIC SERVICE (GES)

Economics is at the heart of many of the issues facing governments. Economics is ubiquitous and government is big so there are a lot of economists working in government and in organizations inputting into government. Government departments and agencies[26] do often advertise directly for economists, particularly for later career economists, but the main recruitment path for new economists into government is through the Government Economic Service (GES). In fact, the GES is the biggest single recruiter of economists in the UK,[27] and so we examine it in some detail. It is a professional body and recruitment service for economists in the UK Civil Service. The GES is gateway to the widest range of interesting and rewarding jobs as an economist, and you would be joining a community of over 3000 economists. GES members are not directly employed by the GES, but rather employed, paid, and managed by the various government departments or agencies that sponsor the GES. Being a government economist is both financially and intrinsically rewarding,[28] but later in your career you may also choose to apply for one of many other non-economist opportunities available across the wider civil service, where economists are well represented.

As well as excellent career prospects, the civil service also provides good pensions, personal development, flexi-working, and other benefits. The GES normally recruits 100 to 200 graduates a year, although higher recruitment numbers may sometimes be sought to cope with times of particularly heavy workloads, such as for BREXIT and Covid-19. Crises increase the demand for economists!

The GES has three entry routes[29] and for all three you must meet the general UK Civil Servant's nationality rules.[30]

Apprenticeship scheme where you would be paid to work and develop as a government economist while you also follow an economics degree at a UK university. This scheme is designed for school leavers with A-levels.

---

[26] A list of departments and agencies can be found at *Departments, agencies and public bodies* https://www.gov.uk/government/organisations (Accessed September 2021).

[27] See Government Economic Service www.ges.gov.uk (Accessed March 2021).

[28] A description of GES roles in some major government departments can be found at *Government Economic Service Fast Stream Job Descriptions* available at https://assets.publishing.service.gov.uk/government/uploads/system/uploads/attachment_data/file/925554/GES-fast-stream-2021-job-descriptions-pack.pdf (Accessed April 2021).

[29] See also Chapter 9.

[30] See Gov.UK Guidance Nationality rules https://www.gov.uk/government/publications/nationality-rules (Accessed March 2021).

The other two schemes on offer require you to have (or be on course for) a first or upper second-class honours degree. At least 50 percent of the courses/modules you take must be in economics, and include both micro and macro. A Master's degree in economics, or certain post-graduate diploma 'conversion courses', are also accepted.

1. Assistant Economist scheme:[31] this focuses on developing the technical skills and experience needed to be a government economist, and the wider behaviours required to be an effective Civil Servant.

2. The civil service GES 'fast stream':[32] an accelerated development programme which seeks to develop future leaders, both in the GES and the Civil Service more widely, and therefore has a specific focus on developing leadership skills and experience.

The GES also offers summer schemes[33] and longer placements for economics students (see below).

Until quite recently the GES was 'Fast-Stream' entry only. Fast Streamer recruits immediately enter a two-year development programme and are expected to aspire to, and eventually reach, Senior Civil Service (SCS) posts during their career, though this may take fifteen years or more. The Civil Service Fast Stream ranks high in the annual Times Top 100 Graduate Employers listing and has topped that list several times. From 2018 the GES has also been recruiting non-fast stream economists as well, and so perhaps a higher percentage of these can be expected to spend their entire career working as economists in non-SCS posts, although this will also entail developing the wider behaviours expected of all civil servants (see Chapter 7). Even if you don't become an SCS you are likely to take on management responsibilities. All that said, your career trajectory as an economist in the civil service will depend more on performance in-service than on your mode of entry.

At the time of writing,[34] in the GES, a recently graduated entrant can expect to earn between £26,000 and £28,000 outside London, and from £27,000 to £33,000 in London. After three to five years' experience GES economic advisers can earn between £43,000 and £55,000. Even if you don't reach the senior

---

[31] Guidance Assistant Economist Scheme 2021 https://www.gov.uk/guidance/assistant-economist-recruitment (Accessed March 2021).

[32] Government Economic Service Fast stream https://www.faststream.gov.uk/government-economic-service/index.html (Accessed March 2021).

[33] Government Economic Summer Scheme https://www.gov.uk/guidance/how-to-apply-for-a-government-economic-service-summer-vacation-placement.

[34] October 2021.

civil service your yearly earnings would climb in time to about £60,000 to £65,000, and that is worth about £75,000 once pension rights are included. You can expect to earn considerably more if your career progresses to the senior civil service.

ADVANTAGES

- A wide variety of economist roles and steppingstones to good career prospects
- Good continuous professional development
- Jobs can be rewarding both financially and intrinsically
- Flexi-time working is available
- Serious commitment to diversity
- You may be 'where the action is' on some high-profile events
- Various job locations across the UK
- Relative job security and good pension

DISADVANTAGES

- You may have to bite your political tongue
- The civil service can be process heavy
- Some departments are still rather hierarchical

LOCATION

Many GES economists work in London but there are also many across the country in Bristol, Leeds, Liverpool, Newport, Sheffield, Titchfield and, of course, in the devolved governments of Scotland and Wales. At Budget 2020, the Chancellor announced that the government would establish a significant new campus in the north of England focused on economic decision-making, to be staffed by 750 civil servants from the Department for Business, Energy and Industrial Strategy (BEIS), Department for International Trade (DIT), Her Majesty's Treasury (HMT), and the Ministry of Housing, Communities and Local Government (MHCLG). Further announcements were made in the Budget 2021, including that the HMT North location would be Darlington. The new infrastructure bank will be in Leeds and MHCLG will have a major campus in Wolverhampton. These changes are framed as part of the Government's wider commitment to move 22,000 civil servants out of London by 2030.

GES INTERDISCIPLINARY WORKING AND A CHOICE OF CAREER PATHS

Most GES members work on policy development, but there are also many jobs providing economic analysis in service and in operational delivery departments, such as the Office of National Statistics and HM Revenue and Customs, and within mixed policy and delivery departments such as the Department of Work and Pensions (DWP). Most have economists working as analysts and almost all government economists will work as part of, or closely with, inter-disciplinary teams with other analytical professions in government, such as Government Social Researchers (GSR), Government Science and Engineering (GSE), Operational Researchers (GORS) and, of course, the Government Statistical Service (GSS).[35] They also often work with natural scientists, to address issues such as health provision and climate change. As we have seen, at the Competition and Markets Authority (CMA), economists also work closely with lawyers.

GES economists also frequently move into policy *per se*, though it should be clear that economics is so intrinsic to most policies that there is often no clear distinction between being a policy adviser as an economist and working in policy formation teams. It is also not unusual for GES economists to move into 'Private Office'. That is, directly supporting a Government Minister. These are roles where rapid, good communication skills and diplomacy are particularly vital for success (see Chapter 5).

The skills of economists serve them well across policy adviser and policy maker roles, but increasingly experience in broader 'operational delivery' is also deemed desirable for more senior roles, that is, for roles in the Senior Civil Service (see Chapter 8 for the importance of operational delivery Page 209). Economists often rise to the highest levels of the civil service, and this entails learning the skills usually associated with CEOs such as having at least some knowledge of all parts of an organization. As a result, some high-flying civil service economists have even spent some time heading operational delivery units before moving even further up in grade. One can do well as an economist in the civil service, but to move up the organisational ladder to the most senior levels requires much more than good economics alone (see Chapter 7).

GES AND THE DIPLOMATIC SERVICE

The UK government diplomatic service recruits from both GES entrants and directly. Not surprisingly, it involves a lot of working overseas, working with other government departments, consultancies, international organizations, and

---

[35] These five professions are often referred to as the 'Analytical Professions', but economists also often work with accountants, lawyers and the policy profession in government too.

partner governments in other countries and academia. Details can be found at https://www.faststream.gov.uk/diplomatic-service-economics/index.html.

The GES provides copious information for applicants, including advice, case studies, job descriptions and even examples of past topics and questions at their Economic Assessment Centre (EAC—see also Chapter 9). A good entry point to explore these resources is at https://www.gov.uk/government/organisations/civil-service-government-economic-service/about.

THE BANK OF ENGLAND

The Bank of England is an active recruiter of policy and research economists. As the UK's central bank, the Bank of England is responsible for monetary policy and for a stable and 'fit-for-purpose' financial system. The Bank of England also has a graduate recruitment programme that hires graduates who have achieved, or are expected to achieve, a 2:1 honours degree, and unlike the GES that ignores A-levels, it requires at least three B-grades at A-levels (excluding general studies) or equivalent. This programme engages with experienced policy makers and academics. For more details see https://www.bankofengland.co.uk/careers/early-careers/our-programmes.

Economist recruits can also gain a Postgraduate Certificate in Central Banking and Financial Regulation accredited by the University of Warwick.

Former Chief Economist of the Bank of England, Andy Haldane (who was in post at the time) explained why he had stayed at the Bank of England, often referred to as simply 'the Bank', for some 30 years despite his original intention to stay for only a few years:

> "The Bank at the time struck me as a very interesting place to work for a bit . . . A bit probably meant two or three years before doing something else. The one thing I did promise myself though, was I'd be there as long as it was interesting. Now it just so happens, somewhat to my surprise and contrary to my expectations that 30 years on it remains interesting. In fact, it remains as, if not more, interesting than the day I first arrived."[36]

Though the Bank is independent of the civil service, its economists are able to join the GES and so enjoy access to the GES internal website, and the GES's regular events and annual conference.

---

[36] In his interview for this book (see Video 16: In conversation with Andy Haldane FAcSS FRS available at www.oup.com/he/pryce-ross1e).

At the Bank of England, the starting annual salary for graduates is, on average, about £29 000 for first degree entrants.

Advantages and disadvantages are more or less the same as for the GES but obviously the work has a strong focus on financial issues and is based in London.

More details of careers at the Bank of England can be found at https://www.bankofengland.co.uk/Home/Careers.

OTHER PUBLIC SECTOR EMPLOYERS TO CONSIDER

THE NATIONAL HEALTH SERVICE (NHS)

As the world's fifth largest employer[37] it is not surprising that the NHS needs a lot of economists. In fact, the NHS was the most named employer of individuals with economics-related skills in job adverts in the Frontier Economics-Burning Glass-Discover Economics survey of job adverts (see Page 28). These jobs obviously include health economists but also some economists more generally. For most health economist jobs in the NHS, you would be expected to have a postgraduate qualification in Health Economics or a Health Technology Assessment (HTA). Health economists use their economics and skills in analysing data to provide advice on the cost-effectiveness of medicines, medical devices, and diagnostic tests for the NHS. They also contribute appraisals and evaluations of the costs and benefits[38] of new or proposed public health policies to the health service and the public.

THE OFFICE FOR BUDGETARY RESPONSIBILITY

The Office for Budgetary Responsibility (OBR) is much smaller than the GES or Bank of England, but also recruits economists from time-to-time, although experience is typically required.

The OBR was created in 2010 to provide independent and authoritative analysis of the UK's public finances. The International Monetary Fund (IMF) estimates that there were 39 similar national bodies in 37 countries in 2016. Despite much public misunderstanding of the nature and purpose of economic forecasting, and contesting of what prudent government budgeting entails, the OBR, under its long-standing former director Robert Chote, established itself as a well-respected expert body.

---

[37] See The Nuffield Trust (2017) *The NHS is the world's fifth largest employer* at (https://www.nuffieldtrust.org.uk/chart/the-nhs-is-the-world-s-fifth-largest-employer) (Accessed September 2021).

[38] See Chapter 10 for an overview of Cost Benefit Analysis (CBA).

THE NATIONAL INFRASTRUCTURE COMMISSION

The National Infrastructure Commission (NIC) was established as an Executive Agency of HM Treasury in January 2017. The Commission operates independently, at arm's length from government, and draws on the advice of eminent academic and practitioner economists. The Commissioners include the former London Mayor adviser, Bridget Rosewell CBE, and the policy-orientated academic Professor Sir Tim Besley of the London School of Economics.

By joining the National Infrastructure Commission you would be helping to deliver independent advice to government on the UK's long-term infrastructure needs.

More details of careers at the NIC can be found at: https://nic.org.uk/careers/

LARGER LOCAL AUTHORITIES

Regional Development Agencies and Local Enterprise Partnerships also often have jobs for economists. For example, the Greater London Authority (GLA) employs about a dozen people as economists in 'GLA Economics'. Some of these have also been members of the GES.

GLA Economics provides expert advice and analysis on London's economy and the economic issues facing the capital for the Mayor of London. Many other local authorities also employ economists; for instance, during the preparation of this book, Cheshire West and Chester Local Authority advertised for a Head of Economic Growth who was to be employed to oversee the borough's strategy for economic growth and to work in partnership with local businesses to achieve this.

Planning authorities will also often employ private sector economic consultants, say, on urban development, such as at Frontier Economics[39] which we mentioned in the 'Specialist consultants' section of this chapter.

JOBS IN THE MEDIA

The media often recruits economists as commentators on economic policies or to do research. On TV they become familiar faces, such as Ben Chu, the Economics Editor of Newsnight, the BBC's flagship news and

---

[39] Frontier Economics describe their contribution to urban development on this webpage: https://www.frontier-economics.com.au/disciplines/urban-economics/.

current affairs programme. And such fame can be the gateway to new careers: Evan Davis, former BBC Economics editor, now hosts popular shows such as *Dragon's Den*; Stephanie Flanders who was the BBC economics editor left the BBC for a role at J.P. Morgan Asset Management, before returning to journalism as Senior Executive Editor for Economics at Bloomberg and Head of Bloomberg Economics; Paul Mason was also a BBC Economics editor and is now a well-known political journalist, author and activist.

The heads of major research units also require good media skills, such as Paul Johnson of the Institute of Fiscal Studies (IFS), and they are regularly asked to comment on economic matters by the media. Jagjit Chadha, a year into his role as Director of the National Institute of Economic and Social Research (NIESR), gave an informative and entertaining account of how he quickly needed to become alert to the way that different media outlets will attempt to spin their reporting to portray very different impressions to the public, even though based on exactly the same NIESR outputs. Economic and financial journalists frequently talk to practising economists when checking out stories and sourcing comment. Indeed, regular interaction with journalists can constitute an integral part of the job of those plying their economics trade in investment banks, asset management, and think tanks.

JOURNALISM

Many news publishers such as the BBC, the *Financial Times*, the *Times* and Reuters run graduate recruitment programmes which may, in turn, offer the economics graduate the opportunity to write about economic and financial affairs. Competition for the jobs offered by such programmes, though, is intense and those interested in such a career path should try to obtain work experience via internship opportunities. It is also advisable to try to gain journalistic experience at university via student newspapers and radio/TV stations. Additionally, various universities offer Masters degrees in journalism though you should be aware that obtaining such a qualification won't necessarily secure you a job in journalism.

Obviously to be an economics reporter communicating on complex matters you will need to practise concision and simplification, and to have a flair for making your outputs interesting. Martin Wolf of the *Financial Times* has even suggested, perhaps somewhat flippantly, that this is more important for economics reporters than their economics![40]

Larry Elliott, the economics editor for the *Guardian*, does not think that being an economic journalist requires mastery of the technical formal models mostly seen in the academic literature:

"I didn't think you needed to have an intimate knowledge of . . . incredibly complex economic models in order to write about economics, and that was never what I thought economic journalism should be about in any event."[41]

Unlike their TV colleagues, newspaper economic editors and journalists are well known mostly only by other economists and those deeply interested in economic policy. For example, such 'big name' journalists include Martin Wolf, Chris Giles and Gillian Tett all of the *Financial Times*, which is an influential and excellent newspaper but hardly the populist *Sun* or *Daily Mirror*. Journalists seldom have the deeply technical knowledge and quantitative skills of academic economists, but the best ones can be far more influential than the vast majority of academics. Of course, media economists do not start-off as 'big names', so it's worth taking a range of lesser opportunities in media organizations just to gain relevant work experience.

There is also a Journalism Diversity Fund Awards[42] scheme that provides bursaries to people from diverse backgrounds who need help funding their National Council for the Training of Journalists (NCTJ) journalism training. Bursaries are awarded four times per year to help cover the costs of NCTJ course fees and/or living expenses. Recipients are paired with a working journalist to mentor them throughout their studies. Lizzy Burden praises this route into journalism in her interview for this book (see Video 6: In conversation with Lizzy Burden available at www.oup.com/he/pryce-ross1e).

ADVANTAGES

- A highly stimulating environment
- The opportunities to 'make a mark' quickly

[40] Lizzie Burden, a young economics journalist now at Bloomberg, gives her 6 top tips for getting into journalism at https://www.youtube.com/watch?v=hyYCW38pNLk (Accessed August 2021).

[41] In his interview for this book (see Video 13: In conversation with Larry Elliott available at www.oup.com/he/pryce-ross1e).

[42] See: *How can the Journalism Diversity Fund help you?* https://www.journalismdiversityfund.com/ (Accessed September 2021).

- The acquisition of highly transferable skills and experience
- Travel opportunities

DISADVANTAGES

- The 24/7 nature of news coverage nowadays can mean long and unsocial hours without the compensatory financial rewards of working, say, for an investment bank
- This is a fast-changing industry, with the print media increasingly challenged. Commercial pressures of this sort can result in limited job security

More details about careers in this area can be found on the London School of Economics and Politics website (https://info.lse.ac.uk/current-students/careers/information-and-resources/employment-sectors/media-and-communcations) and on journalism.co.uk (https://www.journalism.co.uk/media-reporter-jobs/s64/).

ECONOMIST JOBS IN INTERNATIONAL NOT-FOR-PROFIT ECONOMIC ORGANIZATIONS

Though opportunities for travel are often possible at any point in a career, many decide to gain international experience early on in their career, perhaps when domestic ties are fewer. International experience can be both fascinating and CV enhancing. Fortunately, an economics degree is again the gateway to many opportunities.

THE INTERNATIONAL MONETARY FUND

The International Monetary Fund (IMF) is an organization of 189 countries, working to foster global monetary cooperation, secure financial stability, facilitate international trade, promote high employment and sustainable economic growth, and reduce poverty around the world. Its career page offers the following advice with regards to what it can offer its employees:

> "Working as part of the IMF team in a collaborative and supportive environment, you will address many of the most complex and challenging issues facing the global economy and make a measurable and direct impact on the welfare of people around the world. The IMF attracts people who want their work to

matter, are motivated by working in a truly multicultural environment, and are passionate about our mission of achieving global economic stability, either as economists or as part of our highly-skilled specialized professional and administrative staff."[43]

THE ORGANISATION FOR ECONOMIC CO-OPERATION AND DEVELOPMENT (OECD)

Together with the governments of the member countries, and their policy makers and citizens, the OECD works towards establishing international standards and policy recommendations for a range of social, economic and environmental challenges. The OECD's headquarters and Conference Centre are located in Paris, France.

More details of careers at the OECD can be found at https://www.oecd.org/careers/.

WORLD BANK

The World Bank has economists based in many countries around the world. Their staff work with governments, civil society groups, the private sector, and others in developing countries around the world. They assist people in all areas of development, from policy and strategic advice to the identification, preparation, appraisal and supervision of development projects.

More details of careers at the World Bank can be found on their website: https://www.worldbank.org/en/about/careers.

UNITED NATIONS (UN)

The United Nations (UN) has eight 'job networks' one of which is an 'Economic, Social and Developmental Network' (DEVNET) that recruits economists. Opportunities in this department are mostly based in the Department of Economic and Social Affairs in New York, but can also be found in Addis Ababa, Bangkok, Beirut, Geneva and Santiago, the headquarters of the five regional economic commissions of the organization. In their own words, employees of the United Nations 'contribute to the promotion of socio-economic development'.[44]

---

[43] International Monetary Fund (2021) Recruitment page. Available at: https://www.imf.org/en/About/Recruitment (Last accessed July 2021).

[44] United Nations (2021) 'Job Networks'. Available at: https://careers.un.org/lbw/home.aspx?viewtype=JN (Last accessed July 2021).

More details of careers at the United Nations can be found on their website: https://careers.un.org/lbw/home.aspx

THE EUROPEAN UNION

At the time of writing, the impact of Brexit on UK citizens wishing to work in the institutions of the EU is uncertain, but the EU does employ many economists. For example,

> "The Chief Economist team at the Directorate-General (DG) for Internal Market, Industry, Entrepreneurship and SMEs is responsible for the development, coordination and production of economic analysis. It ensures that the initiatives of the DG are based on sound economic evidence."[45]

JOBS IN THE THIRD SECTOR

UK-based and international charities also often employ economists. Together with other non-profit and non-government agencies, charities are known as International Non-Governmental Organizations (INGOs). They include specifically international non-governmental organizations (INGOs) and non-governmental organizations (NGOs). INGOs include charities such as Action Aid, Oxfam, the Red Cross, and Médecins Sans Frontières. These and country-specific NGOs are all in need of economists and so recruit from time to time. But the pay and job security can be comparatively low, and so the work is best suited to those with a strong commitment to the good causes as captured in the missions of these organisations.

PRO BONO ECONOMICS

Volunteering for general charity work is always a good way to enhance your CV and gain satisfaction from your contributions, but you are unlikely to be accepted as a volunteer economist to a charity straight from university. However, it is worthwhile and career enhancing after you have several years of experience working as a professional economist, to volunteer with 'Pro Bono Economics' (PBE).[46]

Pro Bono Economics matches the skills of its volunteer economists with charities and social enterprises that could benefit from their specialist

---

[45] European Commission, *Internal Market, Industry, Entrepreneurship and SMEs* https://ec.europa.eu/growth/about-us/chief-economist_en.

[46] https://www.probonoeconomics.com/

economics input. In particular, PBE charity projects help organizations to measure performance, improve their services and better track outcomes.

Andy Haldane, a co-founder of Pro Bono Economics, explains the origin of the charity.

"The idea was very simple. It was in the tooth [of the] the global financial crisis and the thought was 'could the skills of economists be brought to bear to help the charitable sector?', in particular when measuring their social impact. . . . 10 years on we now have an answer and that answer's the result of us having done . . . hundreds of projects with hundreds of charities to try and better assess their impact. And it turns out that economists absolutely do have the tools of the trade that can help charities tell their story to a wider audience about the social benefits that they are conferring."[47]

As the PBE website says '*PBE has provided volunteering opportunities to 300 professionals. Volunteering is good for you and improves your knowledge and skills*'.[48]

In their interview for the book, recent graduates Jonathan Coller and Nathaniel Greenwold described how rewarding they found it to work on a project with Pro Bono Economics.[49]

PBE also employs some economists directly for paid employment, and these are advertised from time to time as vacancies arise. There are also opportunities through PBE for economists to support and feed into wider debates and development of economists' contributions to 'civil society',[50] a sector that is under measured and underappreciated (see Chapter 10).

JOBS IN POLICY RESEARCH ORGANISATIONS AND 'THINK-TANKS'

The aim of these groups is to analyse, comment on, and influence public policy debate. They engage in research and advocacy across a range of areas such as economics, environment, politics, science and technology, and social policy.

---

[47] In his interview for this book (see Video 16: In conversation with Andy Haldane FAcSS FRS available at www.oup.com/he/pryce-ross1e).

[48] Pro Bono *Economics Celebrating Volunteers' Week: how employers benefit* https://www.probonoeconomics.com/news/celebrating-volunteers-week-how-employers-benefit.

[49] See Video 8: In conversation with Jonathan Coller and Nathaniel Greenwold available at www.oup.com/he/pryce-ross1e.

[50] Chris Giles, 'Voluntary work comes under spotlight in UK's virus recovery', *Financial Times* (2020).

They differ from academic research as there is a direct intention to influence policy and public opinion. There are a host of well-respected research bodies that employ economists, such as the Institute for Fiscal Studies (IFS)[51] and the National Institute for Economic and Social Research (NIESR),[52] and large UK-based organizations with offices around the world like Oxford Economics[53] and Frontier Economics,[54] UK firms like BiGGAR Economics (based in Scotland),[55] as well as the Centre for Economic and Business Research.

There are many influential think tanks that are respected for being balanced even when advocating a certain line, but there are also more dubious think tanks closely linked to political lobbyists, or which are themselves lobbyists. This may suit you if you are keen to push a certain political perspective, but their role in democracy is controversial, especially when their sponsors are not declared.

A useful list of research and think-tank employers in the UK and overseas, including such influential international research and agency bodies as the IMF, OECD and World Bank, can be found on the *Think Tanks Oxford University Careers Service* at https://www.careers.ox.ac.uk/think-tanks/#collapse1529726 and *Smart Thinking* websites (https://smartthinking.org.uk/). On the latter site it is also possible to register your interest in a job in a think tank at *Think Tank & Policy Jobs* (https://smartthinking.org.uk/jobs/). Jobs are also advertised from time to time in the *Economist* and *Guardian*, but individual think-tank websites are the most common source for vacancies. It is also worth directly approaching them, particularly if your research interests match their agenda. They will look for understanding and passion for their area of interest. We'll have more to say about working as an economist in think tanks in the next chapter.

TRADE UNIONS

Trade unions often employ economists to analyse pay comparisons, highlight significant trends, and to comment on government policies and lobby policy makers. For example, Dr Geoff Tily, in addition to his current role as senior

---

[51] Institute for Fiscal Studies-Jobs https://www.ifs.org.uk/jobs (Accessed April 2021).

[52] National Institute of Economic and Social Research—Job Vacancies https://www.niesr.ac.uk/job-vacancies (Accessed April 2021).

[53] Careers at Oxford Economics http://www.oxfordeconomics.com/about-us/careers (Accessed April 2021).

[54] Frontier Economics Vacancies https://www.frontier-economics.com/uk/en/careers/vacancies-and-apply/ (Accessed April 2021).

[55] BiGGER Economics https://biggareconomics.co.uk/services (Accessed April 2021).

economist for the Trades Union Congress, had a long career as a government economist at the Office of National Statistics (ONS) and HM Treasury, and is the author of influential economics articles and the book *Keynes Betrayed*,[56] which is regarded by many as one of the most important recent books on the economics of John Maynard Keynes. Geoff discusses his career and economics and gives advice to those interested in employment with trade unions in his interview for this book.[57]

More details of posts in trade unions can be found on the Prospects website at https://www.prospects.ac.uk/job-profiles/trade-union-research-officer www.prospects.ac.uk/job-profiles/trade-union-research-officer.

POLITICS

Whether working for the public good or for a vested interest, economics has much relevance for politics. As we have seen, some lobbyists are essentially political organizations but there are also the political parties themselves. In her interview for this book, Kitty Ussher describes how economics was integral to her career as an MP, and politicians often employ economists in their private office or as a special adviser (known as a SPAD).

BUSINESS AND EMPLOYER ORGANISATIONS

Hopefully not always on the 'other side' of industry to trade unions are the 'bosses', or employer and trade associations who represent employers in negotiations with policy makers and trade unions. Employer and trade associations often employ or consult economists. The largest umbrella organization for these is the Confederation of British Industry (CBI). The CBI advertises that it speaks for 190 000 businesses in the UK employing nearly 7 million people, about one-third of the private sector workforce. Here is an extract from a CBI job advert.[58]

> "The economics directorate plays a vital function in helping our members to understand the latest intel on the macroeconomy, how to navigate the policy environment, as well as ensuring CBI policy positions are well evidenced.

---

[56] Geoff Tily, *Keynes betrayed: the general theory, the rate of interest and 'Keynesian' economics* (2010).

[57] See Video 25: In conversation with Geoff Tily available at www.oup.com/he/pryce-ross1e.

[58] Econ-jobs.com https://www.econ-jobs.com/economics-jobs/senior-economist-12-month-ftc-13083 (Accessed March 2021).

As part of this function, the Economics directorate has started offering bespoke economic services through our new 'CBI Economics' business that enables businesses to build their economic evidence base on specific areas of interest.

You will play a key role in delivering these projects, supporting the Head of Economic Projects. You will also work closely with the CBI's policy teams to provide economic support through both business surveys and economic analysis to help evidence their policy work."

More details about the CBI can be found on their website: www.cbi.org.uk/careers.

ECONOMIST JOBS PORTALS AND WEBSITES

Portals bring together job opportunities from across a wide range of sectors. Here we include recruitment websites that advertise roles across all manner of industries as well as some more tailored to economic posts.

Subscribing to them will produce a steady stream of job notifications in your email inbox, not all of them very relevant to your ambitions. You may have to tweak your preferences to filter these so that you receive notice of roles that fit your target jobs.

GENERIC SITES

Glassdoor: https://glassdoor.co.uk

Indeed: https://www.indeed.co.uk/

SPECIALIST SITES

Chi square economics: https://chisquare-econ.com/

Econ-Jobs: http://www.econ-jobs.com/

EconomistJobs: https://economistjobs.com/

The Economist jobs board: https://jobs.economist.com/

Murray Mcintosh (a recruiter specializing in economics research, policy, and public affairs roles: https://murraymcintosh.com/

For a more international perspective on jobs, and some UK economist jobs, INOMICS can be useful source which sometimes includes useful articles and links: https://inomics.com/

OTHER MEANS OF FINDING OPPORTUNITIES

UNIVERSITY CAREERS SERVICES

Nowadays they are highly professional units with a wealth of expertise and resources. If you are still at a university, or a recent alumnus, you would be daft not to use their free services!

NETWORKING

Joining *LinkedIn* is also free and allows you to see some notifications of economist posts and to post your CV for others to see and, hopefully, respond to with opportunities.[59]

You can also follow notifications from relevant employer organizations on FaceBook and Twitter, such as at @GES_UK.

SOCIETIES

The Society of Professional Economists (SPE)[60] also circulates a useful list of vacancies for economists to its members. Student SPE membership discounts are available.

STUDENT COMMUNITIES

Organizations that employ economists sometimes have 'student communities' that you can join for free and receive notifications of jobs and recruitment schemes. For example, KPMG is one such organization that does this (https://student.kpmgcareers.co.uk/talentcommunity).

WORK EXPERIENCE, PLACEMENTS AND INTERNSHIPS

Work experience at employers' premises, before you apply for permanent posts, can help you develop new and work-related skills, build professional connections, and help you decide where you eventually wish to work. It could include short placements such as during vacations, internships, vacation jobs, volunteering, insight events and work shadowing, and be paid or unpaid. They can also be an essential element to opening the career door you are targeting. 'Internship' usually refers to work experience over the summer months or directly after graduation, work 'placements' usually refer to a year-in-industry taken as part of a degree, but terms are often used loosely. Any form of work experience can mark you out from other candidates when filling out your CV

---

[59] https://www.linkedin.com/feed/
[60] https://spe.org.uk/

and job application forms, but working as a placement economist is particularly relevant if you want a job where you will directly use your economics. Ideally, if you are aiming to be an economist, for any kind of work experience you should seek work experience that provides you with an opportunity to apply your economics in a real-world setting.

> "A poll of employers by Gumtree showed that work experience makes you 95% more employable. The good news carries on: two-thirds of employers think candidates with work experience were more knowledgeable, 44% think they are more confident and 40% say they are more committed."[61]

A very wide range of organizations offer internship and placement opportunities for undergraduates, from research organizations such as the IFS, to think tanks, from the Bank of England to investment banks. Some employers even use work experience to assess a student or graduate's capability and so recruit employees from their interns, rather than advertise vacancies. The Government Economic Service offers placements across a wide range of government departments, with salaries ranging from £18.5k to £26k (most are just over £20k) and provide a wide range of placement job descriptions[62] to give potential applicants a sense of what they might be doing if successful. The Bank of England also offers paid internships to university students in their first and penultimate year and to those about to start their postgraduate study.

Because of the high demand for placements, it's best to apply to a range of organizations but be wary of 'cut and paste'. It is careless to tell KPMG that you have a lifelong ambition to be a government economist! And because they are usually over-subscribed it's best to apply early, even if a deadline is given. As in this advice from Schroaders, a large British multinational asset management company, shows:

> "Application deadlines will vary by programme so please check the job description for further details. As we recruit on a rolling basis, we recommend you get your application completed as soon as possible. If we receive a large volume of applications, we reserve the right to close applications earlier than the given deadline."[63]

---

[61] Studying Economics, Work experience for Economics students http://www.studyingeconomics.ac.uk/during-your-study/work-experience/ (Accessed March 2021).

[62] government economic service: summer vacation placements, sample job descriptions (2017) https://assets.publishing.service.gov.uk/government/uploads/system/uploads/attachment_data/file/591503/All_Department_JDs.pdf (Accessed March 2021).

[63] Schroder's, *Working here Internship and placement year programmes* https://www.schroders.com/en/people/starting-out/internship-programme/ (Accessed March 2021).

Don't be disheartened if your application is unsuccessful, it is most likely because of the sheer numbers of applicants, it does not necessarily reflect on the quality of your application. We give some practical advice on how to approach applications in Chapter 9.

An alternative to placements can be to do work as an 'interim economist', these contracts can be for just three months or so. These are often advertised though agencies such as at Total Jobs (https://www.totaljobs.com/jobs/economist).

A very useful list of work experience opportunities, including overseas, is offered by Prospects.ac.uk at https://www.prospects.ac.uk/jobs-and-work-experience/work-experience-and-internships/internships.

More information on internships and placements can be found at:

The Studying Economics website which includes information on work experience more generally as well as specific organizations that offer placements:

http://www.studyingeconomics.ac.uk/during-your-study/work-experience/ and http://www.studyingeconomics.ac.uk/during-your-study/work-experience/places-for-economists/

The Government Economic Service: https://www.gov.uk/government/publications/how-to-apply-for-a-government-economic-service-sandwich-student-placement

The Bank of England: https://www.bankofengland.co.uk/careers/early-careers/our-programmes

The Institute of Fiscal Studies advertises for Summer Students on a yearly basis: https://ifs.org.uk/jobs/18

Ernst & Young: https://www.ey.com/en_uk/careers/students/programmes/undergraduates/sip

KPMG:https://www.kpmgcareers.co.uk/undergraduate/vacation-programmes/

Schroders: https://www.schroders.com/en/people/starting-out/internship-programme/

And of course, it is worth researching the organizations we have looked at in this chapter. Universities career services usually also provide help in finding posts for their students and often have advice that can be accessed by all students, regardless of their institution. For example, the Oxford University Career Service provides guidance on internships: https://www.careers.ox.ac.uk/essential-internship-guidance#collapse1553126.

NON-PECUNIARY REWARDS

In addition to the promising pecuniary aspects there are the intrinsic rewards from just being an economist. Economics can be fascinating, is often at the centre of high-profile debates, and in the right hands can be a powerful force for good. Equally, bad economics can wreak havoc and bring much misery! Therefore, there is an important role for economists in countering the economic fallacies that abound in the media and among the general public. These include: 'more for one person must mean less for another'; 'money is itself wealth'; 'tax changes always move revenues in a definite direction'; 'competition is always good'; 'profit is intrinsically good (or bad)'; 'that the state or the private sector is always and everywhere more efficient than the other sectors'. If you are studying economics and take an interest in the media, you should be able to extend this list of fallacies considerably. As an educated economist it is satisfying, if sometimes somewhat depressing, to be able to cut through much of the sheer nonsense we see every day in sections of our media and social media.

Policy economists also frequently work on high profile issues and so have the excitement of being 'part of the action'. Although usually anonymous, they are often at the centre of things in the news. This is also true for a small percentage of academics and is often so for economists engaged in policy analysis in high-profile think-tanks, the media or perhaps trade unions. There is an undeniable thrill from this, from seeing famous politicians and powerful decision makers in action, and it can be a source of great personal satisfaction to contribute to a policy that benefits millions of people, or in harsher times mitigates the adverse effects of what must be done. Even if on occasion you find that your professional role is merely to reduce the unnecessary damage done by non-economist policy makers, that is still a most valuable contribution. And even if your job as an economist does not make you feel you are directly contributing to good causes, if you achieve status and salary as an economist that should provide you with a means of contributing.

SUMMARY

- An economics degree can be the gateway to many exciting job opportunities.
- Economist jobs vary widely and differ in terms of pay, their work-life balance and intrinsic satisfaction.

- There are many ways to work as an economist and many organizations that employ economists, both in the UK and abroad.
- Not only are there many ways to work as an economist, in different roles and for many and various employers, but economist jobs often lead to opportunities to develop your career in new directions.

FIND OUT MORE

'Why study economics?', (2012). *Resource Pack for Teachers and Parents*. Available at: **http://whystudyeconomics.ac.uk/info-for-teachers/** [Accessed May 2022].

QUESTIONS

1. Why do you think there is such a strong demand for economists across such a broad range of jobs?
2. How do the salaries of economics graduates compare with those of other subjects?
3. How is the demand for economists likely to change over the economic cycle?
4. Contrast the advantages and disadvantages of working in the private and public sectors.

EXERCISE

List the things you want from a career and prioritize them. Now compare these criteria with the jobs described in this chapter to create a shortlist of jobs that interest you. Your next task should be to research these sectors and jobs to confirm your selection and to help you prepare for the application and interview process (see Chapter 9).

CHAPTER 3

University and practitioner economics

· · · ●●●●●● · · ·

INTRODUCTION

This chapter explores the difference between academic and practitioner economists, providing insights on what it is like to work as a practitioner economist, in contrast with academic writing and research. For example, writing a briefing for a busy Minister or CEO is very different to writing an article for an academic journal: a practitioner's advice is usually written in a very different style to academic writing and working within a stakeholder's perspective can differ from the objectivity expected of academics. Practitioners often must balance a trade-off between rigour and relevance so as to be useful to their stakeholders (see 'The relevance rigour spectrum' section below page 69). Academics frequently end their journal articles with 'more research is required' rather than commit to a conclusion. That is perfectly acceptable in academia, demonstrating honesty, rigour and balance, but in government, business and commerce, missing the deadline for providing a recommendation would more likely be deemed poor performance. Professional codes, such as for the civil service code, and ethics are also explored in this chapter.

There is an old joke that:

> "Politicians make decisions without any evidence, businesses make decisions with incomplete evidence, and academics never make a decision as there is never enough evidence."

The joke is unfair to academics, but there is a germ of truth in it for practitioners, as this chapter explains. As a student you will get close insights into what it is like to teach and research economics as an academic, but this may not give you a good idea of what it is like to work as an economist outside of academia. University careers staff can be excellent for pointing you towards suitable job opportunities, but they are unlikely to have direct experience of those jobs themselves. In this chapter through to and including Chapter 8, we will often compare working as an economist inside and outside universities, to convey insights that should help you get a better feel for what working as a practitioner would entail. In the next chapter we look at how well UK economics degrees, which are among the best in the world, suit the needs of those working outside academia.

SCIENTISTS, ENGINEERS, AND PROFESSIONAL PRACTITIONER PRAGMATISTS

How might we distinguish between the different ways that economists serve their stakeholders? Greg Mankiw suggested a 'scientists and engineers' distinction for academic research 'scientists', and macroeconomists who advise on real-world policy decisions as 'engineers':

> "Engineers are, first and foremost, problem-solvers. By contrast, the goal of scientists is to understand how the world works."[1]

Perhaps 'engineer' sounds too precise? It might imply that definite answers exist to a problem, whereas economics often can only offer analysis and recommendations that are less than certain, and sometimes highly conditional. Although even then economists are usually a more reliable source than non-economists! Academics, in their work as academics, are more likely to be uncomfortable than practitioners in straying from what can be said with complete 'rigour'. The term 'professional practitioner' is often used for economists working outside of academia,[2] and they are typically nearer the engineering end of Mankiw's spectrum than academics. The terms 'academics' and 'professional practitioners' are often used to split economists roughly into those that work in universities and those who are employed outside universities. However, a division by employer is not a division by task, and there are many economists

---

[1] Greg Mankiw's blog: 'Random Observations for Students of Economics' (2006). Available at http://gregmankiw.blogspot.co.uk/2006/05/scientists-and-engineers.html (Accessed September 2021).

[2] Or just 'professional', though this is more likely to offend academics as they are also typically very professional!

in universities who work on practical problems and many economists outside universities who add to the stock of human knowledge.

We might try to contrast practitioners with academic 'frontier of knowledge economists', but this is far too cumbersome and good policy formation is usually also a learning process. 'Applied economics' can be a useful term, but again it often includes much work that is at the frontier of knowledge and can still be very academic in nature compared to more policy-orientated approaches. The contrast between academics and practitioners can perhaps be best observed by attending the conferences of the learned societies in economics. The Royal Economic Society (RES) conference is more academically orientated than are those of the Society of Professional Economists (SPE) and the Scottish Economic Society. They are all worth going to, they provide a mix of topics and papers to please all economists, and you'll see lots of ideas, data, and graphs at all of them, but the RES conference has a much higher percentage of papers with lots of equations exploring components of models. The more practitioner-orientated societies are more about engagement with 'messy' real world problems, with more eyeballing[3] of data and descriptive statistics, often drawing on more technical results but more concerned with their interpretations than derivations.

THE 'RELEVANCE RIGOUR' SPECTRUM

Again, a lack of a wholly satisfactory definition for something seldom deters the professional practitioner but does trouble an academic, as rigour and precision are hallmarks of academia. So perhaps we can get nearer to a useful taxonomy of economists by understanding the differences in their approaches to economics. If we think of a trade-off along a spectrum between 'rigour and relevance' then a much higher percentage of academic/university economists are towards the 'rigorous end' and a much higher percentage of professional practitioners are towards the 'relevance end'. That is, relevant to the needs of the practitioner economist's stakeholders, usually their employer. An academic may suggest options based wholly on an objective analysis, so too may a practitioner in many cases, but practitioners are wasting their stakeholders' time if they spend much time on options that are inimical to their stakeholders' interests and immoveable beliefs.

---

[3] Using data series and graphics as descriptive rather than inference statistics.

Whereas an academic will want to give a precise specification of a relationship and support this with technical analysis and research, a policy adviser may often have to be content with just coming to a judgement, based on information close at hand, that the effects of a policy are likely to be within a broad direction. Practitioners' audiences are not usually qualified to understand theoretical details anyway, and they don't want a long list of caveats and conditions that seem to them to be just 'analysis paralysis' (see Chapter 5 on communication). Executives and Ministers want 'agency' from advice, more than just 'that's interesting', they want it to help them decide what to do (see below: 'Practitioners need to provide agency for their stakeholders' page 75).

This certainly does not mean that policy economics is easier or that its practitioners are 'sloppier' in their work. It's about using different, but overlapping, skill sets. As Sir Dave Ramsden, former Head of the GES, has expressed it:

> "GES practitioners are engaged in how to produce useful guidance for decision makers from the incomplete information available today, within a multitude of constraints and overlapping considerations, to address an uncertain tomorrow."[4]

Professional practitioners often must compromise on rigour to achieve relevance and to meet deadlines. Often, practitioners are aware of something that is important and so must allow for it, but cannot integrate it in a formal way that would meet academic standards of rigour. Because they know that compromising on precision is necessary for their work, they are usually more comfortable doing it than academics, and they will not be mocked by their peers for it. As the real-world will not wait for them, or more precisely their employers won't, practitioners seldom have the luxury of concluding, as academics so often do, that 'more research is required'. Coming to terms with this difference in approach is something Stephen Le Roux reflects on in his interview for the book.[5]

It is a most unfair stereotype to say that all academic economists live in 'ivory towers'[6] aloof from the real world, but it is still possible for an academic to have a successful career exploring precise answers to questions that no-one has asked or is even interested in: 'Inventing cures for which there is no known

---

[4] In Diane Coyle ed. (2012), *What's the use of economics*.

[5] See Video 22: In conversation with Stephen Le Roux available at www.oup.com/he/pryce-ross1e.

[6] A state of privileged seclusion and separation from the practicalities of the real world.

disease'.[7] This might be justified by saying that one day purely academic research might have applications as yet unknown, but perhaps some academics do prefer to work with highly abstract rigorously precise models rather than the real world of socio-economic phenomenon that can be so very messy and confusing. Even with their often fiendish complexity, economic models are much simpler than the real world, and they have an internal consistency that appeals to those with a bent for this type of 'rigour'.

THE ROLE OF MODELS

None of the above is intended to belittle modellers or to suggest that models are not very important (see Chapter 6). Students will encounter models in economics from the outset: production possibility boundaries; cost curves; indifference curves; and demand and supply—these are all highly abstract models rather than descriptions of 'reality'. Economics degrees are a first step to becoming an economist and so universities understandably put a lot of emphasis on learning the tools of the trade, and models are a major part of an economist's toolkit. There are so many models and techniques that modern economists can use, their sheer volume could easily fill, and overfill, any course in economics. But working hard to understand models in the abstract, often not looking at all like reality, can be off-putting and dispiriting for many students. Good tutors are always careful to explain why models are worth learning about rather than just teaching models as an end in itself (see also Chapter 8). Learning about models[8] is part of becoming an economist as all economists, including practitioners, are ultimately using models whether they are aware of it or not.[9] The important thing is to be aware of the limitations of models, to know when the use of a certain model is warranted and when it is not.[10] The clue is in the name, they are models.

Useful models are *deliberate* simplifications of the real world and so any use of a model in a way that will affect people's welfare must be done with caution

---

[7] With apologies to the late great Victor Borge https://bestmusicquotes.wordpress.com/2014/06/09/victor-borge-quotes/

[8] And the empirical techniques used to test models.

[9] Keynes is alluding to this in his famous quote 'Practical men who believe themselves to be quite exempt from any intellectual influence, are usually the slaves of some defunct economist. Madmen in authority, who hear voices in the air, are distilling their frenzy from some academic scribbler of a few years back': John Maynard Keynes at the end his most famous book, *The General Theory of Employment, Interest and Money* (1936).

[10] And for practitioners, to be able to go beyond what has been formally modelled if needs be.

by analysts who understand these simplifications well. As HM Treasury's *The Aqua Book: guidance on producing quality analysis for government* warns, it is vital that

"model risks, limitations and major assumptions are understood by users of the model, and the use of the model output is appropriate."[11]

Mathematical models are invaluable for revealing how an interrelated system might behave, and because they force precision in the relationships being postulated, models can often be tested rigorously against real data. This is crucial for the mainstream hypothetical-deductive method of scientific advance, that is, of testing hypotheses against data followed by rejection or modification when the model fails the test. This method is what most people mean when they refer to 'the scientific method'. In principle, the interaction between empirical evidence and theory should be what drives scientific progress; unfortunately it is not the whole story. Life is just more subtle and complex than that.

Indeed, it is surprising that students do not challenge the descriptive accuracy of economics even more than they do.[12] For example, no-one literally spends their income so that their marginal utility from the last penny spent on all goods is equalized, and it's odd to have a theory of price determination based on perfect competition where everybody just takes the prevailing price, but no one actually sets the price in the first place! So, economists often like to stress that a degree of artificiality is a necessity to make any progress toward analytically capturing what happens in the real world.[13] And perhaps this is only a problem when economists forget that models are to be used, not believed. It is certainly true that an assumption can be useful even if it is descriptively inaccurate. For example, the notion of sea-level is not descriptively accurate: the real sea is not flat or at sea-level other than momentarily, but sea-level is still a very useful device for navigating boats and ships over shallow waters, and for cartography. Highly abstract artificiality is not necessarily a useless pursuit either, as said, important applications for seemingly arcane discoveries may one day be found. For example, game theory applied to auctions is attributed

[11] HM Treasury, *The Aqua Book: guidance on producing quality analysis for government* (2015). Available at https://assets.publishing.service.gov.uk/government/uploads/system/uploads/attachment_data/file/416478/aqua_book_final_web.pdf (Accessed September 2021).

[12] Joe Earle, Cahal Moran and Zach Ward-Perkins (2017), *The Econocracy: The perils of leaving economics to the experts* is a good example of students of Economics being critically aware (see Chapter 10).

[13] Henry Theil, (1971), *Principles of econometrics* (Wiley), page iv.

with netting vast sums for the Treasury's coffers from the sales of 3G licences,[14] and may be providing new insights into how policy makers interact with those they seek to affect (see Chapter 10).

The hypothetical-deductive model of scientific advance, whereby hypotheses are tested against evidence and rejected and amended as theories in an endless cycle of discovery, suggests a process whereby it might be ultimately possible to accurately model just about everything. A mathematical approach to this is similar to a 'reductionist philosophy' that suggests that ultimately everything in the universe could in principle be explained by physics.[15] Philosophy aside, the practical problem is that working on the basis that 'everything can be explained by physics' or 'we are not allowed to include anything we can't represent in maths', is not always the most fruitful way to tackle most worldly issues, especially when human behaviour is involved. An economist who asserts 'All we have is models' will not make a good policy economist, even though ultimately it may be true. Good economists will heed Henry Theil's insightful warning that 'It does require maturity to realize that models are to be used, but not to be believed.'[16]

All models are simplifications of the real world, and so are prone to an 'omitted variable' problem, where something that turns out later to be important has been left out of the model. This was a common criticism over the omission of a realistic finance sector in most mainstream macro-models before the Great Financial Crisis of 2007–9. It can also just be very difficult to model some vital but elusive factors that might be very important, such as 'Minsky cycles'[17] of increasing financial risk-taking and deregulation as memories of previous crises fade. The relationships being modelled can also change. In econometrics (see also Chapter 6) the phenomena being studied that drive the data generation may be 'non-stationary' and hence their parameters change through time. Ignoring this possibility can lead to spurious results. The 'Lucas Critique' is one well-known type of reason for this, that is, people may learn to adapt their behaviour to changing policy regimes and so relationships that once held may no longer do so.

---

[14] See Economic and Social Research Council, *Design of mobile license auction raised £22.5 billion* (2020) https://esrc.ukri.org/news-events-and-publications/impact-case-studies/design-of-mobile-license-auction-raised-22-5-billion (Accessed August 2021).

[15] Although physics itself casts doubt on that notion.

[16] Henry Theil (1971), page iv, Principles of econometrics (Wiley), page iv.

[17] Named after Hyman Philip Minsky (1919–1996) who argued that this behavioural cycle was a contributor to recurring financial crisis.

The drivers of an economic phenomenon change through time, as real economies are dynamic not static. The institutions that affect a market or economy may undergo changes, the global economy changes, financial instruments change, regulations change, demographics change, technology changes and much else besides. As the Austrian school of Economics has emphasized for a very long time, taken up now by modern complexity modellers, the standard textbook 'comparative statics' approach of moving from one equilibrium to another, the mainstay of elementary to even intermediate economics textbooks, is a limited perspective on the dynamics of real market economies. As Lord Stern notes in his interview for this book:

> "There's quite a bit of economics that says here's an equilibrium, you change this policy, it moves to another equilibrium, and is that second equilibrium better than the first? That's very useful, it's valuable, but where things are changing very fast, we need to understand specifically about how things change."[18]

As we emphasize in Chapter 8, there is much to be gained from a broad pragmatically eclectic approach to economics. Nevertheless, internal consistency within a convergent rather than divergent approach to economics[19] has been a criterion for rigour on which many of the most prestigious economic academic journals have put a heavy emphasis. This does have merits in forcing economists to be explicit and precise, but it can also be rather narrow and hence limit the range of issues that are addressed (see Chapter 10). In contrast, practitioners tend to value what works in practice above internal logic. For policy, 'It is better to be vaguely right than precisely wrong'.[20] Divergence thinking and observation can sometimes be needed in addition to logical concentric thinking. Hence, good policy advisers are 'intellectually permissive' and often inter-disciplinary. Deep discussions of methodology are beyond the scope of this book, but we'll revisit some aspects in Chapter 8, so we'll leave it here for now with a wry poke at overly abstract model-orientated economists from the eloquent practitioner economist and columnist Sir John Kay:

---

[18] In his interview for this book (see Video 24: In conversation with Professor Lord Nicholas Stern available at www.oup.com/he/pryce-ross1e).

[19] Divergent thinking seeks to generate multiple possible answers to problems from multiple perspectives. Conversely, convergent thinking involves finding the one right answer to a problem that has a single solution.

[20] This is the form of a quote often misattributed to Keynes. The original is from Carveth Read in chapter 22 of *Logic, Deductive and Inductive* (1898). Read writes 'It is better to be vaguely right than precisely wrong'.

"The knowledge that every problem has an answer, even and perhaps especially if that answer is difficult to find, meets a deeply felt human need. For that reason, many people become obsessive about artificial worlds, such as computer games, in which they can see the connections between actions and outcomes. Many economists who pursue these approaches are similarly asocial."[21]

PRACTITIONERS NEED TO PROVIDE AGENCY FOR THEIR STAKEHOLDERS

Studying Economics can be just for interest, and in a civilized country university academics should have some space in their contracts for exploration just driven by their own interests, but to be useful to decision makers you must not only be interesting but also provide agency (see Chapter 5 for communicating agency). 'Agency' means helping others to prepare for and/or to decide what to do next. This often means going beyond formal rigour to make a judgement call, even when there is a danger that your judgement call will live on despite new contrary evidence arriving. As Vicky Pryce, one of your authors for this book and former joint Head of the GES, puts it starkly:

"It is easy to see therefore why the relationship between the world of policy making—and politics —and economics will never be an easy one. In politics there is a need to make decisions, and to a timetable, and once having made them—however uncertain the evidence really was—to argue for it, not accept any doubts, not wait for the results of lengthy randomised control group experiments."[22]

Vicky is highlighting here the reality of politics and government while also being acutely aware that practitioner economists are not being professional, or much use, if they simply tell their employers what they wish to hear. Government economists also have the civil service code of 'integrity, honesty, objectivity and impartiality' to live up to (see page 79), and Ministers with integrity understand that policies based on wrong analysis or evidence won't work no matter how popular they may be.

---

[21] John Kay, *the map is not the territory: an essay on the state of economics* (2011) https://www .johnkay.com/2011/10/04/the-map-is-not-the-territory-an-essay-on-the-state-of-economics/. John Kay also adds 'It is probably no accident that economics is by far the most male of the social sciences.' Ibid. But we leave that until Chapter 8.

[22] Vicky Pryce, *The dismal science? Is economics influential enough in government decision making?* Institute of Government (2011) https://www.instituteforgovernment.org.uk/sites/default/files/publications/The%20dismal%20science.pdf (Accessed April 2021).

As we shall explore in Chapter 8, and as is emphasized by Miatta Fahnbulleh,[23] to provide useful agency practitioners must also guard against uncritically applying whatever particular approach to economics they are used to using.

The real world never exactly matches any particular model and so practitioners should eclectically choose from a wide, often interdisciplinary, toolbox to adapt to particular issues, rather than try to shoehorn reality into any particular methodological framework. Again, as Sir Dave Ramsden who was joint head of the GES with Vicky Pryce, observed:

> "McCloskey's (1983) exhortation of the broad and everyday human values of 'honesty, tolerance and clarity' is aligned with the Civil Service Code and is a better guide for GES practitioners than dogged adherence to, say, a set of axiomatic rules for theoretic consistency."[24]

INTELLECTUAL COMPROMISE AND WORKING FOR AN EMPLOYER

Practitioner economists must usually please their boss, and that may restrict what they can say. It also means moving readily and rapidly to new areas of economics if that is demanded by their boss. They are often expected to achieve 'rapid expertise'. One great advantage of working as an academic is not only that you can specialize, and so become a leading expert in your field, but that also you generally enjoy much greater academic freedom and can speak more freely.[25] This is how it should be as academic freedom is a vital part of democracy.

Outside academia and freelance commentary you may have to be more circumspect, particularly if your own views on economics and politics differ from your employer's. For example, a lobby group (see page 59) is not going to employ you to gainsay its mission, and most of the media also have strong editorial control. Similarly, economists working in the private sector are expected to be supportive of their employers' objectives. The civil service has

---

[23] In her interview for this book (see Video 14: In conversation with Miatta Fahnbulleh available at www.oup.com/he/pryce-ross1e).

[24] In Diane Coyle, ed., *What's the use of economics?* (London Publishing Partnership, 2012), page 5.

[25] Well anyway, within the bounds of the law, due respect for students, reputational damage to your university, and the degree of administrative and managerial 'intrusion' into teaching and assessment methods, which has increased since the days when academics were 'only accountable to their peers'.

a code of integrity, honesty, objectivity, and impartiality, but you will still be duty-bound to serve the government of the day and so not publicly criticize it. That does not mean 'sucking-up' to Ministers or the chief executive officer (CEO) of a company—although weaker analyst employees do a fair degree of that. A strong CEO/Minister will want you to be a 'critical friend'. To use a metaphor, a critical friend will tell you if you have body odour but will not tell anyone else! A good analyst is not a lackey. That said, the constitutional duty of a civil servant is to serve the government of the day and so must portray it in a 'favourable light' (see the role of a civil servant page 78. Economists in the private sector also want to earn their crust and must be careful to respect the wishes of their employers too.

The very nature of your role might limit what you can say publicly. For example, journalists may feel restricted by the editorial line of the newspaper, and the advice of an economist can be commercially sensitive. For example, John Llewellyn, former Chief Economist at Lehmans, the investment bank whose failure finally tipped us into full-scale crisis, says many practitioner insiders were alert to the history of financial crises and were acutely aware of the risks that had developed in the financial system ahead of the 2007 crisis. They were not really in a position, however, to broadcast that their institutions might be fragile. Equally, a central bank could find it difficult to warn of a major crisis without risking triggering the very thing they fear. The impact of the economist on the things they are addressing is a phenomenon known in social science as 'reflexivity'.[26]

INDEPENDENT RESEARCH INSTITUTIONS AND 'THINK TANKS'

As we saw in Chapter 2, policy economists are often employed by independent research institutions and 'think tanks'. These tend to have a specific focus and approach and their economists need to understand this for their work to be valued by their employer. Methodology and conclusions are always likely to be contested in Economics, but some non-academic research units are hugely respected and hence influential because of their quality and independence. The Institute for Fiscal Studies (IFS) is an example, as is the Office of Budget Responsibility (OBR), which was set up precisely to remove suspicion of "politicizing" in HM Treasury forecasts by making it independent of the Chancellor of the

[26] Taking account of itself or of the effect of the personality or presence of the researcher on what is being investigated.

Exchequer and the Treasury. That does not mean that the IFS and OBR cannot be disagreed with and challenged, but they are widely respected as honest brokers rather than propagandists. The National Institute of Economic and Social Research (NIESR) is another such influential research organization. NIESR was recently led by Jonathan Portes a former chief economist at the Cabinet Office. Jonathan accepts much of Keynes's prescription for dealing with deep recessions, so though publicly loyal to impartiality and political neutrality while a civil servant he was subsequently openly very critical of the Conservative/Lib Dem Coalition Government's deficit reduction strategy ('austerity') after he left to become director of the NIESR.

LOBBYISTS THINK TANKS

As we noted in Chapter 2, when considering working for a think tank you should be aware that many are implicitly or overtly political. They are there to champion a particular perspective rather than to conduct the open-minded balanced evaluation as expected of academics. For example, the Adam Smith Institute explicitly declares 'we work to promote neoliberal and free market ideas'.[27] The Institute of Economic Affairs gets a great deal of media exposure, often as if they were unbiased experts, but the IEA is again essentially promoting an explicitly left of centre agenda. It describes itself as:

> "The UK's original free-market think-tank, founded in 1955. Our mission is to improve understanding of the fundamental institutions of a free society by analysing and expounding the role of markets in solving economic and social problems."[28]

Most readers of 'The Economist' magazine are probably also unaware that the magazine represents a particular perspective:

> "The Economist remains, in the second half of its second century, true to the principles of its founder. James Wilson, a hat maker from the small Scottish town of Hawick, believed in free trade, internationalism and minimum interference by government, especially in the affairs of the market."[29]

---

[27] https://www.adamsmith.org/ (Accessed August 2021).

[28] https://iea.org.uk/about-us (Accessed August 2021).

[29] The Economist, *About us* https://www.economist.com/help/about-us (Accessed March 2021).

In the UK, our press media ranges from the highly respected *Financial Times* down to the often mischievously inaccurate and highly partisan 'red-top' tabloids. But just because they may be espousing a particular agenda it does not mean that pressure groups, lobbyists and partisan media are not worth listening to, so long as one treats them with appropriate caution. They can be very influential and so are, for better or for worse, part of political debate. At best they tend to over-emphasize their side of a case, or ignore powerful counter arguments; at worst they distort and misrepresent evidence.

An important consideration in assessing the reliability of think tanks is the transparency of their funding. In academia, it would be considered poor form indeed, and a bar to publication in an academic journal, not to declare who is funding one's research. It is an essential point of honesty to declare any possible conflicts of interest. Secrecy about one's funding destroys credibility in academia, but some think-tanks are very secretive about their sources of finance. The clandestine nature of their funding is seldom mentioned when their representatives are being interviewed in the media.[30] But if you wish to be seen as a non-partisan economist then there could be a reputational risk from being closely associated with clandestinely funded lobbyist groups regarded by many as shills for vested interests.[31]

THE ROLE OF A CIVIL SERVANT

Academics often delight in 'speaking truth unto power'. Unfortunately, such a purist attitude is likely to grate with powerful people who may have worked very hard to get to a position specifically so that they can implement their own views. They are likely to ignore 'preaching' experts whom they may regard as having little 'real-world' experience or cannot see the 'bigger picture'. Sometimes it may even be that a powerful person knows what the truth is but it simply serves their interests better to promote an alternative 'view'. A civil servant's role is firmly to serve the Government of the day regardless of their personal support for it or otherwise, but they should do this according to the civil service code, which has four headline behaviours:

[30] For example, see Transparify https://www.transparify.org/.

[31] For example, OFCOM rejected an IEA complaint against the LBC broadcaster James O'Brien 's damning broadcast about them. See https://www.ofcom.org.uk/__data/assets/pdf_file/0026/222965/Complaint-by-Institute-of-Economic-Affairs-about-James-OBrien,-LBC-97.3-FM,-26-February-2019-and-8-March-2019.pdf (Accessed August 2021).

- Integrity: putting the obligations of public service above your own personal interests

- Honesty: being truthful and open

- Objectivity: basing your advice and decisions on rigorous analysis of the evidence

- Impartiality: acting solely according to the merits of the case and serving equally well governments of different political persuasions.[32]

This means they must not lie to their ministers or to the public or seek to thwart or undermine the Government. For example, whatever one's sympathies, this infamous tweet (see Figure 3.1) made by a despairing civil servant about the Government of the day, was rightly condemned, and quickly deleted, by other civil servants.

Civil servants are there to advise and serve their Ministers; only in the most extreme circumstances of a most egregious deliberate constitutional infringement could they ever be justified in seeking to undermine a Government. Civil servants may rightly be held to account if they do try to resist a Minister's clear decision, and serving the Government of the day is less likely to be done well by civil servants who fall-out with their ministers. However, it is true that

FIGURE 3.1 Tweet posted on the official Civil Service Twitter account that was quickly deleted by the Civil Service.

Source: UK Civil Service [@UKCivilService]. (24 May 2020) 'Can you imagine having to work with these truth twisters?' [Tweet]. Twitter.

[32] Statutory guidance, The Civil Service code (2015) https://www.gov.uk/government/publications/civil-service-code/the-civil-service-code (Accessed March 2021).

'portraying the Government in a favourable light' can take civil servants into some rather grey areas in terms of political impartiality.[33]

For example, here is an extract from an HM Treasury Brief from 2012. The briefing gives a good flavour of how civil service economists can skilfully 'portray the Government of the day in a favourable light' even when the economic recovery from the financial crisis of 2007 and consequent recession in 2008 had been badly stalling. Should that Government have lost office and the opposition become the Government then the civil service would have switched to portraying its alternative policies and performance in a favourable light!

SECURITY STATUS: UNCLASSIFIED

Economic Briefing: HM Treasury Date: 05/10/2012
   Headline Economy Brief
   Top Lines
   The action taken by the Government to reduce the deficit and rebuild the economy has secured stability and positioned the UK as a relative safe haven, with interest rates near record lows, benefiting businesses and families.

   Despite the difficult conditions, the economy is healing and rebalancing: the deficit has been cut by a quarter; inflation has halved since its peak in September; over a million private sector jobs have been created under the Coalition Government; and in July the trade deficit fell by its largest monthly cash amount in at least 20 years.

   Official statistics have estimated a contraction in the UK economy of -0.4 per cent in Q2, 2012 (revised up from a previously estimated contraction of 0.7 per cent). This is a disappointing figure, but the UK is dealing with some very deep-rooted problems at home, including recovering from the biggest debt and financial crisis of our lifetimes, as well as a very serious debt crisis.

   The Government has taken action to protect the economy and has set out a comprehensive strategy to achieve strong, sustainable, and balanced growth.

Of course, in an ideal world, the electorate would judge politicians entirely objectively according to a careful assessment of all the facts and their own personal values. Unfortunately, we do not live in an ideal world. It can take more than overwhelming evidence for a policy to be adopted. Political shenanigans

---

[33] The Institute of Government is a respected observer and commentator on the integrity of government and the role Ministers, civil servants and advisers.

can also be frustrating for earnest 'technocratic' civil servants, as Paul Johnson, an ex-Treasury chief microeconomist and now director of the respected IFS, makes clear in an article he wrote for *The Times* in 2017.[34]

IS THERE A PROFESSIONAL CODE FOR ECONOMISTS?

There are no laws against calling oneself an economist, so it would be difficult to impose a general code for all those who claim to be an economist. However, there are rules for submitting articles to many economic journals, such as disclosure of any actual or potential conflicts of interest, and a commitment to provide data and coding for others who wish to replicate or interrogate results. As the GES is the professional body for economists in government its members are bound by the Civil Service Code (see page 79 above), and the RES has recently introduced a code of conduct for its members, which includes:[35]

> "The principal aim of the Royal Economic Society is to promote the study of economic science, which it strives to achieve by supporting its members and others involved in the economics discipline. Promoting the study and development of economics requires a culture in which all professional activities, including research, education, advice and communication more generally, are undertaken collegially, ethically and with integrity. The Society expects its members to adhere to the high professional standards that this requires and to encourage others associated with the discipline to do so. The Society also sets these standards for itself, and hence the code of conduct applies to all involved as members or are associated with the Society through events or other activities.
>
> Research should be conducted and presented with honesty, care, transparency, in compliance with legal requirements, acknowledging limits of expertise and giving due credit to the contributions of others. The provision of advice and other communications in economics should also adhere to these standards. Students at all levels should be treated fairly and with respect. Any real or perceived conflicts of interest should be disclosed in all activities.

[34] See Johnson, P. The truth about making policy is difficult for politicians to swallow' (2017). *The Times* [Online], 4 September. Available at https://www.thetimes.co.uk/article/2234e96a-90cc-11e7-a2ce-ce94682a575d (Accessed May 2022).

[35] Royal Economic Society, *Code of conduct* (2020) https://www.res.org.uk/membership/code-of-conduct.html (Accessed March 2021).

The Royal Economic Society seeks a professional environment in economics where all are able to participate freely, so that equal opportunity and fair treatment apply regardless of characteristics (such as gender, ethnicity, age, disability, political or religious views, status, affiliations or relationships).

Discourse in all forums should be conducted with civility and respect, with each idea or contribution considered on its merits. Under no circumstances will bullying or harassment of any kind be tolerated."

It would be nice but naïve to believe that such high standards are adhered to by all economists.

CONCLUSION

It is a useful over generalization to say that academics are prized by their peers for their rigour and professional practitioners are prized by their masters for their relevance.[36] Although, as we have seen, 'Professional practitioner or academic' is not a dichotomy, and there are certainly economists, such as Sir Richard Blundell, Sir Partha Dasgupta, Dame Rachel Griffith, Dame Carol Propper, Lord Nicholas Stern and Sir John Vickers to name just a few, who straddle both worlds. Hopefully this book and their example will inspire you to try to become such an economist, but if practitioner employers restricted recruitment only to economists of this calibre then they would have fewer economists than they need. So, be reassured that you do not need to be a leading academic to be a successful practitioner (or even an academic!) economist. We look in more detail at what is required to be a practitioner economist in the next chapter.

SUMMARY

- Being a professional practitioner differs from being an academic economist in terms of aims, stakeholders and the context in which tasks are performed.

---

[36] *The pursuit of peer esteem may sometimes even interfere with the pursuit of truth. For example see: Times Higher Educational Supplement, 'How likely are academics to confess to errors in research', https://www.timeshighereducation.com/features/how-likely-are-academics-confess-errors-re-search?utm_source=the_editorial_newsletter&utm_medium=email&utm_content=top_stories&utm_campaign=the_editorial_newsletter.*

- Practitioners seldom have the luxury of concluding, as academics so often do, that 'more research is required'.

- Economists are of no use to their stakeholders and bosses if they only say 'yes' or 'It's all very complicated' (see Chapter 5).

- Practitioner economists are expected to provide agency for their stakeholders.

- The most useful analysts are those who act as 'critical friends' to their bosses.

- Working for a boss or an organization may restrict what you are allowed to say publicly, and sometimes even within that organization.

- Academic and some independent economists have the most freedom in what they can choose to research and to say. That is good for democracy, advancing knowledge, and evidence-based policy. Civil servants have some protection provided by the Civil Service Code from becoming mere shills of Government and, when that is respected, it is also part of a healthy democracy.

- Economists in journalism and think tanks can also be an important part of democracy, but lobbyists and others are often pushing an agenda, sometimes with clandestine funding, and that may be a challenge for an open democracy.

- Policy economics often needs to take account of more than just economics.

- Elegant sophisticated deductive mathematical models may be of less use for policy than more messy inductive heuristic insights, data 'eyeballing' (see Chapter 6) and knowledge of the economic agents involved.

- Sources of economics may be critiqued for rigour, relevance, bias, conflicts of interest and vested interest (see Chapter 8).

- Some employers expect economists to 'spin' on their behalf, but most simply want to benefit from the power and insights of economics.

QUESTIONS

1. How will you do more detailed research on the various types of job that economists do?

2. Pick out what type of economist job most appeals to you. Now compare this with your next best alternative employment.

3. How does being a professional practitioner differ from being an academic economist in terms of aims, stakeholders and the context in which tasks are performed?

4. There is a long-standing debate about whether economics is a science or not. How relevant do you think this debate is to policy economics?

5. Why do civil servant economists work hard to serve a Government even when they are personally strongly opposed to that Government's policies?

EXERCISES

1. Read the Paul Johnson article referenced previously in the chapter and suggest ways that policymaking could be improved. (Johnson, P. (2017) 'The truth about making policy is difficult for politicians to swallow'. The Times [Online] 4 September. Available at: https://www.thetimes.co.uk/article/2234e96a-90cc-11e7-a2ce-ce94682a575d [Last accessed May 2022]).

2. Re-draft the HM Treasury briefing on page 81 in a way that would suit a publication opposed to 'austerity'.

3. Explore the transparency of funding for four think tanks cited or appearing in the media.

4. Read a newspaper article on an economics topic from a popular newspaper and list what elements in it can be said to be based on objective economics and which are political opinions or supposition.

FIND OUT MORE

Paul Anand, Laurence Roope and Andy Ross (2019) *How economists help central government think: Survey evidence from the UK Government Economic Service*, International Journal of Public Administration, 42:13, 1145–1157, DOI: 10.1080/01900692.2019.1575668.

Kay, J. *The map is not the territory: An essay on the state of Economics*, in D. Coyle ed. *What is the use of economics?: teaching the dismal science after the crisis* (London: London Publishing partnership, 2012), pp. 49–59.

Mankiw, G., (2006). *Greg Mankiw's blog: Random Observations for Students of Economics.* Available at **http://gregmankiw.blogspot.co.uk/2006/05/scientists-and-engineers. html.**

Pryce, V. *The dismal science? Is economics influential enough in government decision making? (2011)* **https://www.instituteforgovernment.org.uk/sites/default/files/publications/ The%20dismal%20science.pdf.**

Ramsden, D. *Making economics and economists better: The Government Economic Service perspective,* in: D. Coyle ed. *What is the use of Economics?: teaching the dismal science after the crisis* (London: London Publishing partnership, 2012, pp. 3–9.

The Institute of Government website: **https://www.instituteforgovernment.org.uk/**

CHAPTER 4

How useful are economics degrees?

· · · ·●●●●●●● · ·

INTRODUCTION

This chapter explores the recent debates on whether degrees in Economics are 'fit for purpose' for the jobs that their graduates will do, and looks at the skill gaps perceived in economics graduates as identified by employers. It will refer to the generic skills that benefit all economics students and graduates—for example, good written and verbal communication skills, research skills, critical thinking skills, being an effective team player, self-motivation, self-awareness, and resilience—and skills that practitioners use most often only in their professional work. The nature of these skills will be further developed in Part Two of the book, along with exercises and additional sources.

It may be reassuring to note here that according to Adam Smith, often credited with being the 'Father of Economics',[1] expertise is the result of nurture rather than nature:

> "The difference between the most dissimilar characters, between a philosopher and a common street porter, for example, seems to arise not so much from nature, as from habit, custom, and education."[2]

---

[1] There is a much earlier rival for this honour. Ibn Khaldun, an Arab polymath who has been attributed as the founder of the proto-disciplines that would become historiography, sociology, economics, and demography. See Abdol S. Soofi, 'Economics of Ibn Khaldun Revisited', *History of Political Economy* June 1995 27(2):387–404.

[2] Smith, Adam, *An Inquiry into the Nature and Causes of the Wealth of Nations* (Penguin Classics: London, 1982) (originally published in 1776).

Given the relatively favourable employment outcomes for economics degrees (see Chapter 2), economics degrees could well be regarded as vocational. But in terms of the curriculum, despite recent emphasis on imparting 'employability' in economics degrees, most degrees in economics are still more orientated towards preparing students to become academics rather than professional practitioners. This is understandable as it is difficult to replicate practitioner work environments realistically at a university, hence the desirability of placements. Most university lecturers in economics have not had experience working as a practitioner economist for an employer outside academia or for non-economist stakeholders. It is easier for them to prepare students for the roles with which they are most familiar. Although we emphasize the broader skills for success in Part Two of this book, even the most academic of economics degree is far from being a waste of time. Although it is selling students short to ignore their futures, there is more to a rounded education than employability alone. And there is no doubt that familiarity with the formal theoretical frameworks and objective qualitative and quantitative techniques used by academic economists is important for developing a rigorous approach to economics. The need for rigour is not confined to academia; it also is essential for any more definitive economic research. The best 'low-brow' economics is rooted in 'high-brow' understanding. But too strict an insistence on formal logic and rigour can lead to solving merely the sort of problems and conundrums that only a computer might care about, and it does not prepare you for working with others (see Chapters 6 and 7).

As the eminent American economist Kenneth Boulding is attributed with having amusingly put it:

> "Mathematics brought rigor to economics. Unfortunately, it also brought mortis."
>
> Kenneth Boulding, economist (1910–93)[3]

Indeed, the mathematical problem sets so commonly put before economics degree students are most unlike anything usually encountered when working as a practitioner. As practitioners, we are seldom presented with tasks that are self-contained with definitive answers. There are invariably conditionality issues to make judgements about, areas of sheer doubt and ignorance, and, of course, a dearth of counterfactuals and surfeit of confounders (see Chapter 6). Economics

---

[3] *The Economist*, 'An A-Z of business quotations: Economics', https://www.economist.com/schumpeter/2012/07/20/economics (Accessed May 2021).

briefings to managers and Ministers do not end with 'QED'.[4] We assess the importance and role of mathematics for economists in Chapter 6, where we look at where mathematics in economics is very important indeed and where it is less of a requirement, at least for a wide range of professional practitioners.

For real life problems there are often no definitive answers and a lot more is required than crunching through algebra. Indeed, academics are often surprised by how little attention policy makers wish to give to the algebraic derivations of results, taking the derivations on trust from academics and focussing instead on their interpretations and usefulness. Policy advice usually involves making judgements drawn from a mass of not always consistent data. It even means leaving the office from time to time, perhaps going out and speaking with those actually involved in the markets and agencies in question! That is often called being a 'Dirty Shoes economist' who seeks 'Ground Truth' (see also Chapter 8).

Regardless of where mathematics is necessary and where it is not, there is just no escaping the need for good data skills. You will need a strong understanding of how empirical evidence is formed and used with credibility to be a successful economist (see also Chapter 6).

DIFFERENT WAYS TO SERVE: PRODUCERS AND CONSUMERS OF ECONOMICS

There is something of a division of labour among economists, though there are many ways to serve as an economist. For example, as Treasury economist Mario Pisani points out:

> "There's very little, at least in government, which is about progressing the theoretical body of economics. It's much more about applying it to solve problems."[5]

Academic economists are essential to our understanding of economics and for advancing knowledge, but there are also many more economists who work as

---

[4] QED is the abbreviation for the Latin phrase 'quod erat demonstrandum' used to show that you have proved something that you wanted to prove.

[5] In his interview for this book (see Video 20: In conversation with Mario Pisani available at www.oup.com/he/pryce-ross1e). See also Dame Rachel Griffith's quote on producers and consumers of economics on page 158 and her interview for this book (see Video 15: In conversation with Dame Rachel Griffiths available at www.oup.com/he/pryce-ross1e).

informed consumers and users of economics rather than as producers of new economics. This distinction was very evident in a survey of members of the Government Economic Service:

"We asked our respondents how they might reflect on the best education for economists (see Anand and Leape, 2012) and there is a sense that professional life is something of a surprise to many, following on from their university training. One respondent put it quite succinctly when he said his economics course taught him how to make a car whereas what he wanted for his current job was a training that taught him how to drive a car. There is an important distinction between skill and understanding being made here and the point was well made. In talking to senior economists in government, we found that one of the difficulties new economists have on entry to the service is in applying general economic principles to particular problems. This is a skill very different to model building but one that has, nonetheless, to be taught and practised."[6]

A racing driver has to know the capacity and limits of a racing car, what it is capable of and what it cannot do, and to have an excellent feel for the engine and brakes. Understanding of its construction will help in this, but being able to design and build the component parts is not necessary. Dame Kate Barker explains what her role as a practical policy economist has been:

"In a sense my job was taking the evidence base and thinking about it, but also talking to lots of people who are practical in the fields. If I think about . . . my role as an economist, it's working between people who are very academic and people who are active in business, or politicians, or people planting investment money around the country, and turning the academic stuff into something much more practical."[7]

Of course, economics degrees are far from being an arcane drilling in half-understood techniques. The fundamental concepts that are taught within economics degrees, such as the importance of incentives, opportunity cost, and the role of markets, open-up powerful and distinctive ways of thinking about

[6] Paul Anand, Laurence Roope and Andy Ross (2019) How Economists Help Central Government Think: Survey Evidence from the UK Government Economic Service, International Journal of Public Administration, 42:13, 1145–1157, DOI: 10.1080/01900692.2019.1575668.

[7] In her interview for this book (see Video 3: In conversation with Dame Kate Barker available at www.oup.com/he/pryce-ross1e).

economic and social problems. For policy economists the basic economic concepts taught in economics degrees provide powerful underlying theoretical underpinnings for the five broad categories of government intervention: i) market failure ii) inequality iii) paternalism iv) stability v) growth (see Chapter 10). The fundamental concepts in economics are often called 'threshold concepts' because of their ubiquity and the way that they significantly progress the ability of students to think like an economist and provide deep as opposed to mere surface or even rote learning:

> "The newly developed threshold concepts approach provides a framework for learning that has implications for teaching, learning and assessment. The aim of the approach can be encapsulated as getting students to 'think like economists'. It may help lecturers in Higher Education who are grappling with two widely reported problems: (i) students who acquire formal knowledge of a discipline but who seem unable to use this knowledge when making sense of experience in work or their everyday lives (ii) students who struggle with underpinning theory and resort to verbatim learning of isolated aspects of the subject that they seem unable to use effectively in conjunction with each other."[8]

Of course, in pedagogy just as in economics, there is debate. Not all educationalists think the idea of 'threshold concepts' is the best way to describe these fundamentals. Again, for practitioners the important thing to be grasped is simpler, it is only that the basic tools of economics must be well understood, not merely memorized, so that they can be appropriately selected, or rejected, and applied effectively to new problems and an extraordinarily wide range of issues. As we shall see in Chapter 8, this often involves being eclectic in approach, but used with skill and good judgment the analytical power of the toolbox universities provide for economics graduates is greatly prized by employers.

WHAT DO EMPLOYERS WANT?

Rest assured that economics degrees can develop transferable skills that are held in high regard by employers. The ability to apply theory to specific contexts, as well as data cleaning and processing, time management,

---

[8] Peter Davies and Jean Mangan (2020), *Threshold Concepts in Economics: implications for teaching, learning and assessment*, *The Handbook for Economics Lecturers* (Economics Network). Available at https://www.economicsnetwork.ac.uk/handbook/printable/threshold_concepts.pdf.

teamworking and, of course, the capacity to communicate complex matters in understandable ways are staple skills in practitioner work (see Part Two). All these capabilities are developed to some extent by most economics degrees today and are becoming increasingly evident in degree programmes due to additional emphasis on employability within higher education more generally. However, as research by the Economics Network has discovered, through their questionnaire surveying of employers over a number of years (2012, 2015, and 2019), significant gaps remain between the types of skills that employers want in their recruits and the predominant types of training that are embedded within economics degrees. The gaps can result in students not being aware of and practising skills that will ultimately serve them well as professional economists.

ECONOMICS NETWORK'S EMPLOYER SURVEY—THE FINDINGS

The Economics Network regularly surveys employers of economists to assess whether employers' needs are matched by the education and training that students of Economics receive at university. The latest Economics Network questionnaire survey in 2019, which also involved focus groups and interviews with students, lecturers, and employers, saw 40 employers participate. The main employers involved were from central government, consultancy, and public sector services. One interesting finding was that although employers and lecturers at least speak much the same language about the skills that are needed by economists, they do not always mean the same thing, as we shall see in a moment.

The most highly valued of the skills reported by employers who took part in the 2019 Economics Network survey were, in order of importance: the ability to apply theories to the real world; communication skills; and data analysis. Also highly regarded were collaborative skills and more general transferable skills such as time keeping and critical thinking. In fact, these skills have been consistently among the most valued by employers in all the employer surveys the Economics Network has undertaken. It is therefore encouraging that the three most highly valued skills among employers were the same as those prioritized by academic economists, although academics tended to place data analysis as the most important of the three.

Despite this agreement and the use of common terms, caution is needed in interpreting the findings as there can be a gap between what academia and employers understand to be these skills. For example, the appropriate and careful application of theoretical insights was one of the most highly valued skills for employers. For employers, application to the real world involves the skill of solving commercial or policy-oriented problems and the simplification of complexity to the key variables needed to understand a situation. However, for many of the academic economists that were interviewed in the survey, application merely meant illustrating a theory with real world examples. For example, the theory of international trade might be illuminated by a discussion of why certain countries export certain goods, but this is quite different to, say, advising where the UK or a specific company should concentrate its industrial and trade efforts in the wake of leaving the EU. 'Real world' application for some commercial and operational economist jobs can seem quite parochial compared to the grand themes studied at university.

THE COYLE REVIEWS

In 2012 the distinguished economist Diane Coyle approached the Government Economic Service (GES) to suggest a forum of employers and academic economists on the state of economics and particularly the curriculum of UK Economics degrees. This led to two high profile and influential conferences sponsored by the GES, Bank of England, and Economics Network, both hosted by the Bank of England.[9] The degree of consensus that emerged was perhaps surprising, the academics and employers more or less agreed on the desirable direction but were somewhat perplexed as to how to achieve movement along it. The findings were reinforced in a subsequent survey, conducted by Ian Harwood,[10] one of this book's authors, of what knowledge and skills employers of economics graduates most value, across the membership of the Society of Professional Economists. The prevailing view was that economics students would benefit from:

• Greater awareness of economic history and current real-world context

• More understanding of the limitations of modelling and current economic methodology

• Better practical data-handling skills

---

[9] These events and themes were followed up by Diane Coyle (2012) in the book she subsequently edited *What's the use of economics? Teaching the dismal science after the crisis* (London Publishing Partnership).

[10] See Royal Economic Society (2013), April 2013 newsletter, 'Teaching Economics After the Crisis' https://www.res.org.uk/resources-page/april-2013-newsletter-teaching-economics-after-the-crisis.html.

- Greater ability to communicate economics to non-specialists
- A more pluralistic/eclectic approach to economics and
- A combination of deductive and inductive reasoning.

We shall now look at each of these themes in turn and give our explanations of why they are beneficial for anyone seeking a professional career as an economist, and hence why they should guide your wider professional development as an economist (see also Part Two of this book). It is clear from the outset that the recommendations suggest a more practitioner focus.

GREATER AWARENESS OF ECONOMIC HISTORY AND CURRENT REAL-WORLD CONTEXT

Mastering complex models can lead to an unjustified confidence, even hubris. Over-commitment to what you have already learned can come from the sheer intellectual effort and work required to be an expert in a certain approach. In contrast, reflecting on the shortcomings of past economic policies throughout history is a great antidote to hubris, and a saltatory reminder of the need for scepticism always. It can also highlight the limitations of looking at the world only as an economist. For example, Miatta Fahnbulleh describes how Western economists had characterized economic development failures in Africa as failures of policy, whereas she draws a very different conclusion:

> "The dominant orthodoxy was that that was complete economic madness but you when you go back, and you look at the papers it was very thoughtful and quite rational economic decision making. It was "events, events, events" that scuppered economic strategy!"[11]

As we look at in Chapter 8, trying to fit everything you see into your pre-existing knowledge sets and perspectives is a very common blind spot, and so studying the history of economic thought and policies is a humbling journey through an extraordinarily rich diversity of views and powerful insights. As David Colander puts it:

[11] In her interview for this book (see Video 14: In conversation with Miatta Fahnbulleh available at www.oup.com/he/pryce-ross1e).

"Any time I think I have an even semi-profound thought about economics, all I need do is look at the history of economic thought to rid myself of such hubris. Almost inevitably I find that my thought has been said more profoundly and more elegantly by earlier economists."[12]

Over-confidence during periods of economic stability has been a recurring problem among macroeconomists. Macroeconomists have too often spoken with unwarranted confidence despite the fact that even their most complete models do not fully capture the complexity and unpredictability of real economies. This century, many economists boasted in the long 'Non-Inflationary Continuing Expansion' (NICE) build-up to the 2008 'Great Recession' that they had 'cracked' macroeconomics. The prevailing model was even often called the 'New Consensus'. Nobel Prize winner economist Robert Lucas proclaimed that the 'central problem of depression-prevention has been solved, for all practical purposes'.[13] In contrast, awareness of history tempers an over-reliance on specific models and makes for useful scepticism, as does experience as a practitioner regularly eyeballing datasets and seeing anomalies and unusual developments arise. Among others, Cambridge Professor Philip Arestis and Andy Ross, then at HM Treasury, drew on experience and history to caution against the over-confidence that was so apparent before the financial crisis:[14]

"... experience shows that past consensuses turned out to have been based on inadequate or misleading economics, or at least the parameters of the real world changed rendering them inoperable."[15]

Knowledge of the past avoids hubris in the present. An exclusively model-orientated education in economics can lead to an over reliance on abstract models, in contrast to looking at previous similarities and data. Models are very important ways of thinking about economics and can be crucial for

---

[12] Colander, David in D. Coyle (2012), *What's the use of economics? Teaching the dismal science after the crisis* (London Publishing Partnership).

[13] Lucas, Robert (2003) 'Macroeconomic Priorities' in the *American Economic Review* March 2003, VOL. 93 NO. 1. Available at http://www.princeton.edu/~markus/misc/Lucas2003.pdf (Accessed August 2020).

[14] In a book laudably sponsored by HM Treasury, then serving a Labour government still boasting it had ended 'boom and bust'.

[15] In the introduction by Arestis and Ross (p. 20) in P. Arestis ed. (2007), *Is there a new consensus in macroeconomics?* (Palgrave).

advancing knowledge, but if important real-world determinants are missing—such as for the 'Great Financial Crash' (GFC) and the realistic integration of finance markets—then such models may well fail to predict real events. Indeed, one of the main causes of the GFC was the level of indebtedness and financial exposure built up by financial institutions themselves. This was an aspect of financial risk that was largely absent in the macroeconomic models economists used to understand the economy before the crash. As the Nobel prize winning macroeconomist Thomas Sargent observed about the mainstream models:

> "These models were designed to describe aggregate economic fluctuations during normal times when markets can bring borrowers and lenders together in orderly ways, not during financial crises and market breakdowns."[16]

Although there was an embarrassingly large percentage of the profession that did not see the GFC coming, perhaps the Queen's famous question as to 'Why economists hadn't seen the crisis coming?' should really have been answered: 'Many did'.[17] Many practitioner economists are used to looking at a broad range of historical references and broader data and trends, and so were perhaps better at seeing the crisis coming than those preoccupied with finessing academic models.[18] At least, this is certainly the view of Larry Elliott, the long-serving economics editor of the *Guardian*. Larry Elliott thinks the fact that his history degree did not train him in the technical methods of modern economics might actually have been an advantage! At least for his avoiding what he sees as the 'mathematical myopia' of many university economists:

---

[16] Thomas Sargent (2010), Modern Macroeconomic Models in Economist's View available at https://economistsview.typepad.com/economistsview/2010/09/thomas-sargent-on-modern-macroeconomi-models.html (Accessed August 2021).

[17] In the book *Debunking Economics* Steve Keen provides a list of economists whom he considers predicted the Great Recession for the correct reasons. Many economists would contest Steve Keen's account, but there certainly were economists who were frantically warning of an impending financial meltdown. Of course, some, who didn't but perhaps should have, like to insist no-one did, and it is fair to say some who claim to have seen it coming had been predicting a crisis for a very long-time: a reminder of Samuelson's quip about someone who had predicted 'nine of the previous five recessions'. In fact, most economists are working in microeconomics and most macroeconomists are not involved in forecasting, even for those who are- a dark sky does not tell you when the storm will break, not everyone is looking at the sky all the time and many economists were restricted in what they could say publicly anyway. So, it is hardly surprising that 'most economists did not see it coming'.

[18] Although the very abstract economist Wynne Godley is credited by some for having seen a financial crisis coming from decades before.

"I think the problem has been that universities had a one-track approach . . . that you could learn everything from these fairly standardised models and once you had actually mastered all the differential calculus and equations you were well set up. It created a cadre of economists and a sort of 'group think' which led us to the horrors of the financial crisis. Economics had become divorced from the real world, and one of the problems I think was that it was far too based around mathematical models. The other was it completely tended to downplay, or in some cases eliminate altogether economic history. I think you can learn quite a lot from studying what has gone wrong in the past. In the build up to the 2008 crisis I wrote a lot about how there was a massive financial crisis coming. I didn't have the economic models to prove it but what I did know was that history had shown that . . . every time there was supposedly a new technological paradigm which justified higher share prices, you should go running for the hills!"[19]

Gavyn Davies also says similar in his interview for this book,[20] but most academic economists would disagree with them on the role of mathematics, although the criticism here is with a preoccupation with mathematics rather than maths itself.

Larry Elliot is certainly correct to point out that there were economists before 2007 who were warning of impending financial meltdown. Although some had habitually predicted crisis for a raft of reasons, others were more specific and accurate. Warnings might have been more widespread, but then expressing yourself in ways acceptable to stakeholders is often another important distinction between academic and practitioner obligations (see Chapter 3). As John Llewelyn, former Chief Economist at Lehmans,[21] confided during a seminar for Society of Professional Economist Courses, although no-one could set precise timings, a lot of insiders could see the Great Financial Crisis coming but they were not in a position to add to the fragility of their commercial institutions by making public announcements on the risk. Bankers also have to please their bosses, and equally, economists in central banks must be careful not to trigger a crisis by expressing fears that may or may not otherwise come true.[22]

---

[19] In his interview for this book (see Video 13: In conversation with Larry Elliott. Available at www.oup.com/he/pryce-ross1e).

[20] See Video 13: Video 11: In conversation with Gavyn Davies OBE. Available at www.oup .com/he/pryce-ross1e.

[21] The collapse of Lehmans did much to trigger the potential crisis.

[22] Although many would say the central banks were captured by efficient market ideology and had taken their eye off the ball.

Fortunately for those studying macroeconomics at universities today, there is more focus on the creation of money by bank lending, and of the unintended risks from such lending of a lack of 'macro-prudence'. Research has advanced at institutions such as Rebuilding Macroeconomics, the National Institute of Economic and Social Research (NIESR) and, of course, in central banks such as the Bank of England.[23] Though, as we note in Chapter 10, we are far from out of the woods yet in terms of a complete understanding of finance, and the fact remains that models are necessarily simplified representations of reality, even though they adapt over time to incorporate important new understanding that comes from historical phenomena, such as the financial crash. Analytical models have a great many uses in economics, but a rich understanding of the economy will always require a nuanced approach which supplements economic models with an appreciation of relevant history, talking to people involved on the ground, experience with the data and good judgement. As Robert Chote noted when he left the Office for Budget Responsibility (OBR): its 'Main economic forecast choices have been judgment calls not modelling'.[24]

MORE UNDERSTANDING OF THE LIMITATIONS OF MODELLING AND CURRENT ECONOMIC METHODOLOGY

Practitioners should often 'reality check' models and technique. For example, take the first modelling technique that economists usually learn: supply and demand. Demand is the less problematic of the two. While it is easy to point out that utility maximization is unrealistic and doesn't give unambiguous predictions, overall demand theory does suggest that price rises will normally tend to contract demand and, so long as we keep a look-out for exceptions,[25] this is usually a useful insight. Even then we must still be aware that demand is the amount people wished to buy at that price and not necessarily the amount actually bought, and that as soon as it is measured, that data is out of date. But whether something is 'true' or a good description is often not important for the job in hand, as we saw in 'The role of models' (see page 71) in Chapter 3.

---

[23] Although some economists who have strong claims to have predicted the financial crisis, such as Ann Pettifer, worry that this has not actually stemmed a resurgence of reckless profit seeking by banks.

[24] For example: stated by Robert Chote. Society of Professional Economists, 'The OBR at 10: Lessons learned and challenges for the future', 24 September 2020, 5.00pm–7.00pm delivered live via Webinar. Available at https://spe.org.uk/whats-on/past-events/7399-2/webinar-the-obr-at-10 (Accessed May 2021).

[25] Not only textbook ones such as Giffen Goods and price as an indicator of quality or ostentation, but also operational ones such as when the price is raised to cover the cost of a more persuasive sales drive.

Supply is more problematic. A supply curve asks how much firms would supply at a given price. But prices are not 'given' to firms outside the extreme theoretical case of perfectly competitive markets. It takes good judgement to assess if a market is sufficiency competitive for a supply curve to be a useful simplification. For example, textbooks may show the effects of a food health-scare as a leftward shift of a demand curve and a contraction down an upward sloping supply curve, and so an unambiguous decrease in both price and equilibrium quantity. However, in food retailing there is often a large oligopolistic element, called 'supermarkets', and they may engage in oligopolistic non-price competition where wholesale prices fall but the retail price doesn't follow. And it should always be remembered that supply and demand curves are essentially partial equilibrium concepts, the 'other things constant' assumption and their independence from each other often breaks down in general equilibrium analysis and broader macroeconomics. In short, theories and their models can let you down if you don't pay attention to the specific circumstances and detail of the actual phenomena you are trying to understand (see Chapter 10 for more examples and advice on this).

Admittedly, learning economic theory can be much easier if students 'suspend their disbelief' for a while to concentrate only on how a particular model fits together, but ultimately being critical of all economics is vital to being a good practitioner economist. This is just as relevant for widely used and 'standardized' techniques, such as Cost Benefit Analysis (see Chapter 10), as it is for new approaches.

BETTER PRACTICAL DATA-HANDLING SKILLS

Practitioners also need a wide range of practical data-handling skills. However, recruiters of graduate economists frequently complain that candidates for jobs can recite quite advanced econometric techniques but cannot make use of simple indices, means and modes, pie-charts and histograms, or other descriptive statistics that are useful for getting an overview of the essential aspects of a data set. As professional practitioners are often required to explain things to non-economists, simple descriptive statistics are often more useful for that purpose than advanced statistics. As Dave Ramsden, former Head of the GES reflects:

> "A broad quantitative competency, including descriptive statistics, is also generally more useful within the GES than a narrow training in advanced econometrics, as useful as econometrics can be."[26]

---

[26] Dave Ramsden 'Making economics and economists better: The Government Economic Service perspective' in Diane Coyle ed, (2012), *What's the use of economics?* ch. 1.

Experienced econometricians, such as Professor Ron Smith at Birkbeck, London University, always urge 'eye-balling' data, using graphs and charts, to get a feel for the data before doing anything more complicated with it. This helps avoid the mistake of 'rubbish in rubbish out'. For example, Ron warns that the same regression outputs can result from very different data sets and that knowing about these characteristics can be vital to interpreting the nature of the relationships in the data.[27]

Economics has become increasingly empirical partly due to the wider availability of data and developments in computing power over recent decades. University economics degrees have responded by incorporating more and more data-oriented courses into their degree programmes. However, the Economics Network survey found that while data skills are embedded in academic degrees, the emphasis is more often on the statistical theory underlying data analysis and the use of econometric techniques to analyse that data. In the survey, employers tended to mean something rather different by data analysis skills. They put a far greater value on the ability to identify and select data appropriate to particular empirical questions, the cleaning of data and its collation, and the initial insights that can be gleaned from the descriptive analysis of data. Gathering and organizing data is itself the major task for many organizations, such as from administrative data and larger surveys giving feedback on products and services, whereas university students are often dealing with pre-cleaned finished datasets, which are quickly amenable to more sophisticated econometric analyses. Economists will also tend to use specialized econometric software that is not user-friendly for many people, whereas in most organizations statistical outputs are usually shared using standard packages such as Excel (see also Chapter 6).

GREATER ABILITY TO COMMUNICATE ECONOMICS TO NON-SPECIALISTS

In the case of communication skills, the Economics Network's surveys find that employers value employees who can use economic reasoning to explain complex phenomena to non-expert audiences in a variety of communication modes, written as well as verbal. The focus in most economics degrees still tends to be on academic writing, which is not surprising as a primary concern of academia is to develop producers of economics. For producers of new economics, the communication style that is important is the rigorous explanation

---

[27] Anscombe's quartet provides a striking example of how very different looking distributions when graphed can yield similar summary statistics https://en.wikipedia.org/wiki/Anscombe%27s_quartet.

and justification of one's approach to other economists.[28] In professional settings, it is more usual to be writing for non-economist audiences (see Chapter 5: 'Communicating Complexity Simply').

In practitioner settings, 'wearing one's scholarship lightly' can be helpful. Government Ministers and corporate CEOs are not impressed by overt erudition and complex language: they want their economists to be useful not hard to understand. As we noted in Chapter 3, CEOs and Ministers want their economists to be useful by providing 'agency', that is, giving them a better idea as to what to do next. As Vicky Pryce warns:

> "At the decision point, the economist who tells the decision maker that 'it is all very difficult and uncertain' is not much help and will soon find themselves not invited back."[29]

Communicating to non-economists is vital in most jobs outside academia. For example, economists are often called upon by our media and have increasingly found employment in media and journalism. Romesh Vaitilingam, writer and media consultant noted in his interview for the book:

> "I'm a writer but I wasn't a writer when I was studying economics. I didn't really start off having a career ambition to be a writer or a journalist—I fell into a publishing career, was lucky enough to have some very good mentors in those . . . early days . . . I don't think it was communicated sufficiently to me: the value of good economics communication, although I was taught by some very good economics communicators."[30]

Many UK universities today have begun to take communicating to varied audiences seriously, and there are several new modules on communicating economics emerging. However, some universities still do too little to provide opportunities for students to develop this vital employability skill. Although 'writing short' and 'communicating complexity simply' can take many years

[28.] Along with many conventions in the 'etiquette' of academic writing, such as citation and referencing, that practitioners are less fussy about.

[29] Vicky Pryce (2011), 'The Dismal science? Is economics influential enough in government decision making?' Inside Out 6 (Institute for Government), p. 4. Available at https://www.instituteforgovernment.org.uk/sites/default/files/publications/The%20dismal%20science.pdf

[30] In his interview for this book (see Video 27: In conversation with Romesh Vaitilingam available at www.oup.com/he/pryce-ross1e).

to perfect, there are many simple lessons that can be used to rapidly improve communication. We say much more about communication in Chapter 5 on 'Communicating Complexity Simply'.

WORKING WITH OTHERS

One of the skills that employers value most in graduates of economics is collaborative working with others. (See Chapter 7.) It is true that collaborative working and group work is increasingly integrated into many academic degree programmes, although it is still quite rare in formal assessments for economics. However, when it comes to collaboration, economics departments focus on working with other economists whereas employers are looking for graduates who are confident in working with colleagues from any discipline. This reinforces the importance of communication skills that can be adapted to suit non-economists (see Chapter 5). Placements as part of Economics degrees are rare, so we applaud Bath University Economics Dept in this respect, which has for decades organized placements for economics undergraduates as an integral part of their degree. Sandeep Kapur also describes how the mix of students at Birkbeck, where many are working as professionals in other spheres, enriches the classroom experience, bringing challenge to what is written in textbooks.[31] The London School of Economics LSE100 course is a good example of how interdisciplinary working can be introduced. The aim of LSE100 is to broaden students' skill sets by introducing them to a range of methodologies available for analysing social science issues and problems, as well as issues of causality and the role of induction alongside deduction (see page 215). Sadly, overall, opportunities in universities for working in collaboration with non-economists, outside work placements, remain quite rare.

CONCLUSION

A university degree should not be only about employment, but economics degrees do provide a wide range of transferable skills that are highly valued by employers. Understandably, university degree courses tend to focus on preparing students for producing economics as an academic rather than using economics for stakeholders and communicating this to non-economists. There is a large overlap in the skills required by all economists, and universities

---

[31] In his interview for this book (see Video 17: In conversation with Professor Sandeep Kapur available at www.oup.com/he/pryce-ross1e).

do well with much of this, but the typical university degree tends to leave a skills-gap in terms of employment and using economics in employment outside academe:

> "Economics has come, for a significant number, to be a profession in which the focus is not on the production of new research but rather the application of economic thinking to a range of public sector issues on a daily basis. It is neither a watered-down version of research though being a critical consumer of research is important. Neither is it teaching, though explanation (to non-economists) is a critical aspect of the job. Rather it is emerging into an important new global profession that intermediates the production and consumption of economic ideas and analysis."[32]

Balancing employability with the legitimate academic standards and wider educational purposes of degrees, and integrating such skills into the curriculum at universities, sets a challenge for course design and faculty. It is a challenge worth rising to as there are strong reasons to suppose that economics students would benefit more generally from a move towards a more practitioner-orientated curriculum.

SUMMARY

- Economists of all types use many of the same tools and techniques, but even when the same terms are used, there is a significant difference in the skills prized by academics and employers of economists.

- Economics degrees are useful preparation for many types of jobs, but it is widely agreed that a challenge for academia is to make them more applicable to practitioner economist jobs outside academia.

- The importance of advanced mathematics depends on the economist's job: strong mathematics is vital for academic economists, but not necessarily so for many intelligent consumers of and commentators on economics (see Chapter 6).

- Good data skills are needed by all economists, but the emphasis on what this requires in practice may differ between academics and employers.

---

[32] Paul Anand, Laurence Roope and Andy Ross (2019), 'How economists help central government think: Survey evidence from the UK Government Economic Service', *International Journal of Public Administration*, 42:13, 1145–1157, DOI: 10.1080/01900692.2019.1575668.

- In applying models, it is often crucial to know their limitations, to be alert to relevant developments outside the model and to be eclectic in choosing the most appropriate models for the job in hand (see also Chapter 10).
- Having 'ground knowledge' is useful for all policy economists.

QUESTIONS

1. What are the biggest skills gaps employers identify in economics graduates?
2. Why might serving only the immediate needs of specific employers not be good for careers in the long-run?
3. What are the arguments for and against universities focussing on employability and is there a trade-off anyway for economics degrees?
4. Which of the skills mentioned in this chapter do you think you will need most in your chosen career and how will you develop these skills?
5. A firm successfully sells more by employing a salesforce and charging a higher product price to cover their commission. How easily does that square with standard supply and demand analysis?

EXERCISE

A survey of Government Economic Service members in 2012[33] asked whether they had used the following techniques in the previous year. The percentages show how many had:

Synthesising evidence*	85%
Cost-Benefit Analysis (see Chapter 10)	70%
Analysis involving maths	53%
Econometric Analysis	52%
Game Theory	15%

* Integrating analysis and findings from different research studies across economics and/or across-disciplines.

[33] Anand and Leape (2012), What Economists Do—And how universities might help. Available at https://core.ac.uk/reader/9694770.

Rank how often you have been required to use these techniques in your Economics degree and then compare this with the table.

FIND OUT MORE

Economic Network's Employer Skills survey and recent research: https://economicsnetwork.ac.uk/projects/surveys/employers2019.

Diane Coyle ed. (2012) *What's the use of economics? Teaching the dismal science after the crisis* (London Publishing Partnership).

Paul Anand, Laurence Roope, and Andy Ross (2019) 'How economists help central government think: Survey evidence from the UK Government Economic Service' *International Journal of Public Administration*, 42:13, 1145–1157, DOI: 10.1080/01900692.2019.1575668.

PART TWO

· · · · · ●●●● · · · · ·

Skills for success

CHAPTER 5

Communicating complexity simply

· · ·●●●●●●● · · ·

INTRODUCTION

Good communication is vital for practitioner economists, and yet this is persistently reported as a major skills gap among economics graduates by their employers. The advice on communication typically given at universities is excellent if one wishes to become an academic, but most students will not pursue that path. To be an effective professional practitioner economist one must practise 'communicating complexity simply', being concise, clear, and cogent. It takes considerable practise to learn how to 'write-short'. This chapter outlines how academic writing differs from practitioner writing and provides tips and examples for how to achieve the verbal and written communication skills required to progress your career. The advice we share here is also highly relevant to future job applications, where clear and succinct communication is also an absolute must.

> "To convince people they generally have to understand what you are saying"
>
> (Professor Lord Nicholas Stern).[1]

WHY ECONOMISTS NEED GOOD COMMUNICATION SKILLS

The need for better communication skills among graduates repeatedly ranks high in employers of economists' wish list of skills[2] (see Chapter 4). It is also a

---

[1] Quoted with Lord Stern's permission from a speech he gave to the Government Economic Service circa 2006.

[2] The Economics Network (2019), *2019 Employers Survey*. Available at https://economicsnetwork. ac.uk/projects/surveys/employers2019 (Accessed May 2021).

common reason why people underachieve in their careers. Fortunately, experience shows that, for those whose use of English is merely poor rather than dreadful, taking a short course or using the materials and sources cited in this chapter can dramatically improve communication skills.[3]

Good communication skills, both written and verbal, are vital for practitioner economists. That is why the Government Economic Service (GES) includes 'Effective Communication' as one of its three core professional competencies for economists, of equal status to economics itself. Former Head of the GES, Lord Gus O'Donnell emphasizes in his interview for this book that being persuasive is essential for any economist seeking to influence policies:

> "I always said, when I did talks to new GES people coming in, it's not enough, to be really professional, to come up with really excellent economics. The measure for me is 'Are you influential? Do you actually change things?'. Can you not just come up with the right argument but come up with ways of persuading ministers of the right thing to do."[4]

Good communication skills are important for success in applying for most economist jobs. As we explain in Chapter 9, most interviewers will generally be sympathetic and won't mark you down for being a bit nervous at interviews and presentations, but a poorly written job application will not be excused. Obviously, better use of English is always an advantage, but this chapter also focusses on how academic writing differs from practitioner writing, as well as providing useful tips, examples and sources for further guidance and practice. Nothing beats having an experienced communicator look over your work and provide you with detailed feedback, but you can do a lot to improve even by yourself.

BETTER COMMUNICATION OF ECONOMICS IS IMPORTANT FOR DEMOCRACY

Effective communication is vital for the public understanding of economics and of economic statistics. A recent survey by the Office of National Statistics' (ONS) think tank, the Economic Statistics Centre of Excellence,

---

[3] In the next chapter we also briefly look at how statistics should be presented.

[4] In his interview for this book (see Video 19: In conversation with Lord Gus O'Donnell available at www.oup.com/he/pryce-ross1e).

found that a large proportion of the people they surveyed had little ability to judge how well the government's economic policies or the UK economy are performing:

> "In addition to a relatively limited knowledge of economic concepts, people demonstrated a weak understanding of the size of different economic indicators, and a lack of confidence in assessing and judging economic figures . . . They felt economics was difficult to engage with properly for the average person, and felt it was communicated in an inaccessible way, describing the economy as 'confusing', 'complicated' and 'difficult to understand'."[5]

According to Johnny Runge, senior researcher at the National Institute of Economic and Social Research (NIESR) and the lead author of the report:

> "Many feel economics is confusing and complicated, and regret they are unable to understand it . . . The solution isn't that people should be taught economics in schools, but that statisticians and economists should become better at communication and should listen more to the public's perception and their parallel understanding of the statistics."[6]

This is a sad reflection on our discipline's impact. Ha Joon-Chang, the radical Cambridge economist, berates our discipline as follows:

> "Economists have been fantastically successful in making people believe that [economics] is . . . more difficult than it really is . . . 95% of economics is common sense. It's just made to look difficult through the use of jargon and mathematics."[7]

Ha Joon-Chang is probably overstating his case here, as expertise is often required if only to evaluate which economist is reliable, and not all the concepts are easy, but he is certainly right that in a democracy the voting public should

---

[5] Runge, Johnny and Hudson-Sharp, Nathan (2020), *Public understanding of economics and economic statistics* (ESCoE OP-03), Economic Statistics Centre of Excellence (2nd November). Available at https://www.escoe.ac.uk/publications/public-understanding-of-economics-and-economic-statistics/ (Accessed May 2021).

[6] Giles, Chris (2020), 'Britons understand little about economics, report finds', *Financial Times* (24th November). Available at https://www.ft.com/content/93821297-96ea-4286-8f01-ccb-6fa09161f (Accessed April 2021).

[7] RSA (2016), *RSA ANIMATE: Economics is for Everyone!* [Video] YouTube: https://youtu.be/NdbbcO35arw (Accessed April 2021).

have an understanding of economic policy and how it relates to them. That requires economists being able to make economics accessible to the general public. As Miatta Fahnbulleh, the CEO of the New Economics Foundation, says:

> "We have a propensity to take the most simple idea and turn it into the most complicated and obscure idea. I think it's a double edged sword because people hear us and they think 'Gosh!' they must know what they're talking about . . . but on the other side, you know in a world where people are questioning experts, and . . . challenging the credibility of things that have long been held sacrosanct, our ability to communicate in simple terms that people can understand . . . becomes more important than ever. I think we have a job to do to take the thing that everyone lives and breathes on a daily basis and be able to break it down in a way that someone that isn't of the profession can understand."[8]

It is very welcome, in addition to more general initiatives to 'combine academic rigour with journalistic flair', such as *The Conversation*,[9] to see initiatives by economists aimed at addressing the deficit in public understanding of economics. Such as VoxEU[10] and the Economics Observatory,[11] aimed at bridging the gap between academic research, government policy and the general public. Also, the appointment at the Bristol School of Economics of the country's first Professor of the Public Understanding of Economics, Richard Davies. The new post will help address the gap between people's desire for better understanding of economics and their current low levels of trust in economists. As an author and former journalist, Bank of England economist and adviser to the Chancellor, Richard has extensive experience of communicating economics to public and policy audiences, and will support academics in disseminating their research to the widest possible audiences and help to ensure that communication skills are embedded in the undergraduate and postgraduate curricula. Bristol University is well placed for this post to have impact, with its reputation

---

[8] In her interview for this book (see Video 14: In conversation with Miatta Fahnbulleh available at www.oup.com/he/pryce-ross1e).

[9] The Conversation is an independent source of news and views, sourced from the academic and research community and delivered direct to the public. See https://theconversation.com/uk (Accessed September 2021).

[10] VoxEU provides research-based policy analysis and commentary from leading economists. See https://voxeu.org/ (Accessed September 2021).

[11] The Economics Observatory at https://www.economicsobservatory.com/ (Accessed September 2021).

for policy-relevant research it is also host to the Economics Network, and the city is home to an annual Festival of Economics.[12]

TOP TIPS TO IMPROVE YOUR COMMUNICATION SKILLS

Unfortunately, poor communication can be like bad breath, others notice it more than those who have it! Although the advice on communication given at universities is consistently excellent if one wishes to become an academic, unfortunately it does not always cover the range of non-economist audiences practitioners need to address.

Mid-career economist Toju Anagboso, who has worked for the Office of National Statistics, Shell, and CHC Helicopters, describes in her interview how even after graduating she felt like she had to begin again in her career to learn how to write for non-academic stakeholders:

> "I remember writing lots of different reports, analysing things, and having red pens . . . struck through what I was writing . . . I had to . . . learn like you're back in school, how to write, the art of writing, writing well enough to be featured in the BBC."[13]

To be a useful practitioner economist you must practise communicating 'complexity simply', while being 'concise, clear and cogent'. This is vital for very many jobs that economists do across private, public, and third sectors, but it takes a lot of practice. 'Writing short' is actually more time consuming than writing longer prose. As Pascal once apologized:

> "I have made this longer than usual because I have not had time to make it shorter."[14]

---

[12] In the annual Festival of Economics, economists and experts from around the world debate with each other—and their audiences—some of the key economic questions of our time https://www.bristolideas.co.uk/projects/festival-of-economics/ (Accessed August 2021).

[13] In her interview for this book (see Video 1: In conversation with Toju Anagboso available at www.oup.com/he/pryce-ross1e).

[14] Others may have said similar, but the original seems to be from Blaise Pascal's work 'Lettres Provinciales' in 1657: 'Je n'ai fait celle-ci plus longue que parce que je n'ai pas eu le loisir de la faire plus courte.' This translates to 'I have made this longer than usual because I have not had time to make it shorter.'

THE 'T&CS' OF EFFECTIVE COMMUNICATION

THE THREE T'S

The first and most important things to consider for any communication are summarized by the 'Three T's':

Task: What do you want to achieve with your message? This consideration should drive your choice of medium and content and help you to focus on the points that you are attempting to convey. If time is limited you will have to prioritize, so what are the <u>essential</u> points that must be put across? How can they be driven home? What 'agency' do you wish to provide? (see Chapter 3) What purpose is the message trying to achieve?

Time: This is particularly pertinent to presentations. Your message must fit the time or length allotted for it. If you run over a time limit you may lose important parts of your message and perhaps even your audience. To help you pace your delivery, think about putting a watch or smartphone timer in a visible place, so that you can see how you are doing for time. If you want some interaction with your audience you must allow space for questions and/or discussion. But be warned, just saying at the end 'Have you any questions?' often leads to just an uncomfortable silence. So, have a conversation starter in reserve, such as asking your audience to respond to a question you put, or even prime a friend for the first 'ice-breaker' question. Other questions will often flow once the first question has been asked. If the time allotted is simply inadequate for the task involved, then ask the organizer if another time slot would be better if it were possible to arrange? If not, then you will have to put a lot of effort into making your communication short but effective.

Target Audience: This is usually the most important consideration of all. In everyday life we naturally adapt our communication styles according to whom we are addressing and why we are communicating. We speak differently to strangers than we do to friends, to children differently than to adults, to our work colleagues differently than to our family. Do you want to persuade, inform, motivate or just take the audience through the facts? Understanding the audience is essential for all of these purposes. Unfortunately, experts too often fail to adapt to their audiences in their professional life. As a professional you should always remember that communicating to internal colleagues is often very different than to an external stakeholder, just as an economist communicating with fellow economists is very different to communicating to non-economists.

Perhaps this seems obvious, but the need to communicate to non-economists is still a major key skills gap in terms of what employers want from their economist employees (see Chapter 4), and still seems to be an obstacle for many academics in presenting their work to policy makers and the wider public. Obviously, understanding the needs of your readers and writing accordingly is vital for journalists, as is explained here by Guardian economics editor Larry Elliott:

> ". . . the most important part of being a journalist is to be able to explain to readers what . . . fairly complex issues mean. So, there's no point in trying to fool people or bamboozle them with jargon . . . every time we talk about something like quantitative easing, which is quite a complex issue, you have to actually explain it rather than just assume a level of knowledge which is not there . . . I try and write in a straightforward, easy to understand way that's not patronizing or condescending, and I think that's the balance I try and strike . . . We have . . . a lot of people who read [The Guardian] for our macroeconomic coverage and . . . they're not all specialists . . . some of them are specialists, some of them are economists, but a lot of them are just interested laypeople. They're just interested in the subject and . . . if you want to keep their attention, you have to actually write in a way that's going to be lively, informative and understandable."[15]

Larry Elliot is describing here how journalists, even on the most technical matters, must put their audience before their own expertise. And this is true for very many jobs, as the QAA Subject Benchmarks for Economics notes (see Chapter 1): non-economist audiences are varied, and so practice in communicating to varied audiences should be part of all undergraduate economics degrees. We build upon how to present effectively for your audience in the 'Engage with the audiences' motivations and perspectives' section below (page 123).

THE THREE C'S

The Three T's are about adjusting your communication to the context: Task (including the medium), Time and Target audience. The three C's are more about the content of your message. They are particularly relevant when communicating to busy people:

---

[15] In his interview for this book (see Video 13: In conversation with Larry Elliott available at www.oup.com/he/pryce-ross1e).

Concise: The more important a person is the less time they are likely to have to spend on your message. An executive summary may help, but generally, unless its high importance is known in advance, the longer an email or document is, the less likely it is to be read. This even applies in academia where the advice is 'An author's goal should be to make the paper as short and readable as possible,[16] and so even more so for those who lack a scholar's patience and time for research.

Clear: A common error is trying to impress with one's mastery of vocabulary, expertise, or literary acumen (see 'Wear your intellect lightly' below). This is more likely to irritate busy people than to impress. You may feel your communication to be a 'big moment' but they just want your message to be useful and easy to understand. Sadly, they are much less interested in you. An academic economist once complained that a Minister wanted him to write in 'Baby English', the right response to that is 'If you know what he wants why aren't you doing it?' As even Nobel prize-winning economist Paul Krugman notes 'Nobody cares about your professional credentials, it has to be an argument on the merits, a message that is as simple and vivid as you can make it.[17]

Cogent: Make your message clear, logical, and, when required, convincing. Of course, you want your message to be convincing but trying too hard can lead to the sort of mistakes that come from not 'wearing your intellect lightly'. Let clarity, prioritization of points and driving home the important ones, with a logical flow of narrative, do the convincing. A strong 'story' helps, and for the right audience, vividness lent by memorable graphics or metaphors may help.

You may wish to add 'Correct' to this list of C's, but hopefully this goes without saying, and three points often have more impact that a greater number of points. That said, as with the 'Invisible Hand Theorem' example that we present later in this chapter, there is often a useful compromise between rigour and communication.

In short, a practitioner economist should watch their 'T's and C's' as well as their 'Ps and Qs'.[18]

[16] Weisbach, Michael S., (2021), *The economist's craft (skills for scholars)* (Princeton University Press, Kindle Edition), pp. 60–61.

[17] Communicating Economics (2018), *Nobody cares about your title—Paul Krugman [Video]*, YouTube: https://youtu.be/6KfJNSKXuAA (Accessed April 2021).

[18] 'Mind your P's and Q's is a very old expression but is still used quite frequently today. It means 'mind your manners', 'mind your language', 'be on your best behaviour', 'watch what you're doing'.

KEY PRINCIPLES FOR SUCCESSFUL COMMUNICATION

Here we build upon the 'Three T's' and 'Three C's with some more detailed advice on how to communicate successfully.

ADOPT AN APPROACH APPROPRIATE TO THE SITUATION

- When thinking about the 'Three T's', ask yourself 'What am I trying to communicate and to what audience?' and then adapt accordingly. For example, what is the most useful medium for the message? A short phone call is usually the most direct way to get a quick answer, but an email might be more useful for capturing the details of a more complex situation. A presentation might be the easiest way to get your message across with impact, or failing that perhaps a pre-recorded video for your busy boss to view while travelling is the best opportunity available? Consider also the way that the communication needs to be conducted. Can you go straight to the point, or will the reader need contextualisation to understand the core message? Should you adopt a more informal tone with a colleague you know well, as opposed to a more formal tone, which you might use for a senior colleague or an external stakeholder?

- If you require the reader to do something after reading your communication, then end with a clear call to action explaining what you require of them, and by when.

USE STRUCTURE TO KEEP YOUR MESSAGE ON TRACK AND ACCESSIBLE

Using a clear structure not only helps you get your thoughts in order, but it also helps to satisfy the 'Task' in a 'Concise', 'Clear', and 'Convincing' way.

- Remember that different mediums will require different structures, and you should adapt to this accordingly. Generally speaking, with longer forms of communications—whether an email, report, or presentation—you can structure your message around beginning, middle, and end sections (although as we discuss in 'Communication to Ministers and Managers' below page 131 the content may be very concise indeed!). Most of the time it is best to be up-front about your purpose at the beginning (we build on this in the 'Briefing' section page 135). If you are forming a presentation or executive summary you might want to briefly signpost the key points to look out for in the structure (so that your reader or presentation attendee has a roadmap for what's ahead). If further context and explanation is needed, place this in the middle section (or main body of the email, report, or presentation) to support your core message. End with a summary of the key points and calls to action.

- Find a logical order in which to make your key points, so the reader/attendee can easily follow the flow of argument or information.

- Use lots of short, strong sentences. In presentations work on some short, strong statements.

- Short paragraphs and a lot of blank spaces help break-up 'monolithic' blocks of text.

- In long presentations, at suitable points in the structure, remind listeners about what you have covered and what you are going to cover next. Don't go too fast and do pause for breath occasionally to allow your listeners to take stock of the messages they are receiving.

- In written communication, headlines and subheadings can break up text and help signpost the flow of narrative.

- Lists and bullet points are useful for brevity and clarity, but in reports they lack narrative and can obstruct the flow if overused.

THE LANGUAGE YOU USE MATTERS

Choose the right language for your 'Task' and 'Target Audience'. Obviously language also plays a huge part in how well you are able to satisfy the 'Three C's'.

- Write in plain English for straight-forward communications. If you're struggling to find the words, try saying what you need to say out loud. Verbalizing your message can sometimes help to pinpoint a simpler way to put the point across.

- Avoid obscure acronyms and jargon, particularly when working with external stakeholders. TLAs that are familiar to you may not be to your readers/listeners.[19]

[19] Three Lettered Acronyms—Pryce et al., How to be a Successful Economist 1st edition—annoying if you must search for their meaning!

- Use short, commonly used words, rather than uncommon long ones such as 'sesquipedalian'.[20]
- Use verbs instead of abstract nouns—'prepare' not 'preparation'.
- Choose the more familiar words—'need' not 'require', 'relevant' not 'pertaining'.
- If using slides to support a presentation, limit the amount of information to the core points. Slides should not be treated as a script and are there to support not replace your presentation.
- A large part of your impact comes from your body language. Use eye contact, arm movements and approaching the audience on key points to make impact but learn to suppress nervous habits, such as constant swivelling when sitting in an office chair.

ENGAGE YOUR AUDIENCE

- Use the active, not passive voice, with use of pronouns to show who does what: 'I lowered the test-tube' not 'The test-tube was lowered', 'I shot the sheriff', not 'The sheriff was shot by me'.
- Use concrete examples when you can, avoid piling abstraction upon abstraction. For example, 'Keep your distance' is clearer than 'Observe social distancing'.
- As we've suggested, plain English is best for clarity and formal communications, but it can become dull and unengaging for some tasks—such as for a book on 'How to be a Successful Economist'! So, if the purpose and audience suits, it can be more engaging, compelling, and persuasive to add some variety. A few 'flourishes' can add vividness, but this should all be done sparingly until you write your best-selling novel. Jokes have no place in the most formal communication, and they can be dangerous if unsuited to the audience or badly delivered, but a lighter touch with some humour may make a lengthy exposition or presentation more digestible. The best advice must be 'If in doubt leave it out', as it's probably better for most career prospects to be thought of as a 'bit dull' rather than as 'inappropriate' or a 'loose cannon'.

---

[20] Sesquipedalian is characterized by the use of long words.

- 'A picture is worth a thousand words' is a truth that is utilized by many inspiring economist presenters, such as the Bank of England's former and long-time Chief Economist Andy Haldane, and by the broadcaster, journalist, author, and prolific blogger Tim Harford. Infographics can be used to show statistics more digestibly by integrating statistics with pictures, but avoid 'Junk Charts' full of irrelevant graphics, as the information is <u>always</u> the key message.

- Used appropriately, metaphors can be powerful communicators of concepts that are otherwise difficult to convey. We often use them in economics itself, such as Keynesian 'injections and leakages' and 'homo economicus' and used well they can be particularly helpful for non-economists. Such as the fish stew metaphor used to explain the problem with Collateral Debt Obligations in the film *The Big Short*.[21] Just be aware that pictures and metaphors can look like trying to 'show off' if they are overdone.

- The website *Communicating Economics* provides many great tips and resources for engaging presentations https://www.communicatingeconomics.com/.

We hope that these tips give you a starting point for honing your skills. Next, we probe a little deeper into some of the issues we have touched upon to reinforce the importance of tailoring your communication to your task and audience. We also include some soundbites from the practitioners whom we interviewed for the book, to get their take on the importance of communication.

TROUBLE-SHOOT FOR POTENTIAL MISUNDERSTANDING

'The language you use matters': when giving a presentation, briefing, or a report, you should always consider the language you use and what it will <u>actually</u> mean to the audience. An amusing example of a misunderstanding illustrates this: a statistician was called to give a ten-minute presentation to an important official. Neglecting the importance of putting himself in the listener's non-specialist shoes the statistician explained 'These are my best estimates subject to normal statistical error'. Of course, you will know that the statistician was faithfully reporting that the value of the best linear unbiased estimator they had arrived at was an estimate of the relevant population parameter using the 95 per cent confidence interval. Not surprisingly, that was not what the

---

[21] See for example Watercutter, Angela (2015). 'The Big Short somehow makes subprime mortgages entertaining', *Wired* (12th November). Available at https://www.wired.com/2015/12/big-short-understanding-economics/ (Accessed May 2021).

indignant 'VIP' listener heard. He heard 'I've done my best, but my numbers are probably wrong, they usually are'. The official became angry and stormed off, and the statistician was not invited back.

In fact, many technical terms have everyday meanings that are at odds with their everyday meaning. For example, applying the concept of 'opportunity cost', an economist might see that a firm is earning a negative 'pure profit' when compared to its next best alternative activity. That is, although it is making a financial profit in its current activity it could earn more profit elsewhere. Whereas an accountant might point to the positive number in the accounts for profit, or even to the money itself, the economist is correctly pointing out that opportunity cost is greater than revenue, so that even if there is a positive financial profit there is a negative profit when compared with the profit that could be had from the next best alternative use of the firm's resources. Likewise, 'rent' in economics is not what you pay the landlord, it is profit that is more than 'transfer earnings. 'Investment' in economics is an addition to the capital stock but not savings as it is in common usage. Another commonly misunderstood term, this time again from statistics, is 'significance', statistically significant is often erroneously taken to mean large when it actually refers to probability. For example, when the eminent labour economist Sir Stephen John Nickell reported in a Bank of England research paper that immigration had had a 'statistically significant' adverse effect on the wages of the lowest paid in the UK, this was widely misreported in our national press as if he'd found a big impact. So much so that Sir Stephen later felt obliged to clarify that in fact he had found the impact to be 'infinitesimally small', which of course, ironically, he knew was another example of a technical concept used loosely in everyday communication.[22]

PRESENTATION NERVES

All the tips in this chapter also apply to presentations, but they won't help you much if you are paralysed with fear! With presentations there is an additional skill to be learned—having the confidence to speak in front of an audience. Few of us crave being the centre of attention and so relish doing presentations from the outset. More usually, if you are nervous when speaking in front of a

[22] Chu, Ben, (2017) *Impact of immigration on native wages 'infinitesimally small' says author of study cited by leading Brexiteers,* The Independent (25th January). Available at https://www.independent.co.uk/news/business/news/impact-of-immigration-on-native-wages-infinitesimally-small-a7545196.html (Accessed April 2021).

group of people then be assured that you are just human. Indeed, it is some-thing of an unspoken secret that we all feel insecure from time to time, even those who seem the most self-confident. We are social animals and so fear of humiliation is a powerful human trait; it is nothing to be embarrassed about. It is how you cope with, even learn to use, nervousness that is the issue.

As you become more senior in your career you will almost certainly need to give more and more presentations, and to speak out more at meetings, and even eventually to Chair meetings. These can be challenging ordeals at first. Take comfort in knowing that those who begin as the most nervous present-ers often end up being among the best ones. Perhaps it's because they're more sensitive and so have empathy for their audiences, and they always have that useful surge of adrenaline for presentations: learning to channel natural 'stage fright' into useful energy for an engaging presentation comes with experience and practice at doing presentations—see the 'arousal-performance' curve on page 269.

One way of becoming accustomed to speaking-out in front of others is to look for opportunities to do 'mini-presentations', which are less daunting than doing 'one person shows'. These could be preparing a short piece as a con-tribution to a meeting, or co-presenting with several other colleagues. Over time, and it varies a lot across individuals, through such 'bit parts', you will become more accustomed to speaking in front of others and your stress level will become more manageable. We have seen many painfully shy twenty-year-olds become consummate presenters before they reach thirty. Another way to reduce your fear of humiliation is to practise your presentation in front of friends, or practise before a group at work, while recording it. You will prob-ably be surprised to see that your inward turmoil shows much less on your outside! And, as said, if you never completely conquer your nerves then that that is no bad thing, as with experience it should help you rise to the occasion with energy to impress and hold your audiences' attention.

Of course, nervousness has its downsides. It can make you speak too quickly, or physically pace about too much in a distracting way. Such 'body language' is a large part of how the audience will perceive you and so judge your presentation. Voice control and volume can also be affected by nerves, but with practice you can learn how to 'speak from the chest' and hence pro-ject your voice in a commanding way. Practising with trusted friends and/or videoing can help you learn to control such involuntary behaviour and prac-tise voice control. With time and practice you can learn how to use your body language and voice to have 'stage presence'. Indeed, advice from actors can be useful and has been incorporated into some Economic Network's professional development for lecturers.

Of course, it feels unpleasant to be worried, nerves can keep you awake the night before and mistakes can keep you awake for nights afterwards. But remember this is all very common, we've all been there, particularly as we develop and sometimes even when we have been professional economists for some time. It does not mean you are inadequate or lack potential.

For more tips and information for effective presentations we recommend the website *Communicating Economics* at https://www.communicating economics.com/.

ENGAGE WITH THE AUDIENCES' MOTIVATIONS AND PERSPECTIVES

Understanding the mindset of others and their motivations is important for connecting with your audience and securing their buy-in. Being persuasive in this way is a huge advantage in many careers, and for almost all senior roles. Persuasion is important for:

- making strong business cases
- sales pitches
- motivating colleagues to pursue desired directions
- journalism where persuasion is needed to convince readers of the publication's particular editorial stance
- CEOs and Ministers who want economics expressed in ways that they can then use to convince their own stakeholders
- teaching. Whatever a teacher hopes, many students will be more motivated by getting good grades than understanding. Knowing this, the teacher should construct assessment tasks that do require genuine understanding rather than mere reproduction (see also 'The Rethinking Economics Project' in Chapter 8).

Being convincing through understanding what an interview panel is looking for is also part of the ingredients for a successful job interview (see Chapter 9).

Lord Gus O'Donnell gives this advice to economists seeking to influence politicians:

"... the incentive structure facing a politician is very different to the incentive structure facing you as an economist presenting some policy advice .... a politician will necessarily say, well, actually you know that policy really benefits people in my constituency and I'm in a marginal constituency ... they could argue that actually that's perfectly rational in terms of being what's best for the country, because if they as politicians don't succeed, then this awful lot called the opposition might get voted in and do terrible things. So, you know, they can rationalize what they're doing in a certain way. So understanding their mindset, is one of those absolutely crucial things to actually having your voice heard because you know the way they're going to interpret the advice that you put to them."[23]

An example of the power of understanding your audience could be in making a case for more spending on 'second-chance' further education. An adviser, who is perfectly competent as a social scientist, *per se*, might want to emphasize the contribution to social justice and social mobility from 'second chance' education. But an analyst colleague, with more experience of the particular politician concerned, might know the target politician has very conservative views: 'If you mention social justice he just thinks of a waste of taxpayers' money on misguided social engineering. If you mention social mobility he thinks of more competition for his own kith and kin. So instead, talk about "UK PLC" and "productivity" and the "need to compete" with emerging countries that are now investing more in education and harnessing ever more human capital, then he sees a "risk to profit." '

Finding terms and phrases that give a favourable impression to a particular audience is a common device for persuasion. A free marketeer will say 'flexible labour markets' rather than 'the gig economy', and a 'free enterprise economy' rather than 'capitalism'. More generally, people need a 'story' that they can relate to, as Andy Haldane explains:

"I think there's much further for us to go as economists ... in harnessing the use of stories as well as stats when making points. When I think about ... the instances in my career where I've been able to cut through to a broader audience—— that could be politicians, that could be other policymakers, that could be internationally, that could be the general public—invariably that's come from having a story in narrative about the way the world works ... backed up by the stats, but it's a story that cuts through. Making this resonant and relevant for people's everyday lives."[24]

---

[23] In his interview for this book (see Video 19: In conversation with Lord Gus O'Donnell available at www.oup.com/he/pryce-ross1e).

[24] In his interview for this book (see Video 16: In conversation with Andy Haldane FAcSS FRS available at www.oup.com/he/pryce-ross1e).

Dame Kate Barker in her interview also emphasizes the need for a strong story that resonates with what matters directly to the target audience:

> "To take the Brexit example, for some reason the people who were opposed to Brexit did not really understand the nature of the narrative that the Brexit people had, which was essentially a political narrative. But it was the belief that if we could take our own decisions, things would be better, without bothering to say why. And against that narrative, something that says, 'oh yes, but if you do this GDP will be 3% lower in 10 years' time' is not at all interesting. It had to be about . . . if we do this, it is very likely that we will lose 50,000 jobs in your area . . . or you won't be able to sell your goods abroad, or do you realize you can't take your pets on holiday? . . . the Remainers failed at the right point to make the story human . . . . you have . . . to turn it into 'Why does it matter to you?"[25]

As an example of something that can be explained as a technical result or put in a way that relates to people in their everyday lives, we will look at the 'Invisible Hand Theorem'. A theorem which, for better or worse, is still central to much of microeconomic policy (see also the overview of Cost Benefit Analysis in Chapter 10).

AN EXAMPLE OF EXPLAINING TO NON-ECONOMISTS: PARETO EFFICIENCY AND THE 'INVISIBLE HAND THEOREM'

The First Fundamental Theorem of Welfare Economics (FFTWE) is often called the 'Invisible Hand Theorem', in honour of Adam Smith.[26] It states that ignoring or substituting for a whole host of actual real-world considerations, perfect competition will produce Pareto-efficiency.[27] Students sometimes reasonably ask, and not often enough, 'What is the point of studying something that can never exist?' The usual answer is that by looking at a rarefied 'Ideal Type' model the real-world deviations from this 'ideal' are then highlighted, and so this can provide agency for real policy interventions. Whatever the merits of this argument,[28] it is the case that these 'deviations' from the FFTWE at least provide a useful taxonomy for policy

---

[25] In her interview for this book (see Video 3: In conversation with Dame Kate Barker available at www.oup.com/he/pryce-ross1e).

[26] Whether or not it really represents his insights is contested.

[27] Where it is impossible to make anybody better off without making someone else worse off.

[28] Some might say that it's more like a religious person's view of a perfect human rather than being a sound basis for surgery!

makers, and Cost Benefit Analysis also often implicitly incorporates its assumptions (See Chapter 10). Indeed, in neoclassical economics, the term 'market failure' refers strictly <u>only</u> to a failure to achieve Pareto efficiency,[29] but even this provides a theoretical underpinning for a useful list of the causes of market -failures, albeit only relating to efficiency: imperfect competition; externalities, including public goods and other missing markets'; imperfect information and the rather grey area for neoclassical economics of 'Rationality Failure'. This taxonomy of market-failures is very frequently used by policy economists analysing a case for intervention. As the Treasury's Green Book (See Chapter 10) explains:

> "Perfect markets, as many elementary economics textbooks note are a rarity. While some markets are closer to the perfect model than others the main value of the concept of market perfection lies in providing an abstract thinking tool used by economists to trial economic propositions under a range of market imperfections."[30]

In Chapter 10 we highlight some of the limitations, and distortions, of using this very narrow but still very widely used definition of market failure as a starting point for analysis. In this chapter we focus on how to communicate its core 'message' to non-economists.

Pareto-efficiency can be represented in mathematical form as constrained maximization, using that commonly deployed tool in mathematical economics 'a Lagrangian multiplier'. In that approach it could look like this:

$$L_i((x_j^k)_{k,j},(\lambda_k)_k,(\mu_j)_j)= f^i(x^i)+\sum_{k=2}^{m}\lambda_k(z_k - f^k(x^k))+\sum_{j=1}^{n}\mu_j\left(b_j -\sum_{k=1}^{m} x_j^k\right)$$

In practice, once the first and second order conditions for maximization have been checked, very few economists then go on to work through a more generalized proof, which would then expose some further necessary conditions. Even for academics the level of rigour observed is often restricted by their own understanding and their target audience! Such a mathematical expression would satisfy many economists but is not useful for many practitioners, and it is certainly not helpful for the vast majority of non-economists.

---

[29] Students often write 'a failure to reach equilibrium' as if equilibrium is synonymous with Pareto-efficiency, but equilibriums include many non-Pareto outcomes.

[30] HM Treasury (2020), *The Green Book*. Available at https://www.gov.uk/government/publications/the-green-book-appraisal-and-evaluation-in-central-governent/the-green-book-2020 (Accessed May 2021).

FIGURE 5.1 Diagrammatic Representation of Pareto-efficient General Equilibrium

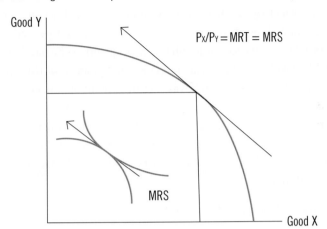

In economics textbooks the link between perfect competition and Pareto-efficiency is often represented graphically, as shown in Figure 5.1:

This diagram is more accessible for those used to using isoquants and feasible set (constraints) diagrams, as in indifference curve analysis. It should be familiar to almost all undergraduate economists, but it is still unhelpful as a means of communication to non-economists. So, we might try words instead:

> "If all markets are perfectly competitive and consumers rational, with no externalities, public goods, or relevant imperfect information and uncertainty, then the resulting equilibrium would be Pareto-efficient."

This could be useful for those policy economists seeking to understand or 'justify' interventions in the market. But non-economists are not going to understand terms such as 'perfect competition', 'externalities' or 'equilibrium'. We need to convey the basic insight without using any technical terms at all- unless we have a year or two to teach our audience a course in economics! Perhaps something like:

> "The basic idea of the invisible hand theorem is that well-informed individuals are the best judge of their own welfare, and so they will freely trade with each other until all the possibilities for mutual gain are achieved."

There is some loss of rigour here. Mutual gain is not quite the same as the Pareto-criterion. The absence of technical terms reveals how useful technical terms are for condensing a great deal of information into a short space.

For brevity we have now had to leave out the causes of market failure. But 'mutual gain' is easier to grasp than the more cumbersome 'at least one person better off without making anyone worse off' of the actual Pareto-criterion. Adam Smith's insight is conveyed, although not as eloquently as he put it himself.[31]

A problem with our statement could be that it paints too rosy a picture of markets. As Adam Smith himself was careful to point out, markets do not always work well in the real world. If we wish only to explain, to our relevant audience, what drives the (static) welfare gains in markets then our statement may suffice as a concise explanation. If we are concerned that it now looks like unalloyed praise for *laissez-faire*, then we might wish to add back in the notion of market failure:

> "In the real world some markets are inefficient in that they fail to maximise mutual gain."

Without being itself technical, this additional sentence primes the audience for a later, perhaps more technical, understanding. Again, depending on the task in hand and the audience to be informed, we might add back in some of the causes of market-failures. For example: the term 'monopoly' is well-understood,[32] 'imperfect information' might be replaced with simply 'lack of information', and 'externality' with 'spill-overs such as pollution'. We might stop there, but again depending on the time, task and the audience, we might not be able to avoid a possible misinterpretation of the term 'public goods', often confused with meaning anything provided for free. So perhaps 'missing markets' might be a more useful phrase. How far you go into these nuances will again depend on the three T's of communication.

Of course, a very different set of T's could involve a full-scale critique of the limitations of the entire neoclassical welfare economics 'paradigm'!

'WEAR YOUR INTELLECT LIGHTLY'

As the quote from Lord Stern at the beginning of this chapter concisely conveys, you are unlikely to influence others if they cannot understand you.

---

[31] For example, 'It is not from the benevolence of the butcher, the brewer, or the baker that we expect our dinner, but from their regard to their own self-interest. We address ourselves not to their humanity but to their self-love, and never talk to them of our own necessities, but of their advantages', quoted from Smith, Adam (1776), *An Inquiry into the Nature & Causes of the Wealth of Nations*, Vol 1, pp. 26–7.

[32] Even when understanding that the objection is efficiency rather than the distributional objections is not well understood.

Far too many experts fail to observe this simple truth. Instead, they feel they have to emphasize their own great expertise and erudition, but high-powered people are interested in how useful someone is rather than how scholarly or learned they are. That is why civil service analysts and policy advisers were told by Lord Gus O'Donnell, when he was the UK's top civil servant and a strong economist and econometrician himself, to 'wear your intellect lightly'. Lord Stern and Lord O'Donnell are both exemplars of deep thinkers who often use simple language in powerful ways. Tim Harford is of course another exemplar of how to vividly communicate 'complexity simply', and entertainingly, to non-economists.

Be warned, people of power and influence are much less prone to say 'I don't understand' than to say 'you've explained that badly'. And if they did not understand you then they have a point, as you have failed in your task. Most likely, they will just not ask you back again—and repeat business is a mark of success in any sphere! Conversely, if you can communicate complexity concisely in clear straight-forward language then you will be actively sought out by your seniors.

AGENCY

Again, always bear in mind that decision makers want you to be useful to them (see also Chapter 3). They are looking for 'agency' from your communication. They want you to help them prepare for and decide what to do next. That is why briefing papers, which we look at below, often begin with the heading 'Purpose'. In effect, it's answering 'Why have you bothered me with this, and how will reading it help me?' Even in academia, where knowledge for knowledge's sake is an entirely legitimate pursuit, it is important to attract the interests of influential colleagues:

> "... for the vast majority of scholars, the importance of their research will not be immediately evident to readers. An important part of the job in writing an academic paper is to explain why the research is important and why a reader should care about it."[33]

A humorous sign in the Norfolk Broads, England, nicely illustrated the difference between mere information and compelling agency. It simply said

---

[33] Weisbach, Michael S. (2021), *The economist's craft (Skills for Scholars)* (Princeton University Press, Kindle Edition), pp. 53–54.

'PLEASE DO NOT THROW STONES AT THIS NOTICE'. Of course, the sign was dented all over from thrown stones!

If you can establish a reputation for helping busy decision makers make their decisions, then your services will be sought by senior people, with obvious career benefits.

EXCELLENT RESOURCES FOR QUICKLY IMPROVING YOUR COMMUNICATION SKILLS

The Plain English Campaign has successfully reduced the use of gobbledegook in the UK. It cajoled, embarrassed and guided many lawyers, executives and officials to use more reader friendly English. The Plain English Campaign's website http://www.plainenglish.co.uk/ provides many resources for rapidly improving the clarity of your communication. Also, invaluable is the 'Economist Style Guide', which is based on the *Economist* magazine's own house-style manual. The Economist magazine is undeniably consistently well-written.

A problem with giving general advice on communication is that, as we noted above, it must be closely tailored to the context, the medium, and the audience. To cover all of this ground would deserve a whole book rather than just this chapter, and so economists are now very fortunate to have a website dedicated entirely to improving their communication. The *Communicating Economics* website has lots of resources covering a wide range of situations, all devoted to improving economist's communication skills.[34] 'Communicating Economics' was set-up by Bob Denham, the founder and executive producer of Econ Films.[35] along with Dame Rachel Griffith[36] and Romesh Vaitilingam. Romesh is a seasoned communicator, journalist and media consultant and the author of numerous articles and several books in economics, finance, business, and public policy.[37]

When asked about the website Romesh explained:

[34] Communicating Economics is available at https://www.communicatingeconomics.com/ [Accessed May 2021]

[35] See Econ Films available at: https://econfilms.tv/about-us/ (Accessed June 2021)

[36] Dame Rachel Griffith was also interviewed for this book (see Video 15: In conversation with Dame Rachel Griffiths available at www.oup.com/he/pryce-ross1e).

[37] Romesh explains why he set-up Communicating Economics in this video: Communication Economics (2017) Communicating Economics—Romesh Vaitilingam [Video]. YouTube: https://youtu.be/TepPCMsIC3E (Accessed July 2021). In recognition of these skills gaps for too many economists, the initiative has been sponsored by the Institute of Fiscal Studies, the Economic and Social Research Council, Manchester University and Econ Films.

"... the Communicating Economics website was really trying to bring together ... all the things that I had learned from working with researchers, from working with the media, from running courses with people like Evan Davis (who ... went to work with the BBC). And then disseminating some advice and saying this is what you can do to write better. These are the ways, these are the lessons for thinking about appearing on a broadcast media program. If you go on the Today programme or Newsnight ... these are the ways you should think about what you want to say. And ... then thinking more broadly, not just about the media but thinking ... how can economists think about communicating more effectively with ... all sorts of audiences they might want to reach. How can they communicate more effectively with policymakers in Whitehall and Westminster or local government, or an international organization such as the ... European Commission?"[38]

Romesh is also on the editorial board of VoxEU,[39] which has a wealth of serious articles on Economics that are far more reader friendly than the more formal academic journals:

"Set up in June 2007 to promote 'research-based policy analysis and commentary by leading economists'. Vox's audience consists of economists working in the public sector, private sector, academia and media—as well as students of economics in the broad sense. Vox columns cover all fields of economics broadly defined and is widely read (the site receives about a half million page views per month)."[40]

COMMUNICATION TO MANAGERS AND MINISTERS

The advice given here is relevant for communicating to busy executives or managers anywhere, but there are additional considerations for government officials. In a survey of GES economists[41] it was found that, over the preceding year, three-quarters of respondents had had to prepare briefing materials and

[38] In his interview for this book (see Video 27: In conversation with Romesh Vaitilingam available at www.oup.com/he/pryce-ross1e).

[39] VoxEU CEPR, Research-based policy analysis and commentary from leading economists. See https://voxeu.org/ (Accessed May 2021).

[40] VoxEU, *About Vox*. Available at: https://voxeu.org/pages/about-vox (Accessed July 2021).

[41] Anand, Paul, Roope, Laurence, and Ross, Andy (2019), 'How economists help central government think: survey evidence from the uk government economic service', *International Journal of Public Administration*, 42:13, 1145–1157, DOI: 10.1080/01900692.2019.1575668.

over two-thirds had prepared policy advice. This underlines how important good communication skills are in government. Writing for managers and Ministers, for CEOs, for journalism and blogs, requires very different styles to typical academic writing. For example, we have noted that briefing for managers and Ministers should be clear, concise, and cogent,[42] but the usual 'golden-rule' of 'Say what you are going to say, say it, and then summarize what you have said' could irritate a high-powered executive or official who has learned to quickly absorb and process information, but who has limited time. Often, a briefing is expected to provide enough information for its purpose on just one to two-sides of A4. It may have another four sides of background that are less likely to be read, and perhaps for the most diligent and interested an appendix, which is even less likely to be read. A long document from outside an organization is likely to be passed to a junior to be summarized. Unless a full report has been commissioned, a short document is more likely to be read than a long one.

Unfortunately, social scientists are notorious for being 'difficult to impossible' to understand. This is not the only reason why social science punches below its weight, but it is an important one that is far too often ignored by social scientists. This is true across all fields of social science, not just economics, and economists are not even the worst culprits. The eminent economist Edward Boulding (1910–1993) once quipped:

> "Physicists can only talk to other physicists and economists to economists . . . sociologists often cannot even understand each other."[43]

Some social science colleagues insist that the onus should be on politicians and other important decision makers to make the effort to understand the language of social science. This is as naïve as it is impotent. For confirmation, ask any Minister or senior civil servant, or read the report from the House of Commons Select Committee on poor communication:

> "Much academic language, especially in the social sciences, is notoriously impenetrable."[44]

---

[42] And, obviously 'correct', but for vividness three points often have more impact than four.

[43] Attributed to Kenneth Boulding in Hans Adriaansens (1980), *Talcott Parsons and the Conceptual Dilemma* (London: Routledge), p. 10.

[44] UK Parliament (2009), *Bad language: The use and abuse of official language*—Public Administration Committee. Available at https://publications.parliament.uk/pa/cm200910/cmselect/cmpubadm/17/1705.htm (Accessed April 2021).

In the following sections we will reinforce the importance of using our key principles for successful communication and then look at how these rules can be put to good effect in briefings.

HOW NOT TO DO IT

The following extract is from the beginning of Chapter 6 in 'The Impact of the Social Sciences—how academics and their research make a difference'.[45] It is an example of how the desire to impress the reader with erudition can make the meaning impenetrable to non-social scientists, and even to some social scientists! That is perhaps counterproductive for a book that had hoped to raise the impact of social scientists in policy:

Government and public policy making

"Since the later nineteenth century, the growth of the social sciences and the expansion of the state have been very closely linked. Both observers sympathetic to this trend, and those critical of it, acknowledge the intimate links between ambitions to reform or improve society using government intervention and 'seeing like a state' (Scott, 1998). This is a top-down gaze that constitutes the field of intervention in terms of synoptic (often statistical) data (and the constructed concept categories that alone make data feasible). Taken in the aggregate, the shifts involved here are never politically or socially neutral. Foucault famously, if controversially, observed: 'There is no power relation without the correlative constitution of a field of knowledge, nor any knowledge that does not presuppose and constitute at the same time power relations.'"[46]

Take a moment to think about the 'Key principles for successful communication'. What do you notice about this passage in contrast to our advice?

This style of writing is far too academic and convoluted for busy non-social scientists. It obscures its meaning by using layer upon layer of abstraction and unfamiliar terms such as 'correlative constitution', and it could well irritate and alienate decision makers who haven't heard of the 'famous quote' from Foucault! To be fair, here we probably have academics writing for other academics, demonstrating their erudition and expertise, but none of this is likely to impress

---

[45] Bastow, S., Dunleavy, P., and Tinkler, J. (2014), *The impact of the social sciences: How academics and their research make a difference* (SAGE Publications Ltd) https://www.doi.org/10.4135/9781473921511.

[46] The quote from Foucault is from Foucault, Michel (1977), *Discipline and Punishment.*

a Minister or manager who wants clear cogent communication. As practitioners we have too frequently seen academics try to impress with such high-brow erudition, often followed with a confidential minute being taken after they have left not to invite them back. Ministers frequently complain that even their own civil servants are difficult to understand, and civil servants in turn complain that they have difficulty understanding academics. So little chance then for an 'arcane esoteric verbose solipsistic sesquipedalian' to impress and influence tired Ministers working through their Red Boxes in the early hours!

A LONG HISTORY OF DISPLEASURE

In fact, there is a long history of politicians complaining about poor communication from their officials and advisors. The revered wartime Prime Minister, Winston Churchill, once chastised an adviser who dared to criticize his draft for a speech.[47] The hapless official had 'reminded' the great orator that a sentence should not end with a preposition. The gist of the story is that the irascible and witty Churchill retorted 'This is the kind of arrant pedantry up with which I will not put.' Such 'pedantic' rules of grammar are less observed than they once were, but traditionalists still get very annoyed if you ignore the more formal rules as laid-down by the bastions of good English, such as *Fowler's Dictionary of Modern English Usage*.[48] It is not wise to unnecessarily upset those for whom you work, and a lack of basic grammar may result in your core message being misunderstood. Sticking to conservative grammatical rules is usually the most appropriate thing to do in formal communication (see 'Does grammar matter?' Below page 144).

In a long line of similar past initiatives, by governments of all complexions, Prime Minister David Cameron circulated a letter calling on all officials to simplify the language they use. He even announced an annual award for 'clarity' for the civil servant who most excelled at telling ministers what they needed to know in the simplest and shortest form:

> "We're surrounded by complex issues on which we must make important decisions . . . we rely on you to cut through the complexity and cut out the jargon. Please be brief and use straightforward language."[49]

---

[47] There are several versions of this story, but the gist is always the same.

[48] Some traditionalists prefer the earlier editions!

[49] Cameron, David (2015), 'The Prime Minister introduces a Civil Service Award for clarity', Civil Service (16 July). Available at *https://civilservice.blog.gov.uk/2015/07/16/the-prime-ministers-award-for-clarity/* (Accessed April 2021).

A good place to start for advice on writing for Ministers, CEOs, and other senior people is 'Working with Ministers: A practical handbook on advising, briefing & drafting'.[50] Chapter 3 of the handbook onwards is particularly relevant. As noted above, the 'Economist Style Guide' is also useful, as is much of the material (a lot of it free) from the Plain English Campaign.[51] University guides to academic writing are usually the most useful for essays and academic journal articles but, unless they include advice about wider audiences, the advice on academic writing should be contrasted with these different styles.

BRIEFING

Briefs, and 'Executive Summaries', are a common means of communication in many organizations. They are short documents, typically only one or two pages long, specifically designed to be read by busy managers and executives. The Three T's are already set by the context of a brief and the Three C's apply very strongly. Often briefs are a condensation of many other much longer dialogues, debates, and documents. Indeed, 'synthesis' was the most common task in a survey of government economists.[52] The format of a brief will vary according to its purpose, but as pointed out in the 'Key principles for successful communication' section (page 117), its purpose should always be stated clearly at the beginning. Larry Elliott, the *Guardian's* Economic Editor, also explains that leading with the main point of the communication is also used in journalism, to grab attention before the reader loses interest. He contrasts this with how academics often write when they submit their proposed articles to him:

> "They've got absolutely no understanding of how a journalist works, or how a newspaper works, which is that you put all the really important stuff in the first two or three paragraphs because unless you actually grab someone's attention when they're reading the paper or reading it online, they'll just click onto another article."[53]

[50] Jary, Christopher, rev., Bryant-Smith, Laura (2015), *Working with ministers: A practical handbook on advising, briefing & drafting*, Civil Service Learning. Available at https://civilservant.org.uk/library/2015_Working_with_Ministers.pdf (Accessed May 2021).

[51] See Plain English Campaign available at: https://plainenglish.co.uk/ (Accessed May 2021).

[52] Anand, Paul and Leape, Jonathan (2012) *What economists do: and how universities might help*. In: Coyle, Diane, (ed.) 'What's the use of economics?: Teaching the dismal science after the crisis'. London Publishing Partnership, London, pp. 15–20.

[53] In his interview for this book (see Video 13: In conversation with Larry Elliott available at www.oup.com/he/pryce-ross1e).

This is advice that academics could also do well to observe even in academia. In a recent book on how to be a successful academic economist the author complains about academic papers with 'introductions that go on and on before they tell the reader what the point of the paper is and why the reader should bother to waste her time on it'.[54]

Briefings usually serve one of two main purposes: to inform or to make recommendations, and frequently they must do both even within the constraints of a few pages. The recommendation may simply be to take no action. This is the 'do-nothing' or 'business-as usual' (BAU) option, which should habitually be used as the benchmark for a comparison of outcomes, to inform whether action should be taken or not (see also CBA in Chapter 10).

HOW TO STRUCTURE A BRIEF OR EXECUTIVE SUMMARY

Below are suggested templates for writing briefs to make recommendations or merely to inform. Obviously, the precise headings and structure to use will depend upon the precise purpose and content of the brief, and both could also be adapted to suit an appropriate executive summary. Much like briefs, executive summaries usually condense and highlight the key points of a much longer report. For example, it might be recommending actions as a result of market research. An executive summary, however, is accompanied by a full-length report detailing the methodology and the full arguments, findings, and conclusions. Typically, briefs are more self-contained with limited additional reference material.

SUGGESTED TEMPLATES

We go on to show how these structures might look in a hypothetical example of briefing. Of course, they may be adapted appropriately according to the specific purpose and content.

INFORMATION BRIEFING TEMPLATE

> **TITLE**
>
> Encapsulate the subject of the brief in a few words.

---

[54] Weisbach, Michael S. (2021), *The economist's craft (skills for scholars)* (Princeton University Press. Kindle Edition.

PURPOSE

Briefly: state what the brief is for and hence how it will help the reader.

BACKGROUND

Don't include too much detail, just the background facts and how the present situation arose.

PROBLEM/SOLUTIONS

If a particular problem has prompted the brief, then briefly describe it and anything that is being done to address the problem.

IMPLICATIONS

Describe the impact of this on the department, policy, the public or other stakeholder, and flag-up any difficulty the Minister should be warned about.

NEXT STEPS

Describe the way forward, including any action to be taken.

RECOMMENDATION BRIEFING TEMPLATE

TITLE

Briefly capture the essence to prepare the reader.

PURPOSE

Briefly define the matter to be decided on, or the problem to be solved.

RECOMMENDATION/ACTION REQUIRED

Briefly set out what you want the minister to agree and by when.

BACKGROUND

Briefly describe how we reached the situation where a decision is required.

Argument or discussion, should include:

Objective: What we are trying to achieve with this recommendation?

Options: List the top options and compare and evaluate. Include the 'do nothing' or 'business as usual' option. List the pros and cons of each of these options, including the weakness of the option you are recommending and the strengths of those you have rejected.

IMPLICATIONS

Highlight significant concerns, such as the possibility of unintended consequences, or perhaps, the response from pressure groups and/or the public.

NEXT STEPS

Note that in both types of briefing templates the 'Purpose' heading comes straight after the title, and that in the recommendation brief the recommendation comes straight after the purpose. This is so the reader knows immediately what is being required of her/him. This can save precious time. If the recommendation is too radical or outlandish for the decision-makers s/he may decline to read on. Or, if the recommendation is from a trusted source and the purpose uncontroversial, the decision-maker may accept it with only a cursory reading of the rest of the brief.

A HYPOTHETICAL EXAMPLE OF AN INFORMATION BRIEFING NOTE FOR A MINISTER OF HEALTH

When major reports are published, especially from major and respected research organizations, Minsters are expected by our media to be immediately up to speed with its details, and to have at least a 'holding position'. Here we show how the Secretary of State for Health's staff might have prepared him for the publication of a King's Fund report led by the eminent practitioner economist Dame Kate Barker.

CLASSIFIED

PURPOSE OF BRIEF

You will be asked questions at tomorrow evening's press briefing on the King's Fund, 'Barker Commission', Report on Health and Social Care called '*A New Settlement for Health and Social Care*', published today, 04 September 2014, and its implied criticisms of the Government's Health and Social Care policy.

RECOMMENDATION

Welcome the Report as a valuable and timely contribution to the Government's thinking.

Make sure to emphasize that:

- The central recommendation of the Report for an integrated health and social care budget had already been acted upon while in Coalition: the £3.8 billion 'Better Care Fund' was set-up in June 2013 to ensure a 'transformation in integrated health and social care' and a local single pooled budget to incentivize the NHS and local government to work more closely together around people, placing their well-being as the focus of health and care services. But naturally such fundamental changes have to be piloted and evaluated and that this work is proceeding. For example, by the Government's backing of the innovative integration pilot in Manchester.

- That the Government is fully committed to a free at the point of delivery health service and that this commitment has been backed-up by a pledge of £8bn in extra funding for the NHS.

- The Report covers many of the options for the continued protection of the NHS that are currently being considered by the Government. This Report has helpfully clarified important issues surrounding these options and will be considered in depth by the Department.

BACKGROUND

The Report's Chair, Dame Kate Barker, is an eminent and influential economist, having been a member of the MPC and led major policy reports such as The Barker Review of Housing Supply. The King's Fund is a well-respected think-tank. The Report is available at http://www.kingsfund.org.uk/publications/new-settlement-health-and-social-care

A summary is attached to this brief (see appendix).

THE ISSUE

The Report is not a direct attack on Government policy, but it could be interpreted as reinforcing recent criticisms of: fragmentation of the NHS; increased inefficiency caused by a separation of health and social care provision; and that ring-fencing the NHS budget has made it harder to address a '£30bn funding gap', as widely publicized by NHS England under Sir David Nicholson. A particular risk for the Department is that planned reductions in funding for local authority social services will be seen as increasing the burden on the NHS and undermining confidence in our commitment to be protecting the NHS from any cuts.

The Report's recommendations are:

1: An end to the historic divide between health and social care.

2: A single, ring-fenced budget for health and social care, with a single commissioner.

3: Simpler access paths to health and social care based on personal budgets.

4: A greater parity by need in access to health and social care.

5: Health and welfare boards that evolve into a single commissioner.

6: No general switch to NHS charges, but a reduction in prescription charges with far fewer exemptions, and new recipients of NHS continuing healthcare should contribute to their accommodation costs on a means-tested basis.

7: Public spending on health and social care planned to reach between 11 per cent and 12 per cent of GDP by 2025. This will involve some significant tax increases, but economic growth will assist their affordability.

8: The older generation should contribute more through reducing non-means tested age benefits and by ending or reducing their exemption from employee National Insurance contributions.

9: Free access for a wider range of social care needs to be phased in, coupled with an additional one percentage point employee National Insurance contribution for those aged over 40 'as a contribution towards the more generous settlement from which they and their parents will benefit.'

10: An increase to 3 per cent in the additional rate of National Insurance for those above the upper earnings limit, again timed to match the recommended extensions of free social care.

11: A comprehensive review of wealth taxation including inheritance tax, wealth transfer tax, changes to capital gains and property taxation.

12: A regular review of the health and social care needs of the country and the spending and revenues required to meet them.

NEXT STEPS

As was arranged with your private office for the publication date, your 8.30am–9.00am session tomorrow has been held. It will have two parts:

a) The Perm Sec and the Department's Chief Analyst will take your questions on the Report.

b) The Perm Sec and your SPAD will conduct a 'Paxman[55] Style' interrogative session to rehearse likely questions and assist with appropriate responses.

ACTION REQUESTED

The Department will monitor media coverage and public responses to produce a more detailed response and analysis for your consideration by mid-September. Please raise any concerns and issues you wish to see addressed.

---

[55] Jeremy Paxman was once a notoriously combative presenter of the BBC news programme, 'Newsnight'.

BRIEFING UPDATES

Often briefings can be little more than simply a set of headline updates from other official sources, such as from the Office of National Statistics. As these real examples below of quick updates demonstrate. The art of producing these is in the brevity and prioritization of detail for busy people.

AN HM TREASURY BRIEFING

The HM Treasury note is clear and concise, it is designed to bring the reader up to speed in as short a time as possible:

RELEASED 7.00 AM 9 APRIL 2020 SECURITY: UNCLASSIFIED

MACROECONOMIC NEW STATISTICS BRIEF UK GDP—FEBRUARY 2020

	February OUT TURN	CONSENSUS FORECAST	January OUT TURN
GDP (3M/3M)	0.1	0.1	0.0
GDP (MoM)	−0.1	0.1	0.0

- This data release is for February 2020 and therefore before the full direct effects of the COVID-19 pandemic took hold.

- However, the ONS note that 'although gross domestic product (GDP) and its top level components were largely unaffected, some small negative impacts could be seen in certain industries, such as travel agents and tour operators within services and manufacture of transport equipment within production.'

- GDP grew by 0.1% in the three months to February, up from no growth in the three months to January and in line with the market consensus.

- On a month-on-month basis, GDP fell by 0.1%, down from 0.0% growth seen between December and January and 0.2ppts below the market consensus.

- In the three months to February, the services sector was the only positive contributor, increasing by 0.2%, whilst both production and construction dragged on growth by 0.6% and 0.2% respectively. Within production, manufacturing fell by 0.4% on the three months to February.

- In the month-on-month series, construction drove the contraction falling 1.7%. Services was flat on the month whilst production grew by 0.1%.
- The full release can be found here.

NEXT RELEASE: GDP first quarterly estimate, UK: January to March 2020–12 May 2020

A BRIEFING TO A COMPANY BOARD

This briefing to a UK company board, one of regular updates from a consultant, is more personalized, but is still concise and goes straight to the main points:

UK ECONOMIC OUTLOOK JUNE 2021

Since we last met, in early March, economic conditions have improved month after month as a result of the successful vaccination programme, easing of social restrictions and increasingly 'smart' ways of working—coupled, of course, with continued government support of the economy.

What is nowadays the most closely-watched business confidence measure, the monthly PMI survey, has gone from strength to strength and stood in May at its highest level since this survey commenced back in 1998. This development has reflected a broadly-based economic recovery on the part of manufacturing, construction and services.

Consumer confidence has also rebounded strongly, with improving employment prospects playing a key role in this. And retail sales have surged as the economy has re-opened.

GDP contracted by 1 ½% in Q1 2021 but the economy had begun to expand once more before the end of the Qtr. And GDP growth forecasts for the rest of the year have been moving upwards as the economic news-flow has steadily improved. Indeed, the NIESR now forecasting a 5.7% GDP gain for 2021 while the OECD's just-released bi-annual forecast is for +7.2%—the strongest among all the developed economies.

Looking ahead, GDP should be boosted by the investment incentives introduced in the March budget and by an enhanced government infra-structure programme.

Though inflationary pressures have increased—and house prices are booming—the Bank of England is unlikely to tighten monetary policy soon. Doves appear still to be in the ascendancy on the MPC.

EXCEPTIONS TO THE THREE C'S: CUSTOMER CARE AND DIPLOMACY IN COMMUNICATION

In contrast to most upwards communication within an organization, there are times when concision would appear to a reader to be brusque, dismissive, insensitive, or downright impolite. Here the 'soft-skills' of Chapter 7 may be more relevant than the Three C's. For example, if a colleague tells you that they have a serious illness it would seem callous to just say 'Noted', without adding something like 'I'm so sorry to hear that'. If customers or clients complain then it could turn their disappointment into anger just to dismiss them with simply 'I don't agree'. There are times when using more words than are necessary to convey the information is important for showing respect and/ or concern.

The following piece of Cabinet Office advice comes from 'Working with Ministers' by Christopher Jary,[56] but it can be adapted for dealing with a wide range of complaints and enquiries to any organization:

> "Defensive lines equip ministers to respond to specific criticisms. Sometimes they are presented in a question and answer format, sometimes simply as lines to take. They often appear in a series of three stages:
>
> - acknowledging the criticism
> - describing what Government is doing to tackle it
> - describing the success Government action is having or will have."

An example of this format being used was when the Academy of Social Sciences wrote to the Government of the day to insist on the reinstatement of the civil servant post 'Chief Social Scientist'. Read the official response and then summarize it as briefly as you can![57]

OFFICIAL RESPONSE (FEBRUARY 2014)

Our priority is that we have people who can champion effective use of social research and social science at the very highest levels in Government.

---

[56] Jary, Christopher, rev. Laura Bryant-Smith, (2015) *Working with Ministers: A practical handbook on advising, briefing & drafting*, Civil Service Learning. Available at: https://civilservant.org.uk/library/2015_Working_with_Ministers.pdf (Accessed May 2021).

[57] Hint: It says No.

David Halpern has been appointed as National Works Adviser, based in Cabinet Office, and is working with departments to advocate the use of robust evidence in decision making. This is a hugely important step towards ensuring that social science evidence has greater influence over policy decisions.

The Government Chief Scientific Adviser, Sir Mark Walport, will be working with David Halpern and is also committed to seeing a social scientist appointed to his network of departmental Chief Scientific Advisors.

DOES GRAMMAR MATTER?

Yes, it does matter for any formal written communication, including for job applications (see Chapter 9). The title '*How to Write Gooder English*' would not be a best-seller! Nowadays though, fewer people insist on those rules and niceties of formal grammar that can seem more like 'polite society etiquette' than prescriptions for clarity. Today we often see split infinitives boldly going wherever they please, 'But' often butts in at the start of sentences[58] and 'who and whom' often meet. Indeed, on social media it would be quite undemocratic to insist on correct grammar! However, official documents, including job applications, are formal communications and so the accepted standard of grammar and general use of English is much higher. In Chapter 9 we list a few of the more common errors that applicants make that jar with potential employers when reading job applications. And remember, whatever your own style and views on grammar, these may not be shared by the person who (whom) you are trying to please. For better or for worse, this could make the difference between being successful in a post or even getting the post in the first place.

Over your career, you will see that your managers and other stakeholders are likely to have personal preferences about grammar and use of English in general. Some can be quite insistent about it. For example, the eminent economist, both academic and practitioner, Sir John Vickers issued guidance on several points about use of English to staff when he headed the Office for Fair Trading (now the Competition and Markets Authority). When Michael Gove was made Justice Secretary[59] he issued his civil servants detailed instructions on grammar, two years after he had circulated similar 'golden rules' to officials

---

[58] Encouraged as an alternative to 'However' by the Economist Style Guide (Wroe, Ann (2018)), *The Economist Style Guide*, 12th edition (Economist Books).

[59] The use of the work 'Secretary' here is an example of government jargon. It is short for 'Secretary of State' and refers to the top minister in a government department.

in the Department for Education as Education Secretary.[60] And, shortly after becoming Leader of the House of Commons, Jacob Rees-Mogg issued strict guidance to his staff.[61] This practice is not just confined to Westminster and Whitehall. SG Warburg, the City merchant bank, famously upheld extremely punctilious standards of grammar and punctuation in its internal communications. And as any BBC Radio 4 listener will know, there are those who get quite livid at any infringement of what they regard as correct grammar.[62]

Sir John helpfully included an explanation of the distinction between 'that' and 'which'. Although the Economist Style Guide helpfully explains that 'Americans tend to be fussy about making a distinction between *which* and *that*. Good writers of British English are less fastidious.'[63] Michael Gove told his officials to write 'make sure' instead of 'ensure', and to avoid using the word 'impact' as a verb or the use of contractions such as 'doesn't', and the deployment of 'yet' and 'however' at the beginning of sentences. He also wrote 'the phrases "best-placed" and "high-quality" are joined with a dash, very few others are'. He also discouraged unnecessary capitalization and repetition. Jacob Rees-Mogg, a self-confessed traditionalist, banned certain phrases and words. These included: 'very'; 'due to'; 'unacceptable'; 'equal'; 'yourself'; 'lot'; 'got'; 'speculate'; 'meet with'; 'ascertain' and 'disappointment'. Here is an extract from the rules J R-M wanted to see followed:

JACOB REES-MOGG'S RULES

- Organisations are **SINGULAR**

- All non-titled males—Esq.

- There is no. after Miss or Ms

- M.P.s-no need to write M.P. after their name in body of text

- Male M.P.s (non-privy councillors—in the address they should have Esq., before M.P. (e.g. Tobias Ellwood, Esq., M.P.)

---

[60] Mason, Rowena (2015), 'Michael Gove issues civil servants with grammar guidelines for correspondence', *The Guardian* (21st June). Available at https://www.theguardian.com/politics/2015/jun/21/michael-gove-justice-secretary-civil-servants-grammar-guidelines (Accessed May 2021).

[61] Hughes, David (2019), *Double spaces and imperial measurements: Jacob Rees-Mogg's aides issue strict style guide to new staff, The Independent* (26 July). Available at https://www.independent.co.uk/news/uk/politics/jacob-rees-mogg-rules-staff-language-grammar-spelling-a9022981.html (Accessed May 2021).

[62] See for example Bailey, Tim (2006) 'Words words words', *BBC News* (10 July). Available at: https://www.bbc.co.uk/blogs/theeditors/2006/07/words_words_words.html (Accessed July 2021).

[63] *The Economist Style Guide* (2018) 12th ed., page 153.

- Double space after fullstops

- No comma after 'and'

- **CHECK** your work

- Use **imperial** measurements[64]

Clearly, some people are stricter than others on rules of grammar, and a few are quite idiosyncratic. Whatever your own views, you can avoid the boss's displeasure by noting her preferences. Some communication tasks in government, however, are so heavily prescribed that they leave little room for any discretion. An example of where strict rules apply is in the writing-up of the minutes of Cabinet meetings where, despite Churchill's protest, the guidance says:

> "Sentences should not end with prepositions. For example 'The Government needed to consider which areas it should intervene on' becomes 'The Government needed to consider on which areas it should intervene' or even better 'The Government should consider where and how to intervene."[65]

There are no hard and fast rules that apply to all communication all of the time, but knowing when and how to adapt your communication is often crucial for career success. In short, 'Task' and 'Target audience' are critical, as a post on Facebook is very different to an official document.

ECONOMISTS' AND SOCIAL MEDIA

Economist Mark Thoma notes that this century has seen a re-engagement of economists with public debate, driven by the rise of social media and blogs.[66] After a long period where there had been a trend for academic economists

---

[64] Hughes, David (2019), 'Double spaces and imperial measurements: Jacob Rees-Mogg's aides issue strict style guide to new staff', *The Independent*, (26 July). Available at https://www.independent.co.uk/news/uk/politics/jacob-rees-mogg-rules-staff-language-grammar-spelling-a9022981.html (Accessed May 2021).

[65] Cabinet Secretariat (2016) *Minute Style Guide* Available at https://www.civilservant.org.uk/library/2016-Minutes_of_Cabinet_Meetings-Style_Guide.pdf (Accessed July 2021).

[66] See for example: Thoma, Mark (2011) *New Forms of Communication and the Public Mission of Economics: Overcoming the Great Disconnect* Social Science Research Council (USA). Available at https://publicsphere.ssrc.org/thoma-new-forms-of-communication-and-the-public-mission-of-economics/ (Accessed September 2021).

to withdraw from public debate, which was seen as 'grubby' compared to an academic rather detached and 'merely scientific' attitude. From what we have said about democracy, this is clearly a welcome development, and, as Thoma notes, reduces a void that was left open for propogandists to fill (see page 77). Clearly, an academic style of communication is unsuitable for social media, and there is evidence that some economists struggle to engage effectively on social media, as highlighted by a study comparing Twitter use with other disciplines:

> "Economics is a discipline with a communication problem: its practitioners have struggled to gain traction in debates over the rise of populism globally and, in the UK, were the target of Brexit campaigners who claimed that the people in the country had 'had enough of experts'."[67]

This failure to connect includes even leading economists' use of social media platforms such as Twitter, which are increasingly key tools in the dissemination of political rhetoric:

> "Researchers at the University of Reading analysed the tweets of the 25 most-followed economists on Twitter—a list led by Paul Krugman, Joseph Stiglitz and Erik Brynjolfsson—and compared them with the accounts of the 25 most-followed scientists, including Neil deGrasse Tyson, Brian Cox and Richard Dawkins. The results, based on analysis of about 128,000 tweets dating between 2008 and last year, were striking. The economists were found to use a more technical register than scientists, which may make their tweets less accessible to a non-specialist reader: there were a number of uses of specialised names and abbreviations, and more than a third of the words used by economists were considered 'complex'. Scientists used fewer specialist names, fewer abbreviations and a 'noticeably smaller' number of complex words, say researchers Marina Della Giusta, Sylvia Jaworska and Danica Vukadinovic Greetham.
>
> Inclusive pronouns such as 'we' and 'our', which indicate a greater degree of involvement with the reader, were used up to twice as often by scientists compared with economists.
>
> Dr Della Giusta, associate professor of economics at Reading, said that academics in her field were seen to not 'have any kind of scientific consensus to offer'. While some blamed the media for this, she suspected that economists themselves were 'not the best "engagers" – we tend to talk at people rather than to people'.

---

[67] Ibid.

This was a sign, according to Dr Della Giusta, that 'readability is not highly regarded in the profession'. It also suggested that greater diversity could lead to more effective public engagement.

The Reading researchers' study was presented at the annual conference of the Royal Economics Society."[68]

A QUICK NOTE ON EVERYDAY VERBAL COMMUNICATION

As your career progresses you are likely to be increasingly called upon to give spontaneous verbal responses to your seniors. As you become more senior yourself you will often have to give presentations and respond to questions and unexpected situations. The standards expected will depend on the culture of the organization. While formal grammar is usually less important than for written communication, your body language and tone of voice, and even accent, can be very important (see also Chapter 8 on diversity):

> "When we judge someone's characteristics based on their accent, we are not judging them on their own merit but making assumptions about their social class, education and ethnicity because of how they speak. Needless to say, these assumptions are often false."[69]

It is prudent to learn to adapt to the expectations and personalities of those to whom you regularly speak. More 'alpha' personality types often prefer more direct and assertive communication styles that others would regard as rude; they can also be quite intolerant of lack of eye contact, hesitancy or lack of assertiveness. Some bosses are hierarchically minded and expect you to show deference, others are more friendly in style and will treat you more as an equal. As verbal communication is in real-time, it requires caution not to unintentionally give a poor impression or to offend. Obviously, in a modern professional workplace raising one's voice in temper, being abusive or bullying, are

[68] Reisz, Matthew (2018), 'Economists' communication problems extend to social media', *Times Higher Education* (24 April). Available at https://www.timeshighereducation.com/news/economists-communication-problems-extend-social-media (Accessed May 2021).

[69] M.Schmid, A. Cole and E. Jeffries (2020), 'Accentism is alive and well—and it doesn't only affect the north of England' (The Conversation and University of Essex).

unacceptable.[70] Such behaviour is unlikely to be forgotten and could lead to formal grievance procedure. Again, developing diplomacy helps. Listening to another's view before responding forcefully can save you much embarrassment, and if you are at a meeting a gentle 'one meeting please' is more friendly than 'shut up'! Much of the skill here boils down to the 'soft-skills' that we look at in Chapter 7.

CONCLUSION

The quality of your communication can make or break your career and will affect the amount of influence you have at work, and in life in general. Always consider the Three T's and the Three C's and use the tips and resources cited here. You will also need good judgment to improve and tailor your communication skills, as what is effective in one context may be inappropriate in another. Feedback from others and courses, even short ones, can be invaluable.

SUMMARY

- Good communications skills are vital, both for crafting a successful job application and in your career.
- Unfortunately, people are frequently unaware that their own communication is poor.
- Fortunately, basic use of English can often be improved quite rapidly.
- Following a few simple guidelines can dramatically improve poor communication, but to become an effective communicator may take a lot of practice.
- Communication is only effective when it is suited to the needs and motivations of the audience.
- Writing for non-academics is usually quite different to writing for academics.

[70] Although it is the case that the language and behaviour between very senior people in some organizations is more 'robust'!

- Communication to Ministers, executives and managers must be clear, concise, and cogent.
- Communication often needs to provide 'agency', that is, it should help the executive, manager or Minister know what to do next.
- Communication skills are highly prized and will advance both your career and influence.

QUESTIONS

1. During the Covid-19 crisis two pieces of advice were issued at roughly the same time, one exhorted 'Practice social distancing' the other 'Stay at home. Get groceries once a week' Which do you think is the more effective message and why?

2. How does the structure of your university coursework essays differ from that of a CEO/Minister's brief?

3. Describe how being daunted by someone's importance can lead to errors from not 'wearing one's own intellect lightly'.

EXERCISES

1. It is vital to compose communications to fit both their purpose and the intended audience. Read the following extracts and describe what the purpose and intended audiences are in each case. Explain why each of these examples of excellent writing is unsuitable for a manager's or Minister's brief:

   a. Opening paragraph of 'A Tale of Two Cities' (1859) by Charles Dickens:

   It was the best of times, it was the worst of times, it was the age of wisdom, it was the age of foolishness, it was the epoch of belief, it was the epoch of incredulity, it was the season of Light, it was the season of Darkness, it was the spring of hope, it was the winter of despair, we had everything before us, we had nothing before us, we were all going direct to Heaven, we were all going direct the other way.[71]

   ---

   [71] Dickens, Charles (1859), *A Tale of Two Cities* (London: Chapman and Hall).

b. Extract from Chancellor of the Exchequer Rishi Sunak's keynote speech at Conservative Party Conference October 2020.

"Being appointed Chancellor in February this year was an immense honour. Even though my first conference speech as Chancellor isn't quite how I expected it to be, it remains a privilege to talk to you today. And I am here today because of so many different people. My family, whose love sustains me. My colleagues in Government and in Parliament, whose backing has never wavered. My association in Richmond, North Yorkshire, who placed their trust in me, and gave me their loyalty, support and this opportunity to serve. And my party, whose members, councillors and activists worked tirelessly to deliver a Conservative government in December last year. Politics is a team sport, and there is always a multitude of hardworking people behind any effort."[72]

c. War time speech by Winston Churchill:

"We shall defend our island, whatever the cost may be, we shall fight on the beaches, we shall fight on the landing grounds, we shall fight in the fields and in the streets, we shall fight in the hills; we shall never surrender."[73]

d. The ending of Nelson Mandela's speech in 1964 at his trial in South Africa, before being imprisoned for 25 years by its racist regime, but who went on to negotiate reform with President Minister F.W. de Klerk and then be elected South Africa's first black president:

"During my lifetime I have dedicated my life to this struggle of the African people. I have fought against white domination, and I have fought against black domination. I have cherished the ideal of a democratic and free society in which all persons will live together in harmony and with equal opportunities. It is an ideal for which I hope to live for and to see realised. But, My Lord, if it needs be, it is an ideal for which I am prepared to die."[74]

[72] Sunak, Rishi (2020) 'Keynote Speech' (5 October), Conservative Party Conference 2020. You can read the speech at https://www.conservatives.com/news/rishi-sunak-read-the-chancellors-keynote-speech-in-full (Accessed July 2021).

[73] Churchill, Winston (1940) 'We shall fight on the beaches' (4 June), House of Commons.

[74] Nelson Mandela (1964). 'The History Place – Great Speeches Collection: Nelson Mandela Speech – I am Prepared to Die'. historyplace.com. 2012. http://www.historyplace.com/speeches/mandela.htm.

e. For outstanding eloquence on the limitations of GDP (or GNP as was the usual measure of national income then) it is still difficult to beat President Kennedy's brother Robert Kennedy and his 1968 critique of Gross National Product:

"Too much and for too long, we seemed to have surrendered personal excellence and community values in the mere accumulation of material things. Our Gross National Product, now, is over $800 billion dollars a year, but that Gross National Product—if we judge the United States of America by that—that Gross National Product counts air pollution and cigarette advertising, and ambulances to clear our highways of carnage. It counts special locks for our doors and the jails for the people who break them. It counts the destruction of the redwood and the loss of our natural wonder in chaotic sprawl. It counts napalm and counts nuclear warheads and armoured cars for the police to fight the riots in our cities. It counts Whitman's rifle and Speck's knife, and the television programs which glorify violence in order to sell toys to our children. Yet the gross national product does not allow for the health of our children, the quality of their education or the joy of their play. It does not include the beauty of our poetry or the strength of our marriages, the intelligence of our public debate or the integrity of our public officials. It measures neither our wit nor our courage, neither our wisdom nor our learning, neither our compassion nor our devotion to our country, it measures everything in short, except that which makes life worthwhile."[75]

2. In a sentence, explain what <u>two</u> main functions prices play in the price mechanism, without using any technical terms such as 'equilibrium' or 'demand and supply'.

3. Summarize for a non-economist friend the gist of a policy-focussed economics article by an academic economist. VoxEU (https://voxeu.org/) would be abundant source for material of this sort but if you want a real challenge try the Royal Economic Society's Economic Journal.

FIND OUT MORE

Jary, C. (2015) 'Working with Ministers: A practical handbook on advising, briefing & drafting', Civil Service Learning. **https://civilservant.org.uk/library/2015_Working_with_Ministers.pdf** (Last accessed May 2022).

The Economist (2018), *Style Guide* 12th edition (Profile Books Ltd.)

The Communicating Economics website: **https://www.communicatingeconomics.com/**

The Plain English Campaign website: **https://plainenglish.co.uk/**

---

[75] Kennedy, Robert F., (1968) 'Remarks at the University of Kansas' (18 March), University of Kansas.

CHAPTER 6

The importance of quantitative skills

· · ●●●●●●● · · ·

INTRODUCTION

> "My belief is that nothing that can be expressed by mathematics cannot be expressed by careful use of literary words."[1]
>
> Paul Samuelson

As an economist, there is no escaping the need to interpret and present data effectively, but practitioners across many industries, for example most of those working in the media, operational delivery, and policy, do not use nearly as much mathematics in their work as you will find in academic economic journals. This chapter will assess the contribution of maths to economics, which is very considerable, and outline the quantitative and data skills most used by practitioners, including sections on presentation, common errors, and how to spot the statistical devices commonly used to mislead.

MATHEMATICS

HOW DOES MATHEMATICS BENEFIT ECONOMISTS?

Some would-be economists, and even including the long-time economics editor of the *Guardian* Larry Elliott,[2] were so daunted by the maths that it put them off studying economics at university altogether.

---

[1] In his interview with Paul Solman. See 'Samuelson on Whether Economics Is a Science' (2009), *PBS News Hour*. Available at https://www.pbs.org/newshour/economy/samuelson-on-whether-economics.

[2] In his interview for this book (see Video 13: In conversation with Larry Elliott available at www.oup.com/he/pryce-ross1e), Larry describes how he came to study history instead of economics because he anticipated that the mathematical content would be challenging.

Mathematics is a very powerful tool, but some students are put off by courses that seem to be overly dominated by learning the techniques used by economists rather than showing how economics can be used to explore the real world of people and issues. This observation inspired the CORE project[3] to seek to transform economics education by leading with the issues rather than with techniques, introducing the formal techniques of economists only as they become useful for the analysis. An approach that recognizes that mathematical techniques are useful tools for economists rather than being the actual economics itself. Even though only about one-quarter of the more than eighty economics degree programmes offered across England, Scotland and Wales require A-level maths for entry, some economists insist that advanced mathematics is essential for all economists. Others, such as the journalist and well-respected *Financial Times* (FT) economist Martin Wolf, freely admit they don't know or use any advanced mathematical techniques at all!

It is sometimes, very unfairly, joked that 'economics is everywhere except in economics where it is all maths!' It is fair to say though, that if you do become an economist without having mastered the most common techniques used by economists, then you are likely to feel at a disadvantage at times. So much of economics is now expressed in mathematics that a lack of mathematical training will be a serious barrier to accessing the academic literature. In his interview, Sandeep Kapur notes[4] that mathematics is, for better or for worse, the language of academic economics, and so is essential for communicating with fellow academic economists. Even some extremely accomplished economists, such as eminent practitioner Dame Kate Barker[5] and former MP Kitty Ussher,[6] say they wish they had done more maths at university. Even so, there are still plenty of opportunities to become a successful economist without much mathematics. This chapter puts mathematics in Economics into perspective, while again noting that good data skills are simply a must for all economists.

---

[3] See https://www.core-econ.org/ (Accessed September 2021).

[4] See Video 17: In conversation with Professor Sandeep Kapur available at www.oup.com/he/pryce-ross1e.

[5] In her interview for this book (see Video 3: In conversation with Dame Kate Barker available at www.oup.com/he/pryce-ross1e).

[6] In her interview for this book (see Video 26: In conversation with Kitty Ussher available at www.oup.com/he/pryce-ross1e).

MATHEMATICS CAN REVEAL THINGS THAT ARE OTHERWISE HARD TO SEE

Mathematics can demonstrate things that are not easy to see without using maths, and sometimes reveals things that are counterintuitive. For example, take just a dozen books from your economics collection and place them on a shelf. Now start rearranging them until you have exhausted all the possible permutations in which the books can be arranged. Return to this book when you have finished.

Or, alternatively, do a little maths. There are twelve options for the first book, and then for each of those twelve options there are eleven more options for the second book. Ten for the next and so on. Spotting patterns is an important skill for mathematics, and so we have that the number of possible permutations is:

$$12\times11\times10\times9\times8\times7\times6\times5\times4\times3\times2\times1 = 479\,001\,600$$

If you were already aware that this calculation is a 'factorial', aptly written '12!', and that such processes quickly produce very large numbers, then you will certainly have declined the earlier instruction. Congratulations! Even without knowing about factorials, if you have developed an 'awareness of number' it would have caused you to pause. In fact, if you were to rearrange the order of the books each second of a twelve-hour day, with no breaks at all, seven days a week, it would still take over 30 years to complete this seemingly simple task. See how much time and energy mathematics can save you!

The human brain is very good at coming-up with things that might affect other things: for example, consumption might be affected by income, wealth, expectations of future income and taxes. Consumption will affect GDP and so there could be feedback effects on consumption, and so they are simultaneously determined and therefore simple estimations by regression will be misleading. But it is hard without mathematics to put all this together to produce an explicit model. Mathematics is powerful in combining many variables and parameters to see what the relationships between them all might be, to assess the likely impacts if the relationships between them or the value of parameters and coefficients change. Indeed, modifying formulae, tweaking parameters, and then re-crunching the mathematics of a model to compare with previous results is perhaps the quickest way for an academic to produce journal articles without even leaving their office!

Modelling is important in economics, but as we point out in Chapters 3 and 4 the real world is too complex to be rigorously captured in its entirety, and so models must be deployed with caution. Some models are constructed merely to show where different assumptions can lead to, they are not necessarily meant to be literal or descriptive. Many are claimed to have direct relevance to the real world, and here modelling plays an important part in sorting out the assumptions that are justified. As Lord Gus O'Donnell points out, models force the modeller to lay bare the relationships and assumptions of the model, and this often means they can be tested against real data:

> "So for me modelling was really important as a way of testing whether all that theory made sense or not."[7]

If we take even elementary economics, say an indifference curve, which you're likely to be introduced to in the first year of an economics degree, then mathematics helps in understanding its properties. For example, intuitively, diminishing marginal utility seems to explain a diminishing marginal rate of substitution, but it turns out from inspecting the cross-partial derivatives of a utility function that diminishing marginal utility is neither necessary nor sufficient for a diminishing marginal rate of substitution (convexity to the origin). And as any positive monotonic transformation leaves the indifference map ordinally unchanged,[8] we see that the 'law of diminishing utility' doesn't even have a literal meaning here.

WHAT KIND OF MATHEMATICS SHOULD BE USED FOR ECONOMICS?

We must accept that mathematics can be extremely useful and provide insights that would be missed otherwise, and indeed, the main difference between studying economics at undergraduate and postgraduate levels is in the extent of mathematical sophistication required of the student.[9] But is being good at the mathematics commonly used by academic economists necessary to be a successful professional economist? Most academics would answer 'Yes', some with wider experience would say it's desirable but not essential, a few will even argue 'No' but because they believe that economists need to use

---

[7] Lord Gus O'Donnell in his interview for this book (see Video 19: In conversation with Lord Gus O'Donnell available at www.oup.com/he/pryce-ross1e).
[8] A positive monotonic transformation maintains the ordering of the indifference curves but changes the magnitude of the 'gaps' between them.
[9] Although there are now a number of Masters in Policy Economics that require less maths.

more advanced mathematics than they typically do. For example, the economist David Colander sets a high bar that many well-respected economists might fail to clear:

> "... the problem is not that economics is too mathematical; it is that the mathematics we use in economics is way too simple to capture the complexities of economic relationships. To understand the economy, an economist must understand how complex nonlinear heterogenous agents operate so that he (sic) is not overly impressed by simple linear models."[10]

IS MATHEMATICS NOW THE 'LANGUAGE' OF ECONOMISTS?

It is true that to become a modern academic economist working with models, for better or for worse, it is pretty much essential to be good at calculus, set theory and linear algebra. Much of the academic literature is now impenetrable without a good knowledge of maths, and economic journals are a vast resource for economists. But the old adage that 'Mathematics is a good servant but a poor master' still holds, and as we have explored in Chapter 4 in truth there are many ways to serve as an economist and (as noted in Chapter 2), not all of them require advanced mathematics.

We saw in Chapter One that there are respected economic journalists who do not take a mathematical approach to their work, and it is also true that many practitioner economists do not make direct use of mathematics in their work. For example, Gavyn Davies has served as a leading macroeconomist and adviser for decades, but he has not needed advanced mathematics to do so. Indeed, he is saddened by what he sees as the overuse of mathematics having become a barrier to many good practical economists:

> "I think academics often use their ability to write things in mathematical ways with techniques that are quite impenetrable in order to maintain their hold over the discipline."[11]

---

[10] David Colander 'What Makes a Good Economist?' In Chapter Two of Diane Coyle, ed., (2012), *What's the use of economics? Teaching the dismal science after the crisis* (London Publishing Partnership).

[11] In his interview for this book (see Video 11: In conversation with Gavyn Davies OBE available at www.oup.com/he/pryce-ross1e).

It is not surprising then that he thinks economics degrees, including his own, place too much emphasis on mathematics rather than on addressing real world issues:

> "I think that there was then and definitely now too much attention on the sort of hard-core mathematical parts of the subject. I include econometrics as well. They are useful but I think are overplayed, and with too little emphasis on understanding the world as it exists."[12]

Academics are often surprised to discover that many economist practitioners do not require much mathematics in their work, and indeed policy makers readily defer to academics on mathematical derivations, focussing instead on the interpretations and usefulness of the results. As such, some practitioner economists complain that their Masters degrees consisted mainly of deriving rather than using technical results, and so have been of little direct application to their careers. Of course, it does depend on whether a technical stream designed for an academic route, or a policy orientated stream for a practitioner route, is pursued.

Dame Rachel Griffiths, a former President of the Royal Economic Society who has worked closely with policy makers, neatly expresses a useful generalization:

> Producers of economics mostly need advanced mathematics but intelligent users of economics mostly don't.[13]

During her interview for this book, Alvin Birdi asked Dame Rachel to expand on her statement:

> "... there's people who do academic research or maybe who work in consultancy firms who need to really understand the nitty gritty of economics. They need to be able to write the formal models and be able to write the programs that use the big data that we have now. So, they need to have advanced maths skills to ... produce new economic research ... But the vast majority of economists, for example, economists working in the civil service, don't really produce a lot of new economics ... mostly they're trying to read large amounts of research that others have done,

---

[12] Ibid.
[13] Quoted with Dame Rachel's permission.

and process and figure out what that means for policy options. In order to do that, you need to not be scared of the maths . . . you need to have some sensibility to understand whether one piece of work is better done than another piece of work and that may rest on some technical detail, but that doesn't mean that you need to know all of that yourself. You just need to be comfortable with seeing it, but not necessarily with understanding the details."[14]

This certainly does not mean that learning techniques is not important or is irrelevant to real issues. As the eminent economist and passionate humanitarian, Professor Lord (Nick) Stern observes:

"You can't just approach these kinds of problems with concern and interest. You've got to have skills as well, otherwise what do you bring to the table?"[15]

In conclusion, it is clear that a degree in Economics needs to be a whole lot more quantitative than a degree in Humanities if it is to equip you to be an economist, and that models can be used in powerful ways. That said, beware of the warning in the old adage that 'Mathematics is a good servant but a poor Master'. As Andy Haldane expresses here:

"Mainstream models have sacrificed too much realism at the altar of mathematical purity . . . economics has become too much of a methodological monoculture [which has] narrowed the economics curriculum in universities . . . Accompanying this has been neglect of disciplines that abut and illuminate economics: economic history, moral philosophy, radical uncertainty, non-rational expectations. In short, neglect of the very things that make economics interesting and economies important."[16]

Fortunately, as we shall see in Chapter 10, Andy Haldane is but one example of many economists who have worked to broadened out Economics this century, and, perhaps more than ever, many economists do demonstrate that it

[14] In her interview for this book (see Video 15: In conversation with Dame Rachel Griffiths available at www.oup.com/he/pryce-ross1e).
[15] In his interview for this book (see Video 24: In conversation with Professor Lord Nicholas Stern available at www.oup.com/he/pryce-ross1e).
[16] See Andy Haldane's foreword to Joe Earle, Cahal Moran, and Zach Wsrd-Perkin ed. (2017), *The Econocracy: The Perils of Leaving Economics to Experts* (Manchester University Press), p. xiv.

is possible to be good at highly mathematical economics without becoming 'trapped' by it.

ESSENTIAL DATA SKILLS

Yet again we stress that if you want to be an economist, there is just no escaping the need to interpret, process, and present data. As we pointed out in Chapter 4 data handling is a skill that employers are looking for in economics graduates and should be considered essential to becoming a successful economist.[17] This section and the following sub-headings outline the data skills most used by practitioners, which as well as some more sophisticated techniques, includes the presentation of data, spotting common errors and not falling for the statistical devices too often used to give biased impressions or even to deceive. A knowledge of how to use and present descriptive statistics can too easily be overlooked in the enthusiasm to learn seemingly more 'impressive' techniques, but when economists share their results with non-economists they will invariably need descriptive statistics and standard software packages. To do this well you do need to be well-acquainted with:

- Means, modes and medians
- Histograms, bar-charts, pie charts, scatter diagrams, graphs, fan charts and other such 'data visualisations'
- Deciles, quartiles and ranges
- Percentages, percentage points and growth measures such as logarithmic scales
- Indices and chaining.

You will also need good judgement to know when and when not to:

- Round numbers (and how many decimal places to use)
- Use a pie-chart (never in 3-D)
- Use illustrative graphics, such as a picture of a 'Couple with one child' for tax and benefit changes (and always to avoid over doing the graphics and ending up with cluttered, 'junk-charts', which are hard to read with any precision).

---

[17] The CORE Project (see Chapter 8), which provides free resources for learning introductory Economics, has a very useful guide *Doing Economics* that aims to introduce students to the art, practice, and excitement of using data to understand economics and policy analysis. Available at https://www.core-econ.org/doing-economics/index.html (Accessed September 2021).

Books such as *Presenting Data: How to Communicate Your Message Effectively* by the celebrated[18] statistician Ed Swires–Hennessy[19] can help. This is a very readable book showing the importance of getting the essentials of presenting descriptive statistics right and how to do it. The technology for presenting data, often called 'data visualisation', has advanced rapidly this century. This is no replacement for the basics of presentation, but technology does make available a much wider range of options for visualisation. As data visualisation software has become more sophisticated and easier to use there has been an increase in the quality of design and animations available to presenters. This sets a higher bar for some presentations, but simple slides are still fine for most work presentations, and a presentation 'fit for purpose' may not need spending hours and hours over finessing your visualisations. The Office of National Statistics also provides free resources on data presentation https://style.ons.gov.uk/category/data-visualisation/ as does the United Nations[20] and other useful free resources are listed in the 'Find Out More' section at the end of this chapter. The Royal Statistical Service is a reliable provider of training courses on data presentation and visualisation (https://rss.org.uk/training-events/training/) and low-cost 'keeping-up' courses tailored for economists are often available from the Society of Professional Economists.

Although not all economist jobs require advanced data processing skills, they are a necessity for a wide range of economist jobs. For example, as we saw in Chapter 3, although some respected economic commentators in the media do not themselves possess advanced data processing skills, they will often rely on other economists in their organization to research and process data on their behalf: division of labour and specialization applies to economists as well as to Adam Smith's pin makers! Their organizations will often have specialist units providing more specialized skills and reports. For example, the extract below is from a job advert for a 'Data Analyst-Economics' to join 'The Economist magazine's 'Economic Intelligence Unit'.

---

[18] At the time of writing, Ed Swires–Hennessy is still the only government statistician to receive a medal from the Royal Statistical Society since Sir Harry Campion (ex-head of Central Statistical Office) some 70 years ago.

[19] E. Swires-Hennessy (2014) *Presenting Data: How to Communicate Your Message Effectively* (John Wiley and Sons Ltd).

[20] For example, UNECE *Making Data Meaningful* at https://unece.org/statistics/making-data-meaningful (Accessed September 2021).

The Economist INTELLIGENCE UNIT

As a research and analysis division of the Economist Group, The Economist Intelligence Unit (EIU) helps leaders prepare for opportunity, empowering them to act with confidence when making strategic decisions. The EIU is the global standard in providing quality, actionable intelligence to the public and private sector, assessing issues that impact the marketplace for over two hundred countries.

We are looking for a data analyst to work within an internationally-focused and diverse team helping to support our macroeconomic & industry databases and models, and to deliver bespoke research projects with a strong quantitative element.

EXPERIENCE, SKILLS, AND PROFESSIONAL ATTRIBUTES

The ideal skills for this role are:

- Graduate/Post-Graduate degree in Economics/Business Economics/Statistics/ Mathematics

- Strong understanding of statistical analysis and econometrics modelling

- A strong understanding of macroeconomic, demographic and international trade concepts, and knowledge of key data series

- Advanced Excel skills—experience with formula auditing, manipulating and cleaning large data sets in excel, knowledge of advanced functions like VLookup/HLookup, Match, Offset, Index, Indirect, Nested If-Then-Else and similar

- Proficiency in any programming language/softwares like R, Python, Eviews, STATA, MATLAB is desirable

- Proficiency in Visual Basic preferable

© The Economist Intelligence Unit, London (2022)

ECONOMETRICS

As with mathematics, econometrics is a good servant but a poor master. And it should be remembered by more economists that a wide range of other statistical methods are available in addition to OLS/Maximum Likelihood regression. Qualitative empirical evidence can also be a valid contribution to the evidence base, such as case studies and history, as well as even narrative and analytical insights.[21] But being good at econometrics opens career doors as an economist that would otherwise be closed even if you are a good economist. Even if you never personally achieve an in-depth knowledge of econometric methods, you are likely to need to incorporate econometric research by others into your own work. Therefore, a knowledge of inference statistics—that is, estimates of population characteristics based on the probability properties of samples—is important for a wide range of economists. You are also likely to have to trouble-shoot econometric analysis done by others. And an insightful knowledge of what statistical inference techniques—wryly called 'sadistics' by struggling students—can and cannot do needs more than just being able to use statistics software.

Although working through the linear algebra in rigorous textbooks is a worthy task,[22] it won't alone make you a good econometrician. The written advice, insights, and warnings in econometric textbooks are just as important as the maths.[23] Being able to crank-out techniques is not the same as being competent in their use and application. Econometric software today makes it all too easy to use sophisticated techniques to produce impressive looking econometric estimates that are meaningless. Indeed, a purely technical approach to econometrics is not likely to develop the insights of extensive hands-on experience; of the gaps and vagaries, pitfalls, twists and turns of empirical work in 'messy' real-world applications.

Experienced data users and econometricians learn to spot when something is wrong without having to do complex calculations. Rather like expert bridge or poker players, they are not constantly performing precise calculations but relying on experience. In our bookcase example (see page 155) we used factorials to calculate the number of permutations and if we apply this to a pack of cards you will know that 52! is a truly stupendous number (= 8.065817517 E+67). Even if we count just combinations for a five-card poker hand the number is still 2 598 960. So, although professional poker players are familiar with intuitively applying the probabilities of playing particular hands of cards, they do not need to be constantly deriving the precise mathematical probabilities. Similarly, practitioner economists develop an intuitive competence in interpreting and trouble-shooting econometric properties and outputs, and then direct the computer accordingly. Hopefully with much less bluff than a poker player!

---

[21] See Shiller, R. J. (2017), 'Narrative economics' *American Economic Review*, 107(4), 967–1004.

[22] For example W.H. Greene (2000), *Econometric Analysis 4th ed.* (Prentice Hall International).

[23] For a well-established book with lots of useful intuition and narrative see P. Kennedy (2008), *A Guide to Econometrics 6th ed.* (Wiley-Blackwell).

That said, all economists dealing with empirical evidence do need to be aware of what inference statistics results mean for their work. For example, anyone using inference statistics will frequently rely on the Central Limit Theorem (CLT). That is, given a sufficiently large sample size the sampling distribution of the mean for a random variable will approximate a normal distribution pretty much regardless of the population distribution of that variable. Most practitioner economists will know what the CLT does, and they may have seen it in action in demonstrations at university and then again in their work, but far fewer would be able to derive the result mathematically, as they won't be required to prove but rather will simply use the CLT result. Though they should know the implications for sample size and the situations where the theorem does not hold, such as for unbounded ranges, lack of independence in the sample or extremely 'lumpy' distributions.

Although it is true that many practitioners use only intuitive understandings of the requirements for reliable econometrics estimators and their diagnostic tests, a strong intuitive grasp of what these possible problems and limitations are is vital for effective troubleshooting of econometric estimates. At the most basic level, if you don't understand the implications of the standard Gauss-Markov conditions for reliable OLS (ordinary least squares) estimates then don't run regressions. If you confuse an 'absence of evidence' with 'evidence of absence', if your knowledge of how biased estimators and a host of other misspecifications can arise is poor, or if you are overly impressed by high R-squared and t-statistics, then steer clear of doing econometrics. If econometrics is vital to the project, then get help if you need it. If the work is important but complicated and sophisticated, then it's probably best to commission a specialist econometrician.

DATA AWARENESS: AVOID 'RUBBISH IN—RUBBISH OUT'

A common complaint about economists from statisticians is that although economists are generally very good at 'above the data-line' econometrics they pay too little attention to what is 'below the data-line'. That is, to the origins and make-up of the data themselves. No matter how sophisticated your econometrics, if you put poor data in you will not get reliable statistics and information out: 'Rubbish in-Rubbish out' as they say. Misleading outputs can often be caused by misunderstanding the nature of the data, and so the Office of National Statistics (ONS), a world-leading and respected data source for UK statistics, publishes comprehensive details of the survey methodology and data compilation rules and techniques that ONS uses. Such 'metadata' that accompanies data must be appreciated and understood when using all data.

For example, extrapolations between infrequent observations may have been used in compiling time series data and/or the weightings used to aggregate data changed. Hence longitudinal and panel data may be taken at face value by econometricians when it does not have the properties required for reliable econometric results. Similarly, some economists complain that the ONS does not chain some data sets across compilation changes to produce a longer time series, but as the former National Statistician, Dame Karen Dunnell emphasized, that may be because the data sets are simply not comparable. This does not stop some economists from constructing their own chained series that would be frowned upon by the ONS, which is understandably diligent in protecting its own high standards. The Economic Statistics Centre of Excellence[24] (ESCoE) was founded 2017 in collaboration with the ONS to improve the understanding of such issues in the measurement and use of economic statistics.

DATA CAN TRIP-UP EVEN THE BEST ECONOMETRICIANS

An interesting example of the importance of understanding and thinking about data before doing any econometrics was provided by the ONS itself:

A recurrent issue on the UK government's economic policy agenda is the productivity gap between the manufacturing sector of the UK and other industrialized countries. In their quest for an explanation and a cure for Britain's weaker performance economists researching this issue using the ARD [Annual Respondents Database] have come across a striking fact: The pattern found in the international comparisons of aggregate data is replicated at the business level. The labour productivity of foreign-owned enterprises in the UK is on average 40% higher than the productivity of domestically-owned enterprises. As both groups of firms operate in the same institutional environment and are supplied from the same pool of labour, this raises issues about managerial performance and inefficient control rather than poor skills or inadequate institutions in explaining the international productivity gap. Moreover, one may conclude that a policy to raise productivity would include the government attracting as much foreign direct investment as possible. The problem with this line of argument can be seen in Figure 6.1.

---

[24] The Economic Statistics Centre of Excellence at https://www.escoe.ac.uk/ (Accessed March 2021).

FIGURE 6.1 Data errors: Foreign owned UK firms are more productive than UK firms so encourage foreign direct investment?

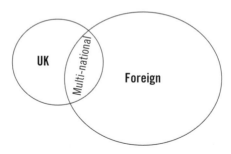

Source: Figure 1 from Matthew Barnes and Ralf Martin (2002) 'Business Data Linking: An introduction' in *Economic Trends* No. 581 April 2002, pp. 34–41, p. 39. Available at https://escoe-website.s3.amazonaws.com/wp-content/uploads/2020/01/01233928/ET-581-Business-data-linking-an-introduction-M-Barnes-R-Martin-Apr-2002.pdf

"... Foreign owned establishments are, by definition, all part of multinational enterprises. The same is true only for a small subset of the population of UK establishments. To find out if the superiority of foreign owned firms is a consequence of their multinational nature rather than a result of poor British managerial abilities, we have to compare foreign-owned firms' performance with that of multinational enterprises which are owned by UK institutions or residents. Although this seems straightforward this has not been possible so far because the ARD data does not contain any marker of UK multinational establishments. It was only after linking the ARD data with information from the Annual Inquiry into Foreign Direct Investment (AFDI) that such a differentiation could be made. Results ... suggest that the foreign effect is indeed a multinational effect. The productivity of UK multinationals in 1998, approximately £40,000 per employee, is only slightly below the average figure for foreign owned firms."[25]

CAUSATION IS BEDEVILLED BY A DEARTH OF COUNTERFACTUALS AND A SURFEIT OF CONFOUNDERS

COUNTERFACTUALS

No matter how good you are at statistics, without a reliable counterfactual it is pretty much impossible to say anything with certainty about causation. As is often pointed out 'correlation is not causation'. Even with a counterfactual

[25] Matthew Barnes and Ralf Martin (2002) 'Business Data Linking: An introduction' in *Economic Trends* No. 581 April 2002, pp. 34–41, pp. 39. Available at https://escoe-website.s3.amazonaws.com/wp-content/uploads/2020/01/01233928/ET-581-Business-data-linking-an-introduction-M-Barnes-R-Martin-Apr-2002.pdf.

there is always the possibility of an alternative explanation you haven't spotted, that is, a 'confounder'. Or, it might just be that you have found one of those weird and wonderful correlations which defy any explanation at all (there is a website dedicated to 30 000 of them at http://tylervigen.com/spurious-correlations).[26]

An old joke illustrates the importance of a counterfactual. That is 'the need to know what would have happened had the thing that happened not happened':

> "A man is walking across Westminster Bridge in London sprinkling white powder. A police officer asks, 'What are you doing?'. 'It's anti-alligator powder' says the man, 'It keeps them off the bridge'. 'But there are no alligators here', says the police officer. The man replies, 'I know, it's marvellous stuff isn't it!'"

We can be pretty confident that there are no alligators in the river Thames under Westminster Bridge, but economics phenomena are often harder to fathom. A New Classical macroeconomist might claim that 'austerity' helps an economy recover from a deep recession, a Keynesian that it would impede recovery, but the only thing we have is the data, often subject to later amendment, on what actually happened. Say the economy took two-years to recover, the New Classical economist could say 'I told you it would recover', but the Keynesian retorts 'It took too long, fiscal stimulus would've greatly sped up the recovery'. This is the familiar problem with much of economics: controlled experiments are seldom feasible for practical, political, and/or ethical reasons, and the economic behaviour of agents may even be affected by the economics to which they are exposed.[27] These problems often make establishing a firm counterfactual problematic.

CONFOUNDERS

In social science there is generally a lack of counterfactuals whereas confounders abound. Indeed, exploring alternative explanations and challenging existing ones not only advances knowledge but is a large part of the fun. A pertinent example for readers of this book might be the returns to a university degree. We would find that a degree is associated on average with higher earnings than being without a degree, but that observation does not tell us why this is. A natural assumption to make is that degrees increase a person's productivity, and this leads to their increased earnings. But are those who study for degrees from the same statistical population as those who don't?

[26] Of course, even a strong relationship between variables may not show up as a correlation if you have tried to fit a linear line to a non-linear relationship, such as a quadratic.

[27] Often called 'reflexivity'.

Perhaps those who don't go to university are not a good counterfactual for what would have been the experience of graduates had they not gone to university? Could an alternative explanation be that degrees are a screening device that merely identifies those with higher natural intelligence, with little impact on their future productivity? Perhaps university degrees have actually become a barrier to social mobility by making it more costly to even be considered for higher paid careers? Perhaps the statistical association between degrees and earnings comes from the children of the better-off having easier access to degrees and also to the social networks that can lead to better jobs? Depending on our interpretations we might favour free or heavily subsidised degrees or see universities as an unnecessary cost and a redistribution of income from the average taxpayer to higher earners!

RANDOM CONTROL TRAILS (RCTS)

Economists have more recently been exploring using Random Control Trails (RCTs). RCTs are used extensively in the medical testing of drugs. This involves the random allocation of respondents to a control and a treatment group. RCTs are held by many to be a 'gold standard' for comparing the treatment group to the counterfactual of the control group. RCT can be powerful evidence, but unfortunately, the same practical constraints to experimentation can apply. Policy makers would not and could not divide the economy into separated treatment 'Keynesian Economy' and control 'Austerity Economy'. The recent excitement over RCTs in economics has subdued somewhat, partly for practical reasons. For example, unless causation is unidimensional then the number of RCTs required to identify multivariate influences can be very large. Enthusiasm has also dwindled because of closer scrutiny of the properties of RCTs. For example, the distinguished philosopher Nancy Cartwright and the Nobel Prize winning economist Angus Deaton write in an article for VoxEU:

> "In recent years, the use of randomised controlled trials has spread from labour market and welfare programme evaluation to other areas of economics, and to other social sciences, perhaps most prominently in development and health economics. This column argues that some of the popularity of such trials rests on misunderstandings about what they are capable of accomplishing and cautions against simple extrapolations from trials to other contexts."[28]

---

[28] Angus Deaton, Nancy Cartwright (2016), 'The Limitations of Randomised Control Trials', VoxEU https://voxeu.org/article/limitations-randomised-controlled-trials (Accessed May 2021).

OBSERVATIONAL EQUIVALENCE

The human capital approach to education v's the 'screening hypothesis' is an example of where observational equivalence may arise. That is, the pattern of data fits different explanations. Further research, using other variables and instruments for sorting out which are the most powerful reasons for the association of degrees with higher earnings, such as independent ability tests, differential returns looking at university drop-outs, sheds light on which are the most powerful drivers. You will be pleased to know that the majority view is that degrees are associated with higher productivity, but it should be clear by now that there is usually room for challenge in any social phenomenon. Trickier examples of observational equivalence arise in explaining economic behaviour. For example, Herbert Simon's[29] non-neoclassical theory of 'satisficing' would be difficult to distinguish using economic data alone from neoclassical 'rational inattention'.[30]

ENDOGENEITY

Even if an equation from a regression 'passes' the battery of statistical misspecification tests (tests for correlation in the residuals, heteroscedasticity etc.) that we must throw at it before we can place any confidence in it, we still usually have the problem that in economics almost everything also depends on something else. That is, variables are likely to be jointly or interdependently determined, and so their values are partly or wholly determined from within the model. They are known as 'endogenous' variables, in contrast to exogenous ones such as pandemics, earthquakes and meteor strikes.

Even in a single equation regression, the causation may flow from Y to X rather than from X to Y, and so distinguishing independent from dependent variables may be difficult. For example, if we found a correlation between nominal GDP and a particular measure of the money supply, does that mean that money affects the economy or that the economy determines the monetary measure? That is, is money endogenous to the economy? Perhaps a missing exogenous variable of aggregate demand determines both nominal GDP and the money 'supply'? Similarly, perhaps in trying to estimate the impacts of immigration on the economy the causation is at least partly the impact of the economy on immigration?

[29] Herbert Alexander Simon (15 June 1916–9 February 2001) was an American economist, political scientist, and cognitive psychologist.
[30] Satisficing assumes than agents are not maximizers but rather use rule of thumb and compromise to arrive at a satisfactory equilibrium, rational inattention maintains that agents are maximisers but that their expectations based on probability lead them to stop when the expected marginal returns to search are equal to the marginal cost of further search.

Not only must a competent econometrician be aware of endogeneity, missing variables, and 'reverse causation', most economic models comprise a system of related equations. In such systems some variables are jointly or interdependently determined. That is, they are wholly or partly endogenous. We saw this earlier in this chapter with consumption and income (page 155), but it can apply to microeconomics too. If you try to trace out a demand curve by regressing quantity on price you may trace out a supply curve instead, or, more likely, a mixture of both. The total impact of changes in exogenous variables on the system as a whole, with all the feedback effects included, must be modelled, to avoid biased and inconsistent estimates.

Apart from the limited opportunity for RCTs, economists do not usually have the advantage of being able to conduct 'laboratory experiments', but 'natural experiments' when they occur can be a useful way to get around endogeneity problems. In addition to meteor strikes etc, other events such as legislative changes or political events can be regarded as outside the economic system. That is, exogenous. In certain circumstances they may provide significant results that are pretty much free from endogeneity issues. David Card, Joshua Angrist and Guido Imbens, won the 2021 Nobel Prize in Economics for pioneering the use and framing of such natural experiments, often called 'the credibility revolution', in economics.[31]

YESTERDAY MAY NOT BE A GOOD GUIDE TO TOMORROW

We haven't even really started on the joys of time-series, where identifying a well-specified statistical model can still leave you puzzling about the economics therein, and of course, Austrian Economics, the Lucas Critique or ever changing structural paraments may be looking over your shoulder suggesting that the past might tell us little about the future anyway.[32] An over reliance on data from yesterday may well be a generic problem in academic economics today. Frey Bruno argues that the top academic journals insisting on econometric evidence from past data tends to stifle and crowd-out other forms of

---

[31] Tim Harford, 'The Nobel Prize economists turned statistics into insight', *Financial Times* 12 October 2021.

[32] Austrian Economics emphasizes that new information is discovered and harnessed through economic activity within an ever changing economy, so any estimates tend to be ephemeral. The Lucas critique was made by American economist Robert Lucas. He criticized naïve structural models that sought to base macroeconomic policies only on past observed statistical regularities. Lucas argued that optimizing economic agents will anticipate and hence adapt to policy changes and hence this behaviour rather than structural parameters should be the basis of modelling-this insight has been widely influential. Institutional economists emphasize that institutions and regimes change through time.

investigation, such as creativity and simply well-informed keeping up-to-date with developments approaches to looking at the future.[33]

A LITTLE KNOWLEDGE CAN BE A DANGEROUS THING!

None of this means that econometrics is not worthwhile or is impotent, it is just a warning that is a vast and complex specialist discipline in itself. Hopefully enough has been said to convince you that the moral of the story is that novices shouldn't rush in where good econometricians tread very carefully. In short, don't do econometrics unless you know your stuff and beware of putting too much trust in econometric estimates unless you are very good at troubleshooting them or they have come from a reliable source.

STATISTICAL SOFTWARE PACKAGES

As we saw in Chapter 5, for practitioner economists the need to communicate with non-economists is paramount. Just about everyone is a Microsoft Word™ user for written documents, but in their eagerness to get to grips with more specialist and advanced packages such as STATA™, some basic spreadsheets skills, such as Microsoft Excel™ may be neglected. Excel is a generic software component of Microsoft Office and is the most common spreadsheet package used by non-economists, and although Excel has limited capacity for inference statistics and graphics compared to dedicated statistical packages, practitioners will often need to produce tables and other descriptive statistics to share with non-economists. As we covered in Chapter 4 (see page 100), being able to use such software packages proficiently is of importance for many employers of economics graduates:

> "Considering data analysis, both employers and economics departments value strong technical/econometric skills. However, employers value more basis skills such as being able to find, clean and organise datasets, as well as being able to use Excel and coding software. There is some, but limited focus on these aspects of data analysis in degrees."[34]

[33] Frey Bruno S. (2021) Backward-Oriented Economics Kyklos. 2021; Volume 74, Issue 2, Pages 187–95. Available at https://www.crema-research.ch/papers/2021-32.pdf (Accessed September 2021).

[34] Clodia Jenkins, Ashley Lait, and Stuart Lane (2019), 'Employability skills in UK economics degrees—Executive summary', Economics Network. Available at www.economicsnetwork.ac.uk/research/employability/executivesummary.

In recent years there has also been widespread adoption, including by many economists, of free statistical software such as RStudio® and Python®. Python is particularly versatile for a range of different tasks. Python provides an excellent tool for both practitioners and academics, being both simple and versatile, it is comparatively easy to use for data management, analysis and visualisations. Python also comes conveniently integrated with user interfaces such as Anaconda®, which again has a free version for individual use (https://www.anaconda.com/products/individual).

'HOW TO LIE WITH STATISTICS'

Hopefully, any economics undergraduate would be able to spot the nonsense in a statement such as:

> "If all regions had grown at just the average rate then overall UK growth would have been higher."

Sadly, genuine statistics are often presented in ways designed to deceive, even though they are not incorrect in themselves. Yes, it is possible to deceive when telling the truth! *How to Lie with Statistics* was written in 1954 by a US journalist named Darrell Huff. It is said to be the all-time bestselling book on statistics and is widely regarded as a classic guide to how statistics can be misused to create false impressions. Unfortunately, as modern-day UK economics journalist Tim Harford[35] points out, the book gives rather a jaundiced view of statistics in general, and Huff was later engaged in a deplorable obfuscation by tobacco companies attempting to obscure the evidence for a link between their products and cancer. But the old cynical jibe that 'There are lies, damned lies and statistics'[36] simply ignores the power of data and statistics to shed light on what does really go on. If the weight of empirical evidence is strong then it requires a strong reason to reject it, glib excuses such as 'you can prove anything with statistics' are no excuse for ignoring statistical evidence. Theory without data is empty and data without theory is blind but using statistics to deceive is always inexcusable.

Alvin Birdi sees facility with data, and learning how to spot when statistics are being misused, as an important part of an economics degree. When asked

---

[35] See: 'Statistics, lies and the virus: Tim Harford's five lessons from a pandemic' *Financial Times* (ft.com).
[36] Attributed to various people.

about the most important thing he got from his own economics degree Alvin replied:

"I think it almost certainly is going to be the facility with data. . . . being able to read data and news stories, things in current affairs and understand when the wool is being pulled over your eyes. You know, things like the difference in correlation and causation. That's quite a simple distinction but being able to actually judge whether what somebody is claiming as causation really is, to look at their methodology and to be able to see whether this is a really viable and robust study or whether it's really just something that you should throw in the bin."[37]

Outside worrying trends in politics, lying is universally frowned upon, but that still leaves a large grey area in which the truth can be used to deceive. For example, by omission of contrary evidence. This could be in the selective representation of facts described as being 'economical with the truth'.[38] Even in the deepest recession there will be some economic success stories to tell, and there can be success stories even with policies that are harmful overall. Selecting only those data and statistics that give a misleading impression of the overall picture is called 'cherry-picking'. As Dame Kate Barker observes in her interview for this book,[39] a trained economist is more likely to be able to interrogate the data presented and to ask 'Which bit of data are you not showing me?'

Emotive associations can also be deployed, which go beyond the information presented yet still leave a strong impression that something factual was added (see also page 178 below). This is surprisingly easy to do, again it should never fool a trained analyst. Consider the message in Figure 6.2.

Ignoring the issue of nuclear power safety, this representation is deliberately construed here to illustrate pulling the wool over the reader's eyes. Unfortunately, it is not far off the misleading persuasive devices we quite frequently see in parts of our press. The association of mutation with nuclear power may seem alarming, especially with those menacing pictures, but apart from the date when Calder Hall started generating electricity, there is no meaningful information here at all. The vast majority of people have more than the arithmetical mean of limbs, as it is, of course, less than four.[40] And why '60 miles'

---

[37] In his interview for this book (see Video 4: In conversation with Professor Alvin Birdi available at www.oup.com/he/pryce-ross1e).

[38] A phrase used by former Cabinet Secretary Sir Robert Armstrong.

[39] See Video 3: In conversation with Dame Kate Barker available at www.oup.com/he/pryce-ross1e.

[40] The average person has slightly less than one testicle and one breast!

FIGURE 6.2 A shocking fact

Consider this shocking fact!

Since 1956 when nuclear power generation began in the UK at Calder Hall, more than 200 children whose parents lived within a 60 mile radius of nuclear power stations were born with more than the average number of limbs.

Source: Left image: TonyV3112/Shutterstock.com; right image: frees/Shutterstock.com

anyway? Is it just to give the appearance of 'statistical facts'? For any comparisons of the rate of unusual births nearby we would also need data from areas without nuclear power stations, as such comparison with 'what would have happened anyway' requires a reliable counterfactual (see page 166). In short, for casual readers the worries in this portrayal may be merely because of their prior assumptions being manipulated by sensationalists playing on populist associations. Good analysts should never be more ready to accept something simply because it seems to support their prior beliefs, that would be to commit the unscientific sin of 'confirmation bias'.[41]

As human evolution has, understandably, equipped us with a greater capacity for absorbing visual information than the messages hidden in large arrays of numbers in data sets, our perception can be easily steered by visual impressions. Such as by changing the axes in a graph to use the same data to present different visuals. Look at the data in the Figure 6.3, it can be presented in absolute numbers to say in effect '*This thing is out of control*' or converted to percentages to say '*Nothing to see here, it's dying away*', when in fact the data are the same for both bar-charts.

Similarly, truncated axes, changing the units of measurement, picking particular starting and end points in time series (see Figure 6.4) and switching from absolute to logarithmic scales can all be used to convey very different impressions of the same data.

---

[41] As the joke goes: 'Since I learned about confirmation bias I've been seeing it everywhere!'

FIGURE 6.3 Uncontrolled expansion or growth petering out?

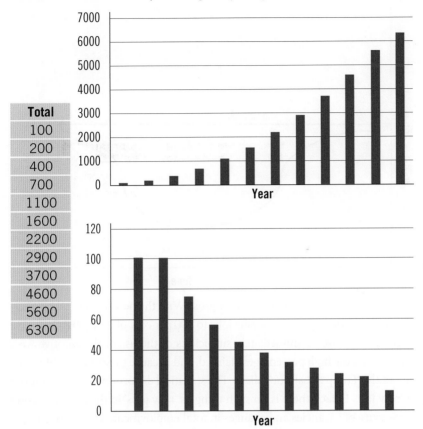

It is worrying to see graduates who have been drilled in advanced econometrics who are poor at descriptive statistics and/or lack an awareness of counterfactuals, confounders and causation. If you are eager to perform, say, Lagrangian multiplier tests for autocorrelation in large samples, to test for stationarity and to crunch-out panel data regression models and other more advanced econometrics, but you can be fooled by statistical 'tricks and quirks', then frankly you are a danger to have around!

STATISTICAL 'FAKE NEWS' IN THE MEDIA

Sometimes there seems to be wilful misrepresentation of data by some sections of our media, particularly often in newspapers playing on resentments and worries. For example, various newspapers repeatedly falsely reported that

FIGURE 6.4 Picking your starting date can be strategic!

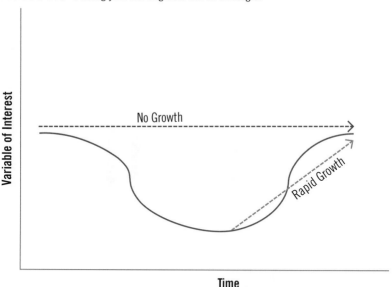

'Immigrants take the majority of new jobs'. With the percentages 'taken' ranging from about 70 per cent of new jobs to 100 per cent of new jobs! Of course, a good economist is immediately suspicious of the use of the emotive word 'taken', and the high percentages claimed, and because they've probably heard about the 'Lump of Labour' fallacy. The statistical distortion is in the notion of a 'new job'. In fact, there is no such thing as 'new jobs' in the data used, only a measure of vacancies and changes in total employment. After strong objections to the misleading impression being given by the Daily Express newspaper, Jonathan Portes, an economist who doesn't suffer fools gladly and actively challenges racism, had agreement from the Independent Press Standards Organisation (IPSO) that the headlines were an abuse of the data.[42]

Figure 6.5 demonstrates how such false statistics might be constructed. You should be able to see how it could just as easily be used misleadingly to claim that the majority of 'new jobs were taken' by people with, say, red hair!

CAN WE TRUST OFFICIAL STATISTICS?

Unfortunately, IPSO is unable to prevent 'fake news' items regularly appearing in our press, partly because it can only respond after the transgression as the result

FIGURE 6.5 A gross abuse of Net

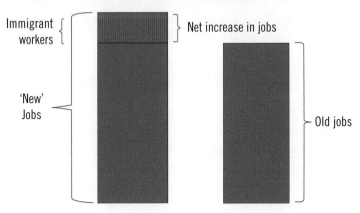

A Gross abuse of Net:
'100% jobs taken by immigrants'

Immigrant workers

Net increase in jobs

'New' Jobs

Old jobs

of a complaint made to it. Fortunately, for official statistics we do have a well-respected watchdog in the UK Statistics Authority. It is a pity that official statistics[43] are often described, or derided, as 'government statistics', for the UKSA is an independent body at arm's length from government with the statutory objective of promoting and safeguarding the production and publication of official statistics that 'serve the public good'. The Office for National Statistics (ONS) is the executive office of the UK Statistics Authority and the largest producer of official statistics in the UK. The quality of ONS statistics has long been improved by having economists working alongside its statisticians. ONS also benefitted from its Economic Experts Working Group (EEWG) a non-statutory body offering independent advice from authoritative economic experts, and since 2017 from the Economic Statistics Centre of Excellence (ESCoE), the UK's first-ever dedicated academic centre of expertise for economic measurement, one of just a handful around the world. ESCoE also provides free courses and publications on economic statistics. Its foundation followed the recommendations of the Independent Review of UK Economic Statistics[44] led by practitioner and academic economist Professor Sir Charles Bean.

---

[43] Official statistics are produced by any organization named by the Statistics and Registration Service Act 2007 and described by that organization as an official statistic or part of a set of official statistics, and any set of statistics produced by an organization named under secondary legislation and described by that organization as an official statistic or part of a set of official statistics.

[44] Independent Review of UK Economic Statistics—Professor Sir Charles Bean, available at: https://www.gov.uk/government/publications/independent-review-of-uk-economic-statistics-final-report.

Although more resources for UK statistics would be helpful, and though there can be, and are, fierce debates on methodological issues, the ONS and UKSA are honest expert bodies that don't deserve the widespread public scepticism about 'government' statistics. That said, politicians and their media advisers have been known to place unwarranted 'spin' on what are independently-constructed statistics.

TIM HARFORD'S 10 STATISTICAL RULES OF THUMB

Fortunately for economics and for the public understanding of statistics, we have Tim Harford. We have already noted Tim's extraordinary ability to communicate complexity simply, and with an even rarer talent, to do it in a very entertaining way. For example, in the programme 'More or Less' on BBC Radio 4, which is an exemplar for explaining, trouble-shooting, and debunking statistics on issues of public interest. In his latest book, *How to make the world add up—Ten rules for thinking differently about numbers*, Tim Harford offers, and elaborates on, ten rules of thumb for the public in approaching the many statistics we see used in politics and the media:

"1. Stop and notice your emotional reaction to a claim, rather than accept or reject it because of how it makes you feel.
2. Try to combine the 'bird's eye' statistical perspective with the 'worm's eye' view from personal experience.
3. Check you understand what the data is describing.
4. Look for comparisons and context and put any claim into perspective.
5. Don't forget to think about where the statistics came from.
6. Query what or who is missing from the data you're looking at.
7. Ask tough questions about algorithms.
8. Pay more attention to official statistics.
9. Don't let yourself be beguiled by beautiful graphs or charts.
10. Keep an open mind and remember that facts can change."

Source: Harford, T., 2021. *How to Make the World Add Up: Ten Rules for Thinking Differently About Numbers.* Bridge Street Press–Little Brown Group Limited. Reproduced with permission of the Licensor through PLSclear.

CONCLUSION

Although mathematical skills always complement economics, the level of mathematics you will need depends on your economist career path, but you will need good data skills wherever you go as an economist.

SUMMARY

- Mathematics is a powerful tool that is essential for many careers in economics, particularly academic careers.
- Mathematics is a good servant but a poor master: mathematics should increase your economics understanding not curtail it.
- Econometrics increases career opportunities and the ability to do empirical research.
- 'A little knowledge can be a dangerous thing', deep understanding is required to do reliable economics and econometrics.
- Statistics are often presented in ways that distort the message of the actual data, a degree in economics should help you spot such deceptions.
- Sophistication of technique in inference statistics should not be at the expense of a thorough grounding in descriptive statistics and data awareness.
- Being able to use more advanced statistical packages is an advantage but most economists will still need to use standard spreadsheet software.

QUESTIONS

1. If an increase in the number of police officers is followed by an increase in crime in official statistics does this mean that the increase in numbers was a waste of resources?
2. If during an overall policy of 'austerity' the Government promises to 'ring fence' the National Health Service budget and then keeps this promise, does that mean that the quality of the health service has been protected?
3. Before lead in petrol was banned, it was noticed that there was a correlation between lead in children and their IQs. How might you challenge the conclusion that the lead was the cause of lower IQ?

4. Shortly after wearing crash helmets for riding motorcycles became compulsory there was a surge in hospitals treating head injuries. Explain why this evidence was perfectly consistent with meeting the objective of the policy.

5. Keynesian economics suggests that more expenditure often leads to more income, but why would it be pointless to use the national accounts to regress national expenditure against national income to test this?

6. Why is 'Get the evidence to support your case' an unscientific approach?

EXERCISES

1. Study the following:

Country	Annual alcohol consumption (litres) per capita over 15 years of age	Life expectancy at birth (years)
Turkey	1.5	71
Poland	8	75
UK	11	78.5
France	14	79

a) Calculate the correlation coefficient

b) Is this a high correlation?

c) Is this good evidence for a claim that drinking alcohol is good for you?

2. Read the following newspaper headline:[45]

Mohammed is top boys' name
MOHAMMED is now the most popular given name for new-born boys in England and Wales

a) How is this headline open to misinterpretation?

b) Explain how a knowledge of descriptive statistics could clear up any confusion.

[45] https://www.express.co.uk/news/uk/208029/Mohammed-is-top-boys-name.

3. List the various reasons why econometrics seldom settles debate beyond all challenge.

4. Practise writing factual but unbalanced cases for and against economic policies that are in the news.

FIND OUT MORE

E. Swires-Hennessy 2014) *Presenting Data: How to Communicate Your Message Effectively* (John Wiley and Sons Ltd).

The ONS Guide to data visualisation: **https://style.ons.gov.uk/category/data-visualisation/**.

The Government Statistical Service (2020) Data visualisation: tables and charts (12 May). Available at: **https://gss.civilservice.gov.uk/policy-store/introduction-to-data-visualisation/** (Accessed May 2021).

Kennedy. P. (2008). *A Guide to Econometrics 6th edition* Oxford Blackwall.

CHAPTER 7

The importance of broader and soft skills

· · · · · ●●●●●● · · · ·

INTRODUCTION

The previous chapter looked at the so-called 'hard skills' of quants and statistics, and we have seen too the importance of analysis for all economists, another 'hard' cognitive skill. Overwhelmingly, the skills listed by the Higher Education Academy and the Quality Assurance Agency (see Chapter 1) for the 'employability profile' of skills that you can expect to gain from an Economics degree, are such technical hard skills.[1] This chapter emphasizes the importance of broader and what are somewhat misleadingly called 'soft skills'.[2] These are required as vital complements to these 'hard skills' across a wide range of careers, and in addition to the good communication skills we covered in Chapter 5. We include a brief overview of these broader and soft skills, including how to 'manage upwards'.

When you first see a list of soft skills, it can look daunting: adaptability; anger management; building productive relationships; communication skills—verbal, written and in the use of media; coaching others; confidence—or at least the courage to 'feel the fear and still do it well'; conflict resolution; constructive challenging; creative thinking; critical thinking; decision making; delivering results; developing others; diplomacy; engaging others; empowering others; emotional intelligence; enthusiasm; flexibility; internalizing corporate values; inspiring others; exercising sound judgement; management skills;

---

[1] Listed at *StudyingEconomics: Employability profile available at* http://www.studyingeconomics .ac.uk/where-next/jobs-and-careers/employability-profile/ (Accessed September 2021).
[2] 'Soft' is really a misnomer, as these skills can be the hardest to learn, but the term soft skills is probably too well-established now to change it.

'managing upwards'; motivation; multi-tasking; networking; prioritization; positive attitude; project management; resilience; self-reliance; teamworking; time management; willingness to learn; and work ethic.

If you search advertised job specifications, you will no doubt find other soft skills to add. Clearly no mere mortal could ever be a paragon of all these virtues! Don't worry, no one ever is or will be perfect in all these respects. We are all, even the best of us, in need of development. You will have many years to develop and you are not expected to be 'the finished product' at the start of your career. We have seen plenty of shy awkward graduates, who, full of self-doubt at 20 years old, go on to become awesome economists and leaders in their careers.

No-one is perfect and change is a constant, so the truth is that professional development can only ever be a journey and not a destination. In an ever-changing world, professional development is more like swimming against a current than climbing a mountain: you will never reach the top but if you stop learning and developing you will go backwards. This is why it's usually called 'Continuous Professional Development' (CPD), with the emphasis on 'continuous'. That said, in most jobs nowadays you are likely to have to regularly demonstrate evidence of professional development to your line manager, for example, for your annual and often mid-year performance and development reviews. Particularly in your early career, you will be expected to show how you have been improving. A poor showing is likely to lead to you having to undergo a 'personal development programme'. Lapses in performance are understood, but if you fail in your development programme you may be ineligible for career advancement, or even eventually shown the exit.

WHY DOES A BRILLIANT ECONOMIST LIKE ME NEED BROADER SKILLS?

It is often said that soft skills are the hardest ones to learn. The irritation that such Human Resources' homilies cause for some hard-nosed analysts is probably in direct proportion to their need for soft skills. It has been joked that an economist with good interpersonal skills is one who looks at your feet and not their own when talking to you, but to be fair this is more a self-effacing reminder by economists to themselves of the need for soft skills, not a particular criticism of economists! Coming across as a 'techy' with no understanding of society is not a good look for any social scientist seeking to have impact. Many soft skills in fact relate to how an employee interacts in professional relationships with others, so they are not just 'nice to have' add-ons, they are vital for personal effectiveness and for success in working in teams and organizations. That's why recruiters of economists typically look for candidates who will combine hard analytical and evidence skills with broader soft skills. Again, we must emphasize that you will not be expected to be the 'finished product' for your early career interviews. It's probably more important at first that you show awareness of the importance of and eagerness to learn soft skills, but for all job applications you are very likely to be set exercises and asked questions that do test for your potential in soft skills (see Chapter 9). Failing to appreciate the importance of soft skills could mean you fail to get a job even if your economics is strong.

Having studied economics at university you'll have acquired many 'hard' skills, such as a thorough understanding of economic theory; the ability to construct hypotheses and marshal data to test them; problem-solving and analytical skills; critical thinking; use of computer software, such as for econometric analysis. But, even if you were lucky enough to have effective courses on wider professional skills as part of your degree, your university course is less likely to have actively taught you the 'soft skills' you are likely to need for a successful career as an economist. This is not all down to a failing of universities, as the most effective learning for these skills is from' learning on the job', and it is difficult to replicate a real workplace in a classroom.

For some economists, relishing the 'real work' of analysis and evidence, 'soft-skills' can seem like an irritating distraction. There are any number of would-be best seller books with catchy or quirky, sometimes even banal, titles out there. Frequently on the shelfs of booksellers at major travel hubs. Some are indeed dross, and to the inexperienced they can all seem full of vacuous homilies, pontifications and such truisms such as 'If you fail to plan you plan to fail', or even worse 'There is no I in Team'.[3] Why does an economist, who has a powerful analytical mind that is used to driving hard logic and empirical data to rigorous conclusions, need to bother with such woolly and patronizing 'life-skills'? Isn't it all just Human Resources (HR) departments and HR consultants justifying their existence, with a few pretentious would-be gurus of management and development thrown-in? Analysts are trained to be sceptical of all things, but if you do take this attitude, perhaps unconsciously and as

---

[3] Although David Brent in the mockumentary 'The Office' did cringeworthily point out that 'There may be no 'I' in team, but there's a 'me' if you look hard enough.' For a tribute to the excruciating wisdom of David Brent see *Farewell, David Brent* available at https://www.standard.co.uk/hp/front/farewell-david-brent-6954179.html (Accessed September 2021).

a refuge from the salutary challenge that personal development can present, then you will learn the hard way how vital these broader skills are for your success, which can be very bad for your own and colleagues' performance and well-being.

You won't be able to avoid completely the need to develop effective broader and soft skills, but you might if you wish seek a more solitary career path that minimizes the need for them. Some individual consultants and researchers seem to prefer this, but to work in any teams or organizations you will need to put as much work into these other skills as into developing your economics expertise. This applies to both the private and public sectors. In any organization it takes more than economics to reach the top.

EXAMPLES OF BROADER SKILLS AND COMPETENCY FRAMEWORKS

WHICH 'BROADER SKILLS' WILL I NEED TO SUCCEED AS AN ECONOMIST?

Prospects.ac.uk lists the skills of an economist on their website.[4] They mention a number of attributes including:

- Research skills
- Project management skills
- Competency in using statistical software packages, including being able to extract and analyse data
- IT skills
- Excellent written and verbal communication skills, including being able to communicate with non-economists
- Good teamworking skills
- Being organized with good time management skills and being deadline orientated
- Being able to prioritize a varied workload
- Being comfortable working independently, sometimes under pressure

---

[4] AGCAS editors (October 2019), 'Job profile: Economist' on Prospects website. Available at: https://www.prospects.ac.uk/job-profiles/economist.

- A self-sufficient and motivated outlook
- Being detail and accuracy orientated
- Having the skills and self-assurance to make sound judgments and recommendations
- A passion for economics and current affairs.

Several of these skills—research skills; utilizing software packages to analyse and extract data; IT skills—are essentially technical in nature. Employers seeking to recruit economists will naturally regard your possession of technical abilities as constituting pre-requisites for the job. The Prospects.ac.uk list is clear though that those employers are also looking for a range of personal and soft skills that are also necessary to perform most economist roles. The ability to work alone under pressure, and being detail orientated for instance, will be generally regarded as a key aspect of any practising economist's role. You have to be task-oriented, able to work on a project unsupervised and capable of delivering it at a specified time—you have never seen the Chancellor of the Exchequer announce on budget day 'Sorry, it's not ready yet'. For most practitioner tasks, achieving perfection is futile if it is after the deadline set. Drawing on the list above, this will require both self-sufficiency and motivation and being organized with good time management skills. It will also necessitate displaying accuracy and attention to detail and, most likely, the ability and confidence to make sound judgements and recommendations.

Reassuringly, coursework assignments at university should have at least helped you in beginning to develop many such skills, insofar as you will have had to answer questions clearly understanding the issues involved; marshal relevant facts and considerations; draw conclusions; and deliver the final version to a firm deadline. In fact, preparing for examinations is not so far-off what practitioners do in preparing for high-profile advice and interrogative sessions with CEOs and Ministers, and especially for select committees.

Multi-tasking is also a skill that it's necessary to develop. Few practitioner economists enjoy the luxury of being able to focus uninterruptedly upon just one particular task for a protracted period. Rather, they face competing demands on their time with colleagues or clients making frequent requests, all of which have to be dealt with in some way but, crucially, in order of importance: a time-management matrix of urgent and important tasks can help prioritization (see Figure 7.1).[5]

---

[5] Often called the 'Eisenhower Matrix' after the American President who is reputed to have utilized it.

FIGURE 7.1 The urgent important matrix

	URGENT	NOT URGENT
IMPORTANT	'Crisis'	Planning & CPD
NOT IMPORTANT	Interruptions	Distractions

In a job with pressure the 'not important and not urgent' quadrant, labelled 'Distractions' is going to effectively be the same as 'ignore'. That's important to know as you will need to ensure some time is spent in the too easy to neglect 'important but not urgent' quadrant, labelled 'Planning and CPD', and to prevent yourself being forever trapped on the urgent side of the matrix. The top left quadrant will be stressful, the bottom left quadrant both stressful and unrewarding. Successfully navigating such an environment can be immensely challenging and demands a combination of calmness, experience and development, sound judgement, being honest with yourself and, often, the exercise of tact and diplomacy with stakeholders—it's always a good idea to explain politely why you can't drop everything else immediately to respond to an out-of-the blue enquiry: 'The impossible we do immediately but miracles take a little longer' is something you may be thinking but are certainly not the words you should choose to use to a valued client or other stakeholder.

Another typical mandatory 'ask' by a potential employer is for a 'team player'. The importance of being able to work collaboratively and amicably in conjunction with colleagues, whether economists or non-economists, towards a common purpose cannot be exaggerated. You must be willing to share ideas, respond constructively to what others have to say, be respectful and supportive of your colleagues and, in particular, regard your work as a collective enterprise. Such an environment, far from stifling personal initiative, should harness and develop the potential of all team members. Happily, most people learn to work well in such circumstances. If not, then to be categorized as 'difficult to work with' is likely to damage promotion prospects or even be a career killer.[6]

Prospects.ac.uk also reiterates the message of Chapter 5, on the fundamental importance of developing excellent verbal and written communication skills in order to explain complicated ideas to those with mixed levels of understanding around economics.

To acquire and develop all the soft skills summarized above may seem a daunting task. Don't worry unduly. Once again, you are not expected to be the finished product on day one of your career. Most economics graduates—once they're aware of the directions in which they need to travel to pursue a successful career as an economics practitioner—demonstrate both the potential and determination to develop soft skills.

NETWORKING

As your career develops you will find that building a personal network can be invaluable. Of course, you will want to have good relations by impressing the lecturers whom you will call upon to write your references, and references usually do ask a lot about character and soft skills. Outside university, finding opportunities to make contact with practitioners in the field you wish to enter can be useful for gauging the right approach and requirements, for learning about opportunities. Obviously, placements provide a great opportunity to do this. You may also make contacts by attending the relevant conferences and networking. Again, the skills used in managing upwards (see page 198) are useful here. You don't have to seek a personal friendship to have cordial productive relationships. Senior successful people are well-used to earlier career acquaintances seeking to include them in their networks and they won't usually resent it so long as they are treated with respect. You should probably avoid trying to form contact through the more personal social media and be

---

[6] The Chartered Institute of Personnel and Development (CIPD) website provides much useful free advice on soft skills such as avoiding conflict at work. For example see: Managing conflict in the modern workplace (2020) https://www.cipd.co.uk/knowledge/fundamentals/relations/disputes/managing-workplace-conflict-report (Accessed 2021).

aware that your details there can be accessed publicly, but the more professionally orientated network sites such as 'Linked-in' are useful for keeping in professional contact. One caveat, never make an unnecessary enemy, as you never know when someone who can influence your career might pop-up unexpectedly!

APPLYING SOFT SKILLS TO COMPETENCY FRAMEWORKS

Dig down into the detail of just about any advert for an economist post and you will find that more than just knowledge and skills in economics will be required. Many of the soft skills included in role requirements are qualities or 'behaviours' that organizations look for in all their staff to contribute to their overall working ethos. This is known as a competency framework. KPMG, for example, requires all its economists to develop the broader KPMG competencies:

"**Search and apply**
When assessing a role, you'll need to consider your own strengths and motivations, and how these compare to our KPMG Competencies . . .

Drive Quality
Delivers high quality products and exceptional service that provide value . . .

Apply a Strategic Perspective
Uses diverse set of inputs to develop a broad perspective on business and people . . .

Foster Innovation
Embraces a culture of innovation and experimentation to create value . . .

Build Collaborative Relationships
Connects with individuals, teams and organisations to build lasting, collaborative relationships . . .

Develop and Motivate Others
Engages teams, instils confidence, and coaches people to find meaning in their work and achieve exceptional results . . .

Demonstrate Self-awareness
Focuses on self-development and continuous learning, using insight to build capability and confidence . . .

Make Sound Decisions
Exercises sound ethical and business judgement when making decisions . . .

Advance an Ethical Environment
Takes personal responsibility for the ethical environment of the firm and encourages others to do . . .

Champion inclusion
Creates an environment in which all people feel like they belong."[7]

The importance of broader skills for government economists was explicitly given equal weighting, some twenty years ago, in the Government Economics Service's (GES) continuous professional development programme, under the leadership of Professor Lord Stern when he was the head of the GES and second permanent secretary at HM Treasury. This equal importance of broader skills with economic skills is well established in the GES today:

> "We take your development seriously and while earning a competitive salary, there will be plenty of support to further your development as an economist. You will broaden your subject knowledge through 50 hours of continuous professional development a year and a further 50 hours on personal skills."[8]

The Civil Service Competency Framework (CSCF),[9] which members of the GES as civil servants are expected to follow in addition to their own professional competency framework,[10] illustrates the wide range of broader skills that contribute to a successful career in any large organization. It demonstrates that beneath the headlines of any framework there are usually many sub-headings (see Figure 7.2). As you would expect, for the civil service some of these sub-headings are tailored specifically to the civil service, but although the wording may differ, the concepts apply pretty much across organizations in general.

---

[7] KPMG, 'KPMG Competencies'. Available at: https://www.kpmgcareers.co.uk/experienced-professional/applying-to-kpmg/kpmg-competencies/ (Accessed September 2021).

[8] Government Economics Service (19 March 2021) 'Assistant Economist Scheme 2021'. Available at: https://www.gov.uk/guidance/assistant-economist-recruitment (Accessed September 2021).

[9] Civil Service Human Resources (2018), 'Civil Service Competency Framework 2012–2017', p. 1. Available at https://assets.publishing.service.gov.uk/government/uploads/system/uploads/attachment_data/file/436073/cscf_fulla4potrait_2013-2017_v2d.pdf.

[10] Note that at the time of writing the GES competency framework is being revisited but is not expected fundamentally to change.

FIGURE 7.2 The Civil Service competency framework

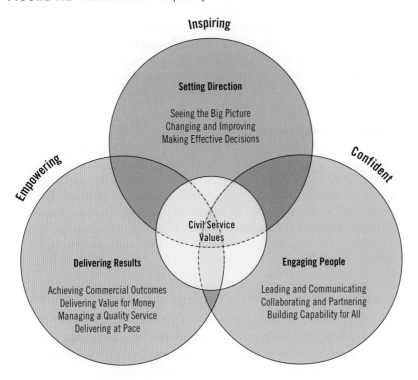

Source: Civil Service Human Resources (2018), 'Civil Service Competency Framework 2012-2017', p. 1. Available at https://assets.publishing.service.gov.uk/government/uploads/system/uploads/attachment_data/file/436073/cscf_fulla4potrait_2013-2017_v2d.pdf

For example, if we look at the 'Engaging People Cluster' we see a further breakdown of the expected behaviours that are needed to fulfil the headline:

"Leading and Communicating
At all levels, effectiveness in this area is about showing our pride and passion for public service, communicating purpose and direction with clarity, integrity, and enthusiasm. It's about championing difference and external experience, and supporting principles of fairness of opportunity for all. For leaders, it is about being visible, establishing a strong direction and persuasive future vision; managing and engaging with people in a straightforward, truthful, and candid way . . .

Collaborating and Partnering

People skilled in this area are team players. At all levels, it requires working collaboratively, sharing information appropriately and building supportive, trusting and professional relationships with colleagues and a wide range of people within and outside the Civil Service, whilst having the confidence to challenge assumptions. For senior leaders, it's about being approachable, delivering business objectives through creating an inclusive environment, welcoming challenge however uncomfortable . . .

Building Capability for All

Effectiveness in this area is having a strong focus on continuous learning for oneself, others and the organisation. For all staff, it's being open to learning, about keeping one's own knowledge and skill set current and evolving. For leaders, it's about investing in the capabilities of our people, to be effective now and in the future as well as giving clear, honest feedback and supporting teams to succeed. It's also about creating a learning and knowledge culture across the organisation to inform future plans and transformational change."[11]

The competency frameworks from such large organizations are worth looking at, especially as they are largely generic rather than specific to that organization. They are readily available, and so can be used to plan your own professional development (see Exercises 1 and 2 below). Obviously, prioritize the organizations that you are interested in. The information provided on the values and skills they value may well come up in questions at interviews for their applicants (see Chapter 9). As you are unlikely to rise to CEO within a year or so, be realistic and honest with yourself. At the start of your career some of the higher-level skills, such as 'setting leadership vision', will be aspirational for the future rather than for the more junior entry level. That does not mean that you shouldn't begin to plan your long-term development, and showing the potential for higher level skills may well get you noticed in the organization.

---

[11] Government Economic Service (year unknown), 'GES Competency Framework'. Available at: https://cabinetofficejobs.tal.net/vx/lang-en-GB/mobile-0/appcentre-1/brand-2/xfaefe81976db5/candidate/download_file_opp/473/37356/1/0/a98c0a91f206d7f64f58259ca374fbf788058eb7.

KEVIN DALY'S TWELVE POINTS GUIDANCE TO BE A SUCCESSFUL FINANCIAL SECTOR ECONOMIST

No matter how long a list of generic knowledge, behaviours and skills, each trade will have its own specific context and emphasis. This may not be explicit in the more general frameworks of the organization and so it is always useful to seek advice on the specifics of the particular job from more experienced practitioners in the field. Kevin Daly discusses his long and distinguished career in the interview he gave for this book,[12] and here we show the brief 12-points guidance that he gives to new Goldman Sachs economists.

Such informal advice from senior colleagues on how to go about tasks is often a vital supplement to the more formal generic and hence more abstract frameworks of the organization. Again, you should note the paramount importance of communication that we looked at in Chapter 5.

"1. Being a successful financial sector economist requires a challenging combination of skills—You need to be an academic, a writer, a charismatic presenter, a forecaster . . . A balance of skills is crucial, so it makes sense to invest time in developing the areas where you are relatively weak.

2. To be a good financial sector economist, your analysis should be academic and rigorous but it also needs to be responsive and user-friendly. The work of many financial sector economists is more akin to financial journalism than economics—as economists, we should be conducting original research, not just reporting on the research of others. In my view, the 'sweet spot' is to produce applied research that is similar to the output of the IMF/central banks, only faster.

3. A key difference between an academic and a financial sector economist lies in how we present our work. As an academic, the methodology underlying your results is at least as important as the conclusion itself, so the methodology needs to be placed front and centre. Writing for a financial sector audience, the rigour and analysis should still be there but it needs to sit more in the background (often in an appendix) and primacy needs to be given to the conclusions that you reach and the implications of those conclusions.

4. Forecasting is only one part of what financial sector economists do. Financial sector economists have to produce forecasts (with all the difficulties that

---

[12] See Video 10: In conversation with Kevin Daly available at www.oup.com/he/pryce-ross1e.

this entails). But a more important part of what we do is to use economic tools and empirical analysis to judge the implications of things that have already happened. E.g., what are the implications of a large change in oil prices and how do these effects differ across countries; how does the valuation of one currency compare with another? etc.

5. Avoid consensus views if possible. In general, this is achievable without coming across as contrarian—one often finds clear errors or a lack of internal consistency in the consensus view.

6. But be honest if your conviction is low. We don't have strong convictions all the time, so make it clear which calls you hold with conviction and which you do not. It is OK to write: 'We think X, but there are significant risks around our view.'

7. Don't belittle the opposing view. Try to present the opposing view as reasonably as you can, before setting out why you disagree with that view. This will help your thought process and will also make your argument more convincing.

8. Don't pick a fight with a 'straw man'. Force yourself to focus on the hard questions that people are asking, rather than fighting with a straw man who has no followers.

9. Do not let your views bias your interpretation of the data. Beware of allowing your underlying view to taint your interpretation of the news flow and acknowledge when a data point provides evidence against your view. This is harder to do in practice than you might think.

10. Honestly acknowledge when your view is wrong. If one of your key views/forecasts is ultimately wrong, acknowledge this graciously.

11. Every piece that you write should have one main point and only one main point. This can be a view that you disagree with, something you expect to happen, etc. You can use various arguments to support your point but, if there is more than one overall point, you should write more than one piece.

12. 'The best way to be boring is to leave nothing out': Strip out any redundant details. You should think of a paper like a movie—you cut scenes in a movie that slow down the narrative."[13]

HOW DO YOU DEVELOP A SOFT SKILL SET?

You should have already begun to develop a number of soft skills through your studies and extra-curricular activities. As you enter a graduate role, many of the broader skills mentioned above will be finessed through on-the-job

---

[13] Quoted with Kevin Daly's permission.

experience. Recognizing the skills you already have and where you need improvement to feel competent, or to progress, is an important step on your professional development journey.

There are usually many support programmes in place in large organizations, expressly designed to help you develop broader and soft skills. For example, training courses and programmes, often organized by Human Resources, such as 'buddy' and coaching systems. But perhaps the most valuable of all is the active and sympathetic mentoring by more experienced colleagues. Good managers ensure that this is an integral part of the workplace and is an essential part of the 'Learning Organisation' concept championed by, among others, Investors in People.[14] Indeed, a smart thing to do to when entering a new job, where appropriate and with diplomacy (see Chapter 5), is to volunteer to give feedback on the induction process and any induction packs. Team induction packs are particularly likely to be neglected by busy people already in post and compiling them is often seen as an unrewarding task. You can get to know the new team by offering the team leader 'fresh eyes' and relieve them of the burden, while affording yourself the opportunity to chat to all the team members about their jobs, and whatever else comes up, with the boss's authority rather than as a 'needy' newcomer.

In the following sections, we consider other ways that you can facilitate constant professional development.

SEEK FEEDBACK

It can be difficult to be honest with oneself, and we all need a certain amount of self- esteem to function well. So, self-criticism should be constructive rather than self-destructive.[15] As we have emphasized in this chapter, no-one is perfect, and be reassured that whatever weaknesses you may have they are shared by millions of other people. That said, recognizing and acknowledging your own weaknesses can still be hard, even unnerving or emotionally painful. To learn from unpleasant experiences, you should not dwell on what you, or others may have done wrong, but on what you can do to improve such situations in the future. Advice from others can be useful for seeing things that you may not be able to see yourself. That is why '360-degree' feedback is now a commonly

---

[14] Investors in People are an accreditation body that recognize organizations that adhere to their person management principles: https://www.investorsinpeople.com/

[15] See also the need to balance welcome nerves with adrenaline in the 'arousal-performance curve' in page 269.

used tool for personal development. 360-degree feedback seeks feedback from those around you, and so contrasts with the regular downward feedback that you should expect from your boss. It could be from those you manage, colleagues, peers, clients and other stakeholders, as well as from self-evaluation.

Lord Gus O'Donnell—hardly a failure!—shared with us a piece of feedback he found hard to take at the time, but that led to a great career move and the path to his becoming the UK's top civil servant. In his interview for this book Vicky Pryce asks him 'And if you're thinking back, then on your career . . . what advice do you wish you had been given at the start of it?' His surprising reply was:

"I think the number one piece of advice would be to really seek out feedback. When I was given tenure by Professor Tom Wilson at Glasgow University and I went to see him to talk about the rest of my academic career he basically said 'Actually, if I were you I'd get out. I'd go and work in the government because you're not going to win a Nobel Prize for economics. You're not going to run some brilliant new theory, but you're really interested in applied stuff. If you really want to make a difference, so go and work in government'. That was very honest feedback. I hated it. I really hated it. It dented my pride."[16]

Constructive feedback of this nature can often be difficult to accept, you can try to ignore it, which is not conducive to continuous improvement, or you can consider it dispassionately and see if it offers an opportunity for improvement, or even a change of direction, as for Gus that worked out so well for himself and others. Of course, you have discretion, and not all feedback is useful. Sometimes it might reflect more on the provider of it than yourself. So, seek balanced feedback including from those whom you respect and know will be candid but proportionate.

A PERSONAL DEVELOPMENT PLAN (PDP)

As professional development is a continuous process, each year you should compile a personal development plan (PDP). This may be with a view to increasing competency in your current role, or with a view to an upwards or lateral move within an organization. Seeking feedback, as described in the previous section, can be a helpful preparation for this process.

---

[16] In his interview for this book (see Video 19: In conversation with Lord Gus O'Donnell available at www.oup.com/he/pryce-ross1e).

There are several ways to approach a PDP, but a standard template will guide you through a set of headings that will help you identify the skills you already have and where further development is required. A template might include prompts for each aspect, such as: 'What do I need to be able to do better?'; 'What knowledge and skills are required?'; 'What are the gaps in my development in this respect?'; 'What action is needed to fill these gaps?'; 'What does the deadline need to be?'; 'How will I measure my success?'

Although some parts of a personal development plan can be kept confidential, or only shared with a non-employer, it is common practice for managers to go through staff development targets and actions as part of the annual performance and development appraisals round. Conversations with a manager may help you identify ways to develop your skillset, such as courses or workshops, and may include allocating funds according to your development needs and potential for future roles.

TRAINING OPPORTUNITIES, MENTORING, AND COACHING

As well as the progress you can make through self-study, practice, feedback and observing others, there is also a plethora of courses in broader and soft skills. Not all are value for money, and so it's worth asking around for recommendations. Working for a large organization with expert HR and Learning and Development facilities can be a great advantage in this respect, at least for the early part of your career. If they don't commission in-house bespoke courses, they will still be able to advise on reliable providers. Organizations also often have coaching and mentoring schemes that can be very useful for linking with more experienced persons. Both coaching and mentoring typically involve one-to-one interactions with skilled exponents, they can be either an internal or external person.[17]

PREPARING FOR MANAGEMENT

As your career and seniority progresses you are likely to manage other people. It is a serious responsibility. Up to this point your career progress will have largely depended on you getting the best from yourself, as a manager your career will largely depend on getting the best from others. And so, good

---

[17] To understand the difference between coaching and mentoring see, for example, the blog by N. Girling (2021) 'Coaching or mentoring: what's the difference?' The Chartered Management Institute (CMI) at https://www.managers.org.uk/knowledge-and-insights/blog/coaching-or-mentoring-whats-the-difference/ (Accessed September 2021).

managers can be vital to the successful shaping of more junior colleagues. Human resource experts will often remind you that: 'If you want to go fast, go alone. If you want to go far, go together.'

Management responsibility will require developing a whole new skill set. You will need emotional intelligence as much as the cognitive intelligence that economists usually have in abundance. Be warned, if you approach being a manager in the wrong way you can damage the health of your staff and yourself! Don't beat yourself up though for the mistakes you are bound to make. It's OK to apologize: so long as it's not too often, it won't mean loss of credibility. Becoming a good manager can take a lot of study and practice, and unfortunately usually learning from a lot of mistakes.

It is unlikely that you will be managing others in the very first years of your new job and we cannot nearly do justice to the importance of good management here. But it could be only a few years before you are expected to manage staff, and you may be asked to host a student on placement before then. You can practise right from the start though by practising how to 'manage upwards'.

MANAGING UPWARDS

This involves the radical perspective of learning to see your boss as a human being. Even when they don't show it, bosses, like you, have fears and aspirations. They have ego, emotions, insecurities, hopes, strengths and weaknesses, good days and bad days. Bosses are really just like people! It can literally pay to treat your boss well, as they are important for your career prospects. Outside academia, whether you like it or not, your boss is your prime stakeholder. Bosses have legitimate authority, unless they abuse it, because they are responsible to their stakeholders for your actions. You have a responsibility to try and meet their legitimate requirements of you, and the more you can exceed these the better it usually is for both of you.

Most, although not all, bosses quickly spot insincere 'sucking-up' and won't respect you for it. But the majority of people do enjoy a bit of flattery and you can subtly combine this with learning on the job: 'You are good at chairing meetings but I'm still nervous just being in a meeting, have you any tips for me, please?' 'Your presentations are compelling; how can I learn to give effective presentations?'. Of course, it's best to avoid confrontation with a 'powerful other' such as a boss, unless it is a really serious misbehaviour in which case use HR or perhaps even a formal grievance procedure. Instead of conflict, you can develop ways to influence their behaviour towards you and to help bring out their strengths. Just as a large part of a manager's job is to get the best from you, so you can learn how to get the best from your boss: that's 'managing upwards'.

Even the way you phrase feedback and responses can be the difference between being seen as difficult and negative or being seen as constructive and positive. If you think that your boss is talking nonsense remember that 'No—that is wrong' is much more aggressive than, 'The part I'm having difficulty in understanding is … '. And if your boss gives you some useful help a 'Thank you for your support, I appreciate it', may encourage more of the same. One very important thing to keep in mind, if you want to keep in with your bosses, is to avoid giving them nasty surprises. They are as worried about answering to their boss as you are to them. So, if you are likely to miss an important deadline give prior warning: 'I won't be able to deliver on all my objectives by the deadlines, please could you help me to prioritise them?'. This allows your boss to prioritize what they need for their boss, and to take appropriate actions. If you are struggling then asking for advice on development is better than appearing not to care about poor performance.

That said, showing some independence will also be appreciated by your boss. For example, by recognizing that managers have limited time (often management is done alongside other accountabilities) and if possible, it's a good idea to be resourceful about solving problems before seeking advice from your boss. For example, by asking more experienced colleagues working at the same level, consulting process documents etc. This means you will have to balance giving your boss command and sight of what you are doing and acting autonomously to reduce their load. As you progress in grade, you will find that the best bosses do not 'micro-manage', rather they empower you to take responsibility, and so long as you have a justifiable reason for any action they will not criticise you for an action they did not authorize, within reason! That said, getting to understand exactly what your boss wants from you and translating that into objectives/targets for yourself, and any team you manage, can significantly reduce potential frictions.

A FEW TIPS TO REMEMBER FOR ASPIRING MANAGERS

When you do reach the level of a manager, remembering what others have learned the hard way may help you to avoid some of the worst mistakes:

- A good manager can't be just 'one of the boys/girls' as they have to take responsibility for their unit's performance, but they seldom have to rely on pulling rank either. Good managers rely mostly on supporting their staff so as to get the best from them, and by earning their respect.

- 'Difficult staff' can be unhappy because they are struggling to cope. Most people want to do a good job and so are unhappy and become fractious when they can't. If you can assist and develop them to do the job better their confidence often grows, and attitude improve.

- Listen first before you provide 'development feedback': Shouting 'Late again, this has to stop!' puts you in a poor position when the response is 'I had to dash my Mother to the hospital as she is very ill'.

Whatever your own attitude towards management is, the 'dark satanic mills'[18] of the industrial revolution are a thing of history, at least for organizations of any size. Modern-day staff have rights and access to the means to redress grievances. They may also have the strength of a trade union. Although they do wield real power, managers can cause a lot of grief and much work and stress for themselves by ignoring these facts.

You may think that becoming a leader can wait for much later in your career, but modern human resource experts point out that leadership qualities are relevant to all levels of an enlightened organization. It is part of the empowerment process and can increase corporate performance. Of course, the degree of leadership you will have, or are expected to demonstrate, will increase as you become more senior. This is yet another new set of skills to learn! The literature for personal development, management and leadership is vast, and there are some rather pretentious books on book stalls, their authors hoping to start or cash-in on a buzzword or phrase and become a best seller. The human resources department in a large organization should be able to provide a guide to more useful reading and courses, and the organization 'Investors in People'[19] is too often neglected as a rich source of advice on how organizations should be run and improved. Reading through their free material can be in effect a crash course for managers.

We end this chapter by noting that good managers tend to surround themselves with people who have complementary skills to their own, rather than seeking to 'recruit in their own image' staff who will merely be compliant. Strong managers and leaders are those who develop and empower others, seek (polite) challenge and use the synthesis and creativity that comes from diversity (see Chapter 8).

CONCLUSION

If you do not develop broader and softer skills you are unlikely to have a successful career.

[18] 'Dark satanic mills' refers to the industrial mills or factories of the industrial revolution and nineteenth century, associated with harsh working conditions and representing exploitative and dehumanizing industrialization.

[19] https://www.investorsinpeople.com/ (Accessed September 2021).

SUMMARY

- It is not enough to be a successful practitioner economist, you will also need to develop a wide range of other skills.

- Professional development is commonly called 'continuous professional development' (CPD). This is to emphasize that it is a continuous life-long process.

- Broader and softer skills can take a long time to develop, and often a lot of learning comes from mistakes.

- None of us are perfect and so everyone can benefit from improving these skills, no matter who they are or at what stage in their career.

- You will have begun to develop some of these competencies through your studies, extracurricular activities, and part time work or volunteering, but there are always opportunities for improvement.

- A successful economist must seek to improve and widen their skills as their career progresses.

- As you become more senior you will need to have a higher level of skills, especially management skills where the emphasis shifts from how good you are at tasks yourself towards how good you are at supporting others to give their best. You can begin practising this even in your early career by learning how to 'manage upwards'.

- Employers will want to see evidence of your potential to develop wider skills, but they will also take your career stage into account.

- The competency frameworks of large organizations, and the 'Investors in People Standard', provide a good overview of the wider skills you will be expected to develop over your career. You can use them to plan your own personal development plan (PDP).

QUESTIONS

1. What broader skills are you most likely to require as your career develops?
2. Why is it likely that those who think that they are near perfect are also the ones who need professional development the most?
3. How honest are you with yourself about your own development needs?
4. Why is it not a weakness to have development needs?

EXERCISES

1. Use one of the jobs portals in Chapter 2 to read through a few job advertisement for economists, and then evaluate the balance of hard and soft skills required by applicants.

2. Use this chapter and the civil service 'Competency Framework' (https://assets.publishing.service.gov.uk/government/uploads/system/uploads/attachment_data/file/436073/cscf_fulla4potrait_2013-2017_v2d.pdf) to identify your own areas for development.

   Use the free resources, and template, provided by the Chartered Management Institute (https://www.managers.org.uk/knowledge-and-insights/research/personal-development-planning/) to compile a personal development plan

3. Watch this video clip on YouTube from Ricky Gervais and Stephen Merchant's 'The Office' (https://youtu.be/IkYUDQCYGHA), to see an hilarious example of how a staff performance/development session should NOT be done (by either party).

FIND OUT MORE

Investors in People provides a host of free resources that are quality tested and cover a wide range of the wider and softer skills required in any organization. Some of their guides can be found at **www.investorsinpeople.com/knowledge/**.

The Investors in People 'Standard' can in effect be used as a crash course in discovering what good management is about. (**https://www.goodmanjones.com/public/downloads/6nOfJ/investors-in-people-goodmanjones.pdf**).

Study the professional competency frameworks of large organizations you may wish to work at. We've looked at KPMG and the civil service, but there are many others saying similar things, such as PwC Professional (**https://tinyurl.com/2p8ntkvt**).

Swain, R. (2019) 'What skills do employers want?' (Prospects), available at: **https://www.prospects.ac.uk/careers-advice/applying-for-jobs/what-skills-do-employers-want**.

CHAPTER 8

Towards a broader economics and a more diverse body of economists

· · •••••• · · ·

INTRODUCTION

A former Head of the Government Economic Service, Dave Ramsden CBE, now Sir David Ramsden and a Deputy Governor of the Bank of England, once wrote:

> "What is certainly wrong and unscientific is to defend one's own field relentlessly with hostility to other approaches: the antithesis of a dynamic self-critical discipline that is genuinely seeking to discover new and better ways of understanding the world."[1]

Sir David, who has very long experience as a very senior policy adviser, is emphasizing here the dangers of a narrow approach to economics. In fact, eclecticism, interdisciplinarity, considering a diversity of viewpoints, and studying historical perspectives are all useful for pragmatic, and therefore more successful, policy formation. And, as we saw in Chapter 4, practitioners must often be able to approach issues from various angles to be able to write from the perspective of their stakeholders and to defend their positions. This requires a pluralistic, or at least eclectic, approach to economics.

---

[1] Ramsden, Dave in Coyle, Diane ed. (2012), *What's the use of economics? Teaching the dismal science after the Crisis* (London Publishing Partnership), p. 5.

This chapter provides examples of how different perspectives and world views can help inform policy formation. Learning about past economic policy is useful for understanding past policy mistakes and is a salutatory exercise for any practitioner of economics. The chapter concludes by reinforcing these insights through highlighting the importance of diversity among economists for better economics, but of course diversity is also vital for moral and democratic reasons. Sadly, economics is one of the worst academic disciplines for the representation of women and certain ethnic minorities. That is damning in a social science. For example, how would we know the range of questions to ask that are important for a diverse range of lived experiences?

TOWARDS A BROADER ECONOMICS

A strong grounding in neoclassical economics and empirical techniques will continue to have vocational benefits, but we believe that to keep up with developments in modern economics economists need to have a broader perspective than has been the focus of most Economics degrees in the recent past (see Chapter 10).

ECONOMICS, ECLECTICISM AND THE NEED FOR INTERDISCIPLINARY APPROACHES

Andy Haldane emphasizes the importance of reflection and being open to new ideas:

"... my career has been either hallmarked or pockmarked by [economic] crises, and each of them has been, among other things, huge opportunities to rethink and refresh both my understanding of the economy, and indeed my understanding of public policy. So, I hope, all these years on, that I'm somewhat better equipped to understand the economy ... I think one of the essences of good economics, and indeed of good public policy, is that inquisitiveness: that capacity to question the pre-existing framework, and indeed to jettison that framework if it breaks in the teeth of crisis."[2]

---

[2] In his interview for this book (see Video 16: In conversation with Andy Haldane FAcSS FRS available at www.oup.com/he/pryce-ross1e).

The frameworks used in economics can be very powerful when appropriately applied, but practitioners must often be able to approach issues from various angles to be able to capture all the important elements, or to write from the perspective of their various stakeholders. We have already seen in this book that eclecticism and interdisciplinarity are often important (see Chapters 1, 3, and 5), this chapter reinforces that insight. This is not only because of institutional constraints and frameworks such as the law, or behavioural responses that must be taken into account, or the feasibility of the politics, but also because real world phenomena are usually multifaceted and have no respect for subject demarcations. As Andy Haldane goes on to say:

> "... with the benefit of glorious hindsight ... I would've loved maybe during the course of my degree to have had a bit more of a blend of the other social sciences ... perhaps a bit more history, a bit more psychology, a bit more anthropology, and sociology. As we're finding latterly from the economics profession, understanding human behaviours, both individually and collectively, is absolutely rudimentary to economics ... a common element of my approach to economic problems ... is to try and draw on as eclectic a range of individuals and of disciplines as possible and try and cross pollinate and cross fertilize some of the ideas."[3]

In her interview for the book, Catherine Connolly advocated listening to other disciplines and professions, something which she feels will result in better-rounded individual economists, but also would be good for the profession as a whole.[4]

Take for example the common practice of buying a round of drinks, or the sequential taking of turns to foot the bill for a restaurant meal. That is, when someone volunteers, or accepts, that it's their 'turn' to buy everyone they are with a drink or the meal. An anthropologist is likely to point to inherited cultural traditions that people feel obliged to observe, the sociologist to point to a bonding ceremony that reinforces membership of the group, the economist might point to the lowering of transactions costs. Which is the correct explanation? Of course, they all are part of this phenomenon. A complete understanding requires all three disciplines and no doubt history and psychology too.

[3] Ibid.
[4] See Video 7: In conversation with Catherine Connolly available at www.oup.com/he/pryce-ross1e.

Lord Adair Turner, an eminent academic and practitioner economist who uses both mainstream and more radical views to understand economic phenomena, echoes that:

> "...really good economic thinking must provide multiple partial insights, based on varied analytical approaches."[5]

Treasury economist Mario Pisani, who also worked in the Chancellor of the Exchequer's private office, observes:

"We're ultimately feeding into policy development and one thing that I wish I'd known earlier is that economics very rarely gives you a complete answer. You need insights from other disciplines, as well and from other considerations and factors, before you can make the final view on an issue."[6]

ECONOMICS COVERS A LOT MORE THAN IS COMMONLY APPRECIATED

As we saw in Chapter 3, it is difficult to pigeonhole the role of economists. This is due in part to the wide scope of things that relate to economics and its many definitions, none of which are wholly satisfactory, and which would have to encompass a wide range of different approaches to economics. As the quotations above from Andy Haldane, Lord Turner and Mario Pisani allude to, whereas the late twentieth century saw a narrowing of the focus of mainstream economics towards neoclassical foundations, this century has seen a renewed interest in a more 'interdisciplinary'[7] approach.

Economics began as a very broad subject. The best-known Islamic scholar who wrote about economics was Ibn Khaldun (1332–1406). In fact, there is a strong case that Khaldun is really the 'Father' of modern economics, even if

---

[5] Turner, Adair (2010), 'The uses and abuses of economic ideology', *Project Syndicate* (15th July). Available at https://www.project-syndicate.org/commentary/the-uses-and-abuses-of-economic-ideology?barrier=accesspaylog.

[6] In his interview for this book (see Video 20: In conversation with Mario Pisani available at www.oup.com/he/pryce-ross1e).

[7] Of course, what is regarded as interdisciplinary may well depend on how broadly you have defined your field in the first place.

Adam Smith (1723[8]–1790) wrote the first 'textbook' of economics. Khaldun wrote about economics in the context of Islamic principles and political theory. For example, in the introduction of his *History of the World* (Kitab al-Ibar) he discusses 'asabiyya' (social cohesion), which he saw as the reason why some civilizations become 'great' and others fail. Smith considered himself to be a 'moral philosopher', he discusses many aspects of the human condition and a wide range of broad themes, such as politics and power; ethics and morality; human 'propensities' (psychology); social structure and transformation.[9] Indeed, Economics was called 'political economy' for most of its history.

In the latter half of the twentieth century there was a narrowing of scope in academic economics, stemming from attempts to make economics 'scientific'.[10] A detailed discussion of this is beyond the scope of this book, suffice to say that 'political economy' and different methodological approaches to, and perspectives on, economics never completely died. Many economists did feel, however, that their work was being 'ruled out of court' by the bulk of academia, and this gave birth to a broad 'heterodox economics' movement. Rather than being a single alternative this included a very wide range of economists from different 'schools of thought' working outside 'Mainstream Economics'. Mainstream Economics has no definitive definition and so is probably best understood simply as the body of theories of economics and methods currently taught across the vast majority of Western universities and colleges, which are generally accepted as the basis for discussion and enquiry. This had become increasingly dominated by neoclassical economics and its extensions in the last decades of the century but did usually retain at least some Keynesian macro elements.[11]

Relations between mainstream and heterodox economists were not always as cordial as one would hope for civilized debate, but this century has seen a wider acceptance that the mainstream had become too narrow to effectively address many of the major challenges faced: economic crises; social

---

[8] Adam Smith's exact date of birth is unknown but he was baptized in June 1723.

[9] A short but useful *Financial Times* article on Adam Smith, by the Nobel Prize winner economist Amartya Sen Adam Smith's market never stood alone (2009) can be found at https://www.ft.com/content/8f2829fa-0daf-11de-8ea3-0000779fd2ac?nclick_check=1 (Accessed September 2021).

[10] This scientific aspiration was epitomized in the best-selling UK textbook of the time: Richard Lipsey (1963), Positive economics (Weidenfeld and Nicolson). It is instructive to read the preface and first chapter across the long run of editions of this famous textbook, to see how it changes to move away from an initial stance of what is often called 'naïve falsification'.

[11] Though the Post-Keynesian school would often argue that these Keynesians elements were usually poor reflections or even distortions of Keynes' actual work.

issues, such as driven by power relations and socio-economic exclusion; the environment and sustainability; incorporating 'real' human behaviour into models and prioritizing welfare. It is rather depressing that this flowering of renewed attention to real and pressing issues and much more interdisciplinary work with other social and natural sciences, politics and history has yet to change the common public perception of economics away from being 'all about money' (see below page 228). There also remains an unresolved debate between pluralists, who assert that various sources of authority as schools of thought should co-exist with more or less equal status, and some mainstream experts who worry that such an approach all too often replaces scientific advance with a political discourse or 'literary appreciation'. They often worry that it could also undermine the authority of economics as a profession and be a distraction from addressing the nitty-gritty of real-world pressing problems. We look at again at aspects of that debate below (page 217).

As practitioners grapple with such real and pressing problems every day, where the limitations of standard models are most quickly exposed, it is perhaps not surprising that they have often been champions of attempts to broaden Economics (see Chapters 3, 4, and 10). Even when their stakeholders are perhaps more constrained! Indeed, there is a strong case that the academic journals that are the most prestigious for advancing academic careers in economics have remained overly narrow despite a widespread dissatisfaction with such narrowness (see Chapter 10). For example, an article in the *Journal of Economic Literature* on the careers and publication histories of economists, as hired by the top-rated 35 US university economics departments between the years 1996 and 2010, refers to 'The Tyranny of the Top Five'[12] (T5) academic economics journals:

> "... academic economics risks becoming (or remaining) a group of top five
> plodders putting one foot in front of the other. Emphasis on the T5 in sorting
> talent creates a culture where vitae [CV] length and publication speed in select
> journals rather than the development of a body of coherent and original ideas is
> most valued. It incentivizes careerism rather than creative scholarship."[13]

---

[12] The American Economic Review, *Econometrica*, the *Journal of Political Economy*, the *Quarterly Journal of Economics*, and the *Review of Economic Studies*.

[13] James J. Heckman and Sidharth Moktan (2020), 'Publishing and promotion in economics: The tyranny of the top five', *Journal of Economic Literature* 2020, 58(2), 419–470.

A similar point was made by another Nobel Prize winning economist George Akerlof in Akerlof, G. A. (2020). 'Sins of omission and the practice of economics'. *Journal of economic literature*, 58(2), 405–418.

In Chapter 10 we look at new, and resurrected, developments in economics that we think it would be wise for practitioner policy economists to become familiar with, as they are topics that are likely to increase in importance. We also use a 'preservation of capitals' conceptual framework to demonstrate that an economist genuinely addressing how the economy affects human welfare must take on board interdisciplinary contributions.

THE IMPORTANCE OF OPERATIONAL DELIVERY

We have seen that for the policy maker 'economics alone' is seldom enough. Effective policy making often requires an interdisciplinary approach and a wide repertoire of sources, inspiration and thought. In the next section we will see how diversity among economists themselves also enhances the effectiveness of economics and economists. Here we note something that is so often underestimated: the practical consideration that it is one thing to draw graphs and to build models to illustrate policy options, but it can be quite another thing to deliver these as real-life policies. Many policies which have impeccable theory and analysis at the abstract stage have failed miserably in practice. This is because the realities of operational delivery have not been understood or have been overlooked. A collection of past examples and insights from neglecting such practical considerations is provided in the wonderful book, *The Blunders of Our Governments* (2013) by Anthony King and Ivor Crewe.[14] For example, the danger of 'too-clever-by-half' sophisticated/complex welfare systems that unintentionally led to the State becoming a mass debt collector from the poorest in society, who had no intention of cheating the system. During the Covid-19 crisis, it was also vividly clear that it takes more than simply announcing a policy, such as 'loans to businesses' or 'track and trace', to ensure its delivery.

A MORE ECLECTIC APPROACH TO ECONOMICS

Eclectic economists pragmatically utilize and combine whatever seems the most useful tools and insights from a wide range of available sources and methods—rather than doggedly following a single approach such as 'Marxism' or 'Neoclassical Economics'. Academic objections to this, such as 'epistemological incompatibility', are very low on a list of practitioner's concerns.

---

[14] Anthony King and Ivor Crewe (2013), *The Blunders of our Governments* (Oneworld Publications).

Using a range of approaches can make for better economists and policies. Agent-based approaches, Austrian, Behavioural, Chinese hybrid, Complexity, Feminist, Green, Institutional, Keynesian and Post-Keynesian, Marxian, Sraffian, and of course, Neo-classical economics, can all provide useful insights.[15] at least when used with the critical scepticism that is the hallmark of any good analyst.

There are strong moral and democratic arguments for plurality too, but the concept of plurality is disliked by some economists. They worry that plurality diminishes the authority of the economics profession to speak out on issues as acknowledged experts, or perhaps even threatens the status of their own field of economic expertise. This is particularly so when it is believed that plurality means 'anything goes'. It should not mean that, and an ideological assertion should never overturn a large weight of contrary evidence. As a Soviet USSR premier, Nikita Khrushchev, is reported to have complained: 'Economics is a subject that does not greatly respect one's wishes'.[16] Plurality should actually set a high bar for accepting any theory through welcoming critical challenge of it, although it does seem ironic that some so-called pluralists challenge other schools of thought a lot more than they do their own!

As one might expect, plurality has more than one meaning. For most practitioner tasks it means plurality of method and hence 'merely' eclecticism. Admittedly, pluralism also allows for different interpretations of the world to co-exist, even when they are in conflict or compete as explanations of social phenomena. For example, a free marketeer will emphasize the freedom to choose your employer and spend your wages as you choose, and so may emphasize freedom in exchange. A Marxist will emphasize that, to access the means of production, and hence income at all, you have to relinquish your labour power to a capitalist for a wage, and so argue that there is inequality in production and unequal power between labour and the owners of capital. That is, 'social classes' as defined by their relationship to capital. Similarly, if unions are found by a researcher to be linked to inflation, is this unions 'causing' inflation or merely

---

[15] An impressively concise introduction to various schools of thought is provided by Liliann Fischer et al. (2018), *Rethinking economics: An introduction to pluralist economics*. For free readings in, and some very useful 'compare and contrast' schematic overviews of schools of thought, see *Exploring economics* https://www.exploring-economics.org/en/ (Accessed August 2021).

[16] The origins of the quote are discussed by Taylor, Timothy (2016) 'Khrushchev: economics does not respect one's wishes'. *Conversable Economist* (2nd May). Available at: https://conversableeconomist.blogspot.com/2016/05/khrushchev-economics-does-not-respect.html#:~:text=Presently%20I%20finished.-,Mr.,not%20greatly%20respect%20one's%20wishes.%22

a legitimate response to an exploitative regime? Such debates go beyond the scope of this book but are certainly relevant to politics, and for equipping citizens for democracy. At a practical level it is certainly true that being able to call readily on a variety of approaches and methods in an eclectic way is an employability advantage. As we have noted, professional practitioners often must work within, or at least respect, the world view of their employer, and hence they need to understand the views of those who disagree with them. Learning alternative perspectives is very good practice for this challenge.[17]

Our advice is to read widely from a range of political perspectives and sources and explore why economic analyses differ, but always be critical as there is 'chaff as well as wheat' out there. And don't discard the work of past economists. It is surprising how often seemingly new problems and crises were actually considered in depth by past economists. Reading widely and considering economics from different perspectives may leave you a bit confused, but that's OK, there are no definitive proofs in real world economics, and so arriving at a considered judgment is part of being an economist. As we noted in Chapter 4, policy proposals do not finish with 'QED'.

However, we also noted in Chapter 4 that practitioners often do have to make day-to-day decisions quickly. This can lead to simply grabbing at the tools one is most used to using but the best practitioners never neglect their continuous professional development (see Chapter 7) and the power of eclecticism that the challenge of broader reading brings. This deepens you as an economist and makes you a more versatile practitioner. The distinction between merely mastering a set of techniques and mastering a subject has perhaps never been better captured than by the eloquence of Robert Graves (1895–1985) in his poem 'In Broken Images'.[18]

Economics has many powerful techniques, learning how to apply them is part of becoming an economist, but you are not really an economist until you also fully understand the weaknesses of any technique and can act accordingly. A broader knowledge will help you understand the inevitable limitations of any one approach.

Eclecticism and a broader knowledge also relate to the constitutional duty of a civil service to serve the government of the day. As no-one can predict

---

[17] Even pluralism needs to be plural. See this piece in the *Financial Times* on different interpretations of pluralism: Samuel Bowles 'How to fix university economics courses: A syllabus that does not integrate the insights of other disciplines fails students' (January 2018) by https://www.ft.com/content/bfd5ac14-fa11-11e7-9bfc-052cbba03425.

[18] See O'Prey, PG (1982), *in Broken images: Selected letters of Robert Graves 1914–1946* (Hutchinson).

which way the future political pendulum might swing, government economists should be equipped and ready to serve a government of almost any political complexion (subject to the law and the civil service code). That requires understanding different belief systems and different approaches to economics.

THE IMPORTANCE OF CHECKING AND INTERROGATING SOURCES

To be more eclectic or pluralistic will sometimes lead you to go beyond well-established 'mainstream' sources. For example, the internet is obviously a useful tool for this, but, as you will know already, one needs to be wary of uncritical acceptance—and good analysts are always sceptical of all sources:[19] 'You can't believe everything you read on the internet.'—Abe Lincoln, 1868. Of course, you easily spotted that this quote is a fake because Lincoln died in 1865.

Besides the more obvious howlers, there is unfortunately a plethora of unreliable, partisan and even downright mischievous sources. Some authoritative sounding think tanks (see Chapter 2) may be more propaganda units than researchers. To help sift out propaganda from research, the Oxford macroeconomist and former HM Treasury economist Professor Simon Wren-Lewis has provided a useful checklist for evaluating the reliability of evidence and so guarding against accepting 'policy-based evidence' or 'alternative facts' uncritically.

Simon Wren-Lewis notes that his tests are not fool proof, but we do find them very useful, and so we summarize and interpret his advice here, (Simon's own words are in quotes):[20]

1) **'Who commissioned the research?'** 'The reasons for suspicion here are obvious, but this—like all the indicators discussed here—is not always decisive on its own.'

   The reasons to be suspicious of some organizations' funding of research are often obvious: turkeys researching Christmas would find it a bad idea, and lobbyists may risk their funding if they attack the interests of their sponsors. But even here, particularly if their research was externally commissioned and meets the following tests, the evidence may be useful.

---

[19] Although best to rein-in this fierce analytical scepticism a bit in your personal life if you wish to have a wider circle of friends!

[20] Wren-Lewis, Simon (2014), 'Policy based evidence making'. *Mainly Macro* (12 August). Available at: http://mainlymacro.blogspot.co.uk/2014/08/policy-based-evidence-making.html?utm_source=feedburner&utm_medium=email&utm_campaign=Feed:+MainlyMacro+(mainly+macro).

2) **'Who did the research?'** 'What about work done in- house by a "think-tank"? Not all think tanks are the same, of course. Some that are sometimes called this are really more like branches of academia: in economics UK examples are the Institute for Fiscal Studies (IFS) or the National Institute (NIESR), and Brookings is the obvious US example. They have longstanding reputations for producing unbiased and objective analysis. There are others that are more political, with clear sympathies to the left or right (or for a stance on a particular issue), but that alone does not preclude quality analysis that can be fairly objective. An indicator that I have found useful in practice is whether the think tank is open about its funding sources (i.e. a variant of (1).) If it is not, what are they trying to hide?'.[21]

Academics are often more reliable than consultants who may feel they have to please their clients.

3) **'Where do the key numbers come from?'** 'If numbers come from some model or analysis that is not included in the report or is unpublished you should be suspicious'.

Are they plucked from the air by some unspecified process? For academic articles the authors should be willing to provide the raw data used.

4) **'Is the analysis comprehensive, or does it only consider pluses or minuses?'** 'If analysis is partial, are there good reasons for this (apart from getting the answer you want), and how clearly do the conclusions of the study point out the consequential bias?'

5) **'What is the counter-factual?'** 'By which I mean, what is the policy compared to? Is the counterfactual realistic?'

As we saw in Chapter 6, without knowing what would have happened in, say, the absence of a policy, then attributing causation is usually very problematic.

Tim Harford warns us of another source of all too often undetected bias—ourselves! That is, our own unconscious bias that all we humans have. This is very different from dishonesty, which is an easier concept than bias: we know when we are being dishonest as it is deliberate. An academic who forges evidence will be disgraced and should rightfully forfeit their career, but it is only human to be biased. As humans we must interpret the world we see, and we can see only via our own perception. The danger here

---

[21] Wren-Lewis, Simon (2014), 'Policy based evidence making'. *Mainly Macro* (12th August). Available at: http://mainlymacro.blogspot.co.uk/2014/08/policy-based-evidence-making.html?utm_source=feedburner&utm_medium=email&utm_campaign=Feed:+MainlyMacro+(mainly+macro).

is to unconsciously see what you want to see, rather than being open to and sceptical of all evidence at all times, whether it fits what you want to believe or not. Tim Harford, an acute interrogator of evidence himself, tells the true story of an art forger who fooled the Nazi Hermann Göring by selling him a fake Vermeer painting.[22] To avoid being charged with the more serious charge of treason, the forger subsequently had to prove that he had himself painted the painting. He did this by revealing how he faked aged materials and by painting another one!

The point of the story is that the expert had been fooled because the forger had studied what the expert wanted to see. The expert had been looking for 'missing Vermeers' and so cunningly had painted the forgery according to the expert's theories of what a missing Vermeer would look like. He saw it as 'validation' that he had been right. The expert was easier to fool than a non-expert, as what he saw matched his predictions and so 'confirmed' his own expertise.[23] As the expert declared when he saw the painting 'I had difficulty controlling my emotions'. As Tim warns us,

'When we are trying to interpret the world around us, we need to realise that our expertise can be drowned by our feelings'.[24]

And so, in response to Simon Wren-Lewis' invitation 'Any further suggestions on how to spot policy-based evidence making?'[25] we add Tim's advice to Simon's list:[26]

6) 'When you are asked to believe something — a newspaper headline, a statistic, a claim on social media — stop for a moment and notice your own feelings. Are you feeling defensive, vindicated, angry, smug? Whatever the emotional reaction, take note of it. Having done so, you may be thinking more clearly already.'[27]

---

[22] Tim Harford 'From forgeries to Covid-denial', Tim Harford on how we fool ourselves, *Financial Times* (January 28 2021) Available at https://www.ft.com/content/13f627fb-eea1-4376-8411-d931c763e27c (Accessed September 2021).

[23] The tendency for humans to see what they want to see is called 'confirmation bias'. Since we learned about confirmation bias we've been seeing it everywhere!

[24] Tim Harford 'From forgeries to Covid-denial', Tim Harford on how we fool ourselves, *Financial Times* (28 January 2021) Available at https://www.ft.com/content/13f627fb-eea1-4376-8411-d931c763e27c (Accessed September 2021).

[25] Ibid.

[26] See Chapter 6 page 178 for the full list of Tim's Ten Top Tips.

[27] Tim Harford 'From forgeries to Covid-denial', Tim Harford on how we fool ourselves *Financial Times* (28 January 2021) Available at https://www.ft.com/content/13f627fb-eea1-4376-8411-d931c763e27c (Accessed September 2021).

DIVERSITY IN METHOD: COMBINING DEDUCTIVE AND INDUCTIVE REASONING

Deduction involves building purely logical models from prior assumptions, such as in indifference curve analysis.[28] You don't even need to leave your desk to do it, and some academics prefer this to getting their hands dirty with the messy indeterminacies and vagaries of a practitioner's job. Whereas deduction involves going from the general to the specific, inductive reasoning takes a series of specific observations and tries to expand them into a more general theory. Practitioners must mix induction and deduction. That is, they mix theory, data and experience, while always being alert to the limitations of any particular model, and they quickly learn that real issues don't come nicely packaged within clear discipline boundaries.

Getting useful insights and context will often involve talking to non-economists and people who are actually involved in the phenomena being studied. So, *Financial Times* journalist Sarah O'Connor calls for economists with 'dirty shoes' to get out of the office and talk to people on the ground! She notes that although anecdotal evidence[29] is unrepresentative and can lead to wrong conclusions, so too can relying too heavily on data: '*Combine the two and you may tease out where they differ. You can also find clues as to why.*'[30]

Andy Haldane calls this 'ground knowledge':

"I don't want to speak just to economists. I want to speak to businesses. I want to speak to public policy makers outside of central banks. I want to speak to communities and the general public—because of course, they are the economy too—and throw together this combination of both stats and stories to build up this jigsaw puzzle of what I think is going on."[31]

Such casual empiricism is sometimes discouraged as 'non-rigorous', but it can help shape understanding of what is going on. It is also good for would-be practitioners to discuss economics informally and to try explaining the immediate

---

[28] When derived from axiomatic assumptions.

[29] Anecdotal evidence is a factual claim relying only on personal observation, collected in a casual or non-systematic manner.

[30] O'Connor, Sarah (2016) 'The best economist is one with dirty shoes'. *The Financial Times*, 19 July. Available at: https://www.ft.com/content/07d4e7c6-4d90-11e6-88c5-db83e98a590a.

[31] In his interview for this book (see Video 16: In conversation with Andy Haldane FAcSS FRS available at www.oup.com/he/pryce-ross1e).

everyday world they see around them using economics (see Chapter 5). Seeing if theory fits what you see around you and if you can identify which theories help explain what you see around you in the everyday brings economics to life and builds 'fluency' in using economics. Interviewers are not impressed by candidates who can only recite theory rather than apply it. For example, think about: 'Why don't parks charge for entry?' 'Why is there a light in my fridge but not my freezer?' 'Why are old buildings often more ornate than new ones even though we have grown richer?' 'Why has much of retailing evolved into a predominance of vast warehouse like stores?' 'Why were basic calculators once expensive items but are now very cheap?' 'Why do supermarkets display selected products on corner-aisles?' 'Why are there so many estate agents on high streets?' 'Is fruit growing wild a public good?' 'Why do more women wear make-up than males?' 'Why do different communities observe different obligations towards relatives?' 'How can it be profitable to deliver even very cheap items bought online?' 'Why do modern highways have lots of turns when Roman ones were straight?' Your explanations may not be correct, but you will hone your skills as an economist by trying to apply your economics to such questions.[32]

THE RIGHT TOOLS FOR THE JOB IN HAND

If you are trying to understand fluctuations in the wholesale price of eggs, then neoclassical economics is very useful.[33] If you want to understand the symbiotic relations between capitalism and associated social structures, then the asocial ahistorical atomistic framework of neoclassical economics is not much use. If you want to understand how capitalism leads to women being disadvantaged, then Feminist Economics has more to offer.[34] If you want to understand the dynamic wealth creating power of capitalism, then Austrian Economics has more powerful insights than the marginal analysis of neoclassical economics. If you are conducting a Cost-Benefit Analysis, then a critical understanding of neoclassical welfare Economics is important for appreciating the strengths and limitations of CBA. If you are looking to understand how market

---

[32] The use of economics as a forensic investigation into things not usually seen as economics was popularized by books such as Tim Harford (2007), *The Undercover Economist* (Abacus) and Stephen J. Dubner and Steven Levitt (2007) *Freakonomics* (Penguin). The latter is a best-selling book which applies a forensic approach applying economic methods to a variety of phenomena—the insights are interesting even if not necessarily definitive.

[33] The retail price is a bit trickier as oligopolistic markets are less determinate than more atomistic competitive ones.

[34] See Vicky Pryce (2019), *Women Vs Capitalism* (C.Hurst & Co (Publishers) Ltd).

mechanisms can fail, then Austrian Economics is less useful than Neoclassical Economics, or, at the macro level, Keynesian insights. But perhaps most of all, if you are crunching data, as economists so often are, then the effort to identify the multivariate relationships therein, and/or a statistical generating mechanism, is more important than any school of thought.

The lesson here is that pluralist or eclectic, choosing the right tool for the job is an essential part of being a good economist. Seasoned professional practitioners learn to be 'intellectually promiscuous', and for pragmatic eclectics the wider the range of tools you have the wider the choice from which to make the best matches. Diversity of knowledge and thought is to be encouraged, but it has to be said again that wider reading must be done with discernment and scepticism, not everything is valid just because someone writes it!

THE CORE PROJECT, THE RETHINKING ECONOMICS PROJECT, AND DIVERSITY OF THOUGHT

As we saw in Chapter 4, calls for reforms to the teaching of undergraduate Economics are not new, but the economic crisis of 2007/08 and aftermath brought a new urgency. In this section we look briefly at two recent major initiatives that each proposed a distinct way forward. Comparing and contrasting these proposals highlights some now well-established agreements but also some very long-standing disagreements that are unlikely to go away anytime soon. Reflecting on these should help you decide how you wish to develop as an economist and therefore what you will want from your continuous professional development and wider reading.

THE CORE PROJECT

The Institute for New Economic Thinking (INET) launched a Curriculum Open-Access Resources in Economics (CORE) Education Project to bring out the real-world relevance and contribution of economics, and so increase the appeal of economics to students.[35] CORE leads with real world issues and develops techniques alongside as they become useful as tools to assist the analysis, rather than these techniques being presented as the subject of economics itself. CORE hopes to dispel misperception that economics is about arcane/irrelevant models that ignore societal and environmental concerns or is only about money and financial matters (see also Discover Economics below page 232).

---

[35] A list of current and past funders of the CORE project can be found at https://www.core-econ.org/about/

The CORE vision is that:

"A radically transformed economics education can contribute to a more just, sustainable, and democratic world in which future citizens are empowered by a new economics to understand and debate how best to address pressing societal problems."[36]

This includes the hope that it will:

"[h]elp change who studies economics to include more women and other un-derrepresented groups by changing content, pedagogy and access to knowledge (We look at diversity among economists below page 223)"

Clearly, these are objectives that deserve to succeed.

A large part of the CORE project consists of preparing and then making freely available teaching and learning materials which are now used in universities across the world. The CORE reports that there are 376 institutions across the world using CORE in instruction, two thirds using the project's textbook, *The Economy*, as the main textbook on a course with some 115,000 students being taught CORE each year.[37] In addition to its free online 'e-tome', *The Economy*,[38] the project has also produced, also freely available online, *Economy, Society, and Public Policy*[39] and its companion workbook with lots of actual data, *Doing Economics*.[40]

The CORE project in *The Economy* has provided an excellent textbook, which is both comprehensive and is easily the best free textbook in the world. Its free access is a boon to students around the world. However, and not surprisingly for anything that attempts to disturb decades of established practice to provide a new way forward, the CORE does have its critics. Some concerns are over losing long established elements seen as desirable in economics textbooks and worries that a well-resourced but free-text book could unfairly undercut

---

[36] CORE ECON: 'Economics for a Changing World' https://www.core-econ.org/about/ (Accessed May 2021).

[37] *Who is teaching CORE?* https://www.core-econ.org/who-is-teaching-core/.

[38] *The Economy is available at https://www.core-econ.org/the-economy/* (Accessed September 2021).

[39] Rather disparagingly, CORE says it has been created 'specifically for students from social science, public policy, business and management, engineering, biology, and other disciplines, who are not economics majors'. Well, we argue that a major in Economics for practitioners of public policy is not only perfectly legitimate but much needed! CORE's *Economy, Society, and Public Policy (ESPP)* is available at https://www.core-econ.org/espp/ (Accessed September 2021).

[40] Eileen Tipoe and Ralf Becker's *Doing Economics* is available at https://www.core-econ.org/project/doing-economics/.

some long established beautifully crafted commercial textbooks, such as *Economics*, now in its eleventh edition, by John Sloman[41] Dean Garrett, and Jon Guest.[42] These authors also share the objectives of CORE about addressing real world issues, being student led and embracing diversity, and economists generally see competition, including among textbooks, as a good thing.

Other objections have been on specific pedagogic details, such as those from teachers who find that the 'Iso-profit curve' approach to the theory of the firm, although capturing nicely the neoclassical notion of a 'duality'—the supposed equivalence of consumption and production theory—is less intuitive and tractable than the 'tried and tested' marginal cost and revenue approach.[43] Because of this, the CORE project does now also contain some material on the well-established marginal cost and revenue approach. More generally, arguably it's more discursive approach makes it harder to pick-out approaches that, for better or for worse, are still used extensively (see Exercise 10.2), and to effectively critique something it is important to have a good understanding of it.

The objection relevant to this chapter is the claim that the CORE initiative is not pluralistic and hence lacks diversity in thought and in representation of a wide range of approaches to economics. The CORE project, of which *The Economy* textbook was a central output, is led by the respected macroeconomist and textbook author Wendy Carling. It was spurred by a growing movement of economists and economic students around the world objecting to what they saw as: a narrowness in mainstream economics that eschewed important real-world features such as the exercise of power and the constraints of social structures; a lack of transparency for the general public, as befits a democracy; failure to address the most pressing real-world problems; and a spurious 'received wisdom' didactic attitude to teaching that fails to develop the critical skills needed to understand the contested nature of economics and indeed to thrive in the very dynamic modern world. The same student discontent, particularly after the 2007/8 financial crisis and recession, also led to the formation of Rethinking Economics.

[41] John Sloman, the original author of the well-respected textbook, is a long-time much-admired ambassador for Economics education and is a most engaging and innovative teacher.
[42] John Sloman, Dean Garrett, and Jon Guest (2021) *Economics* 11th Edition (December) (Pearson Publishing).
[43] An in-depth treatment of which also provides a useful basis for learning the cost and benefit distinctions that arise in Cost Benefit Analysis (see Chapter 10).

THE RETHINKING ECONOMICS PROJECT

Rethinking Economics[44] is a student-led charity that became the spearhead for student objections, in the UK and internationally, to mainstream Economics and its teaching after the 2007/8 crisis. Rethinking Economics paints a dismal picture of economics education:

> "Over the last 30 years, economics education has become increasingly narrow and detached from the real world. Lectures teach one perspective as if it is the only legitimate way to study the economy; seminars ask students to memorise and regurgitate academic theory; whilst exams award those able to solve abstract equations rather than engaging critically with the actual economy and real-world economic problems.
>
> Economics degrees are characterised by a lack of critical thinking, a lack of alternative perspectives, a lack of real-world application and a lack of ethical and political context."[45]

Rethinking Economics undoubtedly makes many telling criticisms of mainstream economics and economics teaching, and the authors of this book admit that they have seen some economics lecturers who have an unnerving ability to take the intrinsically exciting, relevant and fascinating subject of Economics and turn it into a dull, arid drilling introduction to intermediate maths and techniques. Teaching in many degrees has become overly led by empirically doubtful models and techniques for technique's sake, rather than by a critical approach to economics that engages with the most important real-world issues. The models can too often appear irrelevant, or even in stark contrast, to reality. But we also think the portrayal of economics teaching by Rethinking is far too sweeping. There are also very many economics courses and teachers who do regard students as 'candles to be lit' rather than 'bottles to be filled', and who are busy inspiring future generations of students. Teachers such as the late Peter Sinclair to whom this book is dedicated, and award-winning teachers such as Jon Guest, John Sloman and Wendy Carling, recognized for their engaging and insightful teaching and: Oh! Just so very many other inspirational teachers of Economics!

The book *The Econocracy: The perils of leaving economics to the experts* was authored by three prominent members of Rethinking Economics, Joe Earle,

---

[44] Rethinking Economics is available at https://www.rethinkeconomics.org/ (Accessed May 2021).

[45] Why Reform the Curriculum?, Rethinking Economics https://www.rethinkeconomics.org/get-involved/why-reform-the-curriculum (Accessed May 2021).

Cahal Moran and Zach Ward-Perkins.[46] It is a powerful critique, and, yes, a 'wake-up call'. It was welcomed by many high-profile economists, and so it begins with glowing praises from a series of respected economists. For example, Andy Haldane wrote the foreword, in which he also praises the CORE. *The Econocracy* was welcomed even by those who feel that 'We need reform in the way economics is taught, but not a revolution'.[47] However, The Econocracy is scathing about the CORE project:[48]

> "With CORE it remains the case that a narrow, fixed body of knowledge is handed down from one generation to the next, leaving little room for debate. This pedagogy is flawed because it fails to prepare students for living and working in a complex, diverse world in which knowledge is fluid, uncertain and contested."[49]

The authors of this book agree that the CORE project in its current form does too little to invite critical challenge and to represent the highly contested debates around what is currently the 'best' of economics. However, *The Econocracy* is incorrect to say that CORE represents a fixed body of knowledge handed down from generation to generation. In fact, CORE has actively embraced changes and advances in economics and does utilize some different perspectives, such as integrating insights from Austrian Economics and emphasizing incomplete knowledge and contracts, as in 'New Keynesian' macro theory.

> "Instead of seeing all economic activity through the lens of a single model of competitive markets with complete contracts, CORE has invited you to see the economy the way research economists see it, as a diverse combination of institutions and behaviours that is best studied by judiciously choosing among factually tested models."[50]

---

[46] Joe Earle, Cahal Moran and Zach Ward-Perkins (2017), *The Econocracy: The perils of leaving economics to the experts* (Manchester University Press).

[47] For example, Diane Coyle has both praised The Econocracy and heavily caveated its proposals. See Royal Economic Society April 2015 newsletter—A note from Diane Coyle and Simon Wren-Lewis https://www.res.org.uk/resources-page/april-2015-newsletter-a-note-from-diane-coyle-and-simon-wren-lewis.html.

[48] There is a similarly rather scathing critique of the CORE project by experienced economists that goes deeper into conceptual issues using criteria from The Econocracy. It is by Andrew Mearman, Danielle Guizzob and Sebastian Berger (2018) *Whither political economy? Evaluating the CORE Project as a Response to Calls for Change in Economics Teaching* Available at https://eprints.whiterose.ac.uk/131495/3/MEARMAN%20et%20al%20%5BFINAL%20EDIT%5D.pdf (Accessed September 2021).

[49] Ibid., p. 115.

[50] 'Looking forwards to economics after the CORE' at https://www.core-econ.org/the-economy/book/text/50-01-looking-forward.html.

Samuel Bowles distinguishes between two approaches to pluralism:

> "We should distinguish between two variants of pluralism. In one, pluralism by juxtaposition, differing approaches are contrasted, with students encouraged to see the study of economics as a kind of paradigm tournament. But pluralism can also be advanced by marshalling the insights of differing schools of thought and academic disciplines into a common paradigm. Call this pluralism by integration."[51]

And the CORE project does indeed accept the profound truth that all knowledge is ultimately provisional:

> "*The Economy* has been an introduction to what we consider is the best of what economists know at this time. Or, perhaps, we should say what we think we know. As has always been the case, economics is constantly changing."[52]

The Econocracy protests that:

> "Despite the positioning of CORE, we have demonstrated . . . that there are real and fundamental differences between our proposals for reform, and it is important that students, universities, policymakers and the public are aware of this."

Yes, there is a difference in approach: the CORE project seeks to introduce students to what its authors believe has been demonstrated to be the 'best of what economists know at this time' rather than to promote the more pluralistic, competing schools of thought approach advocated by Rethinking Economics and groups such as Promoting Economic Pluralism (PEP).[53] Alvin Birdi expressed it as, 'Rather than simply presenting a number of competing viewpoints . . . CORE has chosen to prioritize explanations that have some basis in evidence.'[54] The CORE project is saying that economics as a disciple has an authority of expertise to inform on some matters, and to say where knowledge is weak, rather than to be merely another voice in debate. *The Econocracy* is correct to say the CORE differs from their own proposals, proposals that many passionately believe are

---

[51] Samuel Bowles 'How to fix university economics courses: A syllabus that does not integrate the insights of other disciplines fails students', *Financial Times* (January 2018).

[52] Looking forward to economics after CORE https://www.core-econ.org/the-economy/book/text/50-01-looking-forward.html#looking-forward-to-economics-aftercore (Accessed September 2021).

[53] See promoting economic pluralism making space for diversity in economics, https://economicpluralism.org/ (Accessed April 2021).

[54] Alvin Birdie (2018) in Annika Zorn, Jeff Haywood, and Jean-Michel Glachant (eds), *CORE: bringing the economics curriculum online in higher education in the digital age. Moving academia online*, (Edward Elgar Publishing: Cheltenham, UK, Northampton, MA, USA).

part of a diversity of thought, but there is no deception. Of course, there are lively debates as to what and who represents 'expertise', but the 'correct' balance between expert discernment and plurality is something that reasonable people can disagree on.[55]

Most economists, including those who do not share all of the prescriptions for economics from Rethinking, do agree with *The Econocracy* that an uncritical drilling in models and techniques is merely training and not education. Yes, we agree there is now too much of this in too many undergraduate degrees. We may have let technique run ahead of economics issues in our teaching. Framing what a problem is, and the choice of the appropriate technique or model for a particular issue or problem does require critical judgment, combined with a good knowledge of the limitations of particular approaches. We have argued, as have members of the Government Economic Service,[56] that for practitioners a more pluralistic approach is useful. We argued in Chapter 3 that at the practical level, pluralism is useful for understanding model limitations, this includes using an alternative 'school of thought' to examine issues, or even to decide what are the issues, and for 'seeing inside the mind' of disparate stakeholders.

TOWARDS A MORE DIVERSE BODY OF ECONOMISTS

Just as an eclectic approach facilitates a deeper understanding of the nature of economics and a richer engagement with policy questions, a diversity of people also brings more creativity, new insights, and more productive team working. As Miatta Fahnbulleh describes in her interview for this book, we all have thought processes that we go through, in which we've been trained, often you're not even aware of it until you are challenged by someone who sees things from a different perspective.[57] This is in addition to the social capital and justice involved in having, for example, a civil service that 'looks like' the

---

[55] Of course, there could be an introductory textbook that covers all schools of thought with a blow-by-blow discernment, but the INET CORE *The Economy* is already dauntingly long, so perhaps the practical issue is not 'What do we include?' in an introduction to Economics but rather 'What do we leave out?'.

[56] See for example Thomas Bearpark, Andrew Heron, and Ben Glover (2017) 'Economics in government: more open, more diverse, more influential' https://quarterly.blog.gov.uk/2017/08/08/economics-in-government-more-open-more-diverse-more-influential/#comments (Accessed September 2021).

[57] In her interview for this book (see Video 14: In conversation with Miatta Fahnbulleh available at www.oup.com/he/pryce-ross1e).

country it serves. Increasing diversity, interdisciplinary working and plurality are explicit goals of the Government Economic Service.[58]

> "Diversity consists of both intellectual—or cognitive—,diversity, and diversity of identity or background. Often these are intertwined, and the absence of either presents significant risks for the quality of advice economists in the Civil Service are able to provide."[59]

Although it is far from unique in this respect, Economics has a diversity problem. To be both more precise and comprehensive, the discipline and its members have a lack of Equality, Diversity and Inclusion (EDI). These issues go back a long way in history (for example—see 'decolonization' below page 245), and the socio-economic structures and cultural norms that today lend them persistence can often be invisible or seen as 'natural' to those who are not disadvantaged by them. This is far from being only to do with active discrimination, but a full analysis would certainly require seeing that people have overlapping characteristics, and so they may experience discrimination in compounded and different ways. This is known as 'intersectionality'. Not only can individuals face discrimination, but they can experience complex and compound discrimination from a combination of elements of their social identity.[60] These include, among other things: gender, ethnicity, disability, age, sexuality, religion and class.

We do not attempt in this short chapter to cover the full range of diversities and their intricate interactions, and so we will focus here on gender, ethnicity, and socio-economic diversity, where the most prominent initiatives from bodies in UK Economics have been.[61]

As the Institute for Fiscal Studies observes:

> "Despite their important role in research and analysis that influences both corporate and public policy, economists are not very representative of society. This reflects unequal representation among those who study economics: women

---

[58] Bearpark, Thomas, Heron, Andrew, and Glover, Ben (2017), 'Economics in government: more open, more diverse, more influential' in *Civil Service Quarterly* (8th August). Available at: https://quarterly.blog.gov.uk/2017/08/08/economics-in-government-more-open-more-diverse-more-influential/ (Accessed December 2017).

[59] Ibid.

[60] See Athena Swan 'What do we mean by "intersectionality?"' https://www.advance-he.ac.uk/equality-charters/athena-swan-charter/FAQs/intersectionality

[61] The authors are aware that his book is very UK orientated, but then the book is primarily focussed on economics jobs in the UK, perhaps a later edition can find room to be more international!

and state school pupils are much less likely[62] to choose to study the subject at university, and previous IFS research[63] has shown that there are big differences between ethnic groups in their take-up of economics as well. Beyond the representativeness of the profession, the low take-up of economics by those from underrepresented groups has broader implications for inequalities in pay and social mobility in light of evidence that economics degrees offer some of the highest financial returns[64] of all subjects in the UK."[65]

CHANGING THE PUBLIC (MIS)PERCEPTION OF 'WHAT IS ECONOMICS?'

There is good evidence that a misperception of Economics may be putting some people off opting to study what is actually a vitally important and exciting subject. But first we will briefly look at a more speculative suggestion that it is not a misperception but rather an actual narrowness of approach in the discipline that had put off some potential economists. This obviously also follows on from our discussion of diversity of thought in the first part of this chapter. For example, completing the quote from John Kay, a professional practitioner economist with enormous 'ground knowledge of economics' (see page 75), that we looked at in Chapter 3. He speculates that part of the problem may be that academic economics had become dominated by an artificiality in the way its models are formulated and used:

"The knowledge that every problem has an answer, even and perhaps especially if that answer may be difficult to find, meets a deeply felt human need. For that reason, many people become obsessive about artificial worlds, such as computer games, in which they can see the connection between actions

[62] Advani, Arun, Griffith, Rachel, and Smith, Sarah (2019), 'Economics in the UK has a diversity problem that starts in schools and colleges'. VoxEU.org (15 October). Available at: https://voxeu.org/article/increasing-diversity-uk-economics.

[63] Advani, Arun, Sen, Sonkurt, and Warwick, Ross, (2020) 'Ethnic diversity in UK economics'. Institute for Fiscal Studies (26 October). Available at: https://ifs.org.uk/publications/15133.

[64] Britton, Jack, Dearden, Lorraine, van der Erve, Laura, and Waltmann, Ben (2020), 'The impact of undergraduate degrees on lifetime earnings'. Institute for Fiscal Studies (29th February). Available at: https://ifs.org.uk/publications/14729.

[65] Advani, Arun, Sen, Sonkurt, and Warwick, Ross (2021), 'A Level economics is a gateway to the economics profession'. Institute for Fiscal Studies (14 January). Available at: https://ifs.org.uk/publications/15261.

and outcomes. Many economists who pursue these approaches are similarly asocial. It is probably no accident that economics is by far the most male of the social sciences."[66]

You might mistake this for a suggestion that girls are not as good at mathematics as boys. Obviously, that is not the case![67] In fact, the share of women among maths undergraduates exceeds that in economics, and of course it is not what John Kay meant at all. He is merely noting that there is some evidence that economists tend to be less socially orientated than their peers[68] and that a higher proportion of boys than girls have an attraction to the artificially of computer games,[69] and so, perhaps a dominance of those attracted by such an approach, particularly in academia, may have put off others. That is, those of all genders who are attracted more by those social sciences that appear to directly focus on the problems people face in real-world issues.[70]

There are indeed branches of Economics that seem more like a 'wonk's[71] paradise' rather than attempts to solve the problems of the real-world. However, as we explore in this book, that is certainly not a fair representation of economics as a whole. That said, some leading economists do worry

---

[66] John Kay (2011), 'The map is not the territory: an essay on the state of economics' (available at https://www.johnkay.com/2011/10/04/the-map-is-not-the-territory-an-essay-on-the-state-of-economics/ (Accessed September 2021).

[67] See for example: Helen Ward (2018), Exclusive: Study shows girls' maths ability equal: educationalists to do more to challenge the gendering of Stem subjects' *Times Educational Supplement*.

[68] See for example Espín, Antonio and Correa, Manuel and Ruiz-Villaverde, Aberto, 'Economics Students: Self-Selected in Preferences and Indoctrinated in Beliefs' (2021). Available at SSRN: https://ssrn.com/abstract=3788857 or http://dx.doi.org/10.2139/ssrn.3788857 (Accessed September 2021).

[69] An American study found 'Boys are substantially more likely than girls to report access to a game console (91%, compared with 70% of girls) and to play games (84% of boys, compared with 59% of girls)'. https://www.pewresearch.org/internet/2015/08/06/chapter-3-video-games-are-key-elements-in-friendships-for-many-boys/.

[70] This echoes the Swedish econographer, Axel Leijonhufvud who as long ago as 1973 wrote an amusing anthropology allegory 'Life among the Econ'. He similarly suggested that economists are seen by many people outside the profession as working within remote and abstract worlds far away from the rest of humanity: 'The Econ tribe occupies a vast territory in the far North. Their land appears bleak and dismal to the outside, and travelling through it makes for rough sledding; but the Econ, through a long period of adaptation, have learned to wrest a living of sorts from it.' Leijonhufvud, A. (1973), 'Life among the Econ,' *Western Economic Journal*, 11(3), 327–337. For an 'update' on the allegory see Thomas Palley (2021) Life among the Econ: fifty years on Post-Keynesian Society Working Paper 2016.

[71] A person preoccupied with arcane details or procedures in a specialized field.

that the teaching of economics too often fails to inspire. Lord Stern, makes an important point:

> "I do think that examining the issues that brought us in to the subject, right from the beginning, at the same time as we learn the technique, is very important"[72]

We worry that the nature of much academic economics may perhaps be a turn-off for those who care about making the world a better place rather than focussing on technical virility if, and it's only a speculative if, women are more likely on average than men to care about the practical application of expertise to real-world policy, then this might help explain why women are better represented among economists outside of academia, and why the CORE hopes its explicitly issues-based approach might attract more women.

> "In the Treasury, 38 percent of economic staff are female; at the Bank of England, 32 percent of senior staff are female, along with 46 percent of their new graduate intake; at the Institute for Fiscal Studies, 40 percent of all researchers listed on their website in May 2021 were female, and of those employed purely by the IFS, 52 percent are female; at NIESR, 45 percent of researchers are female; across UK think tanks, 44 percent of researchers and 29 percent of senior researchers are female. These figures are impressive compared with academic economics, where only 26 percent of those working as economists are female and only 15 percent are professors"[73]

These percentages outside academia are only impressive when compared with academia, especially if we consider that three quarters of those in education as teachers in UK schools are women. It could also reflect the relatively poor treatment of women in universities. Sadly, there is evidence is that women academics in economics are treated less favourably than men.[74]

---

[72] In his interview for this book (see Video 19: In conversation with Lord Gus O'Donnell available at www.oup.com/he/pryce-ross1e).

[73] Victoria Bateman, Danula Kankanam Gamage, Erin Hengel and Xianyue Liu (2021), *the gender imbalance in UK economics: Royal Economic Society Women's Committee Silver Anniversary Report Royal Economic Society. The report marks 25 years since the establishment of the RES Women's Committee, which was set up to monitor and advance the representation of women in UK economics.* Available at https://www.res.org.uk/resources-page/the-gender-imbalance-in-uk-economics.html

[74] See Pryce, V. (2019) *Bias in higher education*, pp. 187–191 and 250–263 in *Women vs capitalism* (Hurst & Company London). Also, for a study of promotion and gender in US academia see Donna K. Ginther (2021)', Available at https://www.nber.org/reporter/2021number3/gender-race-and-academic-career-outcomes-does-economics-mirror-other-disciplines (Accessed October 2021).

"To an extent unimaginable in many other fields, economics seminars are hostile occasions for point-scoring and aggressive challenge. Junior women hardly say a word. Papers written by women are routinely held to higher standards and take longer to get published — in an academic world where publication is everything for career prospects. Peer review rewards peers, and they are mainly men. These phenomena are not unique to economics but the numbers say plainly that there is a particular problem here."[75]

Of course, as there is a preponderance of men in economics, numerically and morally it is men that should be doing most of the work to put 'their' house in order!

MISPERCEPTIONS OF ECONOMICS

Common misperceptions of what Economics is about may deter many people who could in fact become good economists. If you ask the general public about what economists do you will get a range of responses. A vast majority of these responses are likely to revolve around money, forecasting, and taxes, and some will confuse personal finance with economics.[76] Relatively few are likely to say much about topics which relate to other aspects of people's day-to-day living, such as studying people's behavioural responses or advising on and evaluating health, environmental or education policy, or the vast array of topics listed in Chapter One (see page 12). Claudia Goldin, professor of economics at Harvard University, says that to see this you need only play the 'Uber game'. *Take an Uber, tell the driver you're an economist, and nine times out of ten they will ask you to predict the economy or the stock market.*[77] And to quote Sarah Smith, co-Chair of Discover Economics:

"Ask a 15 to 17-year-old to describe an economist and they will tell you that he—because it's usually male—is a man in a grey suit spouting jargon and statistics. As a result, the subject lacks broad appeal. Discover Economics aimed to present a more diverse image of economics."[78]

---

[75] Diane Coyle (2017), 'Economics has a problem with women', The *Financial Times* (28 August 2017).

[76] Economics Network (2017 & 2019) 'ING-Economics network survey of public understanding of economics'. Available at: https://www.economicsnetwork.ac.uk/research/understanding-econ (Accessed September 2021).

[77] Quoted in Gemma Tetlow (2018), 'Where are all the female economists?' *Financial Times* (12 April Available at https://www.ft.com/content/0e5d27ba-2b61-11e8-9b4b-bc4b9f08f381 (Accessed September 2021).

[78] Quoted in Pupils 'Discover economics' with Apprentice-style challenges, University of Bristol News and Features (15 November 2018).

It is becoming clear that this persistent general perception of Economics as a 'male, pale and stale' narrow money-oriented discipline rather than being 'human-oriented' may drive many potential economists away from economics. In her interview for this book, the economist and diversity consultant Toju Anagboso describes how when she first became an economist she saw few Black economists and there was a general image of stuffy white men in suits working alone. Later in time, Toju saw how vital it had become to be able to work as an economist with people from different walks of life, backgrounds and disciplines.[79]

Raising the profile of the social and policy aspects of much of what economists actually do is one of the ways in which the prevailing perceptions of economics can be broadened. As we saw in Chapter 5, there are welcome initiatives to do this by encouraging economists to become better communicators on media and other platforms. Ultimately, economics is a tool that can be used to improve the world, but it is still too often misunderstood just as a means of instrumental self-enrichment.

A-LEVEL CHOICES AND ROLE MODELS

The common public misperception seems to be shared by school pupils thinking about which subjects they want to study at A-level and university. We noted above that the proportion of female undergraduates in economics is low. It is in fact lower than that for other technical subjects like mathematics, statistics, science or medical subjects, so the issue is not to do with the technicality of economics per se. In the work undertaken by Sarah Smith, a former chair of the Royal Economic Society Women's Committee, she found that schoolchildren's perceptions of an economist were typically of a well-paid male in a pin-striped suit, akin to the typical caricature of an accountant.[80] This suggests that the lack of women economist role models may be off-putting for many girls, and this is supported by research that finds that women role models play a key role in attracting students to economics and having women lecturers affects the retention of women students.[81]

---

[79] See her interview for the book: (Video 1: In conversation with Toju Anagboso available at www.oup.com/he/pryce-ross1e).

[80] To be fair, although the accountancy profession at senior levels is still predominately men, Accountancy may well have been doing better than Economics in attracting women students. See Zacharia, Chris (2019), 'Women in accountancy—are the numbers adding up?', London Connection (19 June, University of London). Available at: https://london.ac.uk/news-opinion/london-connection/feature/women-accountancy-adding-up.

[81] Porter, Catherine, and Danila Serra. 2020. 'Gender differences in the choice of major: The importance of female role models.' *American Economic Journal: Applied Economics*, 12 (3): 226–54.

In her interview for this book, Sinéad Boultwood, who is on a graduate scheme at Ofcom, describes how she now 'always wants to be an economist' having been inspired by the women role models at Ofcom such as: Dame Melanie Dawes, who joined Ofcom as an Executive Board Member and Chief Executive in March 2020; Dame Sharon White, the former Chief Executive of Ofcom and first Black person, and only the second woman, to become a Permanent Secretary at the Treasury; and also the 'marvellous' Dr Luisa Affuso, Chief Economist at Ofcom.[82]

Of course, the many factors that affect diversity begin well before A-level age, but the choice of an A-level in economics is correlated with choosing to do a degree in economics. Among current undergraduates, around 20–25 per cent of students with an economics A Level go on to study economics at degree level, compared with 0.6–1.5 per cent of those without A Level Economics. The differential take-up of A-Level subjects is a key factor in the supply pipeline for economists and these differences at A-Level for economics are striking.

"In the 2018/19 academic year, there were nearly 1.7 million UK-domiciled undergraduate students enrolled on their first degree in UK universities, with 2% of these studying economics overall. Among those studying economics, 69% held an Economics A Level, though only 7% of all undergraduates do so. But even this understates the importance of the A Level.

While more than 1 in 5 with an Economics A Level studied the subject at university, only 1 in 150 of those without an Economics A Level did so. Economics A Level is therefore hugely important as a gateway into the discipline, even though no UK university requires prospective students to have taken the qualification and there is no difference in university performance between those that have and haven't taken it after accounting for other student characteristics."[83]

INTERSECTIONALITY

We noted above that 'intersectionality' means two or more characteristics can overlap and combine to compound differences in outcomes. For example, in take up of Economics between private-school educated boys and state-school

[82] See her interview for this book: Video 5: In conversation with Sinéad Boultwood available at www.oup.com/he/pryce-ross1e.

[83] Advani, Arun, Sen, Sonkurt, and Warwick, Ross (2021), 'A Level economics is a gateway to the economics profession'. Institute for Fiscal Studies (14th January). Available at: https://ifs.org.uk/publications/15261.

educated girls, that is, socio-economic background[84] and gender. Each play a large part in determining the take-up of economics and together produce even bigger differences. Both boys and girls without an Economics A Level from state schools are much less likely to take up the subject at university, by around two-thirds in both cases, when compared with their private school counterparts, but girls are less likely to take economics at A Level and less likely to continue to undergraduate degrees even when they do take it. The socio-economic divide is not helped by the fact that, in 2017 for example, only 50 per cent of comprehensive schools offered Economics at A Level, by contrast with 77 per cent of independent schools and 83 per cent of grammar schools:

> "The importance of 'take-up' of A Level Economics for the representation of those from different backgrounds is stark. More than 7% of undergraduate boys from private schools were studying economics in 2018/19, compared with less than 1% of girls from state schools. This largely mirrors differences in the share of students that hold an A Level in economics across these groups, which varies from 25% for private school boys to less than 4% for state schoolgirls."[85]

If we look at gender and ethnicity (see below page 240), we see that only 8 per cent of academic posts with research and teaching duties were held by non-white women (compared with 17 per cent of non-white men) and at no point in the period 2012–18 was a Black woman professor of economics employed on an academic contract in the UK![86]

DID ECONOMICS LOSE ITS WAY?

Dame Rachel Griffith, former President of the Royal Economics Society, suggests that Economics teaching may have lost diversity and its reputation for making the world a better place over the decades, and this is what many

---

[84] As private schools charge substantial fees, this is often used as a proxy for socio-economic background.

[85] Advani, Arun, Sen, Sonkurt, and Warwick, Ross (2021), 'A Level economics is a gateway to the economics profession'. Institute for Fiscal Studies (14th January). Available at: https://ifs.org.uk/publications/15261.

[86] See, for example, Stefania Paredes (2021) 'How can we promote diversity in economics?' Exploring Economics at https://www.economicsobservatory.com/how-can-we-promote-diversity-in-economics (Accessed August 2021).

economists are now actively addressing. For example, the Discover Economics[87] initiative, led by the Royal Economic Society, was launched in 2019 to increase diversity and to encourage 15–17 year olds to see economics as an exciting force for good in the world:

"[Discover Economics] aims are to encourage a broad diversity of people to think about economics as a possible career choice. It comes from seeing that the types of people entering into studying undergraduate economics has really changed overtime. If I go back to when I was young . . . economics was something that a lot of kids from working class backgrounds and diverse backgrounds saw as an interesting thing to study because they saw it as an important way to change the world. A toolkit that they could learn to get to work in government, to work in campaigning organisations and charities and all sorts of different walks of life. Economics taught you a set of things that would help you make the world a better place and somehow, we seem to have lost that a bit, in the UK particularly.

Now what you see is that it's much more likely that boys from fee paying schools enter into economics than kids who are studying in state schools. We think that, from our investigating into why that might be, that it seems that an important reason is that economics is often not offered in state schools anymore. And when you talk to kids about what economics is and what opportunities it provides, there seems to be a real misconception about what economists actually do and what you learn in economics, with people thinking much too much that it's to do with financial markets and banking. Whereas, in fact, most economists work in the public sector, many work in charities, many work in jobs that are really about trying to make the world a better place and address issues like climate change or income inequality, many different topics like that, that really enthuse young people. Discover Economic is about trying to provide better information about what Economics is and what opportunities it opens up for you."[88]

Indeed, it would be very bad for the profession and for democracy if economics ever came to be seen as synonymous with elites making money while turning a blind eye to the problems of everyday people, and it would be very far from what economics is really about.

---

[87] See Discover Economics at https://www.discovereconomics.co.uk/ (Accessed September 2021).

[88] In her interview for this book (see Video 15: In conversation with Dame Rachel Griffiths available at www.oup.com/he/pryce-ross1e).

GENDER

The gender imbalance among economists is well documented. Currently, under a third of UK-domiciled economics undergraduates in the UK are women, even though, overall, well over half of all undergraduates are women. Osama Rahman—the Chief Analyst, Chief Scientific Adviser, and Director of Analysis Directorate at the Department for Education—provides leadership to over 300 analysts and scientists and has been leading a team seeking to boost the number of women among UK civil service economists:

> "My initial thinking was that for some reason female economists were out there but not applying to the Government Economic Service. It was only later I realised there was a problem with women not choosing to study economics."[89]

Figure 8.1 shows, from a recent study, *The gender imbalance in UK economics* by Dr Victoria Bateman et al.,[90] the percentages of UK domiciled men and women students for undergraduate and higher degrees. This under representation in turn contributes to an under representation of women among economists both in the GES[91] (in 2020 women made up around 35 per cent of the GES workforce falling to around 27 per cent at Senior Civil Service level)[92] and in academic departments (around 28 per cent falling to just 17 per cent at professor level).[93] Sadly, growth in women's representation in UK academia economics has stalled since 2012. Reassuringly, the problem of gender representation among UK economics students does not seem to be integral to economics as a subject but to the country where it is studied. It seems to be most pronounced

---

[89] Quoted by Gemma Tetlow (2018),'Where are all the female economists?: Few women reach senior positions—and the root of the problem lies in education' *Financial Times* (12 April).

[90] Victoria Bateman, Danula Kankanam Gamage, Xianyue Liu, and Erin Hengel (2021), *The Gender Imbalance in UK Economics: Royal Economic Society Women's Committee Silver Anniversary Report* (Royal Economic Society). The report marks 25 years since the establishment of the RES Women's Committee, which was set up to monitor and advance the representation of women in UK economics. Available at https://www.res.org.uk/resources-page/the-gender-imbalance-in-uk-economics.html (Accessed September 2021).

[91] To its credit, the GES was a leader in the profession by initiating its Gender in the GES (GiG) initiative in 2018:https://www.gov.uk/government/publications/women-in-economics/gender-in-the-ges-initiative-18-months-note.

[92] Government Economic Service (2020), 'Best Practice – further information' (30th July). Available at: https://www.gov.uk/government/publications/women-in-economics/best-practice-further-information (Accessed August 2021).

[93] Tenreyro, Silvana (2017), 'Royal Economic Society's report on the gender balance in UK Economics Departments and Research Institutes in 2016' (Royal Economic Society) (30 March). Available at: https://www.res.org.uk/uploads/assets/uploaded/8ea564d4-df92-42c9-8d9cf58d3d95f394.pdf.

FIGURE 8.1 UK domiciled economics students by gender

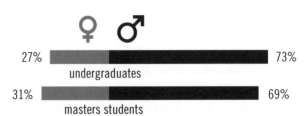

27% | undergraduates | 73%

31% | masters students | 69%

32% | Ph.D. students | 68%

Source: From graphic on page 3 with heading 'UK domiciled Economics students by gender' in Bateman, Kankanam Gamage, Hengel, and Liu, 'Royal Economic Society, Silver Anniversary Women's Committee Report: The Gender Imbalance in UK Economics' (Royal Economic Society and Higher Education Statistics Agency Ltd, July 2021). Available at https://www.res.org.uk/uploads/assets/575c241a-fbff-4ef4-97e7066fcb7597e0/women-in-academic-economics-report-FINAL.pdf (last accessed May 2022).

in English-speaking parts of the world, notably the UK, the US and Australia (see Figure 8.2). Despite notable initiatives, the UK still has a severe underrepresentation of women in its graduate supply pipeline, as Figure 8.1 shows.

"The economy affects everyone, and economists need to represent us all. If they don't, that's a major barrier to building a solid understanding of the economy. Across all students, from undergraduate to PhD, there are twice as many men studying economics as there are women in UK universities. While in many respects the discipline of economics has come a long way in the 21st century, the gender gap is clearly still real, persistent and in some ways getting worse."[94]

Although the under representation among students may not be as acute in some other countries (see Figure 8.2) better representation still does not necessarily translate into women holding leadership positions. Using data from the 2020 edition of the Women in Economics Index (WiE) to document imbalances in the profession's gender distribution, Philip Hanspach, Virginia Sondergeld, Jess Palka report that in the US and Europe:

"Economists hold key positions of power across society—in universities, offices of government, international institutions, and research think tanks. Economists also tend to be overwhelmingly male, with the gender gap increasing with seniority of position."[95]

[94] Ibid.
[95] Philip Hanspach, Virginia Sondergeld, and Jess Palka (2021), Few top positions in economics are held by women (Accessed June 2021).

FIGURE 8.2 Women are more under-represented in economics in some countries

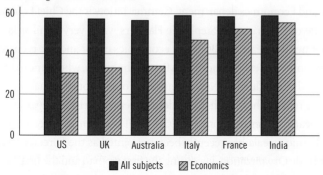

% of undergraduates who are female

US - 2011; Australia, France and India - 2015; Italy and UK - 2016. For France, figures for economics include those studying management. Figures for India relate to those studying for an MPhil.

Source: Featured in Tetlow, G. (2018) 'Where are all the female economists?' *Financial Times* [Online] 12th April. Available at: https://www.ft.com/content/0e5d27ba-2b61-11e8-9b4b-bc4b9f08f381 [Last accessed May 2022].

And although it would not pass any test for statistical significance, a top practitioner and a top academic economist have observed wryly that both the OECD and the EU now call on their member countries to put 'wellbeing' at the centre of their policy framework. The three countries that explicitly do this are Iceland, New Zealand and Scotland- all small countries led by women. So now it's time for a large country led by a man to follow suit![96]

To be sure, there certainly is a very impressive roll call of prominent women economists, too many to list here. Just the list of influential economist Dames is impressive, including: Dame Kate Barker, Dame Melanie Dawes, Dame Rachel Griffith, Dame DeAnne Julius, Dame Susan Owen, Dame Carol Propper, Dame Minouche Shafik and Dame Sharon White. Major economics-based organizations in the UK and around the world employ women in top positions. Just for example, and far from being exhaustive, in the UK at the time of writing, the Royal Economic Society has a woman president; the GES has two women as joint heads;[97] the CBI has women as their Director of Economics and Deputy Chief Economist; Mallika Ishwaran is Chief Economist for Shell International; Janet Henry is Global Chief Economist at HSBC; Bridget Rosewell was Chief Economic Adviser to the Greater London Authority from 2002 to 2012 and holds many

[96] Layard, Richard and O'Donnell, Gus (2020), 'Build back wellbeing and you will truly level everyone up'. *The Sunday Times*. (27 December). Available at: https://www.thetimes.co.uk/article/build-back-wellbeing-and-you-will-truly-level-everyone-up-8lkj806m9.

[97] *Sam Beckett and Clare Lombardelli. Vicky Pryce was the first woman Joint Head of the GES, with Dave Ramsden, and is, of course, a prominent economist.*

major posts such as on the National Infrastructure Commission; for the TUC, an organization headed by a woman, Kate Bell is the Head of the Rights, International, Social and Economics department. Gemma Tetlow is the Chief Economist for the Institute of Government, Stephanie Flanders was a very familiar face on television over her five years as BBC News economics editor and she is currently the head of Bloomberg News Economics. Miatta Fahnbulleh, who came to the UK as a refugee, heads the influential New Economics Foundation. Internationally we have seen: Janet Yellen as head of the US Federal Reserve; Christine Lagarde led the IMF for eight years; Laurence Boone is OECD Chief Economist; Nigerian economist Ngozi Okonjo-Iweala has recently been appointed as the Director General of the World Trade Organization, becoming the first woman and the first African national to lead the global trade body.

Women also figure among the most influential economists of the past: Elinor Ostrom (1933–2012) was the first women to be awarded the Nobel Prize in economics (2009);[98] Joan Robinson (1903–1983) was one of the most influential of Keynes' students and followers, she became the first female honorary fellow of King's College; Anna Schwartz (1915–2012) was the co-author of what was a very influential book *A Monetary History of the United States, 1867–1960* (for which Milton Friedman alone was awarded a Nobel prize in Economics); Harriet Martineau (1802–1876) published books on taxation and political economy in the 1830s and was nicknamed 'one of Adam Smith's daughters' for her interpretations of Smith; Mary Paley Marshall (1850–1944) was one of the first women permitted to study at Cambridge University: she wrote 'The Economics of Industry' with her husband, Alfred Marshall, who became one of the most influential economists in history. Millicent Fawcett (1847–1929) was a feminist campaigner for women's rights and a leading suffragette, she was the driving force behind the Fawcett Society[99] which continues her work today. 100 years ago, Sadie Tanner Mossell Alexander became the first Black woman in the US to earn a doctorate degree in economics, she championed civil rights for marginalized groups, especially black women, helping to create a path for today's black economists, lawyers, and policy practitioners.

The contribution of women economists is clearly impressive even if often overlooked, but, overall, while economists hold positions of power across society in universities, offices of government, international institutions, and research think tanks, they tend to be overwhelmingly men. And the gender gap between men and women widens with seniority of position.

---

[98] Since then Esther Duflo has also received this honour, in 2019.
[99] https://www.fawcettsociety.org.uk/

ACTION FOR DIVERSITY

The poor gender diversity in economics is due to a variety of factors, and we need a better understanding of these to focus efforts to rebalance (see below). Vicky Pryce, in her book, *Women vs Capitalism*[100] undertakes a detailed analysis of the reasons why women do not proportionately enter the top echelons of many professions, including restrictions on the range of feasible opportunities and the biases inherent in recruitment practices, conscious and unconscious, where people tend to like and be impressed by people who are like themselves. Action can't wait until we have a complete understanding: we have good enough evidence to do more now.

ACTIONS FOR UNIVERSITIES

For universities a useful list of seven practical ways to make 'Economics for All' came from a 'Women in Economics' workshop at Warwick University, they were summarized as follows but it is well worth reading the whole report.

"We explain how departments of Economics can start with 7 Action Points to increase inclusivity and female students' satisfaction with the subject:

1. Reshape the image of Economics
2. A curriculum that reflects 'What Economists Really Do'
3. Be Proactive with role models
4. Practice inclusivity in non-academic activities
5. Diversify the sense of belonging
6. Create spaces for women
7. Stop focusing on women!

Points 1 and 2 focus on how to change the perception that students (but also the general public) may have of Economics as a discipline i.e. focus on money, banking and being a men's club. Some may also think of Economics as theoretical and abstract without immediate application to the 'real world'. Points 3, 4 and 5 consider changes to current practices in all aspects of the academic life that may be gender biased. Point 6 and 7 complement each other. The former looks at women specific activities while the latter explains why it is important that male students get involved too and become diversity allies."[101]

---

[100] V. Pryce (2019), *Women vs Capitalism* (C. Hurst & Co. (London) Ltd).
[101] Stefania Paredes Fuentes ed. (2020), Some ideas from the women in economics student workshop Economics for All—7 Action Points to make Economics more inclusive. Available at https://warwick.ac.uk/fac/soc/economics/news/2020/2/women_in_economics_workshop_at_warwick/economics_for_all.pdf (Accessed August 2021).

If you are still at university, you could encourage your university department to adopt these action points.[102] As the authors point out, the action points can also be used to encourage and support ethnic diversity (see below page 240), and it shouldn't be left only to the minorities themselves to press for them!

ACTIONS FOR THE WORKPLACE

More generally, the Behavioural Insights Team, which was inspired by behavioural economics, has worked with the Government Equalities Office to produce a concise guide of evidence-based actions for organizations to take for greater equality (see Figure 8.3).[103]

Despite there being many prominent women economists in public life, we have seen that this has not yet changed the public face of economics and economists for many people. Resolving this problem will involve increasing both the presence of and visibility of women economists. It requires attention to the ways that recruitment and promotion processes work wherever economists are employed. One such initiative is the Gender in GES initiative (GiG),[104] which promotes gender diversity in economics and aims to increase female participation in economics in government and academia. It also provides some great interviews with women economists in the GES[105] that should reassure about a women-friendly working environment. This was echoed by a 2019 GES conference 'Women in Economics' organized in partnership with the Nuffield Foundation.

> "Discussion on inequalities are shaping today's economic debate. OECD evidence is beginning to suggest that there are trade-offs and that inequality could be undermining growth although the relationship is complex. The Gini Coefficient isn't enough to understand the winners and losers from prosperity

---

[102] More suggestions can be found at 'Best practices for economists: Building a more diverse, inclusive, and productive profession'. Available at https://www.aeaweb.org/resources/best-practices (Accessed September 2021).

[103] Behavioural Insights Team (2021), Available at https://www.bi.team/wp-content/uploads/2021/07/BIT_How_to_improve_gender_equality_report.pdf (Accessed September 2021).

[104] Government Economic Service (2020), 'Gender in the GES (GiG) Initiative 18 Months Note' (30 July). Available at: https://www.gov.uk/government/publications/women-in-economics/gender-in-the-ges-initiative-18-months-note (Accessed September 2021).

[105] Government Economic Service (2020), 'Meet the GES GiG committee and our economists' (30 July). Available at: https://www.gov.uk/government/publications/women-in-economics/more-information-on-the-ges-gig-committee (Accessed August 2021).

FIGURE 8.3 Actions for organization to take for greater diversity

Area of focus	▶ Effective actions	❚❚ Promising actions	⇅ Mixed evidence
06 **Leadership and accountability**	Set internal targets for gender, representation and equality Appoint diversity leads and/or diversity taskforces		Diversity statements Diverse selection panels
08 **Hiring and selection**	Offer flexible working by default in job adverts Use structured interviews for recruitment and promotions Use skill-based assessment tasks in recruitment Make expectations around salaries and negotiation clear	Use targeted referrals Remove biased language from job adverts Recruit returners Anonymise CVs Make it possible to list experience In terms of years not dates in CVs Include more women in shortlists for recruitment and promotions Make decisions about applicants in batches	
12 **Talent management, learning and development**	Increase transparency to promotion, pay and reward processes	Request 'advice' for actionable ways to improve instead of 'feedback' on post performance Offer memoring and sponsorship Offer networking programmes	Performance self-assessments Unconscious bias trainning Diversity training Leadership development training
18 **Workplace flexibility**	Share local support for parental leave and flexible working	Improve workplace flexibility for men and women Encourage the uptake of Shared parental Leave	

Source: Behavioural Insights Team (2021), 'How to improve gender equality in the workplace: Evidence-based actions for employers, p. 1. Available at: https://www.bi.team/wp-content/uploads/2021/07/BIT_How_to_improve_gender_equality_report.pdf (accessed September 2021).

Image reproduced with permission of the Behavioural Insights Team from the report 'How to improve gender equality in the workplace: Evidence-based actions for employers' © Behavioural Insights Ltd 2021. Not to be reproduced, copied, distributed or published without the permission of Behavioural Insights Ltd. It is acknowledged that this report was funded by the UK Government Equalities Office.

or growth enhancing policies. We need to look beneath the surface and better understand the drivers that create inequalities in our societies and economies. A potential big win here is to make the teaching and practice of economics more pluralist in principle—bring in other disciplines, critique our models, explain and communicate to the wider public how and why inequality matters."[106]

The Royal Economic Society's (RES) Women's Committee has also done much to highlight the issue within UK Economics Departments and has launched a mentoring scheme for female economists to help them progress in their careers,[107] and of course Discover Economics does much to dispel narrow non-inclusive impressions of economics.[108]

Despite boasting such eminent women economists, economics, in common with all other occupations, also still has a gender pay gap[109] to address. Economics is at least near the top of the UK list of subjects as measured ten years after graduation in terms of female median earnings as a percentage of male median salaries. Economics tops that league for the tax year 16/17 at 89 per cent of male earnings. Economics also tops the list for female upper quartile earnings in both 16/17 and 17/18 tax years.[110] But just because it does well on pay differentials when compared to other subjects, this does not relieve the economics profession of the need to do better. It is pleasing that initiatives to make economics a more 'woman friendly' profession, such as by the GES, RES and Discover Economics as described in this chapter, have been welcomed by the profession, which still has a long way to go in this respect.

ETHNICITY AND ECONOMICS

Some of the statistics on ethnicity representation appear encouraging. Overall, ethnic diversity among economists in academia increased from 19 per cent in 2012/13 to 24 per cent in 2018/19. This is a higher percentage than for

---

[106] Government Economic Service (2019), 'Women in Economics' (2 January). Available at: https://www.gov.uk/government/publications/women-in-economics (Accessed September 2021).

[107] Royal Economic Society (2021) 'Women's Committee'. Available at: https://www.res.org .uk/about/our-structure/women-s-committee.html (Accessed August 2021).

[108] For example in the video interviews that feature on their website at https://www .discovereconomics.co.uk/videos (Accessed May 2021).

[109] The gap between men's and women's median earnings across the jobs within an occupation.

[110] These statistics have been derived from https://www.gov.uk/government/collections/ statistics-higher-education-graduate-employment-and-earnings.

all UK academia at 17 per cent in 2018–19, and higher than for the relevant UK population at 13 per cent among individuals aged 25–64 in 2011.[111] The problem of under participation among women appears greater than that for black and ethnic minority groups, at least on the surface. Non-white students account for 37 per cent of undergraduates in the UK according to a recent report.[112] Again, this is much higher than the proportion of these groups in the UK population, which was around 13 per cent. It is also higher than in STEM subjects.[113] unlike the case for women. However, as in the case of female under-representation, a large proportion of students from ethnic groups studying economics come from private schools having previously studied A-level economics.

These statistics fail to highlight a more granular problem, which is that the high representation of some groups (notably Indian and East Asian) is in contrast to the under-representation of both some non-white and white groups. It is not simply a black and white matter. Working class British whites are very under-represented in universities. As the Office for Students Director for Fair Access and Participation notes:

> "the rate of progression into higher education for white British students who are eligible for free school meals is only 16 per cent. This compares with rates of 47 to 73 per cent for Asian students on free school meals and 32 to 59 per cent for black students in this category."[114]

So, the diversity problem associated with ethnicity is specific to certain groups, mainly Black but also Bangladeshi and Pakistani. Also, non-white economists are much less likely to work at the prestigious, research-intensive Russell Group universities, compared with a 50 per cent share of white academic economists. Less than 30 per cent of Pakistani and Bangladeshi academic economists and less than 20 per cent black academic economists work in a Russell Group university. At higher levels it is primarily black individuals that are most

[111] Advani, Arun, Sen, Sonkurt, and Warwick, Ross, (2020) 'Ethnic diversity in UK economics'. Institute for Fiscal Studies (26th October). Available at: https://ifs.org.uk/publications/15133.

[112] Royal Economic Society (2020). 'Ethnicity report sheds new light on diversity of UK academic economists' (26th October). Available at: https://www.res.org.uk/resources-page/ethnicity-report-sheds-new-light-on-diversity-of-uk-academic-economists.html.

[113] Science, technology, engineering, and mathematics.

[114] *Chris Millward (2021) White students who are left behind: the importance of place Office for Students.* Available at https://www.officeforstudents.org.uk/news-blog-and-events/blog/white-students-who-are-left-behind-the-importance-of-place/ (Accessed September 2021).

under-represented, with this grouping being 64 per cent less likely to work in elite Russell Group institutions. Ethnic minority students' chance of success in the initial GES fast stream programme was 8 per cent compared to 22 per cent for white applicants in 2018.[115] Economics is fortunate to now have *The Black Economists Network* (T-BEN),[116] founded and led by Felicia Odamtten.[117] T-BEN is dedicated to providing a platform through which professionals and students of Black African and Caribbean descent in economics can connect, collaborate, share ideas and support each other. T-BEN also seeks to challenge the lack of diversity within economics-related fields by bringing together and raising the profile of Black people in economics working alongside other organizations on their diversity strategies.

WHY DOES DIVERSITY MATTER?

The desire to increase diversity is about more than its obvious altruism, justice, and social capital aspects, it's also about performance. Even the most energetic pragmatically eclectic approach by an individual is not likely to match the performance of a more diverse team of economists. The creativity and resource that needs to be drawn upon is the diversity across individuals rather than relying only on the pluralism of individual intellects. Here economics has a problem as it does not yet contain the diversity of people and structures within the profession that would ensure representation, social justice, or even some-times- good economics. As the GES puts it:

> "The work of economists in Government touches upon all aspects of life—from living standards and prosperity, an individual's consumption choice to business growth and global trends spanning countries. This is why it is essential that the economists who provide advice for evidence-based policy making are representative of the society that the government serves. Diversity in our backgrounds leads to diversity of perspective with better approaches and more informed decisions."[118]

[115] *BAME economists are under-represented in UK Universities (2020)*. Available at https://diversityuk.org/bame-economists-under-represented-in-uk-universities/ (Accessed September 2021).

[116] The Black Economists Network https://www.tben.co.uk/ (Accessed July 2021).

[117] Meet our Founder T-BEN https://www.tben.co.uk/the-team (Accessed July 2021).

[118] Government Economic Service (2019), 'Women in Economics' (2 January). Available at: https://www.res.org.uk/about/our-structure/women-s-committee.html.

Diversity matters not only for obvious social reasons, but because we know that it is correlated with greater success in business[119] and policy. In particular with more innovation and better decision-making resulting from less 'group-think' and more attention to relevant evidence:[120]

> "Our social knowledge and lived experiences shape our perspectives . . . they also help to shape our research interests. Demographic characteristics such as gender, country of origin or geographical location affect economists' views on contemporary policy issues and the type of research questions asked.
>
> Diversity can help to avoid problems in how we interpret and engage with knowledge in economics. Diverse teams tend to be more objective as they are forced to confront different ways of thinking. If policy-makers are advised by a group of economists sharing common characteristics (such as gender, age and ethnicity), they may not fully understand how diverse groups of people may be affected by the recommended policies, and may fail to rec-ognise or understand how the cost of policies are likely to affect those from groups with different characteristics, or how these groups experience these consequences."[121]

This is a theme that Professor Diane Coyle touches upon in her interview for the book[122]

We noted in Chapter 4 and Chapter 7 the importance of being able to work in a team and the discussion above suggests that teams will work better if di-verse. Diversity is not only a democratic and moral objective- it is a smart one for better performance too!

---

[119] See V. Hunt, D. Layton, and S. Prince (2015), *Diversity Matters,* McKinsey & Company at https://www.mckinsey.com/~/media/mckinsey/business%20functions/organization/our %20insights/why%20diversity%20matters/diversity%20matters.pdf (Accessed September 2021) and Erik Larson (2017), 'New Research: Diversity + Inclusion = Better Decision Making At Work Forbes' https://www.forbes.com/sites/eriklarson/2017/09/21/new-research-diversity-inclusion-better-decision-making-at-work/?sh=7701b0dd4cbf.

[120] Sarah E. Gaither, Evan P. Apfelbaum, Hannah J. Birnbaum, Laura G. Babbitt, and Samuel R. Sommers (2018) 'Mere membership in racially diverse groups reduces conformity' in *Social Psychology and Personality Science,* vol. 9, no. 4 (2018): pp. 402–410.

[121] Stefania Paredes (2021), 'How can we promote diversity in economics? Exploring Econom-ics at https://www.economicsobservatory.com/how-can-we-promote-diversity-in-economics (Accessed August 2021).

[122] See Video 9: In conversation with Diane Coyle CBE available at available at www.oup.com/ he/pryce-ross1e).

WHAT CAN BE DONE TO CREATE A MORE DIVERSE SUPPLY OF ECONOMISTS?

In addition to making economics a welcoming profession for all imbalances can be addressed by improving the 'pipeline' of applicants into universities and jobs.[123] This is where outreach and work with schools, and the perception of economics, becomes most important. For example, as we noted, around half of the state schools within the UK do not offer Economics at A Level while upwards of three-quarters of independent and grammar schools do offer it. Hence, the exposure to economics within the 16–18 age group tends to be unduly concentrated in male and privately educated groups.

DISCOVER ECONOMICS AND APPRENTICESHIP SCHEMES

These issues are the reasons behind UK economists' *Discover Economics* campaign, with the aim of increasing the appeal of economics to a more diverse population of young people thinking about subject choices.[124] *Discover Economics* runs a website and events for schools to give students a taste of the real work that economists do in areas such as the environment or health:

> "Our strategic goals are the following:
> 1. Communicate what economics is and what economists actually do to 15–17 year olds from underrepresented groups
> 2. Amplify the voices of economists and economics students from underrepresented groups in order to provide role models for potential economics students
> 3. Get economics on the national curriculum for all students
>
> The future of UK economics is looking predominantly male and disproportionately privately educated. This column introduces #DiscoverEconomics—a campaign to increase diversity in economics led by the Royal Economic Society and with the support of a wide range of institutions involved in economic research, communication and policymaking, including the Bank of England, the Government Economic Service, the Society of Professional Economists and

---

[123] On the inadequacy of a pipeline for women into economics.
[124] https://www.discovereconomics.co.uk/.

many leading research institutions. The campaign aims to attract more women, ethnic minority students, and students from state schools and colleges to study the subject at university."[125]

The Discover Economics campaign targets 15–17-year-olds who are making choices about what post-16 qualifications to take and what subjects to study at university. It seeks to transform perceptions of economics among students, particularly those attending schools that don't provide it as a subject, and seeks to raise the profile of a more diverse set of economists and expose students to role models already working in the subject.

The Government Economic Service (GES) also introduced a well-received apprenticeship scheme to attract students from a wide range of backgrounds who might otherwise not even think of going to university. The Bank of England is actively promoting diversity and inclusion, and many other employers are beginning to think about new ways to recruit—for example, targeting internship opportunities at under-represented groups, and offering application advice sessions to encourage students from non-traditional backgrounds to apply.

DOES ECONOMICS NEED TO BE DECOLONIZED?

There has recently been a strong flurry of activity within universities aiming to 'decolonise' the taught curriculum across all subjects. Students around the world have agitated for change, initially in colonial universities such as the University of Cape Town, where movements such as 'Rhodes Must Fall' originated. These movements are now very widespread, for example, the 'Why is My Curriculum White' international campaign. Many universities have initiated processes of curriculum decolonization, particularly following the Black Lives Matter protests in 2020.

Colonialism was a process of economic and political expansion and subjugation, supported by reinforcing scientific and cultural ideas disseminated by universities. Indeed, some universities (e.g. Stellenbosch in South Africa, Harvard in the US) were founded in colonies with the purpose of teaching colonized populations supposedly 'universal' ideas that were deemed superior to local and indigenous ideas. Others were set up to support the training of

---

[125] Advani, Arun, Griffith, Rachel, and Smith, Sarah (2019), 'Economics in the UK has a diversity problem that starts in schools and colleges'. VoxEU.org (15 October). Available at: https://voxeu.org/article/increasing-diversity-uk-economics.

colonial administrators or missionaries (such as the East India College where economist Thomas Malthus worked).

The impact of colonial thought is still evident. In economics, for example, it has often been the case that certain benchmark 'models' of the economy produced in Western universities are applied rather indiscriminately to all countries and periods—as was argued by Miatta Fahnbulleh above, regarding Africa (page 223). An example of where this is problematic is the application of formal wage labour models to economies where much of the labour force is employed in informal arrangements. Locally produced knowledge (for example about labour force arrangements) which may have emerged from communities or educational institutions in the Global South may thus be excluded from the curriculum of universities in the Global North. These universal forms of knowledge are typically validated through high-status academic journals and books that are almost invariably published in a handful of countries where the authors are drawn from academics in institutions that are not themselves very diverse or representative (see above in this chapter).

Unwinding and dismantling the inheritance of colonial influence on economics will be a long and arduous task because the complex ways in which colonial practices are embedded in universities are not always obvious or well-understood. One-way students can be alert to this is to be critical of what you learn, and to always question and test assumptions and applicability. That is not just decolonial practice, it is also good academic practice!

As we have seen, many economics departments are not very diverse, while part of the aim of decolonization is to provide learning opportunities to those who have been historically disadvantaged by colonialism. Part of the solution will also be to diversify faculty so that those who produce and validate knowledge are drawn from a wider reference for diversity. The knowledge we produce and teach will need opening up to influences and ideas from other communities and parts of the world. This is not simply a matter of diversifying reading lists, though that is an important aspect of it, it also involves more plurality in economics teaching so that a wider range of ideas is encountered. Our teaching and assessment methods will need to become more participatory so that the student body (and perhaps the wider community) helps to co-produce the curriculum and the knowledge that is valued in our institutions. Our teaching methods will have to be based on learning as an active process involving critical thought, not only the learning of received wisdom. Finally, all these processes will need to result in some improvements to racial and social justice in society at large, or else decolonization becomes meaningless and inward-looking.

Work is taking place to think through the implications of decolonizing economics. The *Decolonising and Diversifying Economics* (D-Econ) group[126] and the *Economics Network* have resources on their websites that explore decoloniality with suggestions of what might be done about it.

There are also useful examples of change from within the mainstream of economics too. One is the economics of Elinor Ostrom, the first female winner of the Economics Nobel Prize. Ostrom spent much of her time as an economist studying the value of local knowledge in successfully managing, for example, environments such as fishing resources. Another example is the work of economist Lisa Cook who has worked on the neglected importance of Black innovators in economic history.

Eclectic approaches to economics are another effective method of ensuring that you remain open to the demands of the context you are studying, and so don't try to make the world look like the economic model you have spent so much time learning. Of course, models are useful abstractions not reality, but one aspect of the art of economics is knowing where to stop with one's assumptions and 'over sophistication'. For example, using a competitive model of the labour market in which supply equates with demand may not be the best starting point to examine an economy such as that of, say, South Africa where there is persistent mass unemployment. Using macroeconomic models of the economy where no individual has any credit constraints and can always borrow against future earnings is probably also not a good starting point.

Having recourse to different approaches and methods can help with giving you alternative ways of approaching diverse contexts. As we have already discussed, one example of a mainstream teaching approach that has encouraged this is the CORE project.

CONCLUSION

Economics is a much wider ranging subject than is commonly appreciated, even by many students of economics. Despite appearances in many courses, economics is defined by its scope not by its techniques (see Chapter 1). It is also a subject that is improved through diversity in thought, culture and

---

[126] This group can be followed on Twitter as @DivDecEcon.

representation. There is still a long way to go, but there are exciting initiatives that provide hope for improvement.

SUMMARY

- Learning a lot of powerful analytical techniques is necessary to become an economist, but you are not really an economist until you also understand the limitations of those techniques.
- Some economist jobs are highly specialized, but economists generally benefit from a rounded approach to economics.
- Practising answering everyday questions using economics can be good preparation for a career in policy economics.
- There has been growing support for greater pluralism in Economics, but not all economists think pluralism by schools of thought is the right approach. However, most do seem to agree that greater eclecticism, including interdisciplinarity, is desirable.
- Diversity of thought means at least eclecticism, but it also comes from the diversity of professionals and being welcoming to a more diverse body of people.
- The formation of good policies often requires diversity, rounded eclectic knowledge, and an acute awareness of the practicalities of operational delivery.
- Diversity in teams generally improves their performance.

As a profession, economics is making genuine efforts to improve its diversity, but has a way to go yet.

QUESTIONS

1. Road congestion is often approached as an 'externality' but explain how a 'pro-motorist' lobbyist could put it down to diminishing returns caused by a lack of investment. What does this tell you about how perspective can frame a problem?

2. What are the arguments for and against pluralism vs eclecticism? Why would this debate matter more to an academic than a practitioner?

3. Why do the National Income Accounts fail to capture the full economic contribution of women, and what could be done about this?

4. What could explain why the Government Economic Service is predominantly men whereas the Government Social Researchers (GSR) service is predominantly women?

5. How many of the actions suggested in this chapter for improving diversity take place at your university/workplace?

6. Why is it important that white middle class men are also champions of diversity?

EXERCISES

1. Contrast how well Austrian and Neoclassical Economics capture the strengths and weaknesses of a market economy. To what extent do they complement or contradict each other?

2. Ask some non-economists about their impressions of what the typical economist looks like and does. How well does this impression match the reality?

3. Assess how eclectic and diverse your own experience of economics has been.

4. Design an action plan for making your university's economics department/workplace more diverse.

FIND OUT MORE

The need to consider operational delivery: For a wonderfully insightful and salutary exploration of failures of governments, usually for practical and human reasons rather than errors of high theory, see *The Blunders of Our Governments* (2013) by Anthony King and Ivor Crewe (Oneworld Publications).

PLURALIST PERSPECTIVES

Exploring Economics, a team dedicated to transforming economics towards pluralism: https://www.exploring-economics.org/en/.

Student campaigns for pluralism: Earle, Joe, Moran, Cahal, and War-Perkins, Zach, (2016) *The Econocracy: The Perils of Leaving Economics to the Experts* (Manchester Capitalism): the book came out of a student-led organization, 'Rethinking Economics'. The book is a detailed examination and critique of the focus of modern economics and of how the subject is currently taught. You don't have to agree with every element of its critique to agree it sends a powerful challenge to economists and so was generally welcomed by the profession. It has a foreword by Andy Haldane and was praised by many other prominent economists, even by those who disagree with central parts of the argument, such as Diane Coyle and macroeconomist Simon Wren-Lewis, who summarize their caveats to the call for a 'pluralist revolution' in the Royal Economic Society April 2015 newsletter—*A note from Diane Coyle and Simon Wren-Lewis* https://www.res.org.uk/resources-page/april-2015-newsletter-a-note-from-diane-coyle-and-simon-wren-lewis.html

The CORE project: see https://www.core-econ.org/

DIVERSITY

Discover Economics: http://www.discovereconomics.ac.uk/

Gender in the GES (GiG) project: https://www.gov.uk/government/publications/women-in-economics

Women in Economics: https://cepr.org/content/women-economics

Vicky Pryce (2019), *Women VS Capitalism* (C. Hurst & Co Ltd).

The Black Economists Network: https://www.tben.co.uk/.

Promoting diversity in economics: https://www.economicsobservatory.com/how-can-we-promote-diversity-in-economics.

Royal Economics Society (2020) *Ethnicity report sheds new light on diversity of UK academic economists,* (26 October). Available at: https://www.res.org.uk/resources-page/ethnicity-report-sheds-new-light-on-diversity-of-uk-academic-economists.html [Last accessed May 2022].

DECOLONIZING THE CURRICULUM

Decolonising the Economics Curriculum (2021) The Economics Network (26th July), Available at: https://economicsnetwork.ac.uk/themes/decolonisation [Last accessed May 2022].

PART THREE

·····•••••·····

Planning for the future

CHAPTER 9

Applying for and passing interviews for economist posts

· · · · ●●●●●● · · ·

INTRODUCTION

This chapter covers the process of applying for posts and how to approach interviews. It describes the most common errors when filling-in application pro-forma and gives suggestions for 'standing-out' from the crowd in a positive way. Advice is given on how to approach job interviews and guidance on 'What to do and what not to do' at interviews. It ends with reports from actual job interviews at a variety of organizations to give you a flavour of actual interview processes.

Obviously, the questions you can expect and the processes you will be expected to pass through as part of a job application will depend a lot on the type of job you apply for, the employer, and the role. As you are likely to be applying for several types of economist jobs, it is worth looking at some of the common requirements and questions candidates have actually been asked and the processes they have been required to pass. So, we list some of these in this chapter.

To give yourself the best chance of securing a job you should do some research on the organizations to which you apply. You are likely to need to tailor your application form, a CV if requested, and your interview responses to that organization. The best jobs will have high standards and will look for knowledge and skills specific to their roles. This means you will have to balance 'putting all your eggs in one basket' with not spreading yourself too thin and wasting time on a mass of weak applications that are bound to fail. Sometimes you can use the same examples for multiple application forms but be careful with your cutting and pasting. If you have a 'life-long ambition to work for PWC' then why tell KPMG!

ADVICE FOR JOB HUNTING

Before you begin the application process, there are some general tips to help you succeed regardless of the industry or organization you would like to work in:

- *Start thinking about your desired career as early as you can.* The best way into many organizations is through an internship, but just focussing on a particular career means you will be alert to people and news connected with the sector and potential employers.

- *Be realistic.* Do not apply to investment banks if you have only three Bs at A-level; you will be wasting the time you could've spent on more realistic possibilities.

- *Research your chosen sector(s).* You may find contacts through your family, friends, and network, and university careers service are often excellent in pointing you in the right direction to learn more, such as from online sources.

- *Don't be disappointed if you don't succeed on the first attempt.* When you are applying to UK internships and graduate schemes you are competing with the best students from around the globe. Getting rejected is part of the normal process for the majority. Sustain your motivation and give every application your best effort. Your experience may well be 'No, No, No, No, No, No, Yes'. If you'd given-up on the sixth 'No' you'd have never reached the 'Yes' that wipes all the Noes away, although they may well have been useful development experience.

- *Be persistent.* Applying to jobs while studying towards a degree can be very difficult, especially when your job applications don't appear to be going anywhere. If you meet the minimum requirements and do your research you will get an interview eventually, so keep going.

- *Try to enjoy it.* Interviews and assessment centres can be nerve-racking and daunting prospects. But the assessors have usually been briefed to be friendly and to try and put you at ease, and to expect some nervousness in candidates. To make these experiences less stressful and rewarding, try to see each interview and assessment centre as an opportunity to learn about yourself and the people that work there. See also the 'arousal-performance' curve below page 269.

- *If you have a disability* you cannot lawfully be discriminated against, but it is also worth checking if the employer is a member of the 'Disability Confident Scheme'. Over 18,000 organizations are in the scheme and Disability Confident organizations play a leading role in changing attitudes. They're changing behaviour and cultures in their own businesses, networks and communities, and reaping the benefits of inclusive recruitment practices (see https://disabilityconfident.campaign.gov.uk/).

COMPONENTS OF YOUR APPLICATION

CURRICULUM VITAE (CV)

Sometimes recruiters specifically ask that CVs are not sent, but it is always useful to keep an up-to-date CV in case you suddenly need one to seize an opportunity against a tight deadline. Although, unless you have literally left it to the last moment, it is important to take some time to adapt your basic CV to the specific employer and the job offered. A CV should highlight your strong features and why your knowledge and skills particularly match the job requirements.

Here is an example of a standard CV template with annotations.

NAME AND CONTACT DETAILS

A PERSONAL STATEMENT

This should highlight your best work-related aspects in a concise and compelling way. For general job search it should describe the sort of posts you are looking for, but for a particular job it should be targeted to the advertised job specification and requirements. Job application packs will usually lay out in detail what the recruiter is looking for in candidates, this should guide how you tailor your CV. For example, a header statement for a CV might look like:

> A recent 2.1 Honours graduate in economics, with several first-class grades, placement experience and strong references. A proven team player keen to apply her excellent communication and data analysis skills, and to develop in challenging roles. Entry to a demanding and rewarding career in PWC, a world-class professional services provider, would be an ideal opportunity.

In short, you are expected to 'sell' yourself, but don't go over the top: 'Future Nobel Prize Winner' would not go down well. If you have a commendation from someone who will impress an employer then that can be a good CV topper too.

EDUCATION

When started and finished. Your degree and grade (or expected) University/College

Briefly describe the most relevant modules to the job. This might be the subject matter of the module itself but can also be more generic: such as IT skills, accessing and processing data, application of statistical techniques.

Dissertations/projects at degree level can be of particular interest to employers, particularly if you can point to the topic's relevance to the job. If you did well in your dissertation, give that emphasis too. Make sure you showcase your best grades, even in modules not as relevant to the job in hand.

Depending on the employer, you may list your A-levels or equivalents, if they are impressive then list them anyway.

PARTICULAR STRENGTHS AND SKILLS

Highlight what you are good at: analysis, communicating, diplomacy, leadership, reliability, taking on responsibility, teamworking, etc.

The success of an application for certain jobs may well depend on your technical ability and training, even on being good at using specific software: spreadsheet and other software skills, such as for Python, R or STATA. Make sure you mention it if you are trained in using them. If you have done something impressive with software make sure to mention it.

RELEVANT EXPERIENCE

This section can draw on relevant things you've done in your personal life, on placements, or any work or voluntary experience. If you have left university for some time then employers will usually want to check your career history, especially any unexplained gaps and so a chronological summary of your career history would be most appropriate, in the form of:

Job role   Employer   Dates of employment

Briefly describe main responsibilities and any standout projects with relevance to the application.

If you are a recent graduate it is OK to start with the most impressive roles and if there are aspects that are particularly relevant to the job being applied to, then highlight them e.g. a placement. If there were aspects that involved demonstrating responsibilities and team working mention these. If there were specific achievements of relevance then make sure to include them. These could be listed under a subheading such as 'Key Achievements'.

EXTRA-CURRICULAR ACTIVITIES

Describe any achievements or positions in clubs, organizations, sports, student societies and student union and volunteering. You can also describe your interests and hobbies and any notable achievements in them. If you can bring out your passion for something it shows your energy and ability to motivate yourself.

REFEREES (ON REQUEST)

A job application pack often specifies how many references are required. But in general list at least two, three is better. The more impressive the post and/or reputation of the referee the better. Conversely, if you do not have such referees and the application does not require them, then it saves space for the rest of the CV not to include this section, or to simply put in brackets 'On Request' as above.

No matter how much you wish to convey, it is best to stick to just two pages in length. Some applications, particularly to the financial sector, will insist upon one page only! If you do happen to have a long list of publications, not expected at the start of your career, then they could be in an annex. Two-sides of A4 is what most recruiters of graduates will expect. If a CV looks like it just waffles on it may well be discarded without being read. As it must be concise, you will need to prioritize what is included in your CV, based on its relevance to the particular job.

Further useful advice on CVs and cover letters can be found on the Prospect[1] and Studying Economics[2] websites.

USE YOUR UNIVERSITY'S CAREER SERVICE!

The days when careers officers were academics spending some time away from their day job, or perhaps being cajoled to cover the role, are long gone. Nowadays, universities have expert specialist and dedicated careers officers. As a university's careers service will have more resources and general advice

[1] Smith, Jenna (2021), *How to write a CV*, Prospects. Available at: https://www.prospects.ac.uk/careers-advice/cvs-and-cover-letters/how-to-write-a-cv (Accessed July 2021).
[2] Studying Economics, *The CV, Cover Letter and Interview*. Available at: http://www.studyingeconomics.ac.uk/where-next/jobs-and-careers/the-cv-cover-letter-and-interview/ (Accessed July 2021).

257

than we can possibly fit into this one Chapter, it would be daft not to ask them for more advice and feedback on your CV, job search, applications and interview techniques. The service is invariably free to existing students and usually to recent alumni too. Universities care about your employability, not only because they care about you but also because it is one of the metrics by which they are measured for their quality. They will usually offer one-to-one advice and coaching sessions as well as a range of online materials and workshops. Often, they are even able to arrange presentations from your target employers.

APPLICATION FORMS AND COVERING LETTERS

Companies and organizations will approach their recruitment process in different ways. Some may require applicants to supply a CV and traditional covering letter in support of their application. Others will use online portals which provide more direct questions as an alternative to a covering letter. Some online application forms will simply ask you to write a personal statement in support of your application as an alternative to the traditional covering letter. Again, unless your covering letter is concise, clear and convincing it can be an own goal.

BEHAVIOUR, MOTIVATION & STRENGTHS AND WEAKNESSES QUESTIONS

Obviously different organizations will seek to identify the particular hard-skills for the role advertised, but they also often use different names for the same generic broader and soft-skills. Even HR recruitment experts often disagree on the precise taxonomy, but they will all usually draw on the same concepts to construct 'blended interviews', a variety of types of questions and tasks that are designed to identify broad and soft skills as well as attitudes and motivations. In the candidates' reports below (see page 272) you will see that even successful candidates often use the wrong descriptors, but in general 'behaviour' questions, often also called 'competency' questions, are about how you've handled various past problems and situations. For these questions you should use the STAR technique below (see page 260). The idea here is that how you dealt with situations in the past is a good guide to how you will address situations in the future. 'Motivation' and 'Strengths' look for core attitudes based on the premise that if you do something regularly with enjoyment it becomes a strength. For these questions it is important to appear positive and to show enthusiasm, but then that is true in general (see 'body language page 270). Of course, given all that we have said about the need for professional development to be a continuous process, you will not be caught out by a 'What is your main weakness?' question. 'I have none' is a very poor answer!

The message here is that you do not have to be an expert HR recruitment designer to do well in these types of questions, but it is important that you practise answering them before you go to interviews. Remember that annoying saying 'If you fail to plan you plan to fail'? Well, it turns out it's very good advice here.

Examples of questions designed to interrogate your broader and softer skills set:

How do you deal with difficult people?

Describe a time when you delivered successful outcomes.

Describe how you go about organizing and prioritising tasks.

Describe a time when you had to use your judgment to make a decision

Tell me about a time when you made a mistake. What did you do to correct it?

How do you go about building constructive relationships with colleagues?

What skills do you see as essential for teamworking?

How do you respond to change?

When these are part of an application form there will be word count limits, such as 'in no more than 250 words, demonstrate your ability to analyse a range of information and evaluate evidence to produce high quality pieces of analysis'. This could be under a heading of 'making effective decisions'. Or: 'In no more than 250 words, demonstrate your ability to communicate analysis and ideas clearly and effectively'. This could be under a heading of 'communicating and influencing'.

This means that you should pack in as much detail as possible while maintaining a good use of English. These word count limits may also apply to writing a longer personal statement. As online forms do not always keep track of the word count as you write, we suggest composing your answer on a word processor first, so that you can edit your answer and check that it sticks to the word count before copying and pasting. It is also worth bearing in mind that a covering letter should follow the same principle applied to CV writing, which is to keep it concise. Try and keep the content to two sides at a maximum, and make sure that every word counts!

The question types outlined here also bear relevance to the interview process. Later in this chapter we include insights from graduates who have been though the interview process at well-known companies. In these examples you will see more questions designed to test your behaviour, competencies, motivations, strengths, and weaknesses.

PROVIDE AS MUCH RELEVANT DETAIL AS POSSIBLE

Amazingly, one of the most common reasons for failing to get a job is that the applicant has simply not filled-in all the boxes on the application form, or at least they have not sufficiently answered the requirements of the job advert in their covering letter. This may be carelessness, but some candidates do seem to think it is beneath their dignity to have to prove that they are a rounded individual by having to justify that they can prioritize tasks or 'Describe when and how you have demonstrated leadership—results, determination etc'. A candidate once complained that the job advertised only required a first degree and as 'I have a PhD from Oxford- isn't that enough?' Generally, the answer is emphatically, 'No!' Unless you put as much effort into proving evidence in response to all the headings given, as you do into listing your formal qualifications, then you are unlikely to be called for interview.

It is important to make sure you address the questions actually asked on the application form, identify the 'buzzwords' from the advert and use your past experiences (from across your studies, extra-curricular activities, work-experience, and volunteering) to craft sentences that show the hiring manager that you 'tick the boxes. 'STAR' is a useful mnemonic for this task. The STAR process can help you to approach direct questions posed in application forms such as 'Describe a time when you had to deliver results to a tight deadline' or in Interviews (see page 264).

STAR

S is for 'situation': Briefly explain the situation you were in to provide some context.

T is for 'task: Explain what you had to do and the success criteria you had to meet. For a group project you should explain the overall group task but be clear about what you did personally.

A is for 'action': This needs to be the major part (around 50–70 per cent). Say what you did, why you did it, how you did it and what skills you used. This is where you will demonstrate your competency, which, as we cover in the next section is crucial to the success of an application.

R is for 'result': What happened because of the actions you took? Would you do it differently or improve on anything next time? If a group task, what impact did the result have on the team task overall?

Don't think that you must come up with exceptional or dramatic examples. You can 'demonstrate initiative' without leading mercy expeditions to a war-torn country and 'determination' can be less than swimming the English Channel! If you've ever worked in a shop, as a waiter or behind a bar, then you will have 'dealt with difficult people'. If you've ever organized a successful social event, then you will have shown you can 'deliver results'. Generally, it is better to use examples from outside university, if you say 'I completed all my coursework on time at university' to prove 'determination, striving, prioritisation, delivering results' and so on, then you are not saying anything to mark you out from all the other applicants who have good degrees. You would certainly fail on 'originality' and 'thinking out-of-the box'.

MAKE SURE YOU DEMONSTRATE YOUR COMPETENCIES

STAR is useful for demonstrating your competencies and behaviour. It is surprising how often candidates can get so engrossed in describing a situation they were involved in that they neglect to demonstrate the skill, behaviour or competency actually specified on the application form. For example, if the heading on the application form is 'Write about a time you had to deliver results', or a job advert asks for 'a results-orientated individual' it is not enough to simply write about a project you were involved in. That is, focusing only on the 'S' and 'T' of the 'STAR' mnemonic. You must say what outputs you actually delivered yourself: the 'A' and 'R' of 'STAR'.

The heading 'Describe a time when you had to prioritise' or an advert searching for an 'organized' individual is often answered with responses such as 'To avoid being overwhelmed I worked longer hours'. That is not prioritization or good organization: that is working longer hours. Do that for too long and you neglect your development and your loved ones, and you risk burn-out.

A tip is to copy and paste the question at the top of the response box, or the key accountabilities and requirements emphasized in the advert, so that you are reminded to focus on only on what is relevant to what has actually been asked.

USE OF ENGLISH AND APPLICATIONS

Poor use of English can prevent you from being short-listed. It is an easy and quick way for busy selectors of candidates to distinguish between a lot of applications. Common grammatical errors that could see your application 'sifted out' include:

- Mixing up 'there' and 'their', 'you're' and 'your', 'affect' and 'effect', 'practise and practice' (for UK).

- The misuse and/or neglect of apostrophes.

- As we noted in Chapter 5, some people object to confusing 'who' with 'whom', to splitting infinitives, mixing up 'that' and 'which', and ending sentences with prepositions. Avoid these in formal communication even though you are unlikely to raise a frown because of them in verbal or informal communication.

As we discussed in Chapter 5, the degree to which it is in your interest to adhere to finer points of grammar depends on the reader and not on your own tastes and views. Unfortunately, it is common for people to be unaware of their own poor communication skills, so seeking feed-back from people who are good at communicating, and using the resources in Chapter 5, will help you identify areas for improvement.

ONLINE TESTS

Sometimes, before you can even access the application form, there may be initial online tests to pass. These can also be utilized as free practice for learning about broader and softer skills, even if you have no intention of applying to that particular employer. If you do well enough in each stage you can move progressively to more intensive tests, again, without necessarily submitting an application. For example, KPMG and others offer practice online assessments[3] and one of your authors recently did a few of the free online tests for the Civil Service Fast Stream as research for this book. Reassuringly he passed (see Figure 9.1).

---

[3] Practice Aptitude Tests is available at https://www.practiceaptitudetests.com/. KPMG tests are available here: https://www.practiceaptitudetests.com/top-employer-profiles/kpmg-assessments/#practice-for-free (Accessed May 2021).

FIGURE 9.1 Email from the Civil Service Fast Stream confirming successful participation in online exercises

```
┌─────────────────────────────────────────────┐
│ 👑 GOV.UK                                     │
├─────────────────────────────────────────────┤
│                                               │
│ Dear Andrew                                   │
│                                               │
│                                               │
│ Congratulations, you've passed the online     │
│ exercises.                                     │
│                                               │
│ The workbased scenarios are now ready for you  │
│ to complete. This will consist of two tests.   │
│                                               │
│ You must finish your workbased scenarious     │
│ before 27 October 2020 at 7:27pm.             │
│                                               │
│ Sign in to your home page to start the        │
│ workbased scenarios.                           │
│ (https://www.apply-civil-service-fast-         │
│ stream.service.gov.uk/fset-fast-              │
│ stream/signin)                                 │
│                                               │
│ Thank you                                     │
│                                               │
│ Fast Stream team                              │
│                                               │
│                                               │
│ If you need more help, call us on 0207 276     │
│ 6969 or email us at                            │
│ faststream.applicationsupport@cabinetoffice.gov.uk │
│                                               │
│ Do not reply to this email.                   │
│                                               │
└─────────────────────────────────────────────┘
```

PSYCHOMETRIC TESTS

These are again mostly online tests. They can be set to evaluate your knowledge and skills but usually refer to a battery of questions designed by psychologists to test 'personality types'. They are quite popular with many large employers, where they use them to try and assess how your character and personality fits with the values and behaviours required by the organization. Some well-known ones, such as Myers-Briggs, classify people into a range of personality types (16 for Myers-Briggs), often become a conversation topic between those who have completed them. The conversation can sound rather like people comparing their star signs! Different people set different store by such psychometric tests, but if you are required to do one you must take it seriously.

Again, using free online ones beforehand is advised, useful advice and links to do this can be found at https://www.prospects.ac.uk/careers-advice/interview-tips/psychometric-tests.

ASSESSMENT CENTRES

This term is sometimes used merely to refer to the physical places where you will take the on-the-day assessments and attend the interview. But more usually it is used to describe the means by which a combination of tasks and activities test your suitability for the job. An assessment centre can last anything from half a day to two-days. Assessment centres are often the final stage of the recruitment process for major graduate recruiters. Often, as with the civil service Fast Stream assessment centre, you will be assessed while working on tasks or 'negotiating' with a group of other candidates, but it's your own performance that is being assessed, often by several observers assessing different aspects of your performance. For example, was the candidate assertive rather than aggressive? Did the candidate hold their position but was prepared to compromise when necessary?

INTERVIEWS

Having heeded all the advice above, you have now got an interview—don't panic!

PREPARING FOR THE INTERVIEW

GETTING TO THE INTERVIEW

If you can, it is best to check how easy and reliable it is to travel to the required location, and on the day leave to arrive with plenty of time. Being late obviously gives a very bad impression for a would-be employee, but even stressing about being late on your journey will both tire you and use up your precious adrenaline before the interview even begins. If you end up being very early, you can usually find somewhere to relax and have a coffee. Obviously, the number of 'virtual' online interviews has increased since Covid struck so you may not need to travel all. But use the most reliable connection and equipment you can access and make sure the background in view of the camera is suitable- not untidy, close to noise, or in front of a window where you will be obscured by background light.

DO YOUR RESEARCH

For many interviews it is an advantage if you can show that you have knowledge of the employer organization. What business lines does it operate in? What significant activities has the organization been involved with recently? Does it face a competitive challenge? Who is the CEO and who are significant Board members? Was there anything in the application materials or on the website about which the organization seems to be particularly committed and/or about which it is proud? Knowing these things suggests a commitment to the organization and shows that it is not just any job you are seeking. It may also provide an opportunity for showing you are committed to the ethos of the organization, and to demonstrate why you could be good match with what is required.

If you have information on who will be on the interview panel it could be advantageous to know a little about them. For example, if a panel member is the lead for a certain project or prominent in an area that is raised during the interview then it may please that person and impress the panel if you at least acknowledge their role in passing. The company website can be a source of such information, and of course social media such as 'Linked-In' but be careful not to confuse their identities with other persons: that would be an own goal!

PRACTISE ANSWERING QUESTIONS

It is very easy to take a video of yourself, so you can check how you will come across at the interview. You can use the questions in this chapter. If you use a friend or careers office to ask the questions that would be even better as it raises your tension a little and so is a bit more realistic. One thing you are likely to notice is that, under pressure, time passes more quickly for you than for the interviewer. That is another reason why it is OK to pause and take a little time at an interview. What feels like a long pause to you is likely to be only a short one for the panel. And be reassured, almost everyone hates how their own voice sounds in a recording!

WHAT MIGHT YOU BE ASKED AT AN INTERVIEW?

Most interviews are structured in a similar way to application forms. They will feature a mixture of behaviour, competency, motivation, strength, and weakness questions. Obviously for an economist role, there will be competency questions on economics, but as we saw in Chapter 7, in most jobs it takes more than economics to be a good economist. Recruiters also want to know about your commitment to their organization (motivation questions) and your personal skills and attributes (competency, but also strengths, weaknesses, and behaviour), such as in your awareness of the need to develop soft skills (see Chapter 7).

Obviously, different employers have different recruitment regimes, so it's worth researching your target organizations and asking fellow job seekers or newly recruited economists for insights as to the interviews and tests conducted by the employers you are interested in. There are also websites that list questions and reports from candidates who applied to certain employers.[4] Non-economics questions may include:

Motivation questions (incorporating questions about your knowledge of the organization):

- Why do you want to join our organization?
- What do you know about our business?
- Which aspects of our work most attract you to this post?
- How do you see the role you would perform if you got this job?
- Where do you see your career heading over the next five years?
- Why do you think you are the right applicant for this job?

Examples of the sort of generic job interview question you should expect include (The first two are often used as 'ice breakers' designed to relax rather than assess you):

- Tell me a little bit about yourself?
- What do you do in your spare time?
- What do you consider to be your strengths?
- Do you have any weaknesses?
- What is the biggest mistake you have made and what did you learn from it?
- Where do you see yourself in five/ten years?

Earlier in this chapter we saw some typical examples of questions about your own behaviours, competencies, and strengths. We list a few more here:

- How do you respond to stressful situations?
- Tell me about a difficult experience and how you dealt with it.

---

[4] Such as 'What will they ask?' available at: http://www.whatwilltheyask.co.uk/index.htm (Accessed July 2021) or *Economics graduate Interview Questions* on Glassdoor, available at: https://www.glassdoor.co.uk/Interview/economics-graduate-interview-questions-SRCH_KO0,18.htm (Accessed July 2021).

- How do you cope with pressure?

- Do you ever get angry?

- What do you see as your biggest successes so far?

- What have you learned from your mistakes?

- Suppose you disagree with your manager or a colleague, how would you go about making this clear?

- What would you do if you saw a colleague being bullied?

- Do you prefer working with others or working alone?

- What is your main weakness and what are you doing about it?

- How would you respond to rapid change?

CURRENT AFFAIRS

If there have been major events near the time of the interview (there often are in economics!) then these could well form the basis for questions. Obviously, you could be asked about significant economic events, but also ones that might affect how you work, such as Covid:

- What did you learn about yourself during the pandemic?

- How well do you think you could do the job if there was a need to work only from home?

- How did you spend your time during the lock-in?

HOW TO GIVE A SUCCESSFUL ANSWER TO INTERVIEW QUESTIONS

We have seen how the STAR method can help you answer behaviour and competency questions. Another tip is that if you are in danger of getting stuck when answering questions then think of what a bad answer would be and then 'reverse' it. For example: 'How do you deal with difficult people? You might answer that you do not lose your temper with difficult people. You calmly explain how you are trying to accommodate them but that you also have requirements, while providing reassurance that you are listening to their feedback. 'How do you cope/adjust to change?' You could say you do not freeze or become demoralized in the face of change You accept change as an inevitable part of a dynamic environment and generally find such challenge exciting and an opportunity to build new relationships and to practise new skills.

'How do you cope with stress?' You might say you do not panic or collapse in the face of stress: you pause to take breath and to take stock of the situation. You accept that stress is likely to arise from time to time in most jobs, but you have learned how to be resilient from coming through stressful situations before, so you will calmly identify and prioritize what has to be done, you use your colleagues, seniors and networks for advice.

An organization's Human Resources (HR) department will often have a say about how interviews, even for economists, should be conducted. Typical HR type questions include 'Give examples of how you have delivered successful outcomes', 'What team working skills do you have?' 'Tell me how you think other people would describe you?' To occasionally seemingly weird and wonderful questions, such as 'For this job, what animal would you choose to be?' It is tempting to be flippant or even humorous in response to such questions. One of your authors once replied to the 'What is your main weakness?' question with 'I sell myself short at interviews', which luckily was well-received that time, but it is generally dangerous to try humour at interviews. It is intrinsically a formal occasion and therefore one that you are expected to take seriously, and anyway the interviewers may not share your particular sense of humour.

MANAGING NERVES

The first thing to remember is that feeling nervous is natural, it is even helpful if you adopt a mature attitude towards your nerves. Interview anxieties can be used to focus the mind and commit to actively researching the organizations you have applied to, and to revise the sort of economics you are likely to be asked about. With a mature approach to 'nerves', anxiety can actually give you the energy to give a better interview. And so, it is helpful to know a secret not often confessed: we all have insecurity feelings. It's a natural part of being a healthy human. Apart from those few who are psychotically confident, even apparently supremely confident people have mostly simply learned how to cope with their tensions and fears, and how to harness their nerves to enhance their performance. Indeed, although your 'stage fright' will decrease with time and experience, you never want to lose it completely as a spur to your performance.

As interview technique is something that can be developed throughout a career, interviewers are usually sympathetic towards a young graduate who is daunted by having to answer questions and explain economics, perhaps for the first time, to older economists for an important interview. All graduates will need

FIGURE 9.2 The arousal performance curve

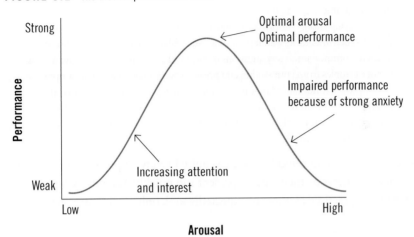

Source: Panel 1 in Figure 2 from Diamond, D. M., Campbell, A. M., Park, C. R., Halonen, J., and Zoladz, P. R. (2007). The temporal dynamics model of emotional memory processing: a synthesis on the neurobiological basis of stress-induced amnesia, flashbulb, and traumatic memories, and the Yerkes-Dodson law. Neural plasticity, 2007, 60803. https://doi.org/10.1155/2007/60803

development once in post, and all experienced interviewers will have seen on occasion sweat and tears, and even once blood from a spontaneous nosebleed! Worrying about being nervous is no good at all, nerves do not invalidate you and may create a vicious circle of underperforming that makes for even more nerves. Psychologists show this as an 'arousal-performance' curve shown in Figure 9.2.

Your aim should not be to deny or to 'conquer' fear but rather to hold your 'arousal' at the optimum level for your performance.

TALKING TOO MUCH OR TOO LITTLE

The wrong level of nerves often leads to talking too much, waffling, or conversely, talking too little, being overly shy or deferential. Prospects.ac.uk provide much sensible advice on interviews, including the following useful advice:[5]

> "Waffling is a common interview mistake and tends to be the result of nerves, but avoid talking about everything all at once. It's important to sell your skills and experience without rambling. Once the interviewer asks a question, pause for a couple of seconds, take a breath and gather your thoughts before

---

[5] Swain, Rachel (2021), 'Top 5 job interview mistakes', Prospects. Available at: https://www.prospects.ac.uk/careers-advice/interview-tips/top-5-job-interview-mistakes (Accessed July 2021).

responding. If you're talking too much or too fast you also run the risk of talking over or interrupting the interviewer.

Not giving enough information and forgetting to mention important points can be just as detrimental as waffling. To make sure this doesn't happen, practise answers to common interview questions beforehand and make sure you have a number of examples from your studies and previous work experience to draw upon.

Employers understand that nerves play a part in the process so, if your mind goes completely blank, politely ask for a couple of seconds to gather your thoughts or ask if it's ok to come back to the question at the end, once you've had some time to think."

Bear this advice in mind if you are required to give a presentation, as when people are nervous they tend to present too quickly. What took ten minutes when you practised at home unexpectedly took only six minutes on the day.

BODY LANGUAGE, DRESS, AND TONE

It is well known that a large part of direct communication comes from manner and body language, and the enthusiasm and engagement of candidates gives a strong impression that can influence interviewers. Indeed, such 'positivity' is often a formal part of the interview assessment criteria. For example, a 'strength' is often defined by HR departments as 'A combination of what someone enjoys doing, and what they are very good at doing'. You should be aware that your body language and tone at an interview can convey much of this message to an interviewer. Slouching lethargically with a lack of eye contact does not convey a positive impression. Good manners, regular eye contact, a smile where appropriate all go down well.

> "Research shows that there is a positive relation between applicant positive nonverbal behavior and recruiter evaluation. Positive nonverbal behavior can be defined as immediacy behavior which elicits proximity and liking in the interaction partner as for example a high level of eye contact, smiling, confirmative nodding, hand gestures, and variation in pitch and speaking rate (Guerrero, 2005). Applicants who used more immediacy behavior (i.e., eye contact, smiling, body orientation toward interviewer, less personal distance) were perceived as being more suitable for the job, more competent, more motivated, and more successful than applicants using less immediacy behavior (Imada and Hakel, 1977)."[6]

---

[6] Cited in Denise Frauendorfer and Marianne Schmid Mast (2015), *The Impact of Nonverbal Behavior in the Job Interview* (University of Neuchatel), p. 4. https://www.researchgate.net/publication/282849027_The_Impact_of_Nonverbal_Behavior_in_the_Job_Interview.

There are usually no explicit dress requirements provided for candidates, but its best to treat an interview as a formal occasion. No-one will turn you down for an economist job because you look too smart. Dressing formally also conveys the message that you are keen to get the job and is a mark of respect to your interviewers, even if they are not dressed as smartly as you. Similarly, your manner should be friendly but at all times appropriate for a formal event, this will again show respect and professionalism. It's also best to use the interviewer's surname unless invited to use first names.

It's also best to avoid expressing strong views or making criticism of others, as you can come across as opinionated and perhaps a 'difficult person'. If you criticize previous colleagues and employers you may be seen as potentially 'disloyal'. If you are invited to ask any questions yourself then avoid ones that may make you look demanding such as 'Can I take additional time off?' or 'How long before I get a pay rise?' Instead ask positive ones, such as 'Can you tell me more about my responsibilities and how I would be expected to develop in my career?'

ADJUSTMENTS FOR DISABILITIES

An employer isn't just being 'disabilities friendly' by offering adjustments at interviews, they are complying with the law. People have a legal right to have 'reasonable adjustments' made for job interviews and other assessments. If adjustments can be made so that a disability does not put you at a disadvantage in meeting the criteria being tested, then employers must provide such reasonable adjustments under the Equality Act of 2010.

Large employers will most probably automatically ask if you need adjustments as part of the applicant process application form, if not you have a legal right to ask. You do not have to 'disclose' your condition when applying for a job, but, if you are going to ask for reasonable adjustments, you will need to say that you are disabled.

For more information and advice on the rights of disabled people applying for jobs see the SCOPE website.[7] SCOPE is a disability equality charity providing practical information and emotional support. It campaigns relentlessly to create a fairer society for disabled people. Employers who care about providing the best opportunities for the disabled are also likely to be members of the Disability Confident Campaign, see https://disabilityconfident.campaign.gov.uk/

[7] SCOPE (2021) 'Asking for adjustments at interview' at https://www.scope.org.uk/advice-and-support/ask-for-adjustments-at-interview/ (Accessed September 2021).

HOW TO RESPOND TO REJECTION

If you fail to get a post after an interview politely ask for feedback. Some organizations provide quite detailed feedback for unsuccessful candidates and this can be invaluable for your personal development, and, of course, for your next successful interview! It is important not to take 'failure' personally. Even the best of us will have experienced failures, and there can be a host of non-personal reasons why you didn't get a job offer. For example, there could simply have been another candidate who was a better match for that particular job, the post itself may have been reconsidered and withdrawn, or, as can quite often be the case, there is already a strongly favoured candidate for the post. This might be an internal candidate who has already performed well in the post on temporary promotion, but the organization may still be required to put the post out for external competition before it can be made a permanent appointment. And if you are already in an organization then demonstrating a positive developmental attitude to an unsuccessful interview can be a strong plus for your next promotion opportunity.

REPORTS FROM ACTUAL JOB INTERVIEWS

Here are a few examples of what might be expected of you at interviews for economist jobs. These accounts are based on feedback from a selection of students from various universities reporting back on their recent job interviews for this book. They are anonymous, partial and self-reported, and although from recent years, they relate only to past interviews, so be aware that that these reports are not a reliably accurate account of what you would experience at the organizations mentioned. However, they do provide a useful overview of interviews for first economist jobs:

BANK OF ENGLAND APPLICATION FOR AN INDUSTRIAL PLACEMENT PROGRAMME

"The process began with a standard online application form which asked . . . about the candidate's motivations for applying to the Bank. There was then a series of stages, including online tests testing candidates' personal values against those of the Bank's. A video interview was used to ask for observations on the Bank's actions in the last ten years and on a case study. If successful, candidates were invited to attend an assessment day after completing a numerical test. The interview on the assessment day consisted of an Excel test, competency and technical questions followed by two group activities, one focused on presentation skills and the other on report writing."

DEFRA GES SUMMER PLACEMENT SCHEME

"About ten minutes were spent on each of competency, macroeconomics and microeconomics. The competency questions included: Why did you choose to study economics? What aspects of economics are you particularly interested in? [these are actually motivation questions not competency ones] Describe a situation where you faced an analytical challenge, how did you go about solving this challenge? [This is a competency/behavioural question].

The macro questions included questions on the association of spending with inflation and demand-pull inflation, and why is government debt a problem. The micro questions were largely about market failure and how the government might go about correcting market failure."

DELOITTE

Some interviews are quite difficult to prepare for in advance. For example, Deloitte has used case studies, of the type of work graduates might be expected to engage with, to test candidates:

"Candidates were asked questions based on briefs about companies facing particular business decisions. Questions were based around prioritising tasks and why, identifying the most important issues and how candidates would deal with them. Candidates were then asked to provide a company plan of action. Deloitte candidates were also asked: Describe any recent project or piece of work you have completed; is there a framework you follow to achieve your goals?; Why did you choose Deloitte out of the Big Four?; How has the economic climate impacted Deloitte?"

ERNST & YOUNG (EY)

An interview for a summer internship at EY consisted mainly of questions, including:

"Give an example of a time when you had to go out of your way to help someone; Have you ever done something differently the second time around? Do you prefer quick action or careful planning? What activities energise you? Do you prefer small or large groups of friends? Give an example of a time when you worked with someone difficult; Tell me about a time that you failed at something; How do you divide your time between different responsibilities? Tell me about a time when you have adapted your behaviour; What is the toughest decision you have had to make? When are you at your best? Which three words would your friends use to describe you? How do you deal with rapidly changing situations? How important is developing yourself to you? There were some more specific questions relating to EY such as: What differentiates EY from other firms?"

THE GOVERNMENT ECONOMIC SERVICE (GES) ECONOMIC ASSESSMENT CENTRE (EAC)

'EAC' of course, tests your economics. To be more precise, it tests your knowledge, application and communication of economics. Here we use information direct from the GES and its assessors.[8]

Candidates were given a topic well in advance of the assessment day and a question on the topic that you would have to write a technical report on, under examination conditions, on your assessment day. Not surprisingly, set topics usually require the application of standard economic tools of analysis to a potential or actual field for government intervention. It's called a technical report as you can assume that the reader is a fellow economist. You are therefore encouraged to use precise technical terms and apply well-known economic principles in your report. Candidates should bear in mind that what is being assessed is their grasp of fundamental economics concepts and principles and their ability to apply them, the topic set is merely a vehicle for doing this. So, don't spend ages memorizing lots of specific statistics and details, concentrate on showing that you can apply the standard tools of economics.

On the day candidates were required to give a verbal presentation on the topic in plain English. Candidates often struggle to avoid using technical terms and to give everyday explanations of economic principles, especially as they get little practice in this important skill at university. The best candidates do not simply try to 'interpret' or 'teach' their technical report but instead shape their presentation around more everyday notions, while also calling on the powerful insights of economics. Candidates must also answer short answer questions. As writing time is limited, time was allowed in the interview itself to gain more marks by verbally completing or correcting questions where maximum marks had not

---

[8] Government Economic Service (2021) *GES Assistant Economist Scheme 2021: Candidate Pack*. Available at: https://assets.publishing.service.gov.uk/government/uploads/system/uploads/attachment_data/file/967275/Assistant_Economist_Scheme_2021_-_Candidate_Pack_Final.pdf#:~:text=The%20GES%20Assistant%20Economist%20scheme%20is%20the%20recruitment,leadership%20skills%20will%20be%20available%20in%20either%20case. (Accessed September 2021).

been obtained in the short answer written test.[9] Finally, the candidate was asked questions on an economic topic of their own choosing, before being allowed to add anything that they felt they may have missed during the interview.

It is important for candidates to prepare for EAC by revising the fundamentals of economics, rather than rehearsing advanced economics at the edge of their understanding. The majority of EAC questions can be answered with simply a good understanding of the economics found in first- and second-year economics texts, such as *Economics* by John Sloman, and then being able to apply these same fundamentals to various issues. There is a useful GES video that gives information on how to prepare for the EAC assessment available on YouTube at https://youtu.be/XscDvh3wWu4.[10]

For the GES Fast Stream you will also have to pass the Fast Stream Assessment Centre (FSAC). For the Assistant Economist scheme, the FSAC is replaced by about 30 minutes of the sort of behaviour and strengths questions we have looked at in this chapter.

HOME OFFICE PLACEMENT INTERVIEW

"This started with a twenty minutes numeracy test, mainly on index numbers and percentage changes. Followed by some general competency questions: When have you worked in a team? What was the main challenge of this? What did you learn from it? When have you persuaded someone to do something? Then the questions turned towards the candidates' interest in economics. Why did you choose to study economics? There were questions on actual economics, starting with macro. Could negative interest rates ever be a good idea? What are the consequences of having a large government debt? What are the social and economic impacts of this? If you were the Chancellor what would you have done to reduce the debt, when and why? How would this affect businesses and who in society would be affected the most? What would be the consequence if banks stopped lending?

The questions on micro included: Do you think the government should intervene more in markets where there are negative or positive externalities and why? How might pollution externalities be resolved without using direct market interventions (Coase theorem)? What is the effect of a minimum wage? If it was raised how would

---

[9] For the Office of National Statistics short answer questions are sometimes used only to screen candidates for interview.

[10] UK Government Economic Service (2017) *The GES Economics Assessment Centre: What to expect* [*Video*]. YouTube: https://youtu.be/XscDvh3wWu4 (Last accessed July 2021).

businesses, government and social groups be affected? What if the minimum wage were set at £60,000 a year? What would be the effect of a maximum wage? The interview concluded with the common question 'Any questions for us?"

HM TREASURY

Sometimes a government department will recruit economists directly, that is, outside of the GES, though often successful candidates will be expected to pass the full Civil Service Graduate Fast Stream (FSAC) assessment process or other means to become a member of the GES within a year or two of commencing work. A recent interview day at HM Treasury consisted of a 20 minute simple maths assessment, e.g. working out percentages and exchange rates; a 15 minute comprehension test reading a report to produce a four sentence summary suitable for the Chancellor of the Exchequer; a ten minute test on economic concepts where the candidate had to choose one A-level standard concept from a list of four and then give two definitions, one for another economist and one that an non-economist could understand; a fifteen minute essay, again choosing one topic from a list of four. One candidate chose the effect of a large-scale investment by government in infrastructure. He included a discussion of the impact on aggregate demand in the short and the long-run, the relationship with productivity, and then he critically analysed the secondary effects of different financing methods, and the possible impacts on the UK fiscal budget deficit.

"The interview consisted of two interviewers, one asking questions on economics, the other general competency questions. The competency questions were: 'Why did you choose to study economics? Why did you choose to apply to HM Treasury and why are you interested in the GES? [These are actually motivation questions!] Can you give an example of when you had to persuade someone to go with your idea?

The economics section of the interview asked both macro and micro questions. Macro questions included: How can the Bank of England use monetary policy to control inflation? How does the low value of the pound affect inflation? How does deflation and a weaker pound affect the UK internationally? The micro questions were: Why might an increase in corporation tax not affect tax receipts as much as expected? How does an increase in income tax affect demand for work and leisure? Then, in a less formal style, interview candidates were asked about how they had been proactive in exploring interests in specific areas of economics and the roles at the Treasury they were interested in."

The applicant was asked a set of general competency questions at interview about her involvement in student societies at university. In particular, she was asked how she had used organizational and communication skills to help steer the direction of the society she led, and how she dealt with difficult people and those not pulling their weight. She was asked how she had responded to the challenges of doing group work and how likely she would be to put herself forward for a future leadership role. She was also asked to discuss a formal piece of writing that she had done recently, such as an essay, and the feedback received on it. This was followed by a question on how she tailors her communications to different intended audiences, including the difference between writing for academics and more general writing. Lastly there was a question on how she prioritised task to meet multiple deadlines.

Her economics questions were on, 'The effects of high inflation, including on prices and wages; how stagflation can come about; the benefits of a large infrastructure project and the relevance of the government multiplier to this; the pros and cons of trade unions; the trade-off between work and leisure and how an individual may alter their choices in the face of varying levels of taxation; the cause of the recent financial crisis and subsequent recession.'

OXFORD ECONOMICS

The applicant reports:

> "I applied online. The process took a week. I was interviewed at Oxford Economics . . . It was a difficult interview but a positive experience. . . . I had to send a CV and a Cover Letter. A week later, I was contacted to do a Skype Interview. I had to do an essay in thirty minutes from three possible economic topics. Followed by a three-quarters of an hour interview when I was asked several technical questions on the essay I had written and then about monetary policy."

CONCLUSION

Writing applications for a job is not to be taken lightly. The quality of your application will determine whether you are called for interview. Equally, do not just 'turn up' for an interview, do the preparation ground work described in this chapter and remember the irritating but important homily 'If you fail to plan you plan to fail'.

SUMMARY

- Start thinking about your chosen career destination early in your studies, be ambitious but realistic in your aspirations, research the specific job that you would like before attempting to complete the application form.

- For most economist jobs, you will need more than just good economics. If you do not take demonstrating these broader skills seriously as part of your application, then you will not be invited for an interview.

- Keep an up-to-date CV handy in case a particularly attractive opportunity suddenly arises, but if there is time tailor it to the specific job.

- A surprising number of applications fail because of seemingly 'trivial' errors, or for not addressing the precise criteria set in the proforma. So, pay close attention to the instructions and all parts of the process.

- Use the headings as specified on the application form, do not drift off topic.

- You could also fail to reach a shortlist simply because of elementary grammatical 'sins'.

- 'STAR' is a useful mnemonic for describing your 'extra-curricular' abilities and achievements.

- Candidates often prepare advanced material but neglect to revise and practise applying the basics.

- Before an interview, practise the sort of questions that are likely to be asked. You will find quite a few in this chapter, but it's sensible to try to find out about an organization's ethos and mission before the interview.

- Make a list of common broader and 'soft-skills' questions and prepare answers you could use if asked them.

- It's OK to be nervous but direct your nervousness into helpful energy rather than let it be a problem.

- Expect to be rejected as part of your learning process but be persistent, try to take pride in watching yourself grow with the experience you gain, knowing that just one success will wipe away all the failures.

- Always ask politely for feedback following any unsuccessful job application, such feedback can be useful for personal development.
- If you have a disability you have the legal right to ask for reasonable adjustments.

QUESTIONS

1. Why is writing on an application form 'I handed all my assignments in on time at university' not a useful way to 'stand out from the crowd'?

2. Why is it important to distinguish between 'presenting yourself in the best possible light' and making false claims?

3. Why will being a brilliant economist not compensate for other weak areas on an application form?

EXERCISES

1. Read the advice on writing CV's at https://www.prospects.ac.uk/careers-advice/cvs-and-cover-letters/how-to-write-a-cv and then write your own CV, then seek feedback on it, this might be from your university's career services.

2. Use the questions in this chapter and then go online and search for job adverts and application forms where you don't actually have to apply for the job. Study the key accountabilities asked for/the headings and questions used and practise your responses. You are likely to find that in the days that follow you suddenly recall events and situations where you demonstrated the required attributes and skills usefully for applications.

3. Find a list of soft skills questions online and plan how you might development them as skills you possess,[11] take advantage of the 'free' online tests mentioned above (page 262).

4. Agree with a friend or colleague to complete and swap CV's and responses to interview questions, troubleshooting and giving advice to each other.

---

[11] For example: Indeed Career Guide (2021) *101 Soft Skill Interview Questions To Prepare For* at https://www.indeed.com/career-advice/interviewing/soft-skill-interview-questions (Accessed September 2021).

5. Arrange a 'mock interview' with a friend, colleague, senior, or your careers service.

6. For a delightfully humorous account of the importance of punctuation read *Eats, Shoots and Leaves: The Zero Tolerance Approach to Punctuation* by Lynne Truss (2003) Profile Books Ltd.

FIND OUT MORE

Your first stop should be your own university or college career service.

Prospects, the central service for careers advice, provides comprehensive guidance and tips for job applications and interviews at **https://www.prospects .ac.uk/careers-advice/interview-tips/**.

CHAPTER 10

How to stay a successful economist

· · • • • •●●● • • · ·

INTRODUCTION

This chapter looks at how you can keep up with economics after leaving university, to keep abreast of new developments and be up to date with data. In Chapter 7, we explained why professional development has to be continuous throughout your career: the skills you will require will change; economies are dynamic and the discipline of Economics itself progresses and evolves; reading more widely, including in other disciplines, will enrich and deepen your economics; there are few skills sets where improvement has no returns. It is true that keeping up will take time and effort. Indeed, you may well not have come across all the developments mentioned below from your study of economics so far. That would not be surprising given how wide-ranging is our discipline. Evidence of a lively interest in economics and so being aware of new developments in the subject is also likely to go down well in interviews (see Chapter 9) and keeping-up to date will certainly be needed when you are in post as a professional economist.

We admit that we cannot know with certainty which new developments will be the most important in the future, but we include those that we judge are particularly likely to be of increasing importance for economists and/or are particularly relevant now for practitioner economists. Cost Benefit Analysis (CBA) is an example of the latter. CBA is not new, but it is a ubiquitous tool used in its various forms across all sectors of the economy and is a tool required in many economist careers. Exploring issues in CBA, including its limitations, also reveals many of the issues in current microeconomic policy. As CBA is nowadays all too often overlooked in economics degrees, we provide an overview and references to help reduce this deficit. Understanding CBA and its techniques will also equip you for many jobs requiring business cases, impact assessments, and investment and options analysis across both the private, public and third sectors.

One thing we must say up front: Economics is a well-established and powerful social science that has many different branches and approaches. Whatever its shortcomings, we do not need to suspend all work while waiting for new developments to come and save our discipline, although new developments are needed and are very welcome!

KEEPING UP TO DATE

Once you have left university and embarked upon your career as a practising economist it's essential not to lose touch with the evolution of economic thinking. It is all too easy to become out-of-date given the vast amount of new research generated by academic economists, year-in-year-out, and by the dynamic nature of the economy. Keeping up to speed with the most recent discourses and debates will also hone your diagnostic capabilities and so sharpen your 'edge'. This was a consideration that Melissa Davies commented on in her interview for the book.[1]

SOURCES TO KEEP YOU IN THE LOOP

Subscribing to economic journals is an excellent way to keep up with what's happening in economics in our universities, but it can be expensive, and the past few decades have seen the emergence of many new journals, so it is important to select with care. The Royal Economic Society's www.res.org.uk/ long-standing *Economic Journal*[2] should be your first port of call. The American Economic Association's (www.aeaweb.org/) regular publications, notably the *American Economic Review*, *Journal of Economic Perspectives* and *Journal of Economic Literature*, are also highly recommended for the more academically minded. There are also many more specialist journals, such as the *Journal of Competition Law and Economics*; the *Journal of Transport, Economics and Policy*, which depending

---

[1] See Video 12: In conversation with Melissa Davies (available at www.oup.com/he/pryce-ross1e).

[2] *The Economic Journal* commenced publication in 1890 and JM Keynes was Editor from 1912 to 1944.

on your career and interests you may find relevant and useful. Often it is possible to enrol for courses, or even a single module, at a university and so also to have access to their library. Some workplaces provide budgets for books and journals and for course enrolments. If you merely have a good reason to use a university library as a visitor, such as researching a topic, you may be granted some level of access.[3]

Much insightful economic research is published outside academe. International bodies such as the Organisation for Economic Co-operation and Development (OECD) (www.oecd.org/), the International Monetary Fund (IMF) (www.imf.org/en/Research) and World Bank (www.worldbank.org/) employ many economists who are encouraged to publish their research. The Bank of England produces a regular stream of updates and research, for example in its staff working papers (https://www.bankofengland.co.uk/working-paper/ staff-working-papers) and central banks in general—including the 'central bankers' bank' the Basle-based Bank of International Settlements (www.bis .org/)—similarly encourage the dissemination of their research to the world at large. The US, with its twelve Reserve Districts and a Board of Governors in Washington, is especially prolific in this respect. A wealth of creative and innovative thinking can also be found on European central bank websites (with 'Bank Underground', where Bank of England staff post short articles, deserving of special mention, at https://bankunderground.co.uk/).

There are also many think tanks whose research output, generally policy-focussed, is well worth monitoring on a regular basis. In the UK the longest-lived of these (established in 1938) is the National Institute of Economic and Social Research (www.niesr.ac.uk). For matters relating to the public finances, the Institute of Fiscal Studies is a well-regarded microeconomic and public finances think tank (www.ifs.org.uk). In the United States, the Brookings Institute (www.brookings.edu) and the Peterson Institute for International Economics (www.piie.com) are especially noteworthy. So too is the US's long-established National Bureau of Economic Research (www.nber. org), under whose aegis the gist of much academic economic research which is subsequently published in academic journals first sees the light of day, in the format of a regular weekly bulletin. Project Syndicate (www.project-syndicate .org), which provides a platform for key macro-economic policy debates, also deserves a mention.

---

[3] For example, the London School of Economics library has a policy of admitting visitors for 'public education'. See https://www.lse.ac.uk/library/using-the-library/secure/join-the-library.

One especially brilliant path-breaking medium for the dissemination of policy-relevant economic research was launched in 2008 in the form of the VoxEU website (voxeu.org/). Contributions are succinct and readable, with virtually no mathematical notation, and VoxEU's 'reach', judged by the site's readership statistics, is impressive. Many academics nowadays also blog regularly on their own websites and following these outputs can be fruitful. Reading The Economist magazine (www.economist.com) and the Financial Times (www.ft.com) on a regular basis will also help keep you up to speed on critical issues. Gavyn Davies, the long-established City economist and FT columnist also observes in his interview[4] that although it is still important to read widely, the digital age has meant he can spend 'days and evenings' watching recent seminars online from a wealth of material from leading economists, even just on *YouTube* alone (see Video 11: In conversation with Gavyn Davies OBE). Treasury Select Committees also often address economic issues and so have expert economist guests (see https://committees.parliament.uk/committee/158/treasury-committee/).

The UK's Society of Professional Economists (SPE) (spe.org.uk/), whose membership encompasses practitioner economists in both the public and private sectors, helps its members keep abreast. Members of the Society have long enjoyed monthly expert speaker meetings and regular Masterclasses have been up and running since 2009, while a Continuing Professional Education programme, including brief and accessible update courses, was launched in 2018. The SPE also publishes regular book reviews, highlighting the most recent publications relevant to practising economists.

Bristol's Festival of Ideas has a regular Festival of Economics programme,[5] which we highly recommend. It provides an impressive programme of interesting economists and contributes to the demystifying of economics. The ninth Festival in 2020 was co-programmed by Diane Coyle (University of Cambridge and Enlightenment Economics) and Richard Davies (Professor of Public Understanding of Economics, Bristol University). Economists and experts from around the world debated key economic questions of our time, both with each other and their audiences.

Later in your career, if you achieve outstanding contributions to Economics, then you could be nominated as a Fellow of the Academy of Social Science

---

[4] In his interview for this book (see Video 11: In conversation with Gavyn Davies OBE available at www.oup.com/he/pryce-ross1e).

[5] Festival of Economics https://www.ideasfestival.co.uk/themes/festival-economics/ (Accessed May 2021).

(AcSS). The AcSS is the National Academy of Academics, Learned Societies and Practitioners in the Social Sciences. Fellowship is a prestigious recognition and the Academy provides updates on what is happening in social science, runs campaigns to raise the profile and funding of social science, and gives access to a very large network of other outstanding social scientists across many disciplines.[6]

KEEPING UP WITH ECONOMIC DATA

Even as you look at economic data, the economy has already moved on, so keeping up is a real challenge. Unfortunately access to subscription data providers such as *Bloomberg* and *DataStream* can be expensive, but universities do often subscribe to them for their students, and there are many ways, short of a full degree course, to be a student at your local university. Continuing to do courses at your local university can both further your professional development and give you access to full university library facilities, including the national inter-library network. Again, to keep up with the main data headlines, reading the *Financial Times* and *The Economist* is useful. Obviously, the Office of National Statistics is a valuable source of up to date and authoritative data, but for a comprehensive list of free data this book will not try to compete with the extensive guide to sources of free data on economics (see https://economics-network.ac.uk/data_sets), provided and updated by John Sloman, the former long-time, Director of the Economics Network and a celebrated teacher and Economics textbook author.

LIMITATIONS OF ECONOMICS

From the 1960's towards the new century, economics became increasingly dominated by applying mathematical maximization principles to individual decision making, aggregated up to produce models of economic systems. This is still the mainstay of the 'neoclassical' approach to economics, although increasingly augmented, rightly, by more empirical content. Neoclassical economics, as with all other paradigms, has limitations. These can be highlighted by comparing it with different approaches. For example, the Austrian School emphasizes that, rather than the copious knowledge of agents and the

---

[6] https://www.acss.org.uk/.

equilibriums of neoclassical economics, market behaviours are constantly creating new information that changes agents' behaviour and hence the dynamics of markets. For Austrian School economists' equilibrium is merely a theoretical extreme, as soon as there is movement towards it the equilibrium has changed. Neoclassical economics is asocial; individualist;[7] based on maximization, including probabilistic[8] expectations; and based largely on comparative statics rather than dynamics. Hence, it fails to include important interdependencies and social relations, institutions, feedback from behaviour and policies, and systemic 'big picture' issues, such as confidence/animal spirits and macro prudence, and the need to understand and so perhaps mitigate, the dangers from true or 'radical' uncertainty,[9] which leads to 'coping' rather than maximizing. It also has some predictions, both micro and macro, that simply run counter to evidence.[10] That said, for all its limitations, neoclassical economics can be a powerful tool for many problems in economics and it still opens the most career doors. We should always be aware, however, as Figure 10.1 shows, and as good economists bear in mind even when using standard neoclassical economics, there is much more to an economy than merely competing individual 'agents' and the neoclassical approach is but one tool in a rounded economist's toolbox.

Limitations matter. At university, making errors simply loses you marks, but in real-world applications of economics making errors can blight or even ruin the lives of so many. To avoid such errors practitioners should have a very good understanding of the limits of the economic tools they use. It is worrying that too many graduates in economics seem to suffer from 'analysis paralysis'. That is, they are unable to relate their economics to real world issues, some even fail to recognize when cranking out a standard technique is leading them to quite ludicrous conclusions. Many of the exercises required for job applications and interviews for economist jobs are designed to 'weed-out' those candidates who have rote learned techniques but have no depth of understanding of their appropriate application. Such economists are dangerous if let loose in the world!

As we have noted, economic models are necessarily abstractions and therefore often deliberately lack descriptive accuracy, but comparing them with

[7] Or 'atomistic'.

[8] That is, it assigns known probability risks to decision-making rather than accepting there can be true, often called 'Knightian', uncertainty.

[9] See for example: John Kay and Mervyn King (2020), *Radical uncertainty: Decision-making beyond the numbers* (W. W. Norton and company: New York, USA).

[10] For example, the neutral impact of a pure profit tax.

what you see around you is a useful way of coming to understand their limitations (see Chapter 3 'The role of models'). For example, have you ever tried to buy something and the shopkeeper says 'I'm sorry, I've just reached equilibrium with my previous customer, please could you come back in my next time period?' Of course not, and that does not, of itself, make equilibrium an invalid theoretical concept, even though equilibrium is much more a theoretical abstraction than a reality. Many criticisms of economics miss the mark as they show a misunderstanding of modelling. This does not mean that realism is unimportant: a theory that captures, albeit in an abstract way, something that is real will be more reliable than one based on arbitrary assumptions that are at odds with reality. The problem is that often we cannot directly see the forces at work, so reasonable people can disagree on what constitutes a 'realistic' model. Nevertheless, no matter how committed we are to any particular model, we should again always heed Henry Theil's warning: 'It does require maturity to realize that models are to be used, but not to be believed'.[11]

In his interview for this book Alvin Birdi expressed this in his response to the question 'What early career advice do you wish you'd been given as an economist':

"Don't get hung up on technicalities of the models and the frameworks that you learn. You spend an enormous amount of time learning technical modelling frameworks, but what you don't learn is how to use them with … an appropriate humility … if somebody had told me that 'you want your economics to adapt to the situation and not the other way around' that would have been quite a useful piece of information to be told."[12]

In job interviews and in our teaching, we have seen many examples of graduates who regard themselves as quite sophisticated economists but who can be confused by even quite basic economics. That is worrying, as it is a deep understanding of the fundamentals that prevents mistakes. For example, take that ubiquitous tool of economics: supply and demand analysis. Economic analysis should always be much more than just sliding a ruler around a page, and so even 'basic' supply and demand analysis can lead to very inaccurate

---

[11] Theil, H. (1971). Principles of econometrics (New York: Wiley).
[12] In his interview for this book (see Video 4: In conversation with Professor Alvin Birdi available at www.oup.com/he/pryce-ross1e).

conclusions in superficial hands. We have seen graduate economists who can recite advanced techniques but who are unable to explain why an unthinking use of supply and demand can lead to misleading conclusions such as:

- Subsidising all products would lead to a lower price and higher quantity for all goods.
- Immigration must lead to lower average wages for incumbent workers.
- A minimum wage must lead to unemployment.
- A food health scare must lead to lower prices for the product in the shops.

The first three are not necessarily so as they are using partial equilibrium supply and demand analysis, as applied to a single market and then unthinkingly extrapolated to many markets. Supply and demand analysis is best used in a single market on the assumption of 'Ceteris Paribus', the Latin phrase commonly used by economists to denote 'all other things constant'. This assumption is unlikely to hold when many markets are affected, there will be feedbacks from changes that affect whole systems of interrelated markets. In short, many things require general rather than partial equilibrium analysis. The third conclusion ignores the oligopoly market structure of supermarket chains, whereas strictly speaking the theoretical underpinning of a supply curve rests almost invariably on the assumption of perfect competition.[13] The lesson is that economists who think they are good economists merely because they have memorized techniques, but who do not have a deep understanding of the basics and therefore the limitations of the models they use, are dangerous for policy makers and decision makers in the wider world. Indeed, as Gus O'Donnell notes,[14] a major part of the usefulness of a model is that by making clear and precise what it is being assumed it can be tested against the data as a 'reality-check'.

'NEW' DIRECTIONS IN ECONOMICS

The last few decades of the twentieth century saw an increase in the pace of technical developments in economics, such as the application of more readily available computing power to econometrics and modelling, and more

[13] A point that was well emphasized in, say, Richard E. Lipsey (1971), *Positive Economics* for example, on page 256, Absence of a supply curve under monopoly, but which many later textbooks seem to ignore.

[14] In his interview for this book (see Video 19: In conversation with Lord Gus O'Donnell available at www.oup.com/he/pryce-ross1e).

technically sophisticated micro foundations for macroeconomics. Indeed, with the increasing focus on the application of individual maximization and econometrics to an ever wider-range of topics, economics was in danger of becoming defined by its techniques rather than its subject matter. By contrast, the twentieth century has seen the rejuvenation of interest in the limits of determinate modelling and in the behaviour of human beings in real world environments, together with their complex economic interdependencies, including through ever-changing institutions that both affect and shape economic behaviour.[15]

In truth, many of these themes were present in the writings of earlier economists such as, for example, Adam Smith, John Stuart Mill, John Maynard Keynes, Freidrick von Hayek, Kenneth Boulding and Tibor Scitovsky to name but a few. Human psychology also featured heavily in the work of organizational behaviourists such as Richard Cyert and Herbert Simon. More recently, the psychology of human economic decision making has been highlighted and explored by psychologists such as Daniel Kahneman and Richard Thaler, who both won a 'Nobel Prize' in Economics for their work on what has come to be known as 'Behavioural Economics'.[16] Behavioural Economics intersects psychology and economics and has reminded economics that human sentiments, limitations, evolution and quirks mean that 'utility maximization' is not always a useful way to model human behaviour. And that 'utility maximization' can be merely a rather vague catch-all for many and varied human motivations including material well-being but also many other things such as altruism, identity, obligation, self-realization, shame, social acceptance, social conscience, socialization[17] and status. Moreover, our preferences are not fixed as in static indifference curve analysis, our choices will determine our experiences, and as we learn from experience, we will change our preferences. We might like to deny it, but our decisions are seldom exclusively our own. We are all influenced by prevailing cultures and socialization, by marketing, media and those around us.

---

[15] Indeed, the narrow portrayal of economics as being only about selfishness in Jonathan Aldred (2019), *Licence to be bad: how economics corrupted us* was already rather out of date by the time of its publication.

[16] As the Nobel prize is not awarded posthumously, Kahneman's co-researcher Amos Tversky did not receive the prize.

[17] In the late 1970s, Andy Ross met a by then quite elderly Tibor Scitovsky at the London School of Economics. Tibor remarked that 'The reason people in the West don't read Russian literature in Russian is not because it wouldn't add to their enjoyment but because they can't read Russian'. Andy was worried at first that the great man was 'losing it', but of course, the more he thought about the statement the more profound it became.

With the power of modern computing, the availability of 'big data' and the application of agent-based modelling (AGM), economists are also making progress in understanding the implications of complexity. AGM can be less modelling than it is experimentation, where behaviours are programmed into sets of agents and the computer then runs simulations allowing them to interact in order to see what happens. Depending on the approach taken, complexity modelling can be used to critique standard economic policy to improve its success rate, or even to take a neo-Austrian stance and claim that many state-led polices are doomed to failure as they just cannot deal with the complexities of a real economy.[18] However, the challenge of climate change and other environmental requirements for sustainability, the persistence of poverty—even in rich countries—concerns that artificial intelligence could marginalize millions, the dramatic success of China's 'hybrid' economy, dependence on fossil fuels and rare earths from troubled countries,[19] the shock of the Great Financial Crisis of 2007–9 and the world recession that inevitably followed, more recently the Covid-19 pandemic and, for the UK, the aftershocks of Brexit, have all reduced the appeal of an asocial 'leave it all to markets' approach to economics.[20] More economists are once again interested in, and not embarrassed to pursue, ideas on how intervention can promote and/or sponsor social progress, sustainable economies, social capital and social cohesion, 'levelling-up' and industrial policy, 'happiness' and well-being, and the fostering and harnessing of civil society for a more inclusive and supportive society. The developments listed in this paragraph have opened, sometimes re-opened, horizons in economics that could well drive work on policy developments for decades to come.

As with previous developments in economics, new developments won't mean that all previous economics is shown to be redundant, but it will expose limitations and suggest new ways to approach problems and issues.

---

[18] *Exploring Economics* has a useful description of complexity modelling, including 'The main difference between complexity economics and the mainstream is the focus on equilibria—static patterns that call for no further behavioral adjustments. Complexity economics portrays the economy not as deterministic, highly predictable, and mechanistic, but as process dependent, organic, and always evolving.' See Joeri Schasfoort (2017), The perspectives of pluralist economics: Complexity economics, Exploring Economics available at https://www.exploring-economics.org/en/orientation/complexity-economics/ (Accessed September 2021).

[19] This book was completed before the war in Ukraine.

[20] Even including among USA economists on the long-standing 'Hayek v's Keynes' macro debate on the efficacy of fiscal policy. See Doris Geide-Stevenson and Alvaro La Parra Perez (2021), *Consensus among economists 2020—A sharpening of the picture* (Weber State University).

BEHAVIOURAL AND NEW WELFARE ECONOMICS APPLICATIONS

Better engagement with what makes human life worth living remains a huge challenge for economics, which is hardly surprising as philosophers have been debating this for thousands of years! Figure 10.1 helps illustrate where economics is currently strongest, portraying human relations as five main types. The easiest to analysis is the individual/atomistic, not surprisingly, the hardest is where there are many interdependences. Economists have powerful theories to analyse individual choices and competition, and much employment of economists in the private sector depends on a good understanding and technical skills in these important areas. However, the allocation of resources and our welfare is also strongly affected by peer pressure,[21] by the leadership and power structures we are in, and by the institutions and relationships in the societies in which we live, which we in turn influence by our collective

FIGURE 10.1   There's more to economics than individuals

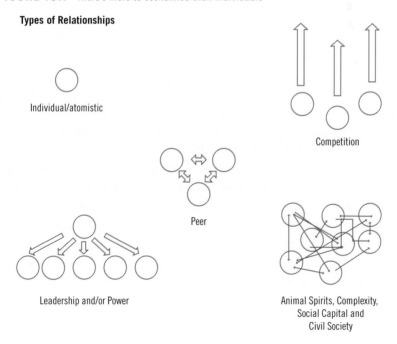

Types of Relationships

Individual/atomistic

Competition

Peer

Leadership and/or Power

Animal Spirits, Complexity, Social Capital and Civil Society

---

[21] As Paul Ormerod notes, this pressure is not necessarily overt: 'People do not decide to copy others deliberately and become obese themselves, but the social pressures and influences on them not to become obese are relaxed when other people in their networks are already obese'. P. Ormerod (2012), *Positive linking: How networks can revolutionise the world.* (Faber and Faber).

behaviours.[22] Most humans seem to be happiest when they combine altruism with self-interest and have a sense of personal achievement. Obviously, to understand these relationships economics requires broader behavioural and interdisciplinary social science. The effectiveness of policies in the public and third sectors can depend on understanding these relationships. Here economics faces tough theoretical challenges and even political challenges as to whether things like 'well-being' and 'happiness' are any business of economists and government at all.[23]

Many economists, such as eminent policy economists Andy Haldane and Gus O'Donnell, are confident that it is very much the business of economists and policy makers to understand better the societal relationships that contribute to human welfare, to learn how to nurture social infrastructures that can reach where other more top-down policies have found it difficult to reach. Wonderful as we economists are, this work obviously needs more than just economists and what is normally regarded as economics:

"Economics is one of the social sciences, and it's actually really useful to understand as many other disciplines as you can, because multidisciplinary work is where real progress is being made now."[24]

Behavioural economics has broadened our understanding of economic decision making and even corrected standard accepted economics in places. It has proved its worth by its fiscal returns alone, such as rephrasing communications and information to increase tax compliance, but it has also proved useful in measures such as providing incentives to insulate homes—including attic clearance as part of the package!—and in explaining why what promised to be very competitive markets turn out in practice not to be such, as in the deregulation of directory enquiries where the ingeniously marketed and easy to remember 118 118 achieved high market concentration. There has also been progress in defining natural and social capital and relating these to welfare (see below page 298). There are also now serious attempts to better understand and hence utilize more effectively 'civil society'. Civil Society refers to the networks of charities, volunteers and

---

[22] Including by economists: this is known as 'reflexivity'.

[23] For example, for a highly critical account see Helen Johns and Paul Ormerod (2007), *Happiness, economics and public policy* (Institute of Economic Affairs). Available at https://www.paulormerod.com/wp-content/uploads/2012/06/happiness-economics-and-public-policy.pdf (Accessed September 2021).

[24] Lord Gus O'Donnell in his interview for this book (see Video 19: In conversation with Lord Gus O'Donnell available at www.oup.com/he/pryce-ross1e).

community networks which can reach into areas of welfare enhancement and support needs that the private and publics sectors fail to reach.

> "At its broadest, it's the space in which individuals and institutions come together for the purpose of generating social good. More narrowly, the social sector—comprising 167,000 charities, upwards of 200,000 grassroot community groups and 100,000 social enterprises (including 7,000 co-operatives)—is often considered the core of civil society."[25]

Andy Haldane explains how important civil society has been in history and recently in the Covid-19 pandemic:

> "We often compartmentalized the economy into convenient silos, something called the public sector, something called the private sector, something called civil society or the third sector … but for me there's very much more that connects those sectors than differentiates them. And I think another common element of what I've tried to do during the course of my career is to join some of the dots. I think of the COVID crisis, which would have been a million times worse had we not seen a joining of hands between the public sector providing its insurance and services, the private sector acting in a purposeful way to support customers, employees and communities, and the charitable sector, providing essential support to those that were suffering most. And that's not a distinctive experience. I look back through history, economic and social history, and the times of greatest strength in our economies and societies is when we've had those three pillars all robust, all strong, and all acting in partnership in shouldering the burden of keeping us growing as economies and individuals, families and communities."[26]

Lord Gus O'Donnell, Chair of the Law Commission on Civil Society also notes that economists have tended to restrict themselves to analysing the role of the private and public sectors when they should also ask:

> "Well, this sort of activity, is it best done by the public sector or private sector or charities or social enterprises? And what are the different incentive structures in all of those things?"[27]

---

[25] *Civil Action: exploring civil society's potential in the 2020s*, Pro Bono Economics (2020). Available at https://www.probonoeconomics.com/civil-action-exploring-civil-societys-potential-in-the-2020s (Accessed September 2021).

[26] In his interview for this book (see Video 16: In conversation with Andy Haldane FAcSS FRS available at www.oup.com/he/pryce-ross1e).

[27] In his interview for this book (see Video 19: In conversation with Lord Gus O'Donnell available at www.oup.com/he/pryce-ross1e).

DEEPENING YOUR UNDERSTANDING OF ECONOMICS

In the rush to learn new techniques and keep-up with whatever new developments are 'trending' in economics, it can be neglected that it is just as important to deepen your understanding by reflecting on the economics you have already covered. Remembering that diagrams and mathematical techniques are only useful tools used by economists—they are not to be confused with economics itself. A deep understanding of concepts and principles is needed to become a successful professional economist. We have argued on page 216 that applying your economics to try and explain the everyday world you see around you is good practice for policy economics. On page 94 we argued that it is often the case that the great economists of the past have had important and insightful things to say about economic approaches that are commonly regarded as 'new'. In this respect, economics can be like great literature, even though you've read it several times before you still gain more from reading and reflecting on it again and again.

On that note, we now wish to alert you to something that seems to have been forgotten to a large extent in economics degrees. Despite economics often being referred to as the 'science of choice' Cost Benefit Analysis (CBA) is no longer included in many economics degrees, even though CBA is an application of basic economics and is a major tool used extensively by practitioners, across all sectors of the economy. Studying the strengths and weaknesses of CBA, its implications for policy and its significant gaps too, is also another salutary lesson in what economics currently can and can't do. It illustrates well the interplay between economic theory and the limits of knowledge that present the hard choices, compromises, and often sheer indeterminacy of real-world policy. Studying CBA, and the HM Treasury's 'Green Book', is important for many economist jobs, and understanding how public choices are made strengthens our democracy.

MICROECONOMICS

Figure 10.2 illustrates the 'traditional' economic mainstream approach to 'justifications' for government interventions. We have been at pains to stress that good policy economists read more widely, keep up with more recent advances in economics, are eclectic, and look for insights from other disciplines. That said, if you do wish to become a policy economist, you will still need to be

FIGURE 10.2 Mainstream economic reasons for intervention by the state

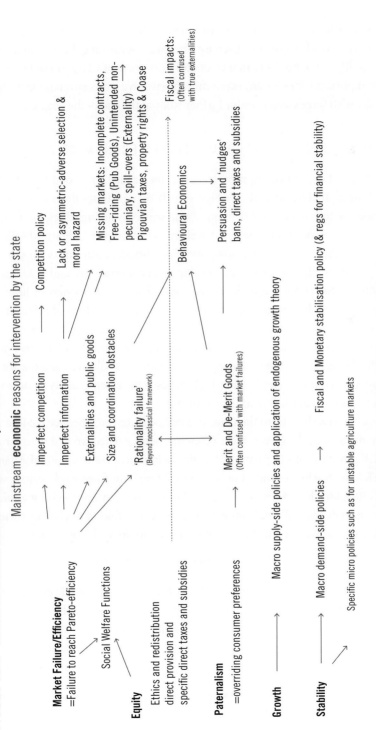

Mainstream **economic** reasons for intervention by the state

Imperfect competition → Competition policy

Imperfect information → Lack or asymmetric-adverse selection & moral hazard

Market Failure/Efficiency
=Failure to reach Pareto-efficiency

Externalities and public goods → Missing markets: Incomplete contracts, Free-riding (Pub Goods), Unintended non-pecuniary, spill-overs (Externality) Pigouvian taxes, property rights & Coase →

Social Welfare Functions

Size and coordination obstacles

Equity
Ethics and redistribution direct provision and specific direct taxes and subsidies

'Rationality failure'
(Beyond neoclassical framework) ←→ Behavioural Economics → Fiscal impacts:
(Often confused with true externalities)

Persuasion and 'nudges'
bans, direct taxes and subsidies

Paternalism
=overriding consumer preferences → Merit and De-Merit Goods
(Often confused with market failures)

Growth ⟶ Macro supply-side policies and application of endogenous growth theory

Stability ⟶ Macro demand-side policies → Fiscal and Monetary stabilisation policy (& regs for financial stability)

Specific micro policies such as for unstable agriculture markets

And always consider the possibility of Government Failure!

familiar with all the concepts shown in Figure 10.2 and be fluent in applying them to real world topics (see Exercise 1 below).[28] Something that you may not find readily in textbooks is an introductory overview of CBA, and so because of its importance for so many economist jobs we give it special attention in this chapter with some references for further study at the end of the chapter.

TOWARDS A MORE INTERDISCIPLINARY ECONOMICS

The 'Social Cost Benefit Approach', sometimes called the 'Total Social Science' conceptual framework (see Figure 10.3), demonstrates the broadness of economics, the challenge of defining it, and why only an interdisciplinary approach to the economy as a whole can claim to be 'complete'. Figure 10.3 illustrates why this is the case. The majority of practitioner economists are always going to be working on more day-to-day practical problems, and academics are often preoccupied with the details and intricacies of models of limited scope, but it is pleasing to note that more recently the teaching of economics has been moving towards encompassing a 'bigger picture' approach, which was the approach of so many of the greatest economists. The CORE free on-line textbook takes a broader perspective than most textbooks, and the Total Social Science approach of Figure 10.3 was used to criticize an overly narrow policy approach to the financial crisis of 2007.

Social researchers from the Government Social Research Service (GSR) and economists from the Government Economic Service (GES) worked together at the UK government's Department for the Environment Food and Rural Affairs (DEFRA) to develop a simple but conceptually rigorous framework that shows why other disciplines are needed, even within a mainstream approach, for a complete understanding of 'The Economy'. The conceptual framework is constructed around the familiar identity that income is the return to wealth or 'Capital':

$$\text{Capital (K)} \times \text{Return (R)} = \text{Income (Y)}$$

This framework helps us appreciate that, when it comes to public policy, economics only contributes to part of the picture. For example, as the framework notes, it is not output in itself that creates welfare but how we experience economic activity and its outputs, or real income, which hopefully should contribute to our wellbeing. But if production has serious downsides- environmental,

---

[28] Any introductory tome should cover these concepts, and an accessible, impressively concise and clearly written account of these can be found in Andrew Mell and Oliver Walker (2014), *Economics: From first principles to the financial crisis* (Rough Guides Ltd).

FIGURE 10.3 The 'Social Cost Benefit Approach', or 'Total Social Science' conceptual framework

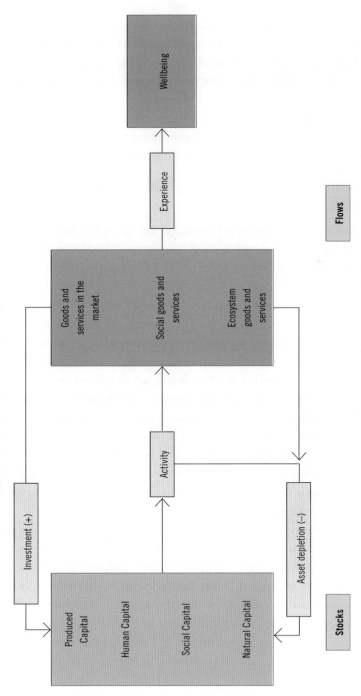

Source: Figure 1 from Department for Environment, Food and Rural Affairs (2011). A framework for understanding the social impacts of policy and their effects on wellbeing (Defra Evidence and Analysis Series, Paper 3), p. 6. Available at (https://assets.publishing.service.gov.uk/government/uploads/system/uploads/attachment_data/file/69196/pb13467-social-impacts-wellbeing-110403.pdf.

psychological or social—then output may not increase well-being. With this in mind, we might try to define economics as the 'science and art of increasing human welfare', but that would certainly encroach upon psychology and philosophy, including ethics, and there is nothing in the framework that says anything must or will be maximized or even increased. Even if we stick to 'things more economic' it is still clear that a wide range of 'capitals' add to useful income and wellbeing, and capital is much more than just machines and physical infrastructure. For example, it includes social cohesion and natural resources, and the system must be sustainable too if it is to maintain the level of welfare.

THE 'PRESERVATION OF CAPITALS APPROACH' TO WELLBEING AND SUSTAINABILITY

Diane Coyle was a pioneer in exploring and describing how new technologies have produced more and more 'weightless' items and activities that makes it harder for GDP to capture the full range of 'Goods and Service in the market' that it is supposed to measure.[29] And Figure 10.3 clearly shows that even if it could measure these more accurately, GDP is still only part of what contributes to human experiences and hence wellbeing. Social goods and services, such as unpaid household production, housework and unpaid caring duties, community production and volunteering, as well as other contributions of 'civil society' (see below) to human wellbeing, are simply not captured in GDP. The ecosystem is also of course often unpriced and so depleted too freely by a plethora of externalities outside of market mechanisms. Again, the ultimate goal of economic activity is not output but well-being, and to get to well-being outputs have to pass through 'experience'. It is a trite saying that 'money can't buy you happiness', and the framework provides a more formal framework for seeing why this is so. GDP may contribute to well-being, but it can never fully compensate for a dysfunctional and therefore unhappy society.

The 'Experience' box between the outputs of activity and Wellbeing also emphasizes that, unless we feel healthy and well-adjusted in ourselves, more output may do little to raise our 'utility'. This emphasis on experience and well-being also suggests that human capital should be defined broadly. In addition to the usual classification as 'investment in knowledge and skills' perhaps human capital should also include investment in mental health. How we experience life is integral to our wellbeing. The eminent economist Lord Layard has argued cogently that there is too little attention given to investment

---

[29] See for example: Coyle. D (1999), *The weightless world—Strategies for managing the digital economy* (The MIT Press).

in mental health and that such investment would often have higher returns, in both well-being and production, than many investments that are included in the usual textbook definition of 'capital', that is machines and infrastructure used for production.[30]

NATURAL AND SOCIAL CAPITAL

The framework in Figure 10.3 also makes it clear that to physical capital and human capital we must add both natural and social capital. Natural capital is the environmental ecosystem, that provides us directly with services such as space and aesthetic satisfaction and natural assets, including air, minerals, soil water and living things. This is obviously a vital consideration for sustainability. 'Deep Green' critics may argue that it is not possible to trade-off natural capital for other capitals so that the capital stock as a whole is not diminished. That is essentially an empirical question, but the framework clearly shows that if the volume of produced capital increases at the expense of natural capital then this could actually lead to a reduction in production. In short, the preservation of capitals makes clear that measured GDP is only part—albeit perhaps an important part—of what contributes to well-being, and that GDP is not sustainable unless the capital stocks base from which it flows are maintained.

> "The 'capitals approach' emphasises sustainability in cost-benefit analysis, which usually focuses on the flows. This is important in terms of whether the stock of wealth-creating and wellbeing-enhancing assets we pass on to future generations is better or worse than what is available to us today, and is a key analytical component of mainstreaming sustainable development."[31]

The work of modern economists, such as Professor Lord (Nicholas) Stern and the renowned Grantham Institute he leads, has done much to integrate natural capital into modern economics and policies. In contrast, social capital, which is the stock of social networks, shared norms and values and understandings that facilitate cooperation and cohesion within or among groups, which was so emphasized by many great economists of the past, remains less integrated. To be fair, experience reveals how problematic it is to operationalize elusive

---

[30] For example, see *UK's 'happiness tsar' on the importance of mental health*: Annie Maccoby Berglof, *Financial Times* (12 September 2014).

[31] *A framework for understanding the social impacts of policy and their effects on wellbeing.* A paper for the Social Impacts Taskforce by social researcher Gemma Harper and economist Richard Price (publishing.service.gov.uk) (April 2011). Available at https://assets.publishing.service.gov.uk/government/uploads/system/uploads/attachment_data/file/69196/pb13467-social-impacts-wellbeing-110403.pdf (Accessed September 2020).

concepts that are immeasurable in any precise way, but then, as in everyday life and in real world policy making, judgements must often be made about many important things that we cannot know with precision. It seems ridiculous that drug dealing is now included in GDP but voluntary work, which would amount to billions of pounds if paid for, is not represented at all in the national income accounts! So, it is pleasing to see that economics is placing more emphasis on the importance of social capital and has exciting new initiatives trying to understand and increase it. For instance, Pro Bono Economics, with the support of the Law Family Charitable Foundation, has launched an ambitious programme of research into how we can unleash the potential of civil society to harness and enhance the powerful community bonds that exist in our nation. The British Academy and the Nuffield Foundation have also launched a research and policy collaboration, awarding over £500,000 in research funding to identify practical solutions to increase the cohesion and resilience of local communities in the UK.

As Matt Whittaker, CEO of Pro Bono Economics, said in 2020:

> "The UK is rightly proud of its civil society, and the coronavirus pandemic has highlighted the crucial role our volunteers, charities, community groups and social enterprises play. The sector has huge amounts of potential to change lives and improve wellbeing in the country. But despite the excellent work charity leaders do with the resources they have, there are systemic challenges in place that prevent the sector fulfilling that potential. And though we have pride in it, public policy focuses on human, financial and physical capital before social capital."[32]

'Social capital' may appear a woolly notion to some hard-nosed policy makers but neglecting it may have serious consequences that swamp and then eclipse narrow economic policies. For example, by focussing only on addressing standard economic concerns, such as GDP, inflation, or even 'sovereign default risk', we may miss potential trade-offs with social capital and societal contentment, and this may eventually create feedbacks and discontents that politically overwhelm our standard economic policy levers. Social capital relates to the level of stability, well-being and trust in a society and hence to productivity as well as directly to welfare. Andy Haldane argues:

---

[32] *Announcing the Law Family Commission on Civil Society* (2020) https://www.probonoeconomics. com/news/announcing-the-law-family-commission-on-civil-society.

"While social capital is built personally and locally, its benefits extend nationally and often globally in an increasingly interconnected world. Social capital is fuel for us as individuals, personally and emotionally. But it is rocket-fuel for us economically and financially too. It is the secret source of economic as well as personal growth ..."[33]

Even the laissez-faire leaning *Economist* magazine has noted that it is dangerous to leave social capital out of the politics of economic policy formulation, as political impacts can eventually overwhelm the relevance of the economics:

"Many economists shy away from such questions, happy to treat politics, like physics, as something that is economically important but fundamentally the business of other fields. But when ignoring those fields makes economic-policy recommendations irrelevant, broadening the scope of inquiry within the profession becomes essential."[34]

Even if someone were still interested in the rather sterile debate as to whether economics is a science or not, it is clear from the preservation of capital framework that in the real world of policy making the economics involved is often intertwined with international relations, politics, sociology and ethics as well as other things that have even less claim to be regarded as 'hard science'. Even the preservation of capitals approach is incomplete: The real challenge of social scientists is not simply to map the forces at work, predict and make warnings about the future, it is to advise on how the future could be improved. More dynamic frameworks that can incorporate potential transformations are also needed, even though this takes us well beyond what would usually be narrowly regarded as 'rigorous science'.

While the drafts for this book were being submitted for publication, Diane Coyle had another new book published: *Cogs and Monsters: What Economics is and what it should be.* She emphasizes how far real economies are from the First Fundamental Theorem we described in Chapter 5 (page 125) and how narrow the membership of the profession and its focus has been compared to the challenges now faced:

---

[33] Andy Haldane (2020), *Social capital: The economy's rocket fuel*, The Law Family Commission on Civil Society. Available at https://civilsocietycommission.org/essay/social-capital-the-economys-rocket-fuel/ (Accessed September 2021).

[34] *The Economist* (2017) 'To be relevant, economists need to take politics into account'. Available at https://www.economist.com/finance-and-economics/2017/01/12/to-be-relevant-economists-need-to-take-politics-into-account (Accessed September 2021).

"… this book [Cogs and Monsters] reflects on the broader character of economics, not only its lack of inclusivity, and how the subject needs to change to be relevant for the rest of the twenty-first century. The issues covered here concern the fundamental paradigm—the subject's roots in utilitarianism, the validity of the distinction between positive and normative economics, the character of dynamic socio-economic systems that do not conform to the standard assumptions, the role of social influence in a discipline built on methodological individualism, and the scope for a powerful social science to alter its own subjects of study."[35]

All this should make it very clear that any perception of economics as only being about 'men in suits making money' is very wide of the truth (see also Chapter 8).

THE UBIQUITOUS ART, SCIENCE, AND POLITICS OF CHOICE: COST BENEFIT ANALYSIS (CBA)

As said, CBA raises many contemporary issues and is so neglected nowadays in economics degrees[36] that we give it special prominence here. CBA approaches choice decisions through estimating the consequences of a decision on future costs and benefits. To compare the size of the benefits with the size of the costs a common unit of account, a 'Numéraire', must be used. The most available and best understood numéraire is money, although in principle it doesn't need to be money at all. To this end, CBA seeks to put a monetary value on as many of the costs and benefits of a decision as possible. This is sometimes confused with the notion that 'only money matters in CBA'. That is incorrect, CBA can include many things that have no market value, such as pollution or even 'social capital' (see page 298). It is not so much conceptual limits as to what could be included in CBA that limits CBA so much as its practical limits, all good economists are well aware of the limits of such 'monetization'. For example, a loving parent has infinite valuations for their children and there is no monetary equivalent—money can't buy you love! Confusion also arises from not appreciating that CBA is only an input to decision making, it is not the decision itself. Clearly real-life decision makers are free to, and do, consider other criteria in coming to their decisions. The purpose of CBA is only to provide

---

[35] Diane Coyle (2021), *Cogs and monsters: what economics is, and what it should be* (Princeton University Press).

[36] With some notable and worthy exceptions.

a consistent and transparent framework for appraising measurable elements that affect the desirability and priority of projects, programmes or policies in terms of net benefits. That is, the value of benefits minus the value of the costs.

CBA AS A TECHNOCRAT'S DREAM

Although it was always accepted that actual decisions involve a wide range of considerations, many of them of a political or social character, a typical article from the time when the use of CBA was being strongly advocated for use by government, A.R. Prest and R.Turvey, 'Cost Benefit Analysis: a survey', *Economic Journal*, Vol 75 (1965) reflected the technocratic aspiration of economists of the time to reduce subjective arbitrariness in government decision making. The emphasis was to place 'positive' economics above vague or 'normative' judgements:

> "... drawing on a variety of traditional sections of economic study—welfare economics, public finance, resource economics ... An important advantage of a cost-benefit study is that it forces those responsible to quantify costs and benefits as far as possible rather than rest content with vague qualitative judgments or personal hunches ... Furthermore, quantification and evaluation of benefits, however rough, does give some sort of clue to the charges which consumers are willing to pay ... The discipline of the market place is so easily and so readily forgotten in these situations that some empirical evidence about benefit projections is highly necessary."[37]

The technocratic aspiration is far from dead today. Cass Sunstein, an American legal scholar known particularly by economists for his joint authorship of the influential book *Nudge*, writes in his book *The Cost Benefit Revolution* published in 2018:

> "Cost-benefit analysis reflects a firm (and proud) commitment to a technocratic conception of democracy ... Cost-benefit analysis insists that difficult questions of fact should be answered by those who are in a good position to answer them correctly."[38]

CBA was to be used in contrast to being vague, emotive or pursuing pet or 'vanity' projects, such as a major public works driven by a CEO's or politician's desire to leave a legacy, or worse, for personal interests or to influence voters. In many ways, although the democratic process must be respected, most economists do

---

[37] A. R. Prest, R. Turvey (1965), 'Cost-Benefit analysis: A survey', *The Economic Journal*, Volume 75, Issue 300, 1 December 1965, pp. 683–735.

[38] C. Sunstein (2018), *The cost benefit revolution* (MIT Press).

tend to champion technocracy over the distortions of populism and politics. Keynes certainly did: '[i]f economists could manage to get themselves thought of as humble, competent people on a level with dentists, that would be splendid'.[39] We all rely on the expertise of dentists rather than ask the patients in the waiting room to vote on the treatment we need! Although decision making is broader, CBA often had a central focus on whether something could be 'justified' by market-failure or distributional considerations. Setting aside the legitimate concerns about how values are distributed to gainers and losers, CBA in effect asked a technocratic question: 'Would the market do this if it could?'. That is, could the gainers compensate any losers and still have a net benefit?

As rehearsed in Chapter 5, 'market failure' in neoclassical economics simply means a failure to achieve a Pareto-efficient outcome. The classic CBA criteria, that the benefits should exceed costs,[40] is in effect a test for a potential Pareto-improvement: could the gainers compensate the losers and still be better off?[41] If that is the case, then in effect CBA can be seen as correcting or 'filling-in' for market failure, such as the 'missing market' of public goods. CBA was originally developed to identify a potential Pareto-Improvement, and although it has seldom if ever been used in such a pure market-failure form, part of its purpose was to reduce, or at least reveal, the arbitrary discretion, whim or vanity, of human decision makers. We should note, however, that the notion that there is no moral element in a Pareto-improvement, as 'no-one loses', is problematic. A quick consideration of, say, prostitution, kidney sales, animal rights or selling the heritage of future generations, should be enough to realize that things are not that straight-forward. In practice, an actual Pareto-improvement was not even the criterion actually used for CBA (see for example the 'Hicks-Kaldor criterion' below). Also, as the final outcomes of output and its distribution are very much affected by the choice criteria used, there is an ethical dimension just in choosing any one choice criteria over another.

In the public sector CBA was seldom, if ever, used in its 'classical' pure neoclassical form. For example, distributional weights were added, and inevitably other factors are brought to bear in addition to just monetized costs and benefits. More recently, incorporating the monetization of wider social and welfare impacts means that 'gainers compensating losers' becomes even more hypothetical. Equally, in commerce, businesses will have strategic aims that may

---

[39] John Maynard Keynes, *Essays in persuasion*, ch. 5.
[40] As large projects typically have impacts over a long period, this criterion is more rigorously stated as 'Is the Net Present Value' positive?
[41] Although as we will note, this is not usually meant in a literal sense.

override their own CBA. In the public sector broader considerations are obviously appropriate for a democracy, although this then opens the door to lobbying by special interests. Nevertheless, the big advantage of CBA over more subjective personal decisions is that it is transparent in method[42] and explicit in the valuations used. This does not mean that CBA calculations are therefore 'correct', but it does mean that its method and estimates can be examined and challenged in detail because of its transparency.

One reason, one of many, why a CBA valuation may be incorrect is that the assumptions made about market values benefits and costs may be misleading. For example, if monopolies are present in construction for a large project then the market prices used to estimate the costs may overstate the true costs and hence the valuations of the alternatives foregone. Or one market failure may be off setting another: a monopoly that raises prices may reduce output and so also reduce a negative externality. These complicated issues of 'second-best' considerations contrast with the simpler and familiar 'first-best' conditions of Pareto-efficiency, such as marginal cost pricing. Even if we take the heroic leap that the rarefied First Optimality Theorem is a meaningful basis for practical interventions at all, it is still fair to say that considerations of second-best conditions tend to be skated over in CBA,[43] as the information requirements to take account of them are simply too great. We describe below some other intrinsic problems that often arise in CBA.

THE THEORETICAL UNDERPINNINGS OF CBA

Clearly, as the theoretical underpinnings of much of CBA are drawn from neoclassical economics, as is still most microeconomic policy, an in-depth understanding of the strengths and limitations of CBA also requires an in-depth understanding of neoclassical general equilibrium theory. And as CBA is used so extensively, this is an argument for including the rarefied neoclassical model of general equilibrium analysis in economics degrees. Not as a description of the real world, which it is far from being, but as a tool of analysis that, for better or for worse, is used extensively in economic policy. As CBA's

---

[42] Well, at least to others who understand CBA!

[43] As are some other thorny theoretical conundrums, such as the 'Scitovsky paradox' and 'Arrow's Possibility Theorem' for consistency of social welfare functions.

theoretical underpinnings lie in neo-classical welfare economics, where equilibrium prices reflect both opportunity costs and monetary valuations, the values used in CBA calculations are often read directly from market costs and market prices. Markets mechanisms automatically attach prices and costs by which people make decisions, and in theory these could reflect willingness to pay and marginal costs, but often these values have to be imputed in CBA estimates for non-market outcomes, such as pollution. These can sometime be estimated through 'revealed preference' where related market prices are affected, or in terms of people's 'willingness to pay' for a benefit, or alternatively how much it would take to 'compensate' them for a loss.

Externalities are an obvious example not weighted by cost or price in the free market, but often it is possible to find at least a proxy measure for how much such externalities are valued by the individuals affected. Economists can be quite ingenious at this. For example, the valuation of street improvements, or neighbourhood crime reduction, might be proxied by measuring changes in house prices, to 'reveal preferences'. But such ingenuity still usually leaves room for challenge. As an exercise, you should consider why estimates of the cost of the noise from an established airport, as measured by the lower house prices around it, may not be a good estimate of the valuation of the noise from the building of a new airport elsewhere. Such thorny valuation issues are very common in CBA (see below page 317).

Markets automatically attach prices and costs by which people make decisions but in the public sector, without markets, estimating 'willingness to pay', or what would be adequate compensation, that is, 'willingness to accept', is fraught with difficulty. Valuations of 'willing to pay' and 'willingness to accept' can also be very context specific. For example, if you ask people what pleasure they get from owning their cars their answers are likely to be correlated with the price of the car, but if you ask them how much pleasure they got from their last car journey they are likely only to complain about the traffic. People are not always good at estimating what things are actually worth to them. Research by Paul Dolan et al.[44] suggests that the very fact of making the respondent focus on a particular thing distorts their valuation of it, as generally they act without such a focus on that thing to the exclusion of other things. Valuations are also likely to depend on perceived incentives. For example, if a

---

[44] See for example Paul Dolan, Henry Lee, Dominic King and Robert Metcalfe (2009), 'Valuing health directly' https://www.bmj.com/content/339/bmj.b2577.extract (Accessed May 2021).

respondent is told that they will not have to personally pay for a project then, if they would benefit from its going ahead, they are likely to exaggerate their valuation. Conversely, if they are told that they will have to pay in accordance with their stated valuation then they may understate their true valuation in the hope of 'free-riding'.

NEW APPROACHES TO WELFARE ECONOMICS

A recent econometric approach that avoids directly asking about specific things uses a utilitarianism approach. That is, people are asked to rank how happy/content they feel in general, and these rankings are then regressed against a selection of characteristics and variables such as wealth, income, religion, marital status, location, health and disabilities. From this, on the rather heroic assumption that self-declared happiness has validity and interpersonal comparisons can be made, values can be indirectly inferred from the estimates for various components of well-being/happiness. There are ardent fans and severe critics of governments directly attempting to increase well-being, and this and other novel approaches to welfare economics have not usually hitherto been part of CBA in government. But 'Wellbeing Guidance for Appraisal' is now explicitly included in The Green Book.[45] The Green Book being the comprehensive handbook issued by HM Treasury that lays down central guidance for the appraisal of projects, policies, and programmes for all government departments (see *HM Treasury's Green Book* below page 307).

DISTRIBUTIONAL IMPACTS

It was always the case that insisting on an actual Pareto-improvement, where no-one is actually made worse off, would paralyse policy. As for any major policy, programme, or project there <u>will</u> be losers as well as gainers. Losers, such as certain businesses that suffer from the impacts of government decisions, or compulsory purchases from people who do not want to vacate their properties to make way for new transport links, or simply those who could have made use of the resources used up in the public sector. Therefore, in practice the Pareto-criterion was pragmatically compromised by using the 'Hicks-Kaldor Criterion'. This criterion, named after two eminent economists,[46] stipulates

---

[45] HM Treasury (2018), the Green Book: central government guidance on appraisal and evaluation.

[46] *Sir* John Hicks and Lord Nicholas Kaldor.

that there need be only a potential Pareto-improvement for a decision to pass the 'benefits exceed costs' test. That is, that the gainers could 'in principle' compensate the losers and still be better off, even if they don't actually compensate the losers. This raises more moral issues of course, but the general idea is that consistency in using this criterion for all decisions will maximize the 'national cake'. That is, the total value-added that there is to share out for everybody.

As the Hick-Kaldor criterion does not relate to redistribution policy, different weights may be placed by the decision makers on the value of income to different groups. Diminishing marginal utility was invoked to try and be less arbitrary in the Green Book, and in 2010 estimated distributional impacts were included in the Chancellor's Budget for the first time. The recent review of the Green Book has incorporated a 'Public Sector Equality Duty' (see below page 309). Of course, if there are more monetized social and welfare impacts with arbitrary weights then the notion of a Pareto-improvement, whereby gainers could in principle compensate the losers if benefits exceed costs, becomes even more abstract.

HM TREASURY'S GREEN BOOK

The Green Book sets out in detail the rules for appraisal/CBA in public policy making. Its methods and rules are also extensively used in the regular 'Comprehensive Spending Reviews', which set the plans for future public spending and assessing spending priorities. As HM Treasury is the UK's Finance Ministry, and so allocates the monies to all the other departments, it can insist that those departments demonstrate that they have used Green Book techniques to appraise their spending plans. All economists concerned with microeconomic policy in the UK should at least skim through the Green Book as it is such an important document for appraising public policies, projects and priorities.

The Green Book has always seen its objective as being to improve social welfare:

> "The Government is committed to continuing improvement in the delivery of public services. A major part of this is ensuring that public funds are spent on activities that provide the greatest benefits to society, and that they are spent in the most efficient way."[47]

---

[47] HM Treasury (2003). *The Green Book: Appraisal and evaluation in central government*, p. v. Retrieved from https://webarchive.nationalarchives.gov.uk/20080305121602/http:/www.hm-treasury.gov.uk/media/3/F/green_book_260907.pdf.

This has not prevented politicians wanting to see the Green Book amended to be more supportive of their own chosen interpretations and policies!

RECENT GREEN BOOK REVISITS

In 2011 David Cameron 'ordered' civil servants to rewrite parts of the Green Book to ensure that his notion of the 'Big Society' would be taken into account. As we have seen above, this is easier said than done. In any case, the Treasury is the lead department for the Green Book and reports to the Chancellor of the Exchequer rather than the PM. Even a Prime Minister's command does not advance the necessary economics! And so, the Green Book was updated at that time mostly with only an annex being added alluding to these wider non-monetised impacts. Although the valuation of wider social impacts and wellbeing was largely work in progress at the time, the OECD had begun measurement projects,[48] and advances in economics may mean broader social and wellbeing impacts are increasingly a part of Green Book appraisal. Prime Minister Cameron's exhortation did, at least, lead the UK's environment Ministry (DEFRA) to develop the theoretical 'preservations of capital' framework we looked at above (see page 297) and was a spur to new work on a broader welfare economics.

In 2018 and 2020 a Conservative Government revisited the Green Book. They insisted that it should take more account of Ministers' policy priorities. They have pushed back further against the original technocratic CBA aim, and so criticized previous versions of the Green Book. The Conservative Party's desire to move away from more technocratic CBA is most explicit in the HM Treasury publication *Green Book Review 2020: Findings and response,* which accompanies the revised Green Book:

> "With a lack of strategic direction now baked into the appraisal process, the selection of the option to be presented as the best becomes heavily reliant on a Benefit Cost Ratio (BCR) that is not aligned to the decision makers' objectives … it reduces decision makers' ability to make informed decisions about which option will best achieve their objectives, ultimately risking undermining their ability to achieve them … the appraisal process will have a clearer focus on the contribution of bids to the Government's explicit policy objectives and less emphasis on purely economic and monetizable benefits."[49]

---

[48] *See* The OECD measurement of social capital project and question databank at https://www.oecd.org/sdd/social-capital-project-and-question-databank.htm (Accessed Autumn 2021).

[49] HM Treasury (2020), *Green Book Review 2020: findings and response.* Sections 1.12, 2.4, and 4.5, pp 4, 9, and 21. Retrieved from https://assets.publishing.service.gov.uk/government/uploads/system/uploads/attachment_data/file/937700/Green_Book_Review_final_report_241120v2.pdf.

The policy review document exaggerates the degree to which the Green Book was ever really a constraint on Ministers' ability to achieve their objectives. As we saw in Chapter 3, civil servants are there to serve their Ministers and a Minister is always at liberty to ask for a broader analysis and to take other things, such as their Government's own policy agenda, into consideration. A Cost Benefit Ratio has never had the authority to veto a Minister, even if occasionally it might embarrass one! The emphasis on 'decision makers objectives', however, seems to be heavier in the rhetoric of the review document, written to introduce the new Green Book, than in the revised Green Book itself. As in the extract on policy making from Paul Johnson: *The truth about making policy is difficult for politicians to swallow*—explained in Chapter 3—this reflects a tension that is always present between politics and economics. Equally, what is part of Government's strategic aim may not be good economics, even in a democracy. In a democracy the Government is entitled to, even obligated, to respond to the electorate's wishes, but bad economic choices can make future trade-offs harsher, and hence reality becomes more of a constraint. For example, decisions that reduce the growth of monetary value-added, and hence GDP, could lead to lower tax revenues and so can make it harder to fund the public services that are also demanded by the electorate.

Nevertheless, human welfare obviously depends on a lot more than even the most perfectly functioning market ideal of neoclassical economics could provide. The revised Green Book reasonably incorporates broader elements that reflect developments in social cost benefit analysis and welfare economics over the previous decade, including the now binding environmental and distributional impact considerations. The Green Book does also integrate environmental targets and a 'Public Sector Equality Duty' (PSED). PSED requires public sector bodies to have due regard to equality of opportunity for persons with protected characteristics and to contribute to 'eliminating discrimination and fostering good relations between protected groups and others'. The Public Sector Equality Duty covers nine protected characteristics: age; disability; gender reassignment; pregnancy and maternity; race; religion or belief and sex and sexual orientation.

Even if the economics of a particular strategic aim or objective of the Government were to be doubtful, it is still worthwhile to have economists clearly spell out the economic pros and cons of the various options for achieving its aims. In fact, the review documents are explicit that the new Green Book is particularly aimed at integrating the Conservative Government's 'levelling-up' agenda, which at the time of writing,[50] appears to be mostly a form of regional policy but would logically include consideration of local deprivations and generic inequality, such as low pay.[51] Unless the criteria and weightings to be used are explicit and well-specified in advance, then there is an inherent risk in integrating the Government's strategic policy objectives into formal appraisal. It may move the weight of decision-making from the original more techno-cratic aspirations of CBA back towards the *ad hoc* interpretations and hence personal motivations of the decision makers. The very thing that CBA was originally developed to reduce. Of course, this is less of an issue if one has little faith in CBA in the first place or is very cynical that CBA ever advanced 'good economics over bad politics'.

Of course, any compassionate policy social welfare criteria will include eq-uity as well as efficiency, so of course a non-Pareto outcome can legitimately be judged to be superior to a less equitable but more efficient outcome. However, increasing the size of the 'national cake' in GDP can also have some advantages, and so shifting focus to other criteria, such as 'levelling-up', might reduce total monetary value-added from the nation's resources. Certainly, it is undesirable that the UK is one of the most regionally unequal countries in the developed world, but what if international competition today is largely between large dynamic cities? There is strong evidence that the close human interaction in major cities enhances productivity and value-added. Called 'agglomeration benefits' in economics. Could diverting resources away from already interna-tionally competitive cities, to reallocate to more depressed regions, decrease national competitiveness and so reduce a nation's potential resources for other forms of redistribution? Also, pockets of poverty, such as in London, can be very different from a region's average earnings, and regional policy has a rather chequered history in the UK anyway. It has not always seemed that regional policy knew better than market forces! Conversely, it might be argued that well-judged development polices could transform the productivity and com-petitiveness of regions and hence increase a nation's economic wealth. Such transformational considerations are intrinsically hard to predict but can be extremely important.

---

[50] End of 2021.

[51] In May 2021 the House of Lords Public Services Committee sent a letter to Boris Johnson to urge him to be more open about funding decisions, as well as other criticisms of 'Levelling-up' as a coherent programme. For example, see UK Parliament (May 2021) *Refocus 'levelling up' strategy and funds, peers tell government* at https://www.parliament.uk/business/lords/media-centre/house-of-lords-media-notices/2021/may-2021/refocus-levelling-up-strategy-and-funds-peers-tell-government/ (Accessed August 2021).

There are no clear answers to these considerations, but clearly, if the criteria are not well-specified and the emphasis is placed on achieving a Minister's objectives as defined by that Minister, then there is a danger that the CBA process becomes circular. At worst, an elaborate exercise within an impressive framework biased towards supporting the Minister's prior decision. For example, if the best options have been excluded then no amount of CBA can guard against waste of valuable resources. There is also the temptation to target politically strategic constituencies or reward supporters. So, it is reassuring to hear, as we complete the writing of this book, that Andy Haldane has been appointed as the Head of the Levelling Up Taskforce.[52]

CBA DOES NOT COPE WELL WITH THE POTENTIAL FOR TRANSFORMATIONAL BENEFITS

It can be difficult to estimate expected values by extrapolating costs and benefits from existing projects into the future, even if similar past ones can be identified. Dynamic effects that lead to transformational change are much harder to estimate. The Green Book defines transformational change as:

> "In Green Book terms transformational change refers to a radical permanent qualitative change in the subject being transformed, so that the subject when transformed has very different properties and behaves or operates in a different way."[53]

And as the review document points outs:

> "The revised Green Book does not provide a step-by-step method that will generate precise valuations of transformational impacts. Such tools do not exist and are unlikely to be developed given the inherent uncertainty of these processes."[54]

Dimitri Zenghelis, a leading climate change economist and Senior Visiting Fellow at the Grantham Research Institute, stresses that decisions taken now

---

[52] GOV.UK (2021) *Press release: Ambitious plans to drive levelling up agenda* https://www.gov.uk/government/news/ambitious-plans-to-drive-levelling-up-agenda (Accessed September 2021).

[53] HM Treasury (2018). *The Green Book: central government guidance on appraisal and evaluation*, Section A7.2 pp. 127. Retrieved from https://assets.publishing.service.gov.uk/government/uploads/system/uploads/attachment_data/file/938046/The_Green_Book_2020.pdf.

[54] HM Treasury (2020). *Green Book Review 2020: Findings and response*. Sections 2.22 p. 15. Retrieved from https://assets.publishing.service.gov.uk/government/uploads/system/uploads/attachment_data/file/937700/Green_Book_Review_final_report_241120v2.pdf.

will affect how the future unfolds, and hence the potential for transformation. In particular, rather than locking in carbon-based infrastructure, the most important impact of targets for reducing emissions are not the 'costly' reduction in emissions that a static approach based on existing technology would suggest, but the transformation of technology that is set in train that leads to renewable energy becoming cost competitive with fossil fuels, and so transforming the carbon footprint from future energy use. Dimitri emphasizes Nobel Prize-winning economist Romer's distinction between 'complacent' and 'cooperative' optimism:

> "Complacent optimism is the feeling of a child waiting for presents. Conditional optimism is the feeling of a child who is thinking about building a treehouse. 'If I get some wood and nails and persuade some other kids to help do the work, we can end up with something really cool.'"[55]

Unfortunately, this doesn't lend itself to precise CBA estimates. As was noted in the recent review of the Green Book, the problem is that even if it there are good reasons to suppose there could be transformational change, from, say, environmental measures, it remains the case, that 'transformation' is harder to detail and predict than is extrapolating current costs and benefits as in standard CBA.

OPTIMISM BIAS

In contrast to potential underestimation of transformational benefits there is the observed and commonplace tendency for 'optimism bias':

> "Optimism bias is the demonstrated systematic tendency for appraisers to be over-optimistic about key project parameters, including capital costs, operating costs, project duration and benefits delivery … The Green Book recommends applying specific adjustments for this at the outset of an appraisal."[56]

---

[55] Quoted in Dimitri Zenghelis, *Nobel for economics 2018—a question of imbalance*, (2009) Available at https://www.lse.ac.uk/granthaminstitute/news/nobel-for-economics-2018-a-question-of-imbalance/ (Accessed March 2021). The original Paul Romer quote can be found on his own blog page: Paul Romer (2018) *Conditional optimism*. Available at https://paulromer.net/conditional-optimism-technology-and-climate/ (Accessed May 2021).

[56] HM Treasury (2018). *The Green Book: Central government guidance on appraisal and evaluation*, Sections 5.43 and A5.4, pp. 48 and 107. Retrieved from https://assets.publishing.service.gov.uk/government/uploads/system/uploads/attachment_data/file/938046/The_Green_Book_2020.pdf.

For example, we saw in page 209 that policy makers dealing in the abstract can be unaware of the practical difficulties in the operational delivery of projects, programmes, and policies. This is guarded against by systematically including an allowance for optimism bias. Even then the margin of error for any large project is speculative, as demonstrated by the spectacular costs and delivery overruns for such as the Scottish Parliament building, London Cross-Rail (Elizabeth Line) and High-Speed Rail HS2.

DISCOUNTING THE FUTURE

Discounting involves using a discount rate to convert a future flow of costs and benefits into their current value, called Net Present Value (NPV). The higher the discount rate is the more it 'discounts' the future, that is, the less the weight given to the future. A central consideration is that by investing in a project, the resources used are not available for something else, so it has an opportunity cost. In private sector investments an opportunity cost takes account of the return from alternative investments. In neoclassical economics the rate of return on capital is often used as the discount rate, as in theoretical equilibrium the rate of return on capital would be equated to the 'time preference' of consumers: the rate at the margin for which consumers are prepared to sacrifice current income for a larger future increase in income. The notion of 'Time Preference' arises from the observation that people generally prefer things now rather than later.[57]

In practice, CBA in the public sector reflects the fact that the available public sector budget is finite and pre-set. This is often known as the public sector 're-source envelope', or colloquially 'the public purse'. The public sector resource envelope is determined by political processes and macroeconomic considerations, rather than by the principles of neoclassical economics. Therefore, for this and for other reasons too, HM Treasury uses a 'Social Time Preference Rate' (STPR) rather than the rate of return on private capital, or indeed any other measure of opportunity cost from the private sector to discount future costs and benefits. In principle, all possible policies, programmes and projects could be converted into discounted NPVs. The ratio of benefits to costs, 'bangs

---

[57] This is sometimes confused with allowing for inflation, but time preference still exists even when inflation effects are removed.

to the buck', could then be used to rank all of these for taxpayer's funding until the public purse is exhausted. Practicalities and the realities of government and democracy has, of course, always meant practice has been at a considerable distance from this 'technocrat's dream'.

WHAT IS INCLUDED IN THE GREEN BOOK'S SOCIAL TIME PREFERENCE RATE (STPR)?

The value of the STPR in the Green Book used to be set at 3.5 per cent and for a long time that was pretty much that. But there have been lively debates since then, and the Green Book has been updated to reflect further theoretical and moral developments. These can be better understood by noting that the Green Book STPR of 3.5 per cent has two main components:

> "'time preference'—the rate at which consumption and public spending are discounted over time, assuming no change in per capita consumption. This captures the preference for value now rather than later.
>
> 'wealth effect'—this reflects expected growth in per capita consumption over time, where future consumption will be higher relative to current consumption and is expected to have a lower utility …
>
> The STPR is expressed as:
>
> $$r = \rho + \mu g$$
>
> where:
> r is the STPR
> ρ (rho) is time preference comprising pure time preference (δ, delta) and catastrophic risk (L)
> μg is the wealth effect: The marginal utility of consumption (μ, mu), multiplied by expected growth rate of future real per capita consumption g."[58]

To put this more simply using an example, you would probably prefer to go on an exotic holiday this year than in five years' time. This can be simply because it is on your immediate horizon of enjoyment rather than a long-time to wait. This is time preference. Also, in five years things may happen to prevent the holiday taking place; your health may deteriorate, there could be a revolution in the destination country, a pandemic may halt flights etc. This is risk, and it reduces the expected likelihood of the more distant holiday taking place and

---

[58] HM Treasury (2018). *The Green Book: Central Government Guidance on Appraisal and Evaluation*, Sections 5.34 and A6.6, pp. 46 and 119–120. Retrieved from https://assets.publishing.service.gov.uk/government/uploads/system/uploads/attachment_data/file/938046/The_Green_Book_2020.pdf.

hence its present value compared to boarding the plane tomorrow. Also, in your employment as an economist you may well expect your income to rise, so perhaps you would find holidays more affordable in the future anyway. Hence the excitement of an exotic holiday by then may have subsided to an extent as they have become more frequent and become just one more of your future luxuries. This is the wealth effect as your marginal utility from income diminishes.

The Green Book notes that time preference applies much less strongly to health and life issues. And so 'the Green Book instructs that a lower discount rate of 1.5% should be applied specifically to relevant health or life impacts. This reflects the principle that the value society places on health does not decrease over time as society grows richer'.[59]

THE DISCOUNT RATE, CLIMATE CHANGE AND FUTURE GENERATIONS

Controversy over the 'correct' discount rate to use became particularly fierce in debates over climate change. This is because a positive discount rate can, in effect, disenfranchise future generations. This is largely because the discount rate works like compound interest in reverse, each year is discounted by the years between today and the future year in question. To take an easy arithmetic example, merely to illustrate this discounting effect: if the discount rate is 100 per cent the 'discount factor' for year N $= 1/(1+1)^N$. Then the discount factors are yr1 $= 1/2$, yr2 $=1/4$, yr3 $=1/8$, yr4 $= 1/16$ etc. Therefore, the Present Value of £100 for 3 years, starting from next year, only has a present value of £100/2 +£100/4 +£100/8 = £87.5. The value of income in the future is rapidly diminished by the compounding effect on the denominator. In fact, at such a high discount rate as 100 per cent, then even £100 a year forever, starting from next year, only has an NPV of £100 today.

Of course, the Green Book standard discount rate of 3.5 per cent is much lower than 100%, but even at its 3.5% rate there is a strong compounding effect, which if left unadjusted would undervalue benefits to future generations and so make light of their costs. The Green Book includes tables to demonstrate the discount factor that arises from using its standard 3.5% discount rate and also for lower discount rates to be used for some long-term projects. For example, the table lists the present value of £100 in 60 years' time as only £14.68. But why should the time preferences of today's population determine the weight

[59] HM Treasury (2020). *Green Book Review* 2020: *findings and response*. Section 3.10 p. 18. Retrieved from https://assets.publishing.service.gov.uk/government/uploads/system/uploads/attachment_data/file/937700/Green_Book_Review_final_report_241120v2.pdf.

to be given to future generations anyway? To answer such questions, we need to turn to the philosophy and ethics:

> "It is the purely selfish 'preference element'of social time preference which Green Book methodology now needs to take into account when addressing significant and virtually irreversible transfers of wealth between generations."[60]

The fact that there is no 'technically correct' intergenerational discount rate is another major reason why economic policy making so often includes ethical considerations rather than being merely a 'value-free science'. But as the Stern Report made clear, the value of the discount rate adopted has important implications for what actions should be taken today rather than be put off to tomorrow. The outcome was that the Green Book guidance became more explicit that long-term projects can involve substantial intergenerational transfers. In particular, it was advised that for projects involving intergenerational transfer the standard discount rate of 3.5 per cent should be supplemented with a lower and declining discount rates that place a greater weight on the welfare of future generations.[61]

THE NEED FOR COUNTERFACTUALS IN CBA

Appraisal differs from evaluation.[62] A distinction often made is that appraisal is before (ex-ante) a project and evaluation is after the project (ex-post). But evaluation can also refer to the evaluation of data from pilots that precede the policy, so the real distinction is that appraisal is based on forecasted estimates whereas evaluation is based on existing data. That is, evaluation uses data from 'what happened' whereas appraisal requires the use of models to predict what 'will happen'. Both require a reasonable counter-factual (see Chapter 6),

---

[60] Joseph Lowe (2008) *Intergenerational wealth transfers and social discounting: Supplementary Green Book guidance* (HM Treasury) Section 1.6, p. 4. Retrieved from https://assets.publishing.service.gov.uk/government/uploads/system/uploads/attachment_data/file/193938/Green_Book_supplementary_guidance_intergenerational_wealth_transfers_and_social_discounting.pdf.

[61] Ibid., HM Treasury website (April 2013) 'Supplementary guidance to the Green Book on intergenerational wealth transfers and social discounting'. Available at https://www.gov.uk/government/publications/green-book-supplementary-guidance-discounting#:~:text=The%20Green%20Book%20recommends%20that,of%20declining%20discount%20rates%20thereafter (Accessed May 2021).

[62] Evaluation in government is led by the Government Social Research (GSR) profession. GSR publishes extensive guidance for evaluation in the 'Magenta Book'. Available at *Magenta Book: Central Government guidance on Evaluation* (March 2020) (Accessed September 2021).

to compare with the forecast of the state of the world in the event of taking the decision to go ahead with the project, or to compare what happened with what would have happened if no changes had been made, or even if something else had been done. In order to compare an option with the state of the world in the absence of taking that decision, the 'do-nothing' or 'Business as Usual' option is routinely included. This is not as straight-forward as it sounds. Take the example of estimating the regulatory impact on business of imposing a minimum wage. We might take the level of wages before the minimum wage as the benchmark comparator, but then wages tend to rise through time and so perhaps we should project the average increase per year forwards as the counterfactual? Or perhaps it would be better to look at the average yearly change only in those markets that are the most likely to be affected by the minimum wage? But is there reason to think that wages in these markets would not have kept rising at a constant yearly average, maybe we attempt to model what the likely level of wages would be in the future in the absence of a minimum wage? Clearly, there is no straight-forward answer, and so sensitivity estimates are often used, these show the estimated effect under several projected scenarios. The point here is that counterfactuals can be complex and sometimes simply indeterminate, but only if we have a strong counter-factual are we able to estimate what the impacts of the decision will be and so arrive at any meaningful CBA estimates.

OTHER ISSUES THAT COMMONLY ARISE IN APPLYING CBA

Multipliers are problematic and even where mutlipliers exist they may cancel out across projects and apply to diverted resourses.

Enumeration: ideally all the costs and benefits associated with a project and its alternatives should be counted, this is usually impossible.

'Second best': considerations can be very complex. First-best efficient allocations of resources where prices precisely reflect marginal social values are most unlikely. Second best considerations are widely ignored on the long standing but rather arbitrary advice that in considering second best 'Only those divergencies which are immediate, palpable and considerable … deserve our attention' (Prest and Turvey 1965).[63]

---

[63] A. R. Prest, R. Turvey, 'Cost-Benefit Analysis: A Survey', *The Economic Journal*, Volume 75, Issue 300, 1 December 1965, pp. 683–735.

Project selection and size of change. In principle, all the various permutations of projects should be simultaneously considered. This can create unmanageable complexity, even within different extents of the same project. For example, people may be indifferent between a heavily littered beach and one that is only half as littered. This would mean the marginal return to clearing litter is at first zero and the gains only come as the beach is completely cleared of litter. It can also be difficult to factor in marginal effects correctly when there are discontinuities in overall effects. For example, marginal changes in climate emissions may be unimportant whereas larger changes are very important.

The sum of individual wants is not necessarily the same as collective wants. For example, an innovation in chocolate bars might attract a million purchasers who each make an individual decision to purchase the new chocolate bar, but if they were all asked if they would rather have seen the development money go to cancer research then they might have collectively made a different decision. In a similar way, Fair Trade campaigns may prevent millions of otherwise small uncoordinated choices leading to the outcome of a 'race to the bottom' of poor wages and conditions for producers in poor countries, even though this would not have been the intention or preference of the consumers. In short, the use of neoclassical-based cost-benefit analysis in the consideration of programmes may tend to bias policies towards individualistic valuations rather than collective ones and to narrower economic concerns rather than broader social impacts.

The social impacts of individual decisions and 'efficiency' can be subtle. For example, by contrast with the mid-twentieth century, people with cars, refrigerators, and washing machines no longer walk to the local shops and laundromats, and so a myriad of casual everyday social interactions cease to occur, in the streets, launderettes, and in the queues in shops where people used to know each other and share chat and concerns. Community cohesion may decrease and loneliness increase. Milk in cartons from supermarkets have replaced milkmen[64] and so no-one notices when elderly people fail to collect the milk bottles from their doorsteps. Social capital (see page 298) can be lost even though it was no-one's intention.[65]

---

[64] They were invariably men.
[65] This is similar to the concept of 'The Tyranny of Small Decisions' coined by the American economist Alfred Edward Kahn (1917–2010).

WITH ALL THESE LIMITATIONS WHAT IS THE POINT OF LEARNING ABOUT CBA?

With all its weaknesses and questionable procedures, it is not surprising that many people, especially non-economists, react against CBA. But the comparative strength of CBA, over other methods of assembling the criteria and valuations for decision making, is that it is transparent. At least, an analyst who is aware of all the above considerations can see exactly what has been done in a CBA exercise and so critique it with precision, unlike judgments made through unrevealed weights, personal opinion and vague rhetoric. As Prest and Turvey (1965) concluded over 50 years ago: 'The case for using cost-benefit is strengthened, not weakened, if its limitations are openly recognised and indeed emphasised'.[66] And anyway, a decision maker is always able to attach their own weightings to supplementary criteria, and usually do, although transparency should require that these weightings are also made explicit. The bottom line is that, for better or for worse, whether you like it or not, CBA is used extensively. Studying CBA illustrates many fundamental issues of how economics can and cannot, should and should not, be applied to policy decisions. It helps reveal what gaps remain to be filled and what might forever remain unanswered, or at least best addressed with the help of other disciplines.

MACROECONOMICS

For all its limitations and areas for development, the progress of microeconomics has been more of a linear progression than has been the case for macroeconomics. Macroeconomics, much more than microeconomics, has been buffeted by, and had to respond to, real world crisis. In macroeconomics, the Keynesian/Neoclassical/Hayekian debates on macroeconomic stabilization, began in the 1930's, still ebb and flow, again largely driven and reignited by events in the real economy. The technical arguments get more sophisticated through time, but the political arguments stay pretty much the same. Similarly, the potential for at least some degree of endogenous (policy driven) growth is pretty much accepted, but the size and extent of the role of the government for fostering growth and stability remain hotly disputed.

---

[66] Ibid.

Macroeconomics, and hence its policy prescriptions, particularly suffers from the 'dearth of counterfactuals and surfeit of confounders' that we looked at in Chapter 6. Moreover, there are still significant conceptual problems in the measurement of aggregates such as GDP and unemployment, and these issues often require the help of other disciplines to advance. At the time of writing, there seems to be a political consensus, unlike in 2010, that when the economy is severely weakened it is not the time to be cutting government expenditure and raising the general level of taxation. But then this has been the majority view among UK macroeconomists since the time of Keynes. Almost all economists accept that likening the government's budget to a household budget is an inadequate and potentially misleading metaphor, but how and when to stimulate the economy and reduce deficits is still contested.

The mainstream 'workhorse' models for teaching, and even for forecasting the macroeconomic economy, still rely heavily on the notion of equilibrium, although shocks, perturbations and lags in adjustments, learning and expectations, have been added to produce fluctuations and 'cycles'. And because of the complexity of macroeconomics and the difficulty of aggregating over millions of economic agents, macroeconomic models often rely on assumptions that are clearly unrealistic. Such as 'representative agents' and 'rational' expectations. Important insights have been gained through this approach, but the real macroeconomy is of course far more complex and is intrinsically dynamic. It follows complex time paths rather than, as in comparative statics, moving from one equilibrium to settle at another. So, some economists seek to develop economics as non-equilibrium analysis, and few economists would claim that our knowledge of macroeconomics is near complete.

Responding to real world events, advances have also been made more recently in integrating the role of the finance sector into macroeconomic models, which was a serious omission in the build-up to the Great Financial Crisis of 2007. Finance has been a source of volatility over the centuries. Modern credit systems, the dynamics of confidence, complexity and estimating macroprudential potential against sudden financial collapse, present difficulties for formalizing mathematical models of finance for use in forecasting. Moreover, the use of ever greater computer power, faster IT connections—even nanoseconds matter in financial trades!—and algorithms that apply billions of calculations to markets before human minds can even register that they are taking place, means that the real world practice in finance is still running ahead of theory. As in the 'Great Moderation' in the long period before the great Financial Crash, this may seem a problem only for the theoreticians, but unless we understand real phenomena we are unlikely to know when it might again run amok and how to act. As part of the unknown lies in the potential for runaway technical processes rather than human intention, the challenges of macroeconomics may well require much more interdisciplinary working with natural sciences, such as IT and epidemiology, as well as other behavioural sciences to advance our knowledge. Such considerations are what led to the creation by the Economic and Social Research Council of a new Network, 'Rebuilding Macroeconomics', ably led by the by the former Treasury macroeconomist Angus Armstrong.[67]

In addition to all this scope for theoretical advances, the world itself is always changing. For example, the call for decarbonization and 'Net-Zero' has become more urgent for both environmental and strategic reasons; Covid-19 has meant a reassessment of fiscal prudence and the role of the state; and global economic power has been shifting Eastwards, particularly as China, and then India, account for an increasing share of the world's GDP. Growing political influence usually follows increasing economic strength, and often growing resentments, and a changing world economy may well bring about wider changes in the world order and hence the macroeconomic environment. Such events are not suitable for precise forecasting models, but their economic implications are profound and so cannot be ignored. This is so not just for media and public sector economists but also for financial economists, as financial sector economist Kevin Daly notes:

"I started my career believing that everything was about forecasting, that forecasting was the main thing if not the only thing that financial sector economists do. What I've learned over my career is that it is really only a small part of what we do, and a much bigger part is using economic and empirical tools, data analysis, to work out the implications of things that have already happened. Forecasting the long-term future is inevitably difficult, and very difficult to be consistently right on that, but what as economists we can do, and what we have to do as financial sector economists, is to be able to understand the implications of things that have already happened, earlier, or at least relatively early, and to be able to convey that to a wider audience."[68]

[67] Angus Armstrong is Director of Rebuilding Macroeconomics and Chief Economic Adviser to Lloyds Banking Group. Former Special Adviser to the International Trade Committee HoC, Economic Affairs Committee HoL, and former Head of Macroeconomic Analysis at HM Treasury.

[68] In his interview for this book (see Video 10: In conversation with Kevin Daly available at www.oup.com/he/pryce-ross1e).

Andy Haldane again echoes the need for, if not precise forecasting, at least some 'futurology' based on consideration of the likely direction of developments, to be better prepared for what might happen in the future:

> "I think that's really crucial if you're in the economics game or the public policy game to have the capacity for some degree of futurology. Some capacity to think about where the world is going because that way you can get some preparation in place to deal with that problem when it looms large."[69]

NOW IS A PARTICULARLY GOOD TIME TO BE AN ECONOMIST

Despite a near consensus on many issues, economics is far from being a definitive discipline. It still has a very long way to develop and is unlikely to ever completely catch-up with an ever-changing world. Many people can bring enthusiasm and interest, but it is your ability to think as an economist and to understand the tools of economics that add value for your stakeholders, that will secure you employment as an economist. Towards a better world, we are confident that society can be improved through a better public understanding of economics and from advances in our understanding of how real humans make their decisions; interdisciplinary synthesis; endogenous and sustainable growth; human welfare and well-being; civil society; cooperative optimism and how to foster transformation (see page 311); our financial systems; social cost benefit analysis; complexity and the dynamics of economic systems-both domestic and global; and the potential for symbiosis between the private, public and third sectors. In the meantime, working on these frontiers of knowledge make it a particularly exciting time to be an economist.

We hope this book has shown you the many rewards from studying economics and that you will join us by choosing to become a professional economist too. We cannot put it better than did Andy Haldane, in his interview for

---

[69] In his interview for this book (see Video 16: In conversation with Andy Haldane FAcSS FRS available at www.oup.com/he/pryce-ross1e).

this book when nearing the end of his long service as Chief Economist at the Bank of England. We will let Andy have the last word:

"My advice to anyone starting off down the path of economics? I will say now what I say to all the incoming graduates at the Bank of England. Actually, you could not have picked a better time, certainly in recent history and possibly in distant history, to be studying economics and to be working on the economy. If you're not enjoying it now you will never enjoy it because the endowment of issues has never been larger … When it comes to rewriting how we think about the economy, and how we best set economic policy to support that economy, you could not wish as an economist or policy maker for a better endowment. And it won't, truth be told, be old wizened lags like me who will solve those problems. It will be the new generation with their new ideas on both how the world works and how the world might work better. What could be more exciting, what could be more uplifting and what could be better as a career."[70]

Bon voyage!

SUMMARY

- Economics provides many well-evidenced theories and well-established policy prescriptions, but economics is, and almost certainly always will be, a 'work in progress' discipline.
- There are many affordable ways to keep up to date with developments in economics.
- Studying Cost Benefit Analysis (CBA) and its applications in government is a great way to explore the issues that arise in microeconomic policy and can have strong payoffs for employment.
- There will always be limits to what we can know, but economists are well-placed to understand the economic implications of change and so make more informed broad predictions earlier than others.

---

[70] In his interview for this book (see Video 16: In conversation with Andy Haldane FAcSS FRS available at www.oup.com/he/pryce-ross1e).

- The limits of our knowledge are particularly obvious in macroeconomics, but there are enormous conceptual, theoretical, and measurement challenges across all areas of economics, this makes it an exciting to be an economist and an opportunity for young economists to go on and make their own mark.

QUESTIONS

1. Why might collective wants differ from the outcomes arising from individual decisions made in isolation?

2. Why does a high discount rate 'disenfranchise' future generations?

3. Explain why there is no technically correct value for an intertemporal discount rate for a project that transfers wealth across generations.

4. How many types of analysis that could involve CBA can you list?

5. Why is the positive normative distinction not clear-cut in practice?

6. Why is it so difficult to model transformational progress?

7. The observation that macroeconomies have unknown properties is used both as an argument for and against Keynesian macro policies, explain how and why that is the case.

EXERCISES

1. i) Use the standard mainstream framework shown in Figure 10.1 to examine the case for intervention in

    a) The provision of education

    b) Addressing climate change

    ii) What are shortcomings in the framework shown in Figure 10.1?

2. Assume a bridge is to be built where there are currently only ferry crossings. Draw a relevant demand diagram and then construct a table of the values that would have to be estimated to do a CBA for the building of the bridge (Hint: remember to include lost profit for the ferry owners and the cost of the bridge construction).

3. Use the headings given in the section 'Common Problems in applying CBA' above to classify the types of issues raised by the House of Lords

Economic Affairs Committee report on HS2 : Houseof Lords, Economic Affairs Committee, 1st Report of Session 2014–15, The Economics of High Speed 2https://publications.parliament.uk/pa/ld201415/ldselect/ldeconaf/134/134.pdf#:~:text=The%20cost-benefit%20analysis%20for%20HS2%20relies%20on%20evidence,HS2%20will%20deliver%20the%20benefits%20it%20claims.%20Conclusion (Accessed April 2021).

4. Read articles from the Financial Times that contain macroeconomic data and use John Sloman's list of free data sources (Available at https://www.economicsnetwork.ac.uk/links/data_free) to locate online the data, or its update, from the sources listed.

FIND OUT MORE

For an early account of the hopes for CBA see Prest, A.R. and Turvey, R., 'Cost-benefit analysis: a survey', *The Economic Journal*, Vol. 75 No. 300, pp. 683–735, (1965).

For an overview of the review of the *Green Book* see HM Treasury (2020) *Green Book Review 2020: Findings and response.* Available at: **https://assets.publishing.service .gov.uk/government/uploads/system/uploads/attachment_data/file/937700/Green_Book_ Review_final_report_241120v2.pdf** (accessed August 2021) and HM Treasury and Government Finance Function (2022) *The Green Book: appraisal and evaluation in central government.* Available at: **https://www.gov.uk/government/publications/the-green-book-appraisal-and-evaluation-in-central-governent** (accessed August 2021).

To learn how CBA is used for business cases see HM Treasury (2018) 'Guide to developing the project business case'. Available at: **https://assets.publishing .service.gov.uk/government/uploads/system/uploads/attachment_data/file/749086/Project_ Business_Case_2018.pdf** (accessed August 2021) and AQA (2022) Teaching guide: investment appraisal. Available at: **https://www.aqa.org.uk/resources/business/ as-and-a-level/business-7131-7132/teach/teaching-guide-investment-appraisal** (accessed August 2021).

Reliable research bodies to follow to keep abreast of developments in the levelling-up initiative include the Academy of Social Sciences (AcSS) (**https:// acss.org.uk/**), The Institute of Fiscal Studies (IFS) (**https://ifs.org.uk/**), The Institute of Government (IoG) (**https://www.instituteforgovernment.org.uk/**) and the National Institute for Economic and Social Research (NIESR) (**https://www.niesr.ac.uk/**).

Index

A

A-Levels 21, 229, 230, 231, 241, 244
academia
  challenge regarding economics
    degrees 103
  declaring funding of research 79
  developing producers of economics
    100–1
  ethnic diversity among economists
    in 240–1
  jobs in 44–5
  rigour and precision as hallmarks
    of 69
  stalled growth in women's economics
    representation 233
academic economists
  earnings of 44–5
  as essential to understanding of
    economics and for advancement of
    knowledge 89
  ethnicity 241–2
  versus practitioner economists 6,
    67–9, 74, 76, 83–4
  questions, exercises and further
    resources 84–6
  'relevance rigour' spectrum 67,
    69–71, 83
  and role of mathematics 96–7, 103,
    154, 156–7
  softening 'ivory towers'
    stereotype 70–1
  sometimes purist attitude of 79
  writing skills 135–6
Academy of Social Sciences (AcSS) 143,
    284–5, 326
actuarial jobs 40–1
actuarial services 33
Adam Smith Institute 78
Affuso, Luisa 230
agency
  from communication 129–30, 150
  meaning of 75, 101
  provision for stakeholders 75–6

agent-based modelling (AGM) 290
'agglomeration benefits' 311
Alexander, Sadie Tanner Mossell 236
Anagboso, Toju xvi, 113, 229
Anand, Paul 90
application forms 258–62
apprenticeships 4, 20, 46, 244–5
Arestis, Philip 95
arousal performance curve 122, 269
assessment centres 254, 264
asset management 31–2
Auckbur, Yasir xvi, 5
audience
  engaging 119–20
  motivations and perspectives of 123–5
  putting before expertise 115
  target 114, 146
Austrian Economics 74, 170, 216–17,
    285–6, 290

B

Bank of England (BoE)
  as actively promoting diversity 245
  advancing research 98, 283
  application for work placement
    interview report 272
  earnings 20–1
  female staff 227
  further resources 51, 64
  internships 63
  as recruiter of economists 50–1
Barker, Dame Kate xvi, 7, 22, 26, 41, 90,
    125, 138–9, 154, 173, 235
Bath University 102
Bean, Sir Charles 177
Beckett, Sam 235
Behavioural Economics 289, 291–3, 295
Behavioural Insights Team 238–9
Bell, Kate 236
'Big Four' 34–5, 40–1
Birdi, Alvin x, 158, 172–3, 222, 287
Birkbeck, University of London 44, 102
'blended interviews' 258

body language 119, 122, 270
Boone, Laurence 236
Boultwood, Sinéad xvi, 5, 230
Brexit 46, 57, 125, 147, 290
briefing
    to company board 142
    comparison with academic
        writing 67, 132
    explanation 135–6
    functions 136
    HM Treasury 81, 141–2
    information briefing templates 136–7,
        138–41
    'Purpose' heading 129, 138
    recommendation briefing
        template 137–8
    structuring 136–41
    updates 141–2
broader skills and soft skills
    applying to competency
        frameworks 189–92
    developing 194–7
    for financial sector economist 193–4
    job application questions 258–60, 278
    list of 182–3
    needed to succeed as economist 185–9
    preparing for management 197–200
    reasons economists need 183–5
    summary, questions, exercises and
        further resources 201–2
Burden, Lizzy xvii, 54
business and employer organisa-
    tions 60–1
business and financial consultancy 32–3
business finance and commerce jobs see
    private sector jobs

C
careers see jobs for economists
Carling, Wendy 219, 220
causation
    confounders 167–8
    counterfactuals 166–7
    endogeneity 169–70
    and historical data 170–1
    observational equivalence 169
    random control trials 168
CBA see Cost Benefit Analysis (CBA)
Central Limit Theorem (CLT) 164
Chadha, Jagjit 53

choosing right tool for job 216–17
civil servants
    earnings 20, 21
    potential move from London 48
    role of 79–82, 84, 310
civil service code 75, 76, 79–80, 82, 84, 212
Civil Service Competency Framework
    (CSCF) 190–2
Civil Service Graduate Fast Stream
    (FSAC) 262–3, 264, 275, 276
civil society 58, 291, 292–3, 298, 300
climate change 7–8, 290, 312–13, 316
coaching 197
codes of conduct 82–3
    see also civil service code
Colander, David 94–95
Coller, Jonathan xvii, 5, 58
communicating complexity simply 25,
    53–4, 92, 101–2, 109, 178
communicating economics
    agency 129–30
    example 125–8
    need for greater ability in 100–2, 109,
        115
    'wear your intellect lightly' 128–9
communication
    as broader skill 185, 188
    in CSCF 191
    customer care and diplomacy in 143–4
    influence on career 149
    to managers and ministers 131–46
    principles for successful 117–30
    summary, questions, exercises and
        further resources 149–52
    three Cs of effective 115–16
    three Ts of effective 114–15
    use of English 262
    verbal 148–9
    via social media 146–8
communication skills
    reasons economists need 109–13
    resources for improving 130–1
    tips for improving 113–16
company board briefing 142
competencies, demonstration of 261–2
competency frameworks
    applying soft skills to 189–92
    civil service 190–2
    KPMG 189–90
    of large organisations 192, 201

competition policy economist and regulators 36–9
complexity economics 290
complexity modelling 74, 290
'confirmation bias' 174, 214
confounders 167–8
Connolly, Catherine xvii, 205
continuous professional development (CPD)
    facilitating 195–7
    firms making large investment in 35
    GES 48, 190
    reasoning behind name 183, 201
Cook, Lisa 247
CORE project
    approach to pluralism 222–3
    benefits of 221–2
    broader perspective of textbook 296
    criticisms of 218–19, 221
    Doing Economics guide 160, 218
    drivers of 219
    ethos 217
    as example of mainstream teaching approach 247
    freely available materials 218
    as hoping to attract more women 227
    and mathematics 154
    number of institutions using 218
corporate banking 33
Cost Benefit Analysis (CBA)
    benefits of studying 324
    'capitals approach' emphasising sustainability in 299
    discounting 314–15
    further resources 326
    Green Book 308–12, 315–17
    importance of studying 294, 320, 324
    incorporation of assumptions 126
    issues commonly arising in application of 318–19
    need for counterfactuals in 317–18
    neglect in universities 11, 281, 294
    overview 302–3
    as of particular relevance to practitioner economists 281–2
    and potential for transformational benefits 312–13
    questions, exercises and further resources 325–6
    as technocratic aspiration 303–5
    theoretical underpinnings 305–7
    and welfare economics 307–12
counterfactuals 166–7, 317–18
covering letters 258–62
Covid-19 pandemic 6, 46, 150, 209, 264, 267, 290, 293, 322
Coyle, Diane xvii, 9, 70, 76, 93–4, 221, 228, 243, 250, 284, 298, 301
Coyle Reviews 93–4
CSCF see Civil Service Competency Framework (CSCF)
current economic methodology, need for greater understanding of 98–9
current real-world context, need for greater awareness of 94–8
curriculum vitae (CV) 255–8, 278
customer care (communication) 143–4

D
Daly, Kevin xvii, 29, 193–4, 322
Dasgupta, Sir Partha 9, 83
data
    appraisal and evaluation 317
    bias in interpretation of 194
    'big' 290
    eyeballing 69, 84, 95, 100
    importance of understanding 164–6
    keeping up to date with 285
    mixing with theory and experience 215
    statistics distorting message of 175–6, 179
    from yesterday, over reliance on 170–1
data analysis jobs 40–1
data awareness 164–5, 179
data skills
    essential 160–2
    need for 89, 99–100, 154, 179
    as prioritized by academics 92
data visualisation 160, 161, 181
Davies, Gavyn xvii–xviii, 97, 157, 284
Davies, Melissa xviii, 282
Davies, Richard 112, 284
Davis, Evan 53, 131
Dawes, Dame Melanie 230, 235
decolonizing economics 245–7, 250
deductive reasoning 94, 215–23

degree in economics
  and A-level economics 230, 231
  argument for including CBA in 305–6
  CBA as often overlooked in 281, 294,
    302
  communication to varied audiences as
    part of 115
  facility with data as important part
    of 172–3, 179
  financial returns comparison with
    other disciplines 15–19, 22, 225
  fundamental concepts taught
    within 90–1
  matching with employer
    requirements 91–103
  and mathematics 154, 158, 159
  most advertised jobs for those with 28
  as opening doors to many career
    opportunities 14, 26–8, 65
  reasons for studying for 4–5
  Rethinking Economics
    perspective 220, 223
  as still more orientated towards
    academia 88
  summary, questions, exercise and
    further resources 103–5
  transferable skills and skills gap 91–2,
    102–3
  usefulness context 87–9
Deloitte
  interview report 273
  as one of 'Big Four' 34
demand see supply and demand
descriptive statistics 69, 99, 160–1, 171,
    175, 179
diplomacy 49, 143–4, 149
diplomatic service 49–50
disability 255, 271, 279
discounting 314–15, 316, 317
Discover Economics 14, 27–8, 51, 228,
    232, 240, 244–5, 250
distributional impacts 307–8
divergent thinking 74
diversity
  actions for universities 237–8
  actions for workplace 238–40
  among economists 22, 223–5, 244
  Bank of England promoting 245
  Discover Economics launched to
    increase 232, 244

ethnic 240–2
gender 237–40
importance of 242–3
summary, questions, exercises and
    further resources 248–50
diversity in method 215–23
diversity of thought 217, 219, 222–3,
    225, 248
dress requirements 271
Duflo, Esther 236

E
earnings of economists 14–22
  2019 salary survey results 20
  academics 44–5
  and degrees 167–8, 169
  distribution of median earnings
    5 years after graduation 17
  government 47–8
  median earnings of UK graduates
    1 and 5 years after graduation 15–16
  upper quartile earnings of UK
    graduates 1 and 10 years after
    graduation 18–19
  women 21–2, 240
eclecticism
  approach to choosing tools for job 76,
    91, 104, 217
  approach to economics 74, 94, 203,
    205, 209–12, 223, 247, 248
econometrics
  causation 166–71
  cautionary notes 164, 171, 175
  importance of understanding
    data 164–6, 179
  increasing career opportunities
    163, 179
  increasing focus on 288–9
  overview 162–4
  role of models 73
economic history
  decolonizing economics research 247
  need for greater awareness of 94–8
Economic Network
  alumni survey 27
  employer survey 92–3, 105
  professional development for
    lecturers 123
Economic Statistics Centre of Excellence
    (ESCoE) 110–11, 165, 177

economics
    communicating to non-specialists 100–2
    dangers of narrow approach to 203
    decolonizing 245–7, 250
    deepening understanding of 294–302
    eclecticism, and need for interdisciplinary approaches 204–25
    and ethnicity 240–2
    as increasingly empirical 100
    keeping up to date with 282–5, 324
    limitations 285–8
    loss of direction 231–2
    mathematics used in 156–7
    misperceptions of 14, 217, 225, 228–9
    new directions in 288–93
    producers and consumers of 89–91
    public perceptions of 208, 225–31
    reasons for studying 4–5, 23
    relation to science 5–6, 10, 11, 294, 301
    relevance of 6–8
    rewards from studying 323–4
    towards broader 204
    types of relationship 291
    as ubiquitous and interdisciplinary 10–13
    wide scope of coverage 206–8, 247
    as 'work in progress' discipline 324
    see also degree in economics
The Economist 78, 88, 130, 152, 161–2, 284, 285, 301
economists
    and broader skills 183–9, 201
    focus on GDP 8–10
    good time to be 323–4, 325
    and mathematics 153–4, 157–60
    professional codes 82–3
    range of topics studied by 12–13
    reasons for needing good communication skills 109–13
    reasons for working as 3, 13–22, 23
    and social media 146–8
    and success 22
    towards more diverse body of 223–5, 244
    see also earnings of economists; jobs for economists
Elliott, Larry xviii, 54, 96–7, 115, 135, 153
employers, requirements of
    better practical data-handling skills 99–100, 160, 171
    Coyle Reviews 93–4

and degree in economics 91–103
further resources 202
greater ability to communicate economics to non-specialists 100–2, 109, 115
greater awareness of economic history and current real-world context 94–8
more understanding of modelling limitations and current economic methodology 98–9
survey findings 92–3
working with others 102, 187–8
employers, working for, and intellectual compromise 76–7, 84
endogeneity 169–70
engineers 68
English language
    plain 118, 119, 130, 135, 152
    use of 110, 144–5, 259, 262
enumeration 318
Ernst & Young (EY)
    as one of 'Big Four' 34
    summer internship interview report 273–4
ethnicity
    and economics 240–2
    and gender 231
European Union (EU) 57
Excel 100, 162, 171
executive summaries *see* briefing
expertise 87, 111, 129, 214, 222–3
externalities 295, 306

F
Fahnbulleh, Miatta xviii, 10, 76, 94, 112, 223–4, 236, 246
'fake news' 175–6
Fawcett, Millicent 236
Fawcett Society 236
feedback
    importance of 149
    post unsuccessful job application 272, 279
    seeking 195–6
finance sector jobs
    asset management 31–2
    business and financial consultancy 32–3
    investment banking 29–31

financial crisis *see* Great Financial Crash (GFC)
financial sector economist, skills for 29, 193–4
Financial Times 53–4, 79, 154, 284, 285, 326
First Fundamental Theorem of Welfare Economics (FFTWE) *see* 'Invisible Hand Theorem'
Flanders, Stephanie 53, 236
forecasting 193–4, 321–3
'free riding' 295, 307
Frontier Economics 27–8, 38, 43, 51, 52, 59

G

GDP
    in company board briefing 142
    consumption affecting 155
    drug dealing and voluntary work 300
    focus on 8–10, 300
    in HM Treasury briefing 141–2
    and wellbeing 298, 299
gender gap 21–2, 234, 236, 240
gender imbalance 226, 227, 230–1, 233–7
Gender in GES (GiG) 233, 238, 250
general economic consultancy 33
GES *see* Government Economic Service (GES)
Giles, Chris 54, 58
Godley, Wynne 41, 96
Government Economic Service (GES)
    advantages and disadvantages 48
    apprenticeship scheme 4, 46, 245
    code of conduct 82
    competency framework 190, 192
    and diplomatic service 49–50
    Economic Assessment Centre 50, 274–5
    'effective communication' as one of core competencies 110
    entry routes 46–7
    equal importance of broader skills with economic skills 190
    ethnic minorities and diversity 242
    expected earnings 47–8
    fast stream 47, 50, 242, 275
    goals of 224
    interdisciplinary working and choice of career paths 49
    interview reports 273, 274–5, 276
    location 48
    nature of 46

placement opportunities 63, 64
policy economics 70, 75
views on best education for economists 90, 99
women in 233, 235, 239–40
grammar, importance of 134, 144–6, 262
Great Financial Crash (GFC) 42, 81, 95–7, 98, 219, 277, 290, 296, 321
Green Book
    discount rate, climate change and future generations 316–17
    objective 308
    optimism bias 313–14
    on perfect markets 126
    purpose 307
    review 309–12, 326
    social time preference rate 315–16
    and transformational change 312, 313
Greenwold, Nathaniel xvii, 5, 58
Griffith, Dame Rachel xviii, 28, 83, 89, 130, 158, 159, 232, 235
'ground knowledge' 104, 215, 225

H

Haldane, Andy xviii–xix, 50, 58, 120, 124, 159, 204–5, 215, 221, 250, 292, 293, 300–1, 312, 323–4
Harford, Tim 120, 129, 170, 172, 178, 213–14, 216
Harwood, Ian x–xi, 93
Henry, Janet 235
'heterodox economics' movement 207
'Hicks-Kaldor Criterion' 307–8
HM Treasury
    biodiversity 9
    briefings 81, 141–2
    interview report 276
    and OBR 77–8
    see also Green Book
Home Office placement interview report 275–6
human bias 213–14
hypothetical-deductive model of scientific advance 72, 73

I

Independent Press Standards Organisation (IPSO) 176–7
independent research institutions 77–8
individual and collective wants 319

inductive reasoning 94, 215–23
inference statistics 163, 164, 171, 179
infographics 120
Institute for Fiscal Studies (IFS) 59, 77, 213, 224–5, 227
Institute of Economic Affairs (IEA) 78–9, 292
intellectual compromise 76–7, 84
intellectual promiscuity 217
interdisciplinary approaches, need for 204–25, 248
interdisciplinary economics 10–13, 296–302
interdisciplinary working 102, 208, 224, 322
International Monetary Fund (IMF) 51, 55–6, 283
International Non-Governmental Organizations (INGOs) 57
international not-for-profit economic organizations 55–7
internships 62–4, 254
　actuarial 40–1
　interview report 273–4
　investment banks 30, 31
intersectionality 224, 230–1
interviews
　adjustments for disabilities 271
　awareness of new developments in economics 281
　being convincing 123
　body language, dress, and tone 270–1
　current affairs questions 267
　getting to 264
　giving successful answers to questions 267–8
　managing nerves 268–70, 278
　practising answering questions 265
　preparation for 264–5, 277–8
　questions on behaviour, motivation and strengths and weaknesses 258–60, 265–7
　reports from 272–7
　research for 26, 36, 254, 265
　responding to rejection 272, 278–9
　summary, questions, exercises and further resources 279–80
　talking too much or too little 269–70
　viewing as opportunities to learn 254–5
investment banking 20, 29–31, 32
'Invisible Hand Theorem' 116, 125–8
Ishwaran, Mallika 235

J
job applications
　application forms and covering letters 258–62
　assessment centres 264
　curriculum vitae 255–7
　deadlines 63
　demonstration of competencies 261–2
　including relevant detail 260–1
　need for research 253–4
　online tests 262–4
　psychometric tests 263–4
　quality of 277
　questions on behaviour, motivation and strengths and weaknesses 184, 258–60
　summary, questions, exercises and further resources 278–80
　university career services 257–8
　use of English 144, 262
job hunting advice 254–5
jobs for economists
　context 25–6
　finding opportunities 61–4
　international not-for-profit economic organizations 55–7
　journalism 53–5
　media 52–3
　non-pecuniary rewards 65
　pictorial representations 28
　policy research organisations and 'think tanks' 58–61
　private sector 29–43
　public sector 43–52
　summary, questions, exercise and further resources 65–6
　third sector 57–8
　wide range of opportunities 26–8
jobs portals and websites 61
Johnson, Paul 22, 53, 82, 310
journalism
　and democracy 84
　earnings 16–19
　importance of economics communication 101
　as job for economists 53–5
　leading with main point of article 135
　persuasion 123
Julius, Dame DeAnne 235

K

Kapur, Sandeep xix, 10, 102, 154
Kay, Sir John vi, 74–5, 225–6, 286
Keynes, John Maynard 289, 304
Khaldun, Ibn 87, 206–7
KPMG
    competencies 189–90
    as one of 'Big Four' 34
    practice online assessments 262
    professional services 34–5, 36

L

Lagarde, Christine 236
language
    importance of 118–19, 120
    of mathematics 154, 157–60
    and potential misunderstandings 120–1
    of social science 132
    straightforward 134
    use of complex 101
    see also English language
large local authorities, jobs in 52
large UK firms, jobs in 41
Leijonhufvud, Axel 226
Le Roux, Stephen xx, 70
Littlechild, Michael xix, 43
lobbyist think tanks 78–9, 84
Lombardelli, Clare 235
London School of Economics 102
Lucas Critique 73, 170

M

'macro-prudence' 98
macroeconomics 95, 98, 320–23, 325
mainstream economics
    versus complexity economics 290
    criticisms of 220
    examples of change in 247
    versus heterodox economics 207
    models 73, 96, 159, 321
    narrowness in 207–8, 219
    need for interdisciplinary
        approach 206, 296
    and neoclassical economics 206–7
    reasons for state intervention 294–5
    simple explanation of 207
management, preparing for 197–200,
    201, 202
management schemes 41
managers, communication to 131–46,
    150, 152

managing upwards 198–9, 201
Mankiw, Greg 68
market failure 8, 91, 126, 128, 295, 304,
    305
market research jobs 41
Marshall, Alfred 236
Marshall, Mary Paley 236
Martineau, Harriet 236
mathematics
    as beneficial to economists 153–4
    criticism of preoccupation with 97
    as good servant but poor master 157,
        159, 179
    as 'language' of economists 154,
        157–60
    as revelatory 155–6
    of use in economics 88–9, 103, 156–7,
        179
    and women 226
McWilliams, Douglas xix, 10, 33
media
    earnings 16–19
    economist role in countering fallacies
        reported in 65
    jobs in 52–3, 54, 101
    percentage of economists working
        in 28
    press 79
    statistical 'fake news' in 175–6
    see also social media
mentoring 195, 197, 240
metaphors 116, 120
microeconomics 294–5, 320
ministers
    and civil servants 80
    communication to 123, 131–46, 150
    and Green Book 309–10
    wanting 'agency' from advice 70, 101,
        123
misperceptions of economics 14, 217,
    225, 228–9
misunderstandings, trouble-shooting
    potential 120–1
models
    artificiality in formulation and use 225
    CORE perspective 217, 221
    and deduction 215
    and endogeneity 169–70
    indiscriminate application of 246
    integrating role of finance sector into
        macroeconomic 321

limitations 95–6, 97, 98–9, 208
Lucas Critique 170
mainstream economics 73, 96, 159, 321
and mathematics 155–6, 157, 159
move towards 'bigger picture'
    approach 296
need for greater understanding of
    limitations 98–9, 104, 223, 288
real world never exactly matching 76,
    155, 220
role of 71–5, 84, 286–7
usefulness 95–6, 155–6, 288
multi-tasking 186
multinational companies 39–40
multipliers 318

N
National Health Service (NHS) 51
National Infrastructure Commission
    (NIC) 52
National Institute of Economic and
    Social Research (NIESR) 53, 59, 78,
    98, 142, 213, 227, 283, 326
natural capital 297, 299–300
neoclassical economics
    CBA 304–6, 314, 319
    choosing right tool for job 216–17
    debate on macroeconomic
        stabilization 320
    limitations 285–6
    and mainstream economics 206–7
    and market failure 126
    notion of 'duality' 219
    towards broader economics 204
nervousness
    during interviews 268–70, 278
    during presentations 121–3
    talking too much or too little 269–70
networking 62, 188–9
New Welfare Economics 291–3
non-governmental organizations
    (NGOs) 57
non-pecuniary rewards 65

O
OBR see Office for Budget Responsibility
    (OBR)
observational equivalence 169
O'Donnell, Lord Gus xx, 5, 6, 110,
    123–4, 129, 156, 196, 227, 235, 288,
    292, 293

Office for Budget Responsibility
    (OBR) 51, 77–8, 98
Office for National Statistics (ONS) 9, 49,
    110–11, 141, 161, 164–5, 177, 178,
    275, 277, 285
Okonjo-Iweala, Ngozi 236
'omitted variable' problem 73
online tests 262–4
operational delivery
    awareness of practicalities in 248, 315
    GES, jobs in 49
    importance of 209
    need to consider 249
opportunity cost 10–11, 121, 314–15
optimism bias 313–14
Organisation for Economic Cooperation
    and Development (OECD) 56, 59,
    235, 238, 283, 309
Ostrom, Elinor 236, 247
over-confidence 95
Owen, Dame Susan 235
Oxford Economics 59, 277

P
Pareto-efficiency 125–8, 295, 304,
    305, 311
Pareto-improvement 304, 307–8
personal development plans (PDPs)
    196–7, 201, 202
Pettifor, Anne 98
Pisani, Mario xx, 89, 206
placements 62–4
    application for 272
    and employability 88
    GES 47, 273
    interview reports 275–6, 277
    in multinational companies 39
    and networking 188
    working with others 102
pluralism
    approach to economics 97, 203, 223,
        240
    choosing right tool for job 217
    and CORE 219, 222
    different interpretations 210–11
    further resources 249–50
    versus mainstreamism 208
    by schools of thought 248
    two approaches to 222
plurality, concept of 210
policy research organisations 58–61

politicians
    as eager for 'hard' statistics 9
    influencing 123–4
    joke about decision-making 67
    long history of displeasure with
        communication 134–5
    as often employing economists 60
    placing 'spin' on statistics 178
    policy making 81–2, 310
    wishing to see Green Book amended
        in their favour 309
politics
    'cherry-picking' 173
    earnings 15–18
    jobs in 60
    relation with economics 11, 60, 75,
        301, 310
    as team sport 151
poverty 7, 8, 9–10, 290, 311
practitioner economists
    versus academic economists 6, 67–9,
        74, 76, 83–4
    intellectual compromise and working
        for employer 76–7, 84
    as needing to provide agency for
        stakeholders 75–6
    questions, exercises and further
        resources 84–6
    'relevance rigour' spectrum 69–71, 83
    valuing what works in practice 74
presentation nerves 121–3
'preservation of capitals' 209, 298–9, 301
private sector
    advantages and disadvantages 43–4
    competition policy 37
    discounting future costs 314
    employees expected to support
        employers' objectives in 76, 77
private sector jobs
    actuarial and data analysis 40–1
    competition policy economist and
        regulators 36–9
    finance sector 29–33
    large UK firms 41
    market research 41
    multinational companies 39–40
    professional services 33–6
    rating agencies 42
    specialist consultants 43
Pro Bono Economics (PBE) 57–8

producers and consumers of econom-
    ics 89–91
productivity gap 165–6
professional codes 82–3
    see also civil service code
professional services 33–6
project selection 319
Propper, Dame Carol 235
Prospects 26–7, 41, 60, 64, 185–6, 188,
    202, 257, 264, 269, 280
Pryce, Vicky xi–xii, xx, 7, 21, 43, 44, 75,
    101, 196, 227, 235, 237
psychometric tests 263–4
public perceptions of economics 208,
    225–31
public sector
    CBA 304–5, 314
    competition policy 37
    estimating 'willingness to pay' 306
    many economists working in 28, 232
Public Sector Equality Duty (PSED) 310
public sector jobs
    advantages and disadvantages 43–4
    Bank of England 50–1
    Government Economic Service 46–50
    large local authorities 52
    National Health Service 51
    National Infrastructure
        Commission 52
    Office for Budgetary Responsibility 51
    teaching and academia 44–5
Python 172

Q

Quality Assurance Agency for Higher
    Education (QAA) 11, 115
quantitative skills
    econometrics 162–71
    essential data skills 160–2
    mathematics 153–9
    statistical software packages 171–2
    statistics 172–8
    summary, questions, exercises and
        further resources 179–81

R

Ramsden, Sir Dave 70, 76, 86, 99, 203,
    235
random control trials (RCTs) 168, 170
rating agencies 42

Rees-Mogg, Jacob 145–6
reflection 204
regulators 37–9
rejection, responding to 272, 278–9
relationships
    types of 291
    understanding 291–2
'relevance rigour' spectrum 67, 69–71, 83
retail banking 33
Rethinking Economics project 220–3, 250
'revealed preference' 306
rigour 68, 74, 88, 116, 126–7
    see also 'relevance rigour' spectrum
Robinson, Joan 236
role models 229–30, 244, 245
Rosewell, Bridget 235–6
Ross, Andy xii, 12, 13, 44, 85, 95, 105, 289
Royal Economic Society (RES) 7, 27, 69,
    82–3, 152, 232, 233–4, 235, 240,
    244, 250, 282
'rubbish in–rubbish out' 100, 164–5

S
satisficing 169
Schwartz, Anna 236
science
    and climate change 7
    of cost benefit analysis 302–20
    and Covid-19 crisis 6
    relation to economics 5–6, 10, 11,
        294, 301
'scientific method' 72
scientists 49, 68, 147
Scitovsky, Tibor 289
Scottish Economic Society 27, 69
'second best' considerations 305, 318
Shafik, Dame Minouche 235
Smith, Adam 87, 125, 128, 161, 207, 236, 289
Smith, Andrew xx, 36
Smith, Ron 100
Smith, Sarah 225, 228–9, 245
social capital 291, 297, 299–302, 319
'Social Cost Benefit Approach' 296–7
social media 146–8, 188–9
social time preference rate (STPR) 314,
    315–16
societies 62, 69, 284
Society of Professional Economists
    (SPE) 20, 27–8, 62, 69, 161, 244, 284
soft skills see broader skills and soft skills

sources
    importance of checking and
        interrogating 212–14
    for keeping up to date 282–5
    for recruitment 61–4
specialist consultants 43
STAR process 258, 260–1, 278
statistical software packages 171–2, 179, 185
statistics
    effective communication of 110–11, 120
    'fake news' using 175–6
    'hard' 9, 182
    lying with 172–8
    'significance' as commonly
        misunderstood term 121
    statistical rules of thumb 178
    summary, questions, exercises and
        further resources 179–81
    trust in official 176–8
    see also descriptive statistics; inference
        statistics
Stern, Lord Nicholas xx–xxi, 7–8, 74, 83,
    109, 128–9, 159, 190, 227, 299
Stern Review 7–8, 317
structure
    of briefings 136–40
    use in keeping communication on
        track and accessible 117–18
student communities 62
summer placement interview re-
    ports 273, 277
supply and demand 98–9, 170, 287–8
sustainability
    challenge of 290
    'preservation of capitals' approach
        to 298–9
    wider metrics for capturing 9

T
teaching jobs 44–5
teams
    in CSCF 192
    developing broader skills 185, 195
    and diversity 243, 248
    'no I in' 184
    team players 187–8
technocratic aspiration 303–5
Tetlow, Gemma 236
'think tanks' 59, 77–9, 84, 212–13, 227,
    236, 283

third sector jobs 57–8
three Cs of effective communication 115–16, 135, 143–4
three Ts of effective communication 114–15, 117, 128, 135
Tily, Geoff xxi, 59–60
time management 185, 186–7
'time preference' 314–17
trade unions 59–60
training opportunities 197
transformational change 312–13

U
UK Statistics Authority (UKSA) 177, 178
United Nations (UN) 56–7, 161
universities
    access to subscription data providers 285
    actions for diversity 237–8
    acquisition of 'hard' skills 184
    careers services 62, 64, 257–8
    and colonialism 245–6
    and communication 101–2, 113, 274
    confounders example 167–8
    and ethnicity 241–2
    and A-Level Economics 230, 231
    neglect of CBA 11
    percentage of economists working in 28
    see also academic economists; degree in economics
urgent important matrix 186–7
Ussher, Kitty xxi, 60, 154

V
Vaitilingam, Romesh xxi, 101, 130–1
valuations 302, 305, 306–7, 319
verbal communication 148–9
Vickers, John 83, 144
volunteering 57–8

W
'wear your intellect lightly' 116, 128–9
welfare economics
    and CBA 216, 306
    new approaches to 307–12
    see also 'Invisible Hand Theorem'; New Welfare Economics
wellbeing
    calls to place at centre of policy frameworks 235

and 'capitals' 296, 298
    framework for understanding social impacts of policy and their effects on 297
    in Green Book 307, 309
    'preservation of capitals' approach to 298–302
White, Dame Sharon 230, 235
'willingness to pay' 306
Wolf, Martin 53–4, 154
women
    Discover Economics campaign 244–5
    earnings of economists 21–2, 240
    economics as one of worst academic disciplines for representation of 204
    and ethnicity 231, 241
    further resources 250
    and misperceptions of economics 226, 227–8
    as under-represented in economics 233, 234–5, 241
    role models 229–30, 235–6
    university actions 237–8
    workplace actions 238–40
    see also gender gap; gender imbalance
work experience
    benefits of 62–3
    further resources 64
    journalism 53, 54
working for employers 76–7, 84
working with others 102, 187–8
workplace actions for diversity 238–40
World Bank 56, 59, 283
Wren-Lewis, Simon 212–13, 214, 250
writing
    academic versus practitioner 67, 100–1, 132, 135–6
    briefs 136–8
    CVs and job applications 255–62
    for non-academic stakeholders 113, 133–4, 135, 149
    skills in 29
    'writing short' 101–2, 113

Y
Yellen, Janet 4, 236

Z
Zenghelis, Dimitri Page 312–13